TAKING SIDES

Clashing Views in
Energy and Society

TAKING SIDES

Clashing Views in
Energy and Society

Thomas A. Easton
Thomas College

McGraw-Hill
Higher Education

Boston   Burr Ridge, IL   Dubuque, IA   New York   San Francisco   St. Louis
Bangkok   Bogotá   Caracas   Kuala Lumpur   Lisbon   London   Madrid   Mexico City
Milan   Montreal   New Delhi   Santiago   Seoul   Singapore   Sydney   Taipei   Toronto

TAKING SIDES: CLASHING VIEWS IN ENERGY AND SOCIETY

Published by McGraw-Hill, a business unit of The McGraw-Hill Companies, Inc., 1221 Avenue of the Americas, New York, NY 10020. Copyright © 2009 by The McGraw-Hill Companies, Inc. All rights reserved. No part of this publication may be reproduced or distributed in any form or by any means, or stored in a database or retrieval system, without the prior written consent of The McGraw-Hill Companies, Inc., including, but not limited to, in any network or other electronic storage or transmission, or broadcast for distance learning.

Some ancillaries, including electronic and print components, may not be available to customers outside the United States.

Taking Sides® is a registered trademark of the McGraw-Hill Companies, Inc.
Taking Sides is published by the Contemporary Learning Series group within the McGraw-Hill Higher Education division.

1 2 3 4 5 6 7 8 9 0 DOC/DOC 0 9 8

MHID: 0-07-812755-6

ISBN: 978-0-07-812755-7

ISSN: 1944-7469

Managing Editor: *Larry Loeppke*

Senior Managing Editor: *Faye Schilling*

Senior Developmental Editor: *Jill Peter*

Editorial Coordinator: *Mary Foust*

Editorial Assistant: *Nancy Meissner*

Production Service Assistant: *Rita Hingtgen*

Permissions Coordinator: *Shirley Lanners*

Senior Marketing Manager: *Julie Keck*

Marketing Communications Specialist: *Mary Klein*

Marketing Coordinator: *Alice Link*

Senior Project Manager: *Jane Mohr*

Design Specialist: *Tara McDermott*

Cover Graphics: *Kristine Jubeck*

Compositor: Macmillan Publishing Solutions

Cover Image: © Digital Vision/Punchstock

www.mhhe.com

Preface

Most fields of academic study evolve over time. Some evolve in turmoil, for they deal in issues of political, social, and economic concern. That is, they involve controversy.

It is the mission of the Taking Sides series to capture current, ongoing controversies and make the opposing sides available to students. This book focuses on issues related to society's use of energy. These issues are political, social, economic, environmental, and technical. The book does not pretend to cover all such issues because not all provoke controversy or provoke it in suitable fashion. But there is never any shortage of issues that can be expressed as pairs of opposing essays that make their points clearly and understandably.

The basic technique—presenting an issue as a pair of opposing essays—has risks. Students often display a tendency to remember best those essays that agree with the attitudes they bring to the discussion. They also want to know what the "right" answers are, and it can be difficult for teachers to refrain from taking a side, or from revealing their own attitudes. Should teachers so refrain? Some do not, but of course they must still cover the spectrum of opinion if they wish to do justice to the scientific method and the complexity of an issue. Some do, though rarely so successfully that students cannot see through the attempt.

For any Taking Sides volume, the issues are always phrased as yes/no questions. Which answer—yes or no—is correct? Perhaps neither. Perhaps both. Perhaps we will not be able to tell for many years to come. Students should read, think about, and discuss the readings and then come to their own conclusions without letting me or their instructor dictate theirs. The additional readings mentioned in the introductions and postscripts should prove helpful, which can be found in the school's library or through the school's access to online magazine and journal databases.

This first edition of *Taking Sides: Clashing Views in Energy and Society* contains 38 readings arranged in pro and con pairs to form 19 issues. For each issue, an *introduction* provides historical background and a brief description of the debate. The *postscript* after each pair of readings offers recent contributions to the debate, additional references, and sometimes a hint of future directions. Each unit is preceded by an *Internet References* page that lists several links that are appropriate for further exploring the issues in that unit.

A word to the instructor   An *Instructor's Resource Guide with Test Questions* (multiple-choice and essay) is available through the publisher for the instructor using Taking Sides in the classroom. Also available is a general guidebook, *Using Taking Sides in the Classroom*, which offers suggestions for adapting the pro-con approach in any classroom setting. An online version of *Using Taking Sides in the Classroom* and a correspondence service for Taking Sides adopters can be found at http://www.mhcls.com/usingts/.

Taking Sides: Clashing Views in Energy and Society is only one title in the Taking Sides series. If you are interested in seeing the table of contents for any of the other titles, please visit the Taking Sides Web site at http://mh-cls.com/takingsides/.

Thomas A. Easton
Thomas College

Contents in Brief

Contents

David Friedman, research director at the Union of Concerned Scientists, argues that the technology exists to improve fuel efficiency for new cars and trucks and requiring improved efficiency can cut oil imports, save money, create jobs, and help with global warming. Charli E. Coon, senior policy analyst with the Heritage Foundation, argues that the 1975 Corporate Average Fuel Economy (CAFE) program failed to meet its goals of reducing oil imports and gasoline consumption and has endangered human lives. It needs to be abolished and replaced with market-based solutions.

Dwight R. Lee argues that the economic and other benefits of Arctic National Wildlife Refuge (ANWR) oil are so great that even environmentalists should agree to permit drilling. The minority members of the Senate Energy Committee objected when the Committee approved a bill that would authorize oil and gas development in the ANWR. They argued that though the bill contained serious legal and environmental flaws, the greatest flaw lay in its choice of priorities: Wilderness is to be preserved, not exploited.

Nina French argues that the continued use of coal is critical for sustainable, inexpensive, secure, and reliable power generation. Coal meets these needs, and the technology exists—and is being improved—to ensure that coal is "clean," meaning that it emits less sulfur, mercury, and carbon. Susan Moran argues that U.S. utilities are building and planning to build a great many coal-burning power plants, often hoping to get them in operation before legislation restricting carbon emissions forces them to find alternatives.

UNIT 2   GLOBAL WARMING   97

Roy W. Spencer argues that the science of global warming is not as certain as the public is told, but even if predictions of strong global warming are correct, it is not at all clear what the best policy reaction to that threat should be. Ralph J. Cicerone argues that though it may be hard to pinpoint the magnitude of future climate changes, there are multiple lines of evidence supporting the reality of and human roles in global climate change. We must decide how best to respond to climate change and associated global changes.

The Union of Concerned Scientists argues that opposition to the idea that global warming is real, is due to human activities, and is a threat to human well-being, has been orchestrated by ExxonMobil in a disinformation campaign very similar to the tobacco industry's efforts to convince the public that tobacco was not bad for health. Ivan Osorio, Iain Murray, and Myron Ebell, all of the Competitive Enterprise Institute, argue that the Union of Concerned Scientists is a liberal-funded partisan organization that distorts facts and attempts to discredit opponents with innuendo.

Sir Nicholas Stern, head of the British Government Economics Service, reports that although taking steps now to limit future impacts of global warming would be very expensive, the economic and social impacts of not doing so will be much more expensive. John Stone finds the Stern report deeply flawed and argues that it would be unforgivable to destroy the world's economic welfare in accord with its charlatanism.

James Allen and Anthony White describe the European Union's Greenhouse Gas Emissions Trading Scheme and argue that it encourages investment in carbon-abatement technologies and depends on governmental commitments to reducing emissions despite possible adverse economic effects. Brian Tokar, recalling the application of pollution credit trading to sulfur dioxide, not carbon dioxide, argues that such "free-market environmentalism" tactics fail to reduce pollution while turning environmental protection into a commodity that corporate powers can manipulate for private profit.

David G. Hawkins, director of the Climate Center of the Natural Resources Defense Council, argues that we know enough to implement large-scale carbon capture and sequestration for new coal plants. The technology is ready to do so safely and effectively. Charles W. Schmidt argues that the technology is not yet technically and financially feasible, research is stuck in low gear, and the political commitment to reducing carbon emissions is lacking.

Professor of astronomy Roger Angel argues that if dangerous changes in global climate become inevitable, despite greenhouse gas controls, it may be possible to solve the problem by reducing the amount of solar energy that hits the Earth, using reflective spacecraft. James R. Fleming, professor of science, technology, and society, argues that climate engineers such as Roger Angel fail to consider both the risks of unintended consequences to human life and political relationships and the ethics of the human relationship to nature.

John J. Grossenbacher argues that there is no realistic alternative to nuclear power as a reliable producer of massive amounts of cost-effective and carbon-emission-free electricity and process heat and that the challenges of high costs, waste disposal, and proliferation risk associated with nuclear power can be managed. Thomas B. Cochran argues that nuclear power is part of the "energy mix." But it is a mature, polluting industry that needs no federal subsidies. New nuclear power plants are not economical in the absence of strong carbon controls.

U.S. Secretary of Energy Spencer Abraham argues that the Yucca Mountain, Nevada, nuclear waste disposal site is technically and scientifically fully suitable and its development serves the national interest in numerous ways. Environmentalist writer Gar Smith argues that transporting nuclear waste to Yucca Mountain will expose millions of Americans to risks from accidents and terrorists.

Phillip J. Finck argues that by reprocessing spent nuclear fuel, the United States can enable nuclear power to expand its contribution to the nation's energy needs while reducing carbon emissions, nuclear waste, and the need for waste repositories such as Yucca Mountain. Frank N. von Hippel argues that reprocessing nuclear spent fuel is expensive and emits lethal radiation. There is also a worrisome risk that the increased availability of bomb-grade nuclear materials will increase the risk of nuclear war and terrorism.

Charles Komanoff argues that the energy needs of civilization can be met without adding to global warming if we both conserve energy and deploy large numbers of wind turbines. Jon Boone argues that wind power is better for corporate tax avoidance than for providing environmentally friendly energy. It is at best a placebo for our energy dilemma.

Issue 16.   Do Biofuels Enhance Energy Security?   322

Bob Dinneen, president and CEO of the Renewable Fuels Association, the national trade association representing the U.S. ethanol industry, argues that government support of the renewable fuels industry has created jobs, saved consumers money, and reduced oil imports. The industry's potential is great, and continued support will contribute to ensuring America's future energy security. Consultant Robbin S. Johnson and Professor C. Ford Runge argue that the U.S. government's bias in favor of corn-based ethanol rigs the market against more efficient alternatives. It also leads to rising food prices, which particularly affects the world's poor.

Issue 17.   Can Hydropower Play a Role in Preventing Climate Change?   340

Alain Tremblay, Louis Varfalvy, Charlotte Roehm, and Michelle Garneau, researchers with Hydro-Quebec and the University of Quebec in Montreal, argue that hydropower is a very efficient way to produce electricity, with emissions of greenhouse gases between a tenth and a hundredth of the emissions associated with using fossil fuels. American Rivers, a nonprofit organization dedicated to the protection and restoration of North America's rivers, argues that suggesting that hydropower is the answer to global warming hurts opportunities for alternative renewable energy technologies such as solar and wind and distracts from the most promising solution, energy efficiency.

Issue 18.   Will Hydrogen Replace Fossil Fuels for Cars?   355

Professor David L. Bodde argues that there is no question whether hydrogen can satisfy the nation's energy needs. The real issue is how to handle the transition from the current energy system to the hydrogen system. Michael Behar argues that the public has been misled about the prospects of the "hydrogen economy." We must overcome major technological, financial, and political obstacles before hydrogen can be a viable alternative to fossil fuels.

Thomas Valone argues that the solution to the world's need for large amounts of energy lies in "zero-point energy" (ZPE), a sea of energy that pervades all space. We need but develop means to tap this energy. Physicist Robert Park argues that though many inventors have claimed to have working "free energy" devices, none of them work or can work. Their proponents are guilty of "voodoo science."

Introduction

The history of human civilization is in large part the story of how people have increased their use of energy. Ten millennia ago, when people were changing from hunting and gathering to more settled lives centered on herding and farming, each person was limited to the energy of their own body plus whatever could be gained from fire for cooking, heating, pottery-making, and a few other uses. A plain-English definition of "energy" is "the capacity to do work," and at that time no one had any way to magnify the work they could do with their own muscles and hand-held tools.

J. R. McNeill, in *Something New under the Sun: An Environmental History of the Twentieth-Century World* (Norton, 2000), notes that when people adopted shifting agriculture, they increased the amount of available energy by a factor of ten, largely because agriculture increases the amount of sunshine turned into food for people and thus the number of people and the work they can do. Settled agriculture gave another ten-fold increase by increasing productivity. Domesticating large animals such as horses, cattle, elephants, and camels gave another large boost by greatly increasing the amount of work even a well-fed person can accomplish. By the beginning of the Industrial Revolution (about 1800), however, human muscle still supplied a large portion of all the energy used in civilization (estimates vary from 70 percent to 85 percent). Since then, per capita energy use has climbed very rapidly. David Price, "Energy and Human Evolution," *Population and Environment: A Journal of Interdisciplinary Studies* (March 1995), notes that in 1860, humans used about 100 kilograms of coal equivalent per capita. In 2000, the figure was about 2000 kilograms. The amount of work done around the world, using energy other than that of the human body alone, was the same as what could be done by 280 billion human beings. Price translates that as meaning that every human being on Earth has the equivalent of 50 invisible slaves working for them and adds that in highly technological countries such as the United States, every person has more than 200 such slaves.

The historical increase in energy use has been paralleled by growth in the human population. It has also required changes in technology. Wind was harnessed very early to drive ships, and later windmills. Water power also has a long history of being used to grind grain and saw wood. The Industrial Revolution truly began when the steam engine was invented and the energy content of fossil fuels (coal only at first) could be released. The first major uses were industrial, but coal furnaces made central heating available for homes, coal gas made gas lighting available, and when electrical generators were developed and installed, the use of energy in the home and in industry climbed very rapidly. To supply that energy, the scale of water power (hydroelectric dams) grew, fossil fuel use grew, and new energy sources such as nuclear power were devised. The internal combustion engine and the automobile also greatly increased the per capita use of energy.

This brief account glosses over an immense number of details. History is more than changes in energy use and more than the development of technology. But many of the other aspects of history—religion, trade, war, even art—are enabled by energy use and technology, for only when people need not spend all their time meeting essential needs such as food and shelter do they have time to devote to other pursuits. When agriculture first made it possible for some people not to spend their time getting food, it also made possible priests and generals, sculptors and musicians, masons and plumbers, merchants and lawyers, scientists and engineers (among others). Modern agriculture requires large amounts of energy for fuel, fertilizers, pesticides, irrigation, and more and is so productive that a very small portion of the population can feed the rest. On-farm employment has dropped from 90 percent in 1800 to 2 percent today.

It also ignores environmental impacts of energy use. Those impacts were small when per capita energy use was small, as well as when population was small (population is 6.5 billion today, but it did not reach 1 billion until 1800). The account above makes it clear that agriculture is an energy technology, and even thousands of years ago it led to deforestation, erosion, desertification, and soil salinization. An energy technology with surprising effects is the use of wind to power ships. The British Empire dominated the world with sailing ships built of wood. The need for raw materials for building ships played a major role in exhausting Britain's forests, which sparked the nineteenth-century shift from wood to steel as ship-building material. But steel production needs coal, which means coal mines, which have a tendency to flood with groundwater. The first steam engines (in the eighteenth century) were built to pump the water out of the mines. Once they had been sufficiently improved, they powered the steel ships as well as a vast amount of industry on land.

The use of coal—and later oil and natural gas—produces its own environmental problems, including pollution of air and water and global warming (see Issues 6–8), which prompt us to find other ways to meet our energy needs. We must also consider that the amount of fossil fuel buried in the ground is finite (see Issue 1). "Finite" means that eventually we must use it all. To this thought we must add that demand is increasing as other countries strive to improve standards of living and levels of technology. China alone increased its production of passenger vehicles by almost 30 percent in 2006, and according to the U.S. Energy Information Administration's *International Energy Outlook 2007* (http://www.eia.doe.gov/oiaf/ieo/highlights.html), world energy consumption is projected to increase by 57 percent between 2004 and 2030. Problems thus threaten to grow worse, and the time when we have in fact used all the planet's stock of fossil fuels grows ever closer. It seems clear that we must find replacements for fossil fuels before that day. Fortunately, fossil fuels are by no means the only way to generate energy for human use.

How Do We Use Energy?

One of the most revealing portraits of how modern civilization uses energy can be seen at http://svs.gsfc.nasa.gov/vis/a000000/a002900/a002916/. This image shows outdoor electric lighting around the world, as seen from space. The lights are brightest in urban centers and dimmest in rural areas and in urban areas with less technological infrastructure. As a corollary, they are also brightest in areas where population is dense and numerous. If we reflect on the past, we must recognize that the lights have brightened as population and urbanization have grown, but that before the adoption of electric lighting, urban and population centers must have been nearly as dim as the countryside. If we project the situation into the future, with world population projected to be increasingly more than 50 percent urban after 2008, we can see the lights growing brighter and the bright zones spreading. Yet it is worth noting that any light that can be seen from space represents wasted energy ("wasted" in the sense that it is not going where it is wanted, on the ground). This waste is reduced when cities adopt directional lighting, parking garages, and enclosed shopping districts (such as malls); if cities do so widely enough, future space cameras may actually see a less brilliant picture of the Earth. Cameras sensitive to heat (infrared) radiation today map hot spots that correspond well to the bright spots. Heat too is waste, and this waste can also be reduced. But the laws of thermodynamics dictate that any use of energy will unavoidably emit waste heat.

We do not use energy only for electric lighting. Electricity itself powers some trains, appliances, computers, communications, and industrial machinery. Fossil fuels power steel mills, factories, cars, trucks, trains, airplanes, ships, farm equipment, electrical power plants, and home heating, and provide the energy needed to make the fertilizers (and other chemicals) that maintain our food supply. They also provide the energy used to manufacture the rocket fuel that puts communication and weather satellites in orbit and carries people to and from the International Space Station. Many of these uses benefit the consumer. Much also goes to military uses. Either way, they provide jobs and incomes, boost the economy, and raise the modern standard of living far above what was attainable in the past.

How Do We Obtain Energy?

In the United States, 40 percent of the energy used comes from petroleum, of which 69 percent goes to transportation (and accounts for 96 percent of the energy used by transportation); 22.4 percent comes from natural gas, with roughly a third going to residential uses and a third going to industrial uses; 22.6 percent comes from coal, 90 percent of which is used for generating electricity. A mere 8 percent is nuclear, all of which goes to generating electricity. Alternative or renewable energy sources (e.g., sun, wind, biomass, hydroelectric, tidal, geothermal) provide only 6.8 percent of the mix, mostly as electricity. (See the Energy Information Administration's Annual Energy Review 2006 [Report No. DOE/EIA-0384(2006), http://www .eia.doe.gov/aer/, posted June 27, 2007].)

Heat and motion are at present the twin keys to making energy useful to humans. Most of the energy we use today—85 percent—comes from burning fossil fuels in internal combustion engines, heating furnaces, and power plants. By itself, burning releases heat, and sometimes, as is the case with home heating, that is the desired form of the energy. Heat also causes gases to expand, and in an internal combustion engine, that phenomenon is harnessed to cause movement of pistons, crankshafts, and wheels. In an electrical power plant, the heat is used to boil water and produce steam under pressure, which is used to spin the generators that make electricity.

Nuclear power (Issues 12–14) also generates heat to make steam and spin generators to produce electricity. Geothermal power plants tap underground heat to do the same thing. Hydroelectric and tidal power plants use the force of falling water to spin the generators (see Issue 17). Wind power relies on the force of moving air to do the same job (see Issue 15). Only photovoltaic power (solar cells) uses an entirely different phenomenon—the interaction of light with the electrons in a semiconductor—to generate electricity. At present, it accounts for only a small fraction of total electricity production (roughly a tenth of wind power use), but its use has been increasing rapidly. Ken Zweibel, James Mason, and Vasilis Fthenakis, in "A Solar Grand Plan," *Scientific American* (January 2008), describe how solar power could be developed, with the aid of government funding, to supply 69 percent of the U.S.'s electricity and 35 percent of its total energy by 2050. By 2100, it could supply all the nation's electricity and 90 percent of its energy.

The statistics are both illuminating and frightening. Eighty-five percent of the energy used in the United States comes from fossil fuels. Transportation is almost totally dependent on petroleum, most of which is imported (see Issue 2) and all of which could be used more efficiently (see Issue 3). If we run out of petroleum—as we will, since it is finite in supply—we will need other liquid or gaseous fuels to power cars, trucks, trains, ships, and airplanes. This may mean converting coal to liquid form, as has been done in the past. It may also mean increasing use of biofuels (see Issue 16) or hydrogen (see Issue 18). Each of these alternatives has problems: Coal too is finite in supply, and biofuels compete with the human need for farmland and crops. If the alternatives cannot meet the need for liquid fuels, and if we cannot find other power alternatives, transportation must be much reduced. One "other way" is electricity, but electric vehicles need improved methods of storing electricity.

Physics holds out the very theoretical possibility of tapping the structure of space-time for energy (vacuum energy or zero-point energy), but so far that is the realm of science fiction (see Issue 19).

Environmental Issues Related to Energy

Historically, energy use did not strike people as causing many significant problems. It was seen as a source of benefits. But by the 1600s, a few people had begun to comment on the smoke that plagued cities and suggested moving workshops and factories to the countryside (see, e.g., John Evelyn, *Fumifugium: Or the Inconvenience of the Aer and Smoake of London Dissipated* [1661]). Since then, the human population has grown, and industry has come to occupy more of the landscape, provide more jobs, and meet more needs. It has also grown much more energy-intensive.

During the twentieth century, people began to recognize the damage that energy use could do to the environment. People protested the building of dams that would flood scenic landscapes (John Muir, founder of the Sierra Club, led and lost the fight to stop the damming of the Hetch Hetchy Valley). By the 1960s, air pollution was an issue, and the U.S. Clean Air Act was passed. Nuclear power provoked concern about leakage of radioactive materials from both power and reprocessing plants (see Issue 14) and about the hazards of nuclear wastes (see Issue 13). Concern over coastal flooding by tidal power projects has blocked wider implementation of this energy source. People object to the noise associated with windmills, as well as the threat they pose to migratory birds (see Issue 15). People argue against the damming of rivers in part because of the damage done to fish populations (see Issue 17). Today, prime concerns are biofuels (Issue 16) and global warming (Issues 6–8), an inevitable consequence of adding carbon dioxide to the atmosphere by burning fossil fuels and a potential threat to wildlife, forests, coastlines, and human communities. Fossil fuel use also poses other problems, including oil spills, landscape destruction, and disruption of wildlife, and attempts to increase the supply are leading the fossil fuel industry into fragile areas such as the Arctic National Wildlife Refuge (see Issue 4). Coal is plentiful, and the coal industry believes it can be used cleanly, without continuing its infamous problems (see Issue 5).

Energy—in large quantities—is essential to modern civilization. Since it seems unlikely that we can ever find a source of energy whose use does not affect the environment, we may have to accept environmental problems as a necessary part of the price (in addition to money and political turmoil) we must pay for energy. However, this is not to say that we should ignore those problems. It serves human interests to be aware of the problems and to seek to minimize them and their consequences. Among other things, this must mean choosing energy sources that create fewer problems as well as repairing damage already done and finding work-arounds (such as fish-ladders to help migratory fish get past dams).

Fortunately, there are alternatives to the energy sources (fossil fuels) that dominate the current market. They include nuclear, solar, wind, tidal, geothermal, and hydroelectric power, and they do have less environmental impact. But at present they play only a small role. If fossil fuels vanished overnight, it would take many years to expand that role to the point where civilization could function as it does today. Fossil fuels will not vanish that quickly, but as noted above, their supply is finite. There will come a day when they will no longer be able to meet our needs. It thus behooves us to develop and implement alternatives before they are needed.

Global Warming

The energy-related environmental problem of most concern to governments and environmentalists today is of course global warming. In 2007, the Intergovernmental Panel on Climate Change (IPCC; http://www.ipcc.ch/) issued its Fourth Assessment Report, saying in no uncertain terms that "Warming of the climate system is unequivocal, as is now evident from observations of increases in global average air and ocean temperatures, widespread melting of snow and ice, and rising global average sea level." The warming is due to human activities, notably including the burning of fossil fuels, which over the course of a few decades releases carbon dioxide originally removed from the atmosphere many millions of years ago. Since carbon dioxide is a greenhouse gas—meaning that it slows the release of heat to space—it causes warming. The impacts on ecosystems and human well-being (especially in developing nations) are expected—despite the difficulty of making precise predictions—to be serious. Indeed, analysts are saying that even though measures to prevent or minimize global warming will be expensive, they will be much less expensive than just letting global warming run its course (see Issue 8). It is thus not surprising to see momentum gathering for action, although the U.S. government remains opposed to mandatory controls on carbon emissions, and the pro-action and anti-action sides continue to accuse each other of deceptive practices (see Issue 7).

What sorts of steps might be taken to fight global warming? Burning less fossil fuel is an obvious answer to the question, but it is also a difficult one because of civilization's dependence on oil, natural gas, and coal. Researchers are developing ways to keep carbon emissions from reaching the atmosphere (see Issue 10) and to keep solar heat from arriving (see Issue 11), while economists are developing ways to encourage compensatory actions (see Issue 9). Some people—even some environmentalists—are arguing that part of the answer must be increased use of nuclear power (see Issue 12). We will also surely need wind power (Issue 15), biofuels (Issue 16), hydroelectric power (Issue 17), and perhaps hydrogen (Issue 18).

Coping with Consequences

The twin issues of global warming and the finiteness of fossil fuels force us to face some hard questions. Because we are not about to run out of or stop using fossil fuels in the near future, we need to say only a little about what the sudden loss of 85 percent of the current energy supply would mean for civilization. If we resist the temptation to be pessimistic, we can say that it would probably *not* mean the end of civilization. There would be a period of adjustment while alternatives were rapidly deployed and people found ways to live using less energy (by moving closer to work and decreasing their standard of living), but over time we would adapt. Many people would find the necessary changes difficult and painful. The changes will not be impossible, but knowing that they may lie ahead should motivate us to deploy alternative energy sources before the crisis is upon us.

Global warming is a more urgent matter. Changes in climate can mean changes in our ability to produce food, and late in 2007, the UN Food and Agricultural Organization reported that the world food supply is dwindling and the world's poor face a serious crisis. Both the supply and the price of food are already being affected by high fuel prices, diversion of land and crops to biofuels, and global warming. Residents of poor countries face the prospect of not being able to afford adequate food even if it is available. In addition, high prices for food and fuel mean that aid agencies are finding that their budgets cannot supply as much aid as in the past. Millions of people face the prospect of starvation. Though this does not threaten civilization itself, it would be a major disaster. By the spring of 2008, some 30 countries had already seen food riots driven by rising prices and short supplies.

Climate change also means that sea levels will rise. Some South Pacific island nations are already protesting that this will inundate their islands. Others, such as Bangladesh, face the loss of low-lying coastal zones that are currently home to millions of people. However, the Netherlands (Holland) is already preparing to cope. David Talbot, in "Saving Holland," *Technology Review* (July 2007), describes how planners there are carefully studying potential impacts of global warming on a country much of whose land is already below sea level and kept habitable by extensive dikes. Among other measures, they are contemplating building houses, greenhouses, and even roads that can float on the rising waters.

Other potential impacts of climate change include the loss of arctic ice (and the gain of new shipping routes), increases in hurricane frequency and strength, spreading droughts, and migration of tropical diseases such as malaria into temperate zones. Environmentalists are also concerned that many species will die out. However, the other impacts mentioned are of more immediate concern to humans because they threaten drastic change to people, landscapes, and economies. Many of these impacts will be measured in terms of money; in Issue 8, the Stern report says that the prospective monetary impact of global warming is so great that it justifies spending a great deal of money now to forestall it.

Can we forestall such impacts? Michael M. Crow, in "None Dare Call It Hubris: The Limits of Knowledge," *Issues in Science and Technology* (Winter 2007), argues that "we seem to be operating beyond our ability to plan and implement effectively, or even to identify conditions where action is needed and can succeed." Furthermore, he says, current issues (such as the response to Hurricane Katrina's impact on New Orleans) "are child's play compared to the looming problems of global terrorism, climate change, or possible ecosystem collapse; problems that are not only maddeningly complex but also potentially inconceivably destructive." There are limits rooted in human psychology, politics, economics, and more that define "the boundary conditions that we face in learning how to manage our accelerating impact on Earth," and an important question is, How can we create knowledge and foster institutions that are sensitive to these boundary conditions? It is hubris (overweening pride that defies the gods) to think that we can always "predict, manage, and control nature," while at the same time devoting "little effort to the apparently modest yet absolutely essential question of how, given our unavoidable limits, we can manage to live in harmony with the world that we have inherited and are continually remaking."

Yet no one finds it acceptable to say "we cannot cope." We *must* cope, because the alternative is unthinkable. Fortunately, powerful voices say we *can* cope. In June 2008, the International Energy Agency released *Energy Technology Perspectives 2008* (http://www.iea.org/Textbase/techno/etp/index.asp). Among its points is that in our use of energy, we are not living sustainably. In order to reduce carbon emissions by 50 percent and avoid harmful climate change while still having sufficient energy for human needs, the world will need to spend $45 trillion on technology and deployment by 2050. The technologies needed already exist, and many of them are discussed in this book.

Why Should We Care?

To some people, what is at stake in connection with energy is wealth. Enormous sums of money flow to energy companies, who see changing from fossil fuels to something else as an unmitigated economic disaster. The governments of oil-rich nations will also suffer if the oil runs out or people stop using it. The governments of oil-using countries gain through taxes on fuel use, and in late 2007, states were complaining that because of high gasoline and diesel prices, people were driving less. The movement toward more efficient cars also promises to decrease fuel use, and therefore the tax revenue from fuel use. Since that revenue is used to maintain roads and bridges, some people are already expecting problems unless other sources of funds are found.

Some people—notably countries that supply fossil fuels to the rest of the world—believe that what is at stake is political power. They too see changing away from fossil fuels as disaster. But many see continuing with business as usual—using fossil fuels, adding to global warming, delaying the shift to alternative energy sources—as the disaster. Civilization may need energy, but it does not need mass starvation, rising sea levels, and the many other problems that accompany energy use.

Still others dream of a better future. At present, this means a rising standard of living defined by improving incomes and the ability to afford cars, computers, refrigerators, air conditioners, and other energy-intensive possessions that the people of industrialized nations (the United States, Europe, Japan, Australia, and a few others) take for granted. China is rapidly industrializing and increasing its consumption of energy, largely in the form of fossil fuels. It increased its production of passenger vehicles by almost 30 percent in 2006. The nation is very conscious of the accompanying problems because Chinese cities are infamous for their air pollution. But reducing the use of fossil fuels, lacking a viable alternative, would be seen as a giant step backward. To countries that have not yet taken even China's steps forward, reducing fossil fuel use would be seen as oppression. Indeed, there are already complaints that trying to prevent global warming by restricting the use of fossil fuels amounts to a conspiracy to keep poor peoples poor.

Why should we care? Some people argue that we should protect the environment from the effects of human actions. Some say that we should protect *people* from the effects of human actions (which can also protect the environment). If we fail to do so, people will suffer. The basic question is one of priorities. We must make choices about what matters to us most: people or the environment? The present or the future? Convenience or responsibility? Most people would agree that it is important to meet human needs, to see to it that everyone has enough food, clean water, and at least basic health care and education. These are among the UN's eight Millennium Development Goals:

1. Eradicate Extreme Hunger and Poverty
2. Achieve Universal Primary Education
3. Promote Gender Equality and Empower Women
4. Reduce Child Mortality
5. Improve Maternal Health
6. Combat HIV/AIDS, Malaria and other diseases
7. Ensure Environmental Sustainability
8. Develop a Global Partnership for Development

The use of energy appears here in Goal 8. Development means improving standards of living. Unfortunately, there is a conflict between development and sustainability that some feel is irreconcilable. Can we increase global energy use without destroying the environment, and in a way that can be kept up for the long-term future? If we can, it will not be easy.

False Hopes

We must cope, or at least hope that we can do so. Lacking hope, it makes little sense to attempt to foresee problems and devise ways of warding them off or repairing them. Yet it does not seem to be a lack of hope that leads some people to say that we do not face energy-related problems. Instead, it is commitment to the status quo, to business as usual, to careers rooted in the customary ways of doing things, to investments, to political backers who make their money from established energy industries (such as oil and coal companies). It is refusal to contemplate any need to change standard of living by driving a smaller car or giving up summer air conditioning and vacation travel. It is even just plain denial; people are often reluctant to see problems before they are imminent, and politicians too often reinforce that reluctance in order to win votes. It is hard for a bearer of bad news to win an election.

Hope clearly marks those who spend their careers developing workable alternative energy sources, identifying future problems, and looking for solutions to those problems. It also marks those who wax enthusiastic over "fringe" ideas such as "cold fusion" or the "free energy" addressed in Issue 19. At the moment, both cold fusion and free energy look like false hopes because neither one can be demonstrated, and physicists are highly skeptical of the theory behind them.

Are there other false hopes? The greatest may be the hope that all the problems will just go away, that the scientists will prove to be wrong about finite oil or global warming, or that a technological breakthrough will make all our worry a waste of time. A lesser false hope is that conservation can solve all our energy-related problems. It can help, and it is even essential if we are serious about minimizing environmental impacts, but it is not enough.

The Need for Critical Thinking

Many energy-related issues, both in this book and elsewhere, prompt vigorous and noisy debate. Students and voters alike must struggle to make sense of the arguments and decide which side seems most likely to be right. It is not enough to take a politician's or a newscaster's word. People must examine and assess the data themselves, in a process often called "critical thinking." *Taking Sides* books like this one are designed to help develop the necessary skills by presenting opposing sides, providing background and context information, and pointing users toward additional information.

To assess opposing views on energy issues, it can help to have had a course or two in physics and chemistry, but even without that it can help to identify vested interests, if any. Vested interests can take many forms. For instance, government projects are infamous for their inertia, with critics of excess funding saying that they have only two stages: "too soon to tell" (whether they will work) and "too late to stop" (even if they don't work) because politicians have staked their reputations on them, bureaucracies have extended power structures into them, and jobs have been based on them. Should we believe anyone who argues in favor of a project in the "too late to stop" stage?

We can identify other vested interests by asking who pays the debaters. Can they be trusted if they support the views of those who pay them? A representative of a fossil fuel company, or a researcher funded by the fossil fuel industry, who argues against restraints on the burning of fossil fuels may deserve some skepticism. So may a politician whose party is known to favor business interests, arguing against measures that would reduce corporate profits, or a politician whose party is known to favor the environment, arguing *for* such measures. A proponent of a vested interest who argues for measures that would harm that interest may seem more trustworthy.

"May" is a key word here. It can be helpful to identify a debater's biases, but bias alone need not invalidate an argument. What is their attitude toward the data? Do they cite only data that supports their view? Do they recognize conflicting data and try to fit it into an overall understanding of the situation? Are they open to other interpretations of the data?

What are their values or their priorities? This is another kind of bias. Some debaters value the natural world over the human world. Some put economic values over spiritual or aesthetic values. Some may seem too willing—or too unwilling—to accept risk. And though all values have their places in human life, it can be extraordinarily difficult to reconcile them in these debates, where so much is at stake.

Thomas A. Easton
Thomas College

Internet References . . .

Life after the Oil Crash

Attorney Matt Savinar's "Life after the Oil Crash" page with its "Civilization is coming to an end" message may seem alarmist, but it gathers a great deal of pertinent information.

http://www.lifeaftertheoilcrash.net/

The Energy Bulletin

The Energy Bulletin's "Peak oil primer" is a more sober—but also sobering—look at the situation.

http://www.energybulletin.net/primer.php

Energy Independence Now

Energy Independence Now is a California-centered non-profit organization dedicated to catalyzing a rapid transition to a clean, renewable energy and transportation economy.

http://www.energyindependencenow.org/

CAFE Overview

The National Highway Traffic Safety Administration's CAFE Overview page provides a wealth of basic information on the new vehicle fuel-efficiency standards.

http://www.nhtsa.dot.gov/CARS/rules/CAFE/overview.htm

The Arctic National Wildlife Refuge: A Special Report

This site offers cogent review of the debate over exploiting the Arctic National Wildlife Refuge (ANWR) for oil.

http://arcticcircle.uconn.edu/ANWR/anwrindex.html

U.S. Department of Energy—Clean Coal

The Department of Energy's Clean Coal information page outlines work being done to make coal a cleaner fuel.

http://www.fossil.energy.gov/programs/powersystems/cleancoal/

Fossil Fuels

Modern civilization is powered by fossil fuels—coal, oil, and natural gas. Unfortunately, the supply of these fuels is finite, they are not evenly distributed around the world, and their waste products pose problems of pollution and climate change. What can we do if and when an important fuel runs out? How do we deal with the vulnerability inherent in depending on other nations for supplies of essential resources? What is the role of those vested interests that have grown rich on the status quo?

Understanding these controversies is essential preparation for understanding the debates that will shape politics and headlines, as well as the changes in energy use that must come over the next few years.

- Can the United States Continue to Rely on Oil as a Major Source of Energy?

- Is It Realistic for the United States to Move Toward Greater Energy Independence?

- Should Cars Be More Efficient?

- Should the Arctic National Wildlife Refuge Be Opened to Oil Drilling?

- Should Utilities Burn More Coal?

ISSUE 1

Can the United States Continue to Rely on Oil as a Major Source of Energy?

YES: Eric Gholz and Daryl G. Press, from "U.S. Oil Supplies Are Not at Risk," *USA Today Magazine* (November 2007)

NO: Mimi Swartz, from "The Gospel According to Matthew," *Texas Monthly* (February 2008)

ISSUE SUMMARY

YES: Eric Gholz and Daryl G. Press argue that predictions that global oil production must slow are based on scant evidence and dubious models of how the oil market responds to scarcity.

NO: Mimi Swartz argues that the coming peak in global oil production and the subsequent decline is a worse threat to civilization than is global warming.

T he world's supply of oil is finite. The amount oil companies can take out of the ground depends on how many oil deposits have been found and how easy it is to get the oil out of the ground. How long the oil companies can keep pumping oil depends on how quickly they discover new oil deposits to replace the ones they have exhausted and on improvements in methods of getting oil out of the ground (essential once the easy-to-pump oil has been removed). If the rate of pumping slows, the price of oil rises, giving the oil companies more money. With more money, they can fund improvements in technology and searches for new deposits, which then increase the rate of pumping. Optimists say the cycle can continue for the foreseeable future. Pessimists say there must come a point where the amount of oil that can be pumped in a year reaches a maximum; this is the "peak oil" moment. After that, the yearly supply must decline.

The January/February 2006 issue of *World Watch* magazine was devoted to the debate over whether "peak oil" poses a real problem. Red Cavaney, president and chief executive officer of the American Petroleum

Institute, a trade group, titled his contribution "Global Oil Production about to Peak? A Recurring Myth." Christopher Flavin, president of the Worldwatch Institute, argued in "Over the Peak" that it is no myth. Oil extraction from the ground has exceeded new discoveries for two decades. Flavin also noted oil industry studies that predict peak production within a decade and called continuing to expand use of oil and expecting supply to continue to meet demand "irresponsible and reckless." Robert K. Kaufmann, professor in the Center for Energy & Environmental Studies at Boston University, said in "Planning for the Peak in World Oil Production" that we will not run out of oil overnight. The decline will be gradual, but if society does not begin taking steps now—for instance, increasing energy taxes to reduce demand and stimulate development of alternate energy technologies—"the effects could be disastrous."

Jim Motavalli, "The Outlook on Oil," *E Magazine* (January/February 2006), says that "one conclusion is irrefutable: The age of cheap oil is definitely over, and even as our appetite for it seems insatiable (with world demand likely to grow 50 percent by 2025), petroleum itself will end up downsizing." Peak oil may in fact have already happened, in 2005; if it hasn't, it will soon; see Robert L. Hirsch, Roger H. Bezdek, and Robert M. Wendling, "Peaking Oil Production: Sooner Rather than Later?" *Issues in Science and Technology* (Spring 2005). Talk against the problem may be motivated by the enriching effects of high oil prices on corporate and investor bank accounts. If we do nothing, tough times—even disaster—loom ahead. Some peak oil believers, says Bryant Urstadt in "Imagine There's No Oil," *Harper's* (August 2006), go so far as to say that as oil supply declines,

> "The economy will begin an endless contraction, a prelude to the 'grid crash.' Cars will revert to being a luxury item, isolating the suburban millions from food and goods. Industrial agriculture will wither, addicted as it is to natural gas for fertilizer and to crude oil for flying, shipping, and trucking its produce. International trade will halt, leaving the Wal-Marts empty. In the United States, Northern homes will be too expensive to beat and Southern homes will roast. Dirty alternatives such as coal and tar sands will act as a bellows to the furnace of global warming. In response to all of this, extreme political movements will form, and the world will devolve into a fight to control the last of the resources. Whom the wars do not kill starvation will. Man, if he survives, will do so in agrarian villages. It is a terrible scenario . . ."

In the following selections, professors Eric Gholz and Daryl G. Press argue that predictions of "peak oil"—the moment when global oil production must slow and begin to decline—are based on scant evidence and dubious models of how the oil market responds to scarcity. Oil supply depends more on economics than on geology, and there is plenty of oil to go around. Mimi Swartz, executive editor of *Texas Monthly*, argues that the coming peak in global oil production and the subsequent decline is a worse threat to civilization than is global warming.

YES    Eric Gholz and Daryl G. Press

U.S. Oil Supplies Are Not at Risk

It is past time for political and ecological alarmists to stop spreading unfounded fears that America's energy security somehow is endangered.

Many Americans have lost confidence in their country's "energy security" over the past several years. Oil prices already were high by historic standards in 2005 when Hurricane Katrina ravaged the Gulf Coast and temporarily shut down the refineries, pipelines, and offload terminals at that large port complex, highlighting the apparent vulnerability of U.S. oil infrastructure. Furthermore, growing chaos in Iraq reminds Americans of their country's limited ability to control events in the oil-rich Persian Gulf region. Finally, the reliability of even America's domestic oil supplies was called into question last year when poor maintenance temporarily closed the pipelines that carry oil from Alaska to the contiguous 48 states. That a foreign company (British Petroleum) manages the Alaska pipeline only reinforces the overarching feeling that the U.S. has little control over the energy supplies it vitally needs.

Because the U.S. is a net oil importer, and a substantial one at that, concerns about energy security naturally raise foreign policy questions. One set of arguments is based on fears about dwindling global oil reserves and their increasing concentration in politically unstable regions. Those so-called peak oil worries have led some foreign policy analysts to call for increased U.S. efforts to stabilize—or, alternatively, democratize—the politically tumultuous oil-producing regions. A second concern focuses on the rise of China and Beijing's alleged strategy for "locking up" the world's remaining oil supplies through long-term purchase agreements and aggressive diplomacy. According to a number of analysts, the U.S. must respond to China's energy policy, outmaneuvering Beijing in the "geopolitics of oil," or else American consumers will find themselves shut out from global energy markets. Finally, many analysts suggest that even the "normal" political disruptions that sometimes occur in oil-producing regions—occasional wars and revolutions—hurt Americans by disrupting supply and creating price spikes. U.S. military forces, those analysts claim, are needed to enhance peace and stability in crucial oil-producing regions, particularly the Persian Gulf.

Each of those fears about oil supplies is exaggerated. Peak oil predictions about the impending decline in global rates of oil production are based on scant evidence and dubious models of how the oil market responds to scarcity. In fact, even though oil supplies increasingly will come from unstable regions, the ongoing investments designed to reduce the costs of finding and extracting oil are a more effective response to that instability than trying to fix the political problems of faraway countries. Furthermore, fears of China are overstated as well. Chinese efforts to lock up supplies with long-term contracts will, at worst, be economically neutral for the U.S. and even may be advantageous. The main danger stemming from China's energy policy is that current U.S. fears may create a self-fulfilling prophecy of Sino-U.S. conflict. Finally, instability in the Persian Gulf poses surprisingly few energy security dangers, and the U.S. military presence there actually exacerbates problems rather than helping to solve them.

Those arguments do not mean that the U.S. can ignore energy concerns. Global demand for energy is soaring and shows no sign of relenting. Furthermore, oil supplies, though currently abundant, eventually will begin to run low, and the world will need to develop other energy sources. Yet, neither of those problems requires the sort of activist military policies that many foreign policy analysts suggest. . . .

Geologic features determine the location and quantity of oil deposits, but they do not determine "oil supply" in any meaningful sense. Supply depends on the difficulty (and hence cost) of oil exploration and production and on companies' economic decisions about how much money to spend looking for new oil fields, developing pumping capacity from the fields they find, and filling pipelines with oil. In any given region, geologic factors, such as the porosity of the rock, determine whether meaningful oil deposits exist and how expensive they are to discover and tap. However, geology merely creates the playing field for oil exploration and extraction. The amount of oil that actually can be "produced" at any given time, that is, extracted from the ground, transported to refineries, refined, and then transported in various forms to end users, depends on how much money oil companies have invested in a given field.

Prices drive fluctuations in oil supply. High prices encourage producers to pump their working fields at a higher rate to maximize profits before prices drop; lower prices lead them to reduce production. Companies with large inventories of oil generally respond to high prices by selling their stocks, unless they expect prices to rise even higher in the future. Price troughs encourage them to hold (or expand) their inventories, reducing supply in the short term.

Similarly, expectations about future petroleum prices shape long-term trends in oil supply. Oil companies, some of which are owned by the governments of countries with large reserves, decide how much to invest in exploration, new extraction technologies, and refining and transportation infrastructure and whether to pay large up-front costs to tap difficult-to-reach fields (such as those under deep water). Those major decisions, far more than geologic constraints, determine how much oil can be produced in the coming decades. Moreover, in the oil industry, like all others, investment decisions are driven by expectations about future prices—if the companies expect oil prices to be high, they will invest more heavily today since the enormous up-front expenditures will be recouped by high per barrel prices in the future but, if they expect prices to be low, they will trim investment, reducing future supplies.

Supply and Demand

Oil prices do not merely affect supply; they also play a key role in determining global demand. In the short term, demand does not change much in response to price fluctuations. People need to drive to work and heat their houses even if oil prices soar, so they tend to cut expenses elsewhere rather than go without oil. Higher prices, though, will reduce long-term demand. As prices increase, companies spend money on more efficient equipment and production processes, and individuals buy more efficient cars and improve the insulation in their homes. Finally, high prices spur investment in equipment that uses nonpetroleum energy sources, reducing the demand for oil.

Although rising prices generally dampen demand, in the short term, climbing prices actually may spark additional demand. If the factors pushing up prices seem likely to continue, then consumers, brokers, and producers may decide to fill their inventories so that they can profit from the even higher price they expect in the future. Such speculation is the principal mechanism at work when fears of war or political instability drive up oil prices. Yet, this dynamic occurs only in the short term. Eventually, inventories become full or the price rises sufficiently that speculators start to sell their inventories. Demand returns to a level commensurate with actual consumption, and the price temporarily is depressed because the market draws supply from ongoing extraction and from the excess inventory. Day-to-day prices may bounce around quite a bit as consumption, extraction, and inventory strategies adjust, but that volatility is centered on a price level determined by "real" supply and demand.

The overall point is that the oil market has its idiosyncrasies and arcane details, but it generally functions like other markets. Rising prices increase supply, stimulate investment, and reduce demand. Price fluctuations match up the amount of supply on the market at any given time with the amount of demand, such that there are no "gaps" between supply and demand on a day-to-day basis.

Market forces shape oil prices, but they do not act alone. More than in most other industries, political risk tempers companies' enthusiasm for making expensive investments because many oil-producing regions are politically volatile. Will local governments nationalize companies' investments or raise taxes and fees for future extraction? Will terrorists destroy key equipment, or will a war disrupt the flow of oil to markets? In essence, companies explore and drill less intensively in unstable regions than they would otherwise because the expected costs due to political risks must be added to the purely economic costs. Companies must expect oil prices to rise by an extra margin before they are willing to invest in volatile regions.

Oil companies understand political risk; they have made their profits by dealing with it for their entire history. The big corporations manage portfolios of investments in different parts of the world, increasing the likelihood that at least one of their investments will be affected by political events at any given time, but reducing the probability that a substantial fraction of their oil revenue will be disrupted all at once. Because oil companies' investments account for a baseline level of political risk, that baseline is built into the overall level of today's available oil supply. In especially "lucky" times, when little goes wrong politically, an unexpectedly high level of oil will be available on world markets, and oil prices may fall; conversely, in especially "unlucky" times, oil prices temporarily may rise. In sum, political risk affects the overall level and geographic location of investments in the oil industry, but it does not change the fundamental supply dynamic. The quantity of oil available today depends on the investment decisions made in previous decades. Future levels of supply hinge on current investments.

Supply disruptions and political risk are not the only necessary adjustments to the basic supply-demand framework in oil markets. The world's major oil exporters have formed a cartel, the Organization of Petroleum Exporting Countries, to try to affect prices by controlling supply. The cartel members negotiate agreements to mute the normal, competitive market pressure to produce up to the point where price equals marginal cost. Although the logic is simple, making a cartel work is difficult. First, even monopolists are uncertain about the actual strength of demand for their product, and OPEC members often disagree about how much to restrict supply. They also often are at odds about how much production to expect from countries that are not members of the cartel. Second, even if the members can agree about the ideal level of production, they have to allocate market shares among themselves. Huge sums of money are at stake in this zero-sum negotiation; not surprisingly, agreements often are hard to reach. Finally, even when OPEC members completely agree about total production and the allocation of production quotas, each has a short-term interest in cheating, because each producer can increase its own profit by exceeding its quota.

OPEC's difficulty managing oil supply varies depending on political and market conditions, if investment and production patterns or political events change the number of key players in the OPEC negotiations, the cartel management task will change, too. Agreements are simpler to reach and cheating is easier to detect and punish if fewer players are involved. Furthermore, cartels work better when the members are willing to sacrifice some of today's profits for the long-term benefits of a strong cartel, and the political and market conditions in the OPEC member states determine how much each country will sacrifice for future gains.

Each time the global oil supply-and-demand situation changes, OPEC members have to adjust their cartel agreement. Given that, before the disruption, the cartel was at least somewhat effective at increasing profits above the normal competitive level, most disruptions should hinder cartel cohesion. Each market disruption is an opportunity for intracartel conflict, hence an opportunity for the amount of oil flowing onto world markets to increase compared to the level that OPEC had preferred to offer in the past.

Like political risk, cartel behavior does not change the underlying importance of supply and demand in oil markets. Political risk and cartel behavior merely modify the expected responses across the oil industry to price changes and political shocks.

In the past decade, the authors of several widely read books and articles have raised alarms about the quantity of the world's remaining oil reserves. According to the peak oil hypothesis, the world recently passed an ominous milestone: half of the recoverable oil already has been consumed, and the rate of global oil production therefore has begun, or soon will begin, an irreversible decline. The implication, according to proponents of that hypothesis, is that, in the coming decades, oil prices will soar as supplies dwindle and demand grows. Some observers argue that the U.S. should use foreign policy tools to ensure access to the "American share" of oil supplies in that difficult environment; others ominously warn that it is exactly that sort of "mercantilism," which they view as an inevitable consequence of passing the oil supply peak, that will draw the U.S. into resource wars.

Plenty of Oil to Go Around

These pessimistic claims about peaking oil supplies should be treated with skepticism. For decades, analysts have contended that oil supplies were dwindling and that the peak rate of production soon would be reached. In fact, one prominent advocate of that argument once predicted that the global production peak would occur in 1989 but, since then, global crude oil production has grown by 23%, and oil supply (crude oil and other petroleum liquids) has risen by more than 28%. More telling, the world's ultimately recoverable resources (URR) have been growing over time, largely because many fields contain substantially more oil than originally was believed.

One reason URR is growing despite the world's continuing consumption of oil is that improved technology has allowed a far greater fraction of reserves to be extracted from oil fields. In 1980, 22% of the oil in the average field was recoverable but, with better technology, average recovery now is up to 35%, effectively increasing URR by more than 50%. The results of the growing URR and recovery rate are striking: in 1972 the "life-index" of global oil reserves (the length of time that known reserves could support the current rate of production) was 35 years; in 2003, after 31 more years of accelerating oil extraction, the life index stood at 40 years. In short, no one knows how much oil ultimately is recoverable from the Earth, and there is no compelling evidence that reserves are running out or that production is near its peak.

Although the simplest version of the peak oil hypothesis exaggerates the likelihood of impending oil shortages, there is a subtler cause for concern that has some merit—the world's remaining oil supplies increasingly are concentrated in politically volatile regions, particularly the Persian Gulf and Central Asia. Fears of instability in those regions could suppress investment in exploration and development of oil fields, which could raise prices. In addition, pessimists maintain, unstable oil production in the future could leave the U.S. vulnerable to sudden supply shocks.

Concern about the effect of peak oil on the geographic concentration of oil supplies has led foreign policy analysts to advocate costly initiatives to attempt to mitigate the instability in key oil-producing areas. One proposal is for the U.S. to do more to police the Persian Gulf and the oil-producing sections of Central Asia. More ambitious policies would aim at addressing the underlying political instability directly. Traditional realpolitik logic might suggest that the U.S. should support authoritarian leaders in oil-producing regions and even help them to quash unrest, although that option rarely is expressed openly. Alternatively, the U.S. could sacrifice the short-term stability provided by regional dictators in the hope that robust U.S. democracy-promotion efforts might enable peaceful democratic regimes to provide long-term stability. All three strategies are based on the view that the growing concentration of the world's oil reserves in unstable regions requires an enhanced U.S. effort to reduce that instability.

Those foreign policy prescriptions for responding to instability in oil-producing regions are unnecessary and unwise. If oil production becomes more and more concentrated in politically unstable regions, suppressing investment in the oil industry (raising prices) and increasing the frequency of supply disruptions (also raising prices), then possible policy responses should be evaluated on the basis of their ability to enhance supply and reduce price. Using that metric, investments in oil exploration and extraction technologies are far more attractive than foreign policies that support dictators or attempt to police or democratize violent regions.

Oil industry research and development has a solid track record for increasing oil supplies. Decades of investment in exploration technology have made it easier to find deposits, and improvements in extraction technologies have made it possible (and economically feasible) to recover oil from locations that once were inaccessible, such as under deep water. Improved extraction technology also has increased the fraction of the oil that can be recovered from fields. As a result, the average finding and development cost of a barrel of oil (adjusted for inflation) plummeted from $21 in 1979–81 to six dollars in 1997–99. The steady stream of technological innovation in the oil industry explains why URR has grown over the past half-century.

In contrast, past efforts to increase stability in oil-producing areas by supporting dictators, policing violent regions, or spreading democracy have a dubious track record. . . .

China's Huge Appetite for Oil

China's soaring demand for oil is one of the biggest changes to affect energy markets in recent times. China's growing thirst for oil, part of the broader global surge in energy consumption, will drive up prices, imposing costs on the U.S. economy. Some analysts see an even graver threat ahead stemming from Beijing's energy policy: China is negotiating preferential long-term purchase agreements that could deny Americans even the opportunity to bid for some oil. Those analysts fear that competition for oil supplies will lead the U.S. and China into a struggle they describe as "the geopolitics of oil." They implicitly recommend that the U.S. shift its foreign policy to work against the Chinese strategy—in essence, creating its own preferential agreements to guarantee U.S. access to oil and perhaps exclude China.

Fears about the implications of China's energy policy are blown way out of proportion. First, on the demand side, China's efforts to reach long-term oil purchase agreements will not affect aggregate global demand for oil; the prepurchase agreements merely will change the patterns of global oil trade—which specific barrels of oil China consumes—but not the overall level of consumption. The long-term agreements, therefore, will not affect oil prices significantly. Second, on the supply side, China's leap into the oil exploration and extraction business either will be economically neutral for the U.S. or, if Chinese investments increase aggregate global supplies, possibly advantageous to the American economy.

Until the mid 1990s, China produced more oil than it consumed; since then, China's consumption greatly has outpaced domestic production. China's economic growth creates a voracious appetite for oil, especially because much of the manufacturing investment that fuels the Chinese expansion is energy intensive, and Chinese consumers view personal cars as a symbol of their middle-class status. Each unit of Chinese gross domestic product increase therefore bumps up global energy consumption more than a comparable GDP increase in many other countries. Many oil analysts believe that Chinese demand accounts for a substantial part of the oil price jumps since 2000.

Meanwhile, as the appeal of communist ideology has faded, Chinese leaders have staked their political future on the country's economic performance and the ongoing rise in living standards. As a result, they have used price controls to insulate domestic consumers and industries from price increases for petroleum products. Protected from rising prices, Chinese consumers and industries unabatedly increase their consumption. The traditional geopolitics of oil argument goes like this: without a fundamental shift in Chinese political strategy, Chinese demand for oil may threaten the energy security of other consuming countries, notably the U.S. Because the Chinese recognize their sustained need for oil, the government encourages companies to sign long-term contracts to buy large quantities of oil from producers around the world, allegedly establishing "preferential relationships." They also have bought access to overseas fields by investing in established foreign oil companies and obtaining concessions to develop oil fields and rights to explore for new fields. Those acquisitions give the Chinese decision-making control over future oil supplies.

Meanwhile, Chinese diplomats cultivate relationships with the governments of countries with large oil reserves. Some analysts allege that such statecraft especially is helpful in the oil industry, because government-owned oil companies control the fields in many countries and, perhaps those governments will be persuaded to sell to the Chinese at below-market prices, particularly during an oil shock. Finally, the Chinese government and oil companies are negotiating overland pipeline deals to bring oil to China from Russia, the Caspian basin, and even the Middle East. Other analysts and a number of American politicians are worried that all of those moves reflect a coherent Chinese national energy policy, one that might lock up sources of oil supply, leaving less oil on the word market for relatively laissez-faire countries like the U.S.

The economic arguments against those fears are compelling. Whether or not China arranges its oil purchases years in advance, it will consume the same amount of oil. If China buys concessions from foreign governments to pump oil from their wells or to prospect for new fields on their territory and then chooses to ship the crude to Chinese customers rather than to sell it on the open market, the Chinese actions simply will free up oil pumped by other companies so that they then can sell to non-Chinese consumers. In other words, the Chinese arrangements may lock up supply, but they also sate a substantial portion of world demand. Even the Department of Energy study mandated by Congress—a study prompted by an overwhelming congressional vote to "protect" American energy security—found that the consequences of the Chinese oil strategy are "economically neutral."

Defenders of the geopolitics of oil argument attack those rebuttals by questioning a key assumption of the economic view. They ask, what if the Chinese government were willing to sacrifice profits to keep oil for the Chinese market—that is, what if China imported all of the oil from its foreign concessions, holding down oil prices on the Chinese domestic market, and refused to resell its oil, even if world market prices soared above the Chinese domestic price? That would reduce the supply of oil available to non-Chinese consumers, dramatically driving up oil prices outside China. Current Chinese price controls on petroleum products, after all, demonstrate the Chinese government's willingness to sacrifice economic efficiency for noneconomic goals, such as the political stability that they think cheap oil enhances.

What the pessimistic analyses overlook, however, is that a Chinese decision not to resell the oil China pumps (whether from foreign concessions or domestic production), despite the opportunity to make big profits, would be the same thing as China deciding to pay more for oil than other consumers. Remember, China's hypothetical decision not to sell oil to Americans even if world prices rose dramatically—during a supply disruption, for instance—would cost the Chinese the same amount of money that they could use to outbid Americans in a "free" oil market in which China had not made long-term deals with suppliers. The point is that China's current activities, whether or not they are characterized as mercantilist efforts to lock up oil supplies, make no difference to Americans' long-run ability to buy oil in the market. What might hurt American consumers is China's growing demand for oil, because that demand drives up prices.

In the end, though, Chinese ownership of oil, like political risk and cartel behavior, does not matter much when it comes to the U.S. being able to acquire and use the oil it needs to keep its economy and society humming.

The Gospel According to Matthew

The Coronado Club, in downtown Houston, is an unlikely place to contemplate the end of life as we know it. Plush and hushed, with solemn black waiters in crisp black jackets, the private enclave practically exudes wealth and stability. Captains of local industry enter and exit purposefully, commanding their usual tables, wearing the best suits. Everybody knows everybody else. The light is flattering. The wine room is nicely stocked.

But here is Matthew R. Simmons, the head of one of the largest investment banking firms in the world, stabbing at his salad greens and heatedly discussing the chaos to come when, as he has long predicted, global oil production peaks and for the rest of our time on earth we struggle and suffer and barely endure under a diminishing supply of fuel until it disappears entirely. This idea is known as "peak oil," and Simmons is its most fervent and fearsome, apostle. As he puts it, "I don't see why people are so worried about global warming destroying the planet—peak oil will take care of that." . . .

Slashing through his entrée, barely stopping for breath, be describes a bleak future, in which demand for oil will always surpass supply, the price will continue to rise—"so fast your head will spin"—and all sorts of problems in our carbon-dependent world will ensue. As fuel shortfalls complicate global delivery routes and leave farmers unable to run their tractors, we will face massive food shortages. Products made with petroleum, from asphalt and plastic to fabrics and computer chips, will also become scarcer and scarcer. Standards of living will fall, and people will not be able to pay their debts. Lending will tighten, and eventually there will be major defaults. Growth will cease, and hoarding will set in as oil becomes increasingly rare. Then, according to Simmons, the wars will begin. That is the peak oil scenario.

Simmons is an unlikely Cassandra in this, the energy capital of the world. He is a consummate insider—a friend of Mayor Bill White's and of innumerable nabobs in the local as well as global energy business, a graduate with distinction from Harvard Business School, a Republican who advised presidential candidate George W. Bush on energy policy, and an extremely wealthy man. In 2006 his investment firm, Simmons and Company International, closed 35 transactions worth $8.7 billion and co-managed 19 offerings worth $6.7 billion. He lives with his wife, Ellen, in one of the city's most exclusive neighborhoods and also owns a vacation house in Maine.

Yet at 64, Simmons opts to spend his days traveling the globe at his own expense, speaking at universities and business forums and to tiny alumni groups and just about anyone else, trying to convince an uninformed, uninterested populace that the end is very, very near. Like a lot of prophets, he has little patience for those who disagree with his message. He is an intense man, smallish and ruddy-complexioned, with a high, wide forehead and marble-blue eyes. Old ways of thinking—that the market will correct for skyrocketing prices, that the Saudis will always provide—drive him buggy. "Price has no impact on slowing demand," he insists, as an anxious waiter hovers. "We've seen a stealth growth of eighteen million barrels a day, while the demand between the end of 1995 and last week went up tenfold." What about when everyone said that Saudi Arabia was hiding vast reserves, ready to flood the world market and cause a price collapse? "That was the dumbest thing I ever heard," he snaps. "What giant new oil finds have they reported in the last decade or so?" . . .

"People used to talk about how tech had changed the name of the game in oil field development," he reminisces, barely able to conceal his disgust with earlier industry predictions. "They said costs would come down. I thought it was BS. Tech sped up the decline curves." He shoots his left arm nearly straight up, his palm stiff, like a rocket on takeoff. Then, hardly pausing to chew his food, he continues: "I spent two decades convincing myself that most conventional oil myths weren't true. People thought I was nuts. They called me Matt the Alarmist." Now he believes—"knows" might be a better word—that his conclusions spell doom for the American way of life unless people heed his warnings.

"The best we can hope for is a ten-year plateau," Simmons says, skipping coffee. "This controversy is the single biggest risk for the twenty-first century,"

So can anything be done?

He looks sharply at me, the Coronado Club's soft light reflected in his glasses, and shrugs, suddenly out of gas himself. "I'm a lot more concerned than I was three years ago," he says,

The term "peak oil" was coined by M. King Hubbert, a geophysicist with Shell in the forties and fifties. At the time, the United States was the largest producer of oil in the world. But in 1956 Hubbert predicted that American off dominance would peak fourteen years into the future. Though he was considered a serious crank by some contemporaries, just about everyone now knows that Hubbert was right. American crude production has been in decline since 1970, resulting in our current reliance on—some might say addiction to—foreign oil.

Hubbert's model proposed that production of resources with a finite supply could be expected to follow a more or less symmetrical bell curve, meaning that the rate of decline once the peak was reached would be the same as the rate of increase had been. In other words, if worldwide oil production peaked in 2000, as Hubbert predicted it would, the rate of production in 2010 would match the rate in 1990. While Hubbert was wrong about his second prediction, many peak oil theorists believe he wasn't wrong by much—that, in fact, peak oil was reached in 2005. Others put the date further into the future. The most optimistic peak oil supporters estimate that production will begin to decline after 2037.

Meanwhile, the peak oil debate has become one of the most fractious of our time, with Simmons and other advocates squaring off against their critics, not just over the timing of this supposed disaster but indeed over whether it will happen at all. Analysts like Yergin, who runs Cambridge Energy Research Associates (CERA), contend that we are decades away from a peak, that there is plenty of oil left in the ground, and that new technologies will soon come online to help extract it more efficiently. This view, known as "nondramatic peak oil," has a number of proponents, including the U.S. Geological Survey.

Other critics dispute Hubbert's premise itself, arguing that oil production may never peak (this idea has been dubbed "cornucopian" by peak oil followers). There's even a radical idea known as the Abiogenic Theory, that holds that most petroleum comes not from dinosaur fossils but from naturally occurring carbon deposits, possibly dating to the formation of the earth, which are being regenerated as we speak. All attempts to understand production are vexed by the fact that off reserves are always subject to debate. Just as it can be difficult to determine the status of a weapons program halfway around the world, it's never easy to verify a country's claims about how much oil it has.

In fact, Simmons and many others believe that Saudi Arabia, the largest supplier of oil to the U.S., has been fudging its production numbers for quite some time. In 1989 the famously secretive country claimed to have 170 billion barrels of oil in reserve. In 1990 the number had risen to 257 billion, despite the fact that no substantial fields had been discovered in Saudi Arabia since the Ghawar Oil Field, in the forties. Furthermore, oil in a new field gushes easily from the ground, and the complex technology now required to coax the oil from Ghawar and other large Saudi fields suggests that they are in deep decline.

Simmons believes that the worldwide peak was reached in 2005. He estimates the rate of decline for all oil production at somewhere north of 5 percent a year. At the same time, the global need for oil is expanding exponentially, particularly as China and India claim their places on the world stage. In India energy needs are expected to grow 72 percent by 2025; China's are expected to roughly double during the same time frame. In seventeen years the world's demand for oil may well be more than 50 percent greater than it is today, while production capacity may well sink to 1985 levels.

Most of the globe remains oblivious to this impending crisis, but the number of people who have come to see its logic is growing. The once-skeptical Energy Information Administration, a U.S. government bureau that keeps tabs on oil production, is slowly buying the argument, as is Sadad Al-Husseini, the former executive vice president of exploration and producing for Saudi Aramco. Simmons spends much of his day strategizing via Black Berry with other peak oil believers, like Colin Campbell, the famed geologist; David Rutledge, a Caltech electrical engineering professor and wireless-communications expert; Robert L. Hirsch, a senior energy program adviser at the government-friendly Science Applications International Corporation; Maryland congressman Roscoe Bartlett; Randy Udall, the son of former Arizona congressman Mo Udall; and yes, T. Boone Pickens.

Simmons's Web site . . . which had just shy of 10 million visitors in 2006 alone, is designed to spread the word with a helpful if somewhat daunting compendium of gloomy speeches, papers, and PowerPoint presentations ("A Hungry World in Search of More Oil," "Autopsy of Our Energy Crisis," "Summer's Over: Preparing for a Winter of Discontent"). There is an ever-growing list of Web sites [that] hail Simmons as a hero and pose the kinds of questions no one much wants to think about answering. For instance: "If your family were permitted to purchase only five gallons of gasoline per week, how would this change your lifestyle?" . . .

This growing anxiety may help to explain why one resource that seems to be in decline along with the availability of fossil fuels is the optimism that was always so intrinsic to the oil-and-gas business. It used to be that if you went broke today, you could always start over tomorrow, and in the meantime the country club would keep your membership on the books until your next well came in. But suddenly people in Houston and beyond are beginning to suspect that there might not be many more giant deposits—in the North Sea, the Middle East, Venezuela, or even the deep end of the ocean—so somebody had better start talking about life after oil.

That job has fallen to Simmons, thanks in large part to his evangelical zeal. "Peak off is not as complicated a topic as people think it is," he likes to say. But getting people to grasp the ramifications and adapt—is much harder.

It is a suspiciously warm Tuesday in early December, and Simmons has just flown from Houston to Miami on a chartered plane to give a speech to the International Regulators Offshore Safety Conference, a worldwide organization dedicated to offshore rig safety. Simmons never charges for these presentations because he feels they are the perfect marketing opportunity for his investment firm. "Merrill Lynch and Goldman Sachs have spent billions of dollars on advertising. We don't spend any," he says, his eyes twinkling with the thought of more than a few pennies saved. "When I speak, I get a sublime introduction. It's branding of the highest order."

Today he wears a natty battleship-blue suit set off with a white monogrammed shirt and a theme-appropriate camel-patterned Ferragamo tie. Simmons' speech is titled "Is Our Energy System 'Sustainable'?" He has already told me on the ride over that the answer is no, but after a decade of being known as Dr. Gloom, he likes to present his information as coolly as possible, "If you try to make it dramatic . . . well, it's dramatic enough," he says, He's convinced too that "reasonably intelligent people can absorb bad news as long as it isn't presented smugly."

After what is indeed a very florid intro given by a Swede (more than twenty nations are represented at this meeting). Simmons takes the stage confidently. Screens on either side of trim display his slides of doom. In about fifteen minutes, he goes through a variation on his usual speech. Our refineries are decrepit. Demand from developing countries will exponentially increase. Seventeen percent of out daffy supply comes from only ten supergiant fields, and if their reported production numbers are correct, all are in decline. The North Sea is depleted. Brazil is problematic. The "easy era" of offshore oil and gas is over.

"These aren't new fields," Simmons tells the crowd. "The newer fields are aging at an even faster rate, because the production is so intense to satisfy demand." He moves on to the incredible increase in the price of drilling ($2 billion to $4 billion is now the norm; estimates for a new project in the Caspian Sea are about $137 billion) and the protracted time it will take to get new wells online.

The optimism espoused by critics of peak off is "faith based," he tells the crowd, dependent on questionable reserve reports, the unproven ability of technology to come to the rescue, and the highly theoretical availability of vast Canadian tar sands to replace the light, sweet crude of today. To counter those who say that market corrections will bring oil prices down, he projects a slide showing that demand for oil is currently "insatiable" at a time when many oil basins have already peaked. Need is so great here in the U.S. and in developing countries that improved technology only speeds the depletion of what's left in the ground. Oil demand, Simmons says, could exceed 115 million barrels a day by 2020, an amount that will still leave China and India "energy paupers."

Simmons's critics often cite past price collapses, which theoretically indicate that there remains plenty of oil that can be provided with the well-timed turn of a spigot. But price declines have been short-lived, Simmons says, and while production has accelerated over the past decade, prices have soared. The best he has to offer is that high oil prices—up to $200 and $300 a barrel—could have a positive outcome, but only if the profits are spent on exploring, rebuilding infrastructure, and closing the ever-widening economic gap among people in the politically unstable nations of the oil-rich Middle East.

Clicking to his last slide, titled "It Is Easy to Miss an Approaching Crisis," Simmons quotes Alexis de Tocqueville: "Revolutions, before they happen, appear to be impossible and after they occur they appeared to have been inevitable." The illustration is of a rearview mirror reflecting rusting oil barrels, a drilling rig, storage tanks, a list of rising oil prices, and the words "Objects in mirror are closer than they appear."

Afterward, Simmons makes his way quickly to the elevator. He usually stays around to pick up industry scuttlebutt about declining fields and faulty data, but he's headed for South Africa the next morning, so he punches the button briskly.

A tall gray-haired man stops to say hello. "Great presentation," he says.

"It's not great news," Simmons responds.

The man nods. "Most of us are gonna go jump off our balconies about now." . . .

Simmons was one of the first to see that the oil field services industry could be more than just an adjunct to the oil business; instead, it could be—should be—a separate entity. ("The profit margins were so good!") . . . One year after the 1973 energy crisis, Simmons opened his own firm with his brother, L. E. Simmons, in Houston. They drew business from companies in Texas, Louisiana, and Alaska and from firms in the United Kingdom working in the North Sea. In 1975 he did an IPO for Handelman's company, now known as Oceaneering, in which the investors' value grew sixfold. Times were great. By 1979 oil was on its way to $50 a barrel, and Simmons was becoming a very rich man. Oil and gas had been good to him. He diligently studied the best journals and newsletters and thought he knew everything there was to know.

So, like everyone else, he was dumbfounded when oil collapsed in 1982. "For two or three years I couldn't believe we'd survive," he says, and in fact, Simmons and Company came perilously close to shutting its doors.

The devastation, however, led Simmons to an epiphany. Instead of attributing his losses to plain old bad luck, he began analyzing the raw data himself. Looking at the numbers, he realized he should have seen the crash coming: Then and there he decided he would never again rely on "a club of energy economists." He would rely on his own instincts and his own raw data and disregard the so-called experts.

Simmons's research further suggested that the depression in oil prices was going to last for quite some time. He began traveling the country, offering this prediction and his analysis that the industry would not survive without consolidation. "Boy, did people in energy think that was stupid," he says. . . .

Then, of course, oil prices collapsed again, in the late nineties, the result of tremendous oversupply. The size of the glut was estimated at about 3.5 million barrels a day. Conventional wisdom held that this had been created by the failure of the Asian markets, OPEC's overproduction, and the collapse of the Soviet Union. Experts claimed that demand had peaked just as new technologies were getting the off out of the ground faster than ever.

Simmons's private research showed something very different. He didn't believe there was a glut at all. Instead, he thought the oil business was being ruined by bad math and a lack of common sense. "I don't think we were understanding demand," he says. During this time, he took a trip to China and got a glimpse of the future as he watched the country muscling its way into the modern age. He realized that, with developing nations driven by mobility and a passion for prosperity, "there is no glass ceiling to how big demand can grow." As Simmons began to speak on this topic, he once again became the odd man out, disparaged this time for not being a trained economist.

In February 1999 oil was at $10 a barrel, and the experts believed that the price would stay low indefinitely. Instead, just a few days after the *Economist* published a story called "Drowning in Oil," the petroleum ministers of Venezuela, Mexico, and Saudi Arabia took two million barrels off the market and prices went back up again, to $37 a barrel. Simmons, who had always suspected that the glut was a product of smoke and mirrors, was vindicated. He had come to distrust the International Energy Agency's accounting. "I thought [that] either they had found data I'd never seen or they're lazy," he says. Or, perhaps, they just didn't know: in 2000 Simmons served on a government energy task force; at meetings there was often no one else in the room who could name the largest oil fields in the Middle East, Mexico, or Angola.

Simmons went back to his studies, teaching himself not just more about oil but also about electricity and natural gas and how the businesses worked together. In 2001, drawing on the lesson he'd learned in high school debate, he conducted a personal examination of the world's largest off fields, generating his own research data. His analysis suggested that production was already in decline throughout the Middle East. Though the Saudis were claiming to control 25 percent of the world's off field reserves. Simmons began to suspect that, in fact, their oil fields were aging rapidly and already required expensive and complex technology to extract their remaining reserves. This could only spell trouble for a world that was predicted to increase its oil needs by more than 50 percent by 2025. It seemed like a good time to hold the first peak oil conference. Fifty people attended the event, which was held in Sweden, in May 2002.

Shortly afterward, in 2003, Simmons was invited to Saudi Arabia by oilman Herbert Hunt. On a visit to an oil field there, he noticed the Saudis were using water pressure to get the oil out of the ground—a sure sign of an aging well. When he got back home, Simmons undertook another study, assembling 240 peer-reviewed papers on Saudi oil fields written by the Society of Petroleum Engineers—"It was about a foot tall," Simmons says—and spending the end of a Maine summer reading through the stack, pinpointing evidence of decline. The research finally proved his long-held suspicions: Saudi supply was nowhere near what had been claimed for years.

But proving his hypothesis was bittersweet. Feeling something like a surge of panic, Simmons reported his findings in *Twilight in the Desert: The Coming Saudi Oil Shock and the World Economy,* a dense, four-hundred-page tome published by John Wiley and Sons in 2005. The book became an international best-seller, and Matthew Simmons became a true prophet of doom, the global authority on peak oil. . . .

Daniel Yergin's CERA believes there is enough oil in the ground to keep us going for quite some time—3.74 trillion barrels, as opposed to the 1.2 trillion barrels the peak off proponents claim. The group has produced a $499 downloadable report titled "Why the 'Peak Oil' Theory Falls Down—Myths, Legends, and the Future of Off Resources." Yergin likes to point out that this is the fifth time the world has been said to be running out of off and that new sources or technologies always appear on the horizon to save us. CERA has argued that oil production won't peak but will follow an "undulating plateau," which should leave us plenty of time to come up with a solution to the problem of diminishing resources.

These opinions aren't as reassuring as they sound. If Simmons believes the end is upon us, CERA's time frame is just a few decades away.

According to one of its papers: "During the plateau period in later decades, demand growth wilt likely no longer be largely met by growth in available, commercially exploitable natural oil supplies. Non-traditional or unconventional liquid fuels such as production from heavy oil sands, gas-related liquids (condensate and natural gas liquids), gas-to-liquids (GTL), and coal-to-liquids (CTL) will need to fill the gap."

Simmons does not believe that the great industry hopes of Canadian tar sands or South American oil shales can ever fill this gap in time. They simply cannot produce the volume necessary to sustain the current levels of 80 million barrels used around the world every day. Simmons further counters that CERA's plan to use this remaining time to squeeze the last drop of oil from declining wells is a fool's errand. Companies will be spending more to get less and less out of the ground. "I've always said Dan [Yergin] was a fabulous historian," Simmons says. "He'll write the best history of how we crash."

Then there are those who argue that simple economics will keep the oil business from imploding: As prices go up, demand will go down, until the price goes down and demand goes up again. "These were the same old arguments as to why oil would never stay above thirty dollars a barrel," Simmons counters with impatience. "Free markets do not work when demand outstrips supply." . . .

For a Republican zillionaire who thinks Nobel Prize winner Al Gore's movie was "crappy," Simmons's proposals are surprisingly green. First, he believes the workforce should be liberated from the nine-to-five grind, because 70 percent of our oil is used for transporting people and goods. "The biggest inefficiencies are long-distance commuting and traffic congestion," he says. "People shuffle into work and get on the Internet. You can have staff meetings by webcam."

Simmons also thinks we should put an end to the global food distribution system that allows us to have Chilean watermelon in December. "We can't afford to do this anymore," he says. We should also harness the power of the oceans and move more goods over water, a proposition that isn't as quaint as it sounds, It's currently being done off the coast of Washington State. Most important, the public should insist on data reform that includes quarterly reports on reserves and field production numbers. It isn't just the Saudis who are stretching things, he says. Exxon Mobil, for instance, ran into trouble with its 2004 data; after the company boasted that it was replacing its own production to the tune of 125 percent, the SEC calculated that the actual number was 83 percent. "We've wasted four years," Simmons says. . . .

"If we keep our head in the sand, we'll be like Tulsa in 1965," he says, referring to a city that, until the seventies, was more important in the world of off than Houston. "I am trying to scare people. To tell them to wake up. This is a real defining moment."

POSTSCRIPT

Can the United States Continue to Rely on Oil as a Major Source of Energy?

By May 2008, skeptics of "peak oil" were having a harder time defending their views. Oil was not running out, but conflicts between supply and demand had already driven oil prices well above 2006's $60 a barrel (which had seemed alarming at the time), and much higher prices were being forecast. "Peak oil" was in the news, with the Reuters agency saying on May 28, in "Peak Oil: Fact or Fallacy?" that "The price of crude oil has hit record levels above $135 a barrel, pushing industry analysts to take more seriously peak oil, or the idea that global production is near an apex after which it will decline sharply." In England, financial analyst Nadeem Walayat, "The Solution to Peak Oil—A Crude Oil Super Spike!" *The Market Oracle* (May 29, 2008) (http://www.marketoracle.co.uk/Article4869.html), was suggesting that it "may take a super spike in crude oil towards $200 to really inflict major psychological damage upon consumers that will make their stomachs churn at the gas pumps, thus forcing near permanent behavioral changes." Walayat expects oil prices to drop toward $110 per barrel before shooting above $150 before the end of 2008. Mark Hertsgaard, "Running on Empty," *Nation* (May 12, 2008), notes that peak oil is imminent and is likely to trigger an economic crisis.

Paul Roberts, "Tapped Out," *National Geographic* (June 2008), regrets that so far discussion of changing our energy-hungry lifestyles is "off the table," but behavioral change was already being detected in some reports. According to the U.S. Department of Transportation, thanks to high gas prices, Americans drove fewer miles in March 2008 than in any March since 1979. CNN called the driving decline more rapid than at any time since the government started keeping records in 1942 (when gas rationing went into effect). It is fair to say that many people are already feeling the pinch and taking what steps they can to adapt. Yet a great deal more can be done. Charles H. Eccleston, "Climbing Hubbert's Peak: The Looming World Oil Crisis," *Environmental Quality Management* (Spring 2008), calls for an international program to make energy alternatives more available. Timothy J. Considine and Maurice Dalton, "Peak Oil in a Carbon Constrained World," *International Review of Environmental & Resource Economics* (2007), note that continuing use of oil conflicts with efforts to reduce greenhouse gas (carbon) emissions. "A clear policy direction for carbon regulation that encourages technological innovation is imperative as peak oil approaches."

Despite warnings that peak oil is a looming disaster, it seems unlikely that modern civilization will grind to a halt. Oil is not the only fossil fuel available. Vast amounts of coal are already used for electricity production, and coal can be used to make liquid fuels (see Zhang Ruihe, "Should China Develop Coal to Oil?" *China Chemical Reporter*, December 6, 2007). We are thus unlikely to run out of gasoline for our cars or heating oil for our homes. Fuel will, however, be more expensive. We can also use natural gas and biofuels. If we wish to get away from fossil fuels, anything that generates electricity (such as nuclear, solar, and wind power, among others) will help keep people on the road, either in electric cars or in hydrogen-fueled cars. Developing these alternatives will, however, require rapid action and extensive funding to minimize the severity of the crisis so many people are prophesying.

ISSUE 2

Is It Realistic for the United States to Move Toward Greater Energy Independence?

YES: Richard N. Haass, from Testimony on "The Geopolitical Implications of Rising Oil Dependence and Global Warming" before the House Select Committee on Energy Independence and Global Warming (April 18, 2007)

NO: Paul Roberts, from "The Seven Myths of Energy Independence," *Mother Jones* (May/June 2008)

ISSUE SUMMARY

YES: Richard N. Haass argues that energy independence cannot be achieved if it means being able to do completely without imports of oil and gas. We can, however, move toward energy independence by raising gasoline taxes, making cars more fuel-efficient, and developing alternative energy sources.

NO: Paul Roberts argues that despite its immense appeal, energy independence is unlikely to succeed. We have no realistic substitute for the large amount of oil we import, many of the alternatives to oil come at substantial environmental and political costs, and even if we had good alternatives ready to deploy, it would take decades—as well as energy from present sources—to replace all the cars, pipelines, refineries, and other existing infrastructure.

T he United States gets most of its energy from coal, not oil. But oil does fuel the transportation sector—meaning cars, trucks, and airplanes—and the nation imports over 60% of the oil it uses. That comes to almost 400 million barrels of oil per month, at a price in June 2008 of over $135 per barrel. The nation sends huge amounts of money overseas and is at the mercy of international politics, which can cut off the flow at will, and terrorism, which can destroy pipelines and oil tankers. It lacks what is often called "energy security," the ability to ensure a steady and affordable flow of energy to consumers. To remedy this lack, politicians and others have long urged that the United States achieve "energy independence." In the extreme, this means producing all energy used within the United States within U.S. borders. More practically, it means reducing dependence on vulnerable foreign supplies—by stockpiling oil in the Strategic Petroleum Reserve and by developing stronger national sources—to the point where a disruption in supply of foreign oil will not cripple the country.

In February 2006, Barack Obama, speaking to the Governor's Ethanol Coalition, said that "for all of our military might and economic dominance, the Achilles heel of the most powerful country on Earth is the oil we cannot live without." The Bush administration has recognized that the problem exists but has not made "a serious commitment to energy independence. The solutions are too timid—the reforms too small. America's dependence on oil is a major threat to our national security, and the American people deserve a bold commitment that has the full force of their government behind it." Obama's suggested solutions began with more fuel-efficient cars and biofuels and move on to "a national commitment to energy security" exemplified by the appointment of "a Director of Energy Security to oversee all of our efforts [and] coordinate America's energy policy across all levels of government."

Would such an approach work? Philip J. Deutch, "Energy Independence," *Foreign Policy* (November/December 2005), does not believe the United States can stop relying on imported oil any time soon. Nor can it burn less coal. Nuclear power is needed. Energy conservation may help, but it can't get the energy monkey off our backs. "Energy independence may be hopeless in the next 20 years, but there is no doubt that emerging technologies will eventually bear the brunt of our energy burden." Steve Stein, "Energy Independence Isn't Very Green," *Policy Review* (April/May 2008), argues that replacing dependence on oil with dependence on coal (which adds to global warming) does not improve our security; nuclear power is the better answer. Robert Bryce, *Gusher of Lies: The Dangerous Delusions of "Energy Independence"* (PublicAffairs, 2008), finds that there are just no substitutes for oil in the near future.

In the following selections, Richard N. Haass, president of the Council on Foreign Relations, argues that energy independence cannot be achieved if it means being able to do completely without imports of oil and gas. We can, however, move toward energy independence by raising gasoline taxes, making cars more fuel-efficient, and developing alternative energy sources. Author Paul Roberts argues that despite its immense appeal, energy independence is unlikely to succeed. We have no realistic substitute for the oceans of oil we import, many of the alternatives to oil come at a substantial environmental and political cost, and even if we had good alternatives ready to deploy, it would take decades—as well as energy from present sources—to replace all the cars, pipelines, refineries, and other existing infrastructure. "Paradoxically, to build the energy economy that we want, we're going to lean heavily on the energy economy that we have."

YES

Richard N. Haass

Geopolitical Implications of Rising Oil Dependence and Global Warming

. . . The geopolitical implications of rising oil dependence and global climate change for the United States are great and likely to become even greater with time.

Let me address each of the questions you have posed to me and my fellow witnesses.

I will begin with how ever-increasing dependence on imported oil affects U.S. national security. The short answer is that it does, in many and important ways. Four stand out:

First, American and global dependence on the Middle East for oil artificially increases the importance of this part of the world. This is not to say it would not be important even if there were no oil in the region or if the United States and the world were not dependent upon the region's oil. The United States would still have important, even vital concerns relating to terrorism, non-proliferation, conflict resolution, Israel, and so on. But there is no denying that energy makes this part of the world far more vital than it would otherwise be and reduces American willingness and ability to tolerate developments that were they to occur in other regions would provoke less of a response. And just to be clear, let me stress that this concern for oil and gas is not tied to protecting the interests of the large oil companies but rather to maintaining adequate access on acceptable terms to a vital raw material.

Second, the fact that the United States imports roughly 60% of the oil it consumes leaves the U.S. economy vulnerable to supply interruptions that even in small amounts can cause price increases and in larger amounts cause not only price increases but economic disruption. The United States would be vulnerable economically to supply interruptions (and price spikes) even if it imported far less oil given the extent to which others are vulnerable and the degree to which U.S. economic fortunes are tied to those of others.

Third, the need to pay for oil imports exacerbates the already considerable current account deficit, which in turn further weakens the dollar and makes the United States more dependent on (and vulnerable to)

From House Select Committee on Energy Independence and Global Warming by Richard N. Haass, (April 18, 2007).

the decisions of other governments. Approximately one-third of the annual current account deficit, or some $250 billion, is attributable to oil imports.

Fourth, American demand for oil contributes to upward pressures on prices and provides massive revenues to producers. One of the top five oil exporters to the United States is Venezuela, whose foreign policy is anti-American in large measure. The top two exporters of oil in the world, Saudi Arabia and Russia, carry out policies at home and abroad that at times run counter to American values and interests. Iran, the world's fourth largest exporter of oil, is in large part able to conduct the problematic foreign policy it does because of high oil revenues. In addition, massive inflows of oil revenues can be as much a liability as a windfall in another way in that they often work against efforts to promote market economies and the rule of law.

The second question posed asks whether it is urgent that the United States do something about this state of affairs. It is. It is also a national failure, a bi-partisan failure, that this country is consuming and importing as much oil as it is today, more than three decades after the first oil shock that accompanied the October 1973 Middle East conflict. It is a matter of some debate as to whether U.S. energy security has actually deteriorated despite that and subsequent crises: the United States is more dependent than ever on imports, but U.S. energy intensity is down and international markets seem better able to weather disruptions. But whatever the relative judgment on energy security, it is not what it needs to be in absolute terms. That said, it has taken us decades to get to where we are today, and will take decades for the situation to change fundamentally. There is, however, no reason to delay. Every day we as a country wait to act only increases the price we pay for the current state of affairs and makes it that much more difficult and costly for us to change them.

Should climate change be treated as a national security matter? The short and clear answer is "yes." Countries are unlikely to go to war over levels of greenhouse gas emissions, but they may well go to war over the results of climate change, including water shortages and large-scale human migration. Climate change, by contributing to disease, extreme weather, challenges from insects that attack both food production and people, water shortages, and the loss of arable land, will also contribute to state failure, which in turn provides opportunities for activities such as terrorism, illegal drugs, and slavery that exploit "sovereignty deficits." Development, democracy, and life itself will not thrive amidst such conditions.

The last two questions can best be answered together, as they ask for recommendations for reducing oil dependence and greenhouse gas emissions and addressing both climate change and energy security.

Energy security is not easy to define. It is a relative concept, in the sense that it is impossible to achieve total energy security—just as it is impossible to achieve full security (or complete invulnerability) in any realm. A traditional definition of energy security would be one that emphasized minimizing U.S. vulnerability to supply interruptions and price increases. This "reliability and affordability" approach to energy security is inadequate, as it does not capture the additional rationales for reducing consumption of oil (imported or otherwise) in order to curtail the flow of resources to unfriendly governments and to reduce the adverse impact on the world's climate. As a result, we need to adopt a broader definition of the concept. Energy security is directly related to the ability to manage the form and amount of energy produced, consumed, and imported so that the United States reduces its vulnerability to supply and price fluctuations, the flows of resources to unfriendly producer countries, and the adverse impact on the global climate.

A range of prescriptions, some familiar, some not, flows from this broader approach to energy security. One is the desirability of diversifying sources of oil and other energy supplies. Such diversification reduces the impact of losing for whatever reason access to the output of any single producer. The United States has done this in the oil realm, as only Canada provides the United States in the range of 20% of its total oil imports. 90% of U.S. crude oil imports are distributed to more than ten countries.

The United States can also help reduce its vulnerability to supply interruptions through contingency planning, including the maintenance of the strategic petroleum reserve (SPR) and various stand-by international sharing arrangements. Congress would be well-advised to assess both the adequacy and guidelines for use of the SPR. Also in need of overhaul is the International Energy Agency, which needs to be amended (or complemented by the International Energy Forum) so that major countries such as India and China are fully included in global planning.

The entire energy infrastructure—production areas, pipelines, pumps, refineries, terminals, power plants, and so on—needs to be made more robust and made more resilient. This involves better intelligence and law-enforcement cooperation, enhanced protection of critical sites, and provision for the redundancy of critical components. There is also no substitute for the ability to protect and clear critical transitways.

Supply diversification and related measures have their limits, however. The price of oil reflects global supply and demand, so the price of oil will rise if more than a negligible amount of oil is taken off the market. In addition, the United States is in principle more vulnerable to supply interruptions given the rise in terrorism and the increased role of national oil companies, who are more likely to reflect government policy when it comes to making decisions about production and sales.

Another way to increase diversification of supply is to increase domestic production, which is now below 7 million barrels a day. Expressed differently, the United States imports some 2/3 of the oil it consumes. It is doubtful new drilling (even with new technologies that increase recovery rates) could appreciably affect this number given the falling output of many mature wells and fields and the growing domestic demand for oil. Still, the United States ought to increase the amount of exploration and development that it allows, especially in coastal areas. Again, though, no combination of diversification of external oil supplies and increased domestic production can satisfy the demands of a comprehensive energy security posture.

Alternative forms of energy, including coal, natural gas, nuclear, solar, wind, geothermal, and biofuels, are also central to any discussion of energy security. One reality to contend with though is the fact that most of the oil produced and imported is used in the transport sector—and that most of what fuels the transport sector is oil. Massive substitution is not a near-term option. In the medium and long-term, fuel-efficient "pluggable" hybrids that use electrical power appear promising. So as well does cellulosic biomass, which can substitute in significant quantities for gasoline without disrupting food supplies or requiring anything near the amount of energy to produce corn-based ethanol. One short-term step that should be taken is the removal of the tariff on ethanol imports.

Coal is and will remain the principal fuel for electricity generation. It generates half the electricity in the United States. Coal is readily available in the United States as well as in both China and India. It is also relatively inexpensive. China is building large coal-fueled plants at the rate of two per week; India is building them at a rate closer to two per month. The problem is that coal is a major contributor to greenhouse gas emissions. As the recently-released MIT study *The Future of Coal* makes readily apparent, the climate change problem will continue to worsen unless something can be done about coal. The reality, though, is that there is no realistic alternative to coal; the principal question is whether technology can be developed, proven and introduced with sufficient speed and on a sufficient scale to capture and then sequester the massive amounts of carbon dioxide existing and planned plants will produce. Governments ought to work with industry in creating an investment and regulatory environment that accelerates the emergence, testing, and fielding of such technology in the United States and around the world. In the meantime, the government should only authorize the construction of coal plants that use the most advanced, efficient and clean technologies and that are designed to incorporate emerging technologies designed to capture carbon.

Nuclear power is the ideal form of fuel for electricity production given that it adds hardly at all to climate change. Nuclear power stations now provide some 20% of U.S. electricity. There will be hurdles to maintaining, much less increasing, this percentage. Politics is one problem. The last reactor to be completed was ordered nearly four decades ago and became operational in 1996. There are currently 103 reactors operating. Even with 20 year extensions of their planned lifespan all existing reactors will be decommissioned by the middle of this century. Just replacing them will require building two reactors a year for the next fifty years. It is not clear this rate of construction in the United States (coupled with ambitious building programs elsewhere) is sustainable. Indeed, a forthcoming study (*Nuclear Energy: Balancing Benefits and Risks*) written by Charles D. Ferguson of the Council on Foreign Relations concludes that "Nuclear energy is not a major part of the solution to further countering global warming or energy insecurity. Expanding nuclear energy use to make a relatively modest contribution to combating climate change would require constructing nuclear power plants at a rate so rapid as to create shortages in building materials, trained personnel, and safety controls." Other analysts are more bullish about the prospects for nuclear power, although even if they are correct it will not prove transformational for decades if then. In addition, a greater emphasis on nuclear power will raise security challenges as well as demands for safe storage of spent fuel.

In short, developing alternatives will over time make a difference. But no energy security policy can be considered comprehensive without a significant emphasis on reducing the consumption of oil and oil products. The United States daily consumes some 21 million barrels of oil and oil products. The policy question is how best to slow or better yet reverse this growth.

Increasing the tax on gasoline would have the most immediate impact. U.S. taxes (18.4 cents per gallon at the federal level) are low by world standards. If politics required, an increase in the federal fuel tax could be offset by reductions or rebates in other taxes or in designating revenues for energy-related investments.

Tightening fuel efficiency standards is a good mid-term approach given the time it will take for more efficient cars and trucks to be built and to replace the existing fleet. One area deserving exploration is what might be done to accelerate the replacement of low-mileage vehicles with hybrids and relatively fuel-efficient cars and trucks.

All of the above would affect climate change. Climate change policy, however, is something different. Congress and the administration should start developing guidelines for the post-Kyoto Protocol, post-2012 world. They should work with state governments, business, and academic experts. It is essential that the United States be a full participant in any negotiations and in any resulting regime—and that it approach such negotiations with a national policy in place. Developing countries need to be a central (although not necessarily equal) participant in a post-Kyoto framework. Some sort of carbon tax or cap and trade system will likely work best. Factored into any plan should be a positive credit for forested areas that absorb carbon dioxide. Even before then, U.S. aid policy should be adjusted to provide financial incentives to discourage deforestation and encourage reforestation.

We will also need to consider whether and how future trade negotiations and the WTO process itself address climate change. Many of the innovations that will reduce emissions (such as nuclear power stations and cleaner coal plants and capture and sequestration technology) are costly. Questions such as how to treat subsidies and the role (if any) of tariffs to deal with producers who give short shrift to climate concerns require study.

I want to close with a few thoughts on this subject. Despite the formal name of this select committee, "energy independence" is beyond reach if by independence is meant an ability to do without imports of oil and gas. A recent Task Force (*National Security Consequences of U.S. Oil Dependency*) sponsored by the Council on Foreign Relations concluded "During the next twenty years (and quite probably beyond) it is infeasible to eliminate the nation's dependence on foreign energy sources." A more useful and realistic task is how to manage energy dependence or, better yet, how best to promote energy security.

Similarly, energy security cannot be promoted through any single policy or breakthrough. Rather, what is required is a family of policies. The U.S. government will need to adjust to help bring this about. The creation of this select committee is a step in the right direction; so, too, would be a directorate in the National Security council staff devoted to energy security and the inclusion of the secretary of energy more regularly and centrally in national security meetings. Energy security properly defined is now too intimately a part of overall security to be left out of the most important deliberations of our country.

Paul Roberts  **NO**

The Seven Myths of Energy Independence

MYTH #1

Energy Independence Is Good

On February 1, 2006, Prince Turki al-Faisal, Saudi Arabia's ambassador to Washington, arrived at the White House in a state of agitation. The night before, in his State of the Union address, President Bush had declared the United States to be "addicted to oil, which is often imported from unstable parts of the world." He had announced plans to "break this addiction" by developing alternatives—including a multibillion-dollar subsidized ramp-up of biofuels—and had boldly stated that by 2025, America could cut imports from Gulf states by three-quarters and "make our dependence on Middle Eastern oil a thing of the past." "I was taken aback," Prince Faisal later told CNN, "and I raised this point with government officials."

Two years on, anyone who's been to a gas station or a grocery store knows the prince had very little to worry about. Despite supposedly bold initiatives such as last year's Energy Independence and Security Act, America is no freer from foreign oil: Since 2006, imports have remained steady at about 13 million barrels every day, while the price for each of those barrels has jumped by $30. And though federal efforts to encourage biofuel production have significantly boosted output, our heavily subsidized ethanol refiners now use so much corn (closing in on a third of the total crop) that prices for all grains have soared, sparking inflation here at home and food riots abroad.

Okay, so maybe ethanol's critics are right, and turning food into fuel isn't the smartest way to wean ourselves from imported oil. But the deeper lesson here isn't that Washington backed the wrong weapon in the war for energy independence, but that most policymakers—and Americans generally—still think "energy independence" is a goal we can, or should, achieve. Nine in ten voters say the country is too dependent on foreign crude. Every major presidential hopeful formulated some kind of strategy for energy liberation (Rudy Giuliani unveiled his at a NASCAR race), and

From *Mother Jones*, 33(3), May/June 2008. Copyright © 2008 by Foundation for National Progress. Reprinted by permission.

between 2001 and 2006 the number of media references to "energy independence" jumped by a factor of eight.

And on the surface, the argument seems solid. Imported oil, some 60 percent of the oil we use, exposes our economy and politics to stresses halfway around the world (bin Laden calls it "the umbilical cord and lifeline of the crusader community"). It also increases our already massive trade imbalance, Which must be corrected by ever-greater federal borrowing, and funnels tens of billions of dollars to the likes of Saudi Arabia, Russia, and Venezuela—countries that are unfriendly and, in some cases, actively anti-American. What's not to like about energy independence?

In a word, everything. Despite its immense appeal, energy independence is a nonstarter—a populist charade masquerading as energy strategy that's no more likely to succeed (and could be even more damaging) than it was when Nixon declared war on foreign oil in the 1970s. Not only have we no realistic substitute for the oceans of oil we import, but many of the crash programs being touted as a way to quickly develop oil replacements—"clean coal," for example, or biofuels—come at a substantial environmental and political cost. And even if we had good alternatives ready to deploy—a fleet of superefficient cars, say, or refineries churning out gobs of cheap hydrogen for fuel cells—we'd need decades, and great volumes of energy, including oil, to replace all the cars, pipelines, refineries, and other bits of the old oil infrastructure—and thus decades in which we'd depend on oil from our friends in Riyadh, Moscow, and Caracas. Paradoxically, to build the energy economy that we want, we're going to lean heavily on the energy economy that we have.

None of which is exactly news. Thoughtful observers have been trying to debunk energy independence since Nixon's time. And yet the dream refuses to die, in no small part because it offers political cover for a whole range of controversial initiatives. Ethanol refiners wave the banner of independence as they lobby Congress for massive subsidies. Likewise for electric utilities and coal producers as they push for clean coal and a nuclear renaissance. And it shouldn't surprise that some of the loudest proponents of energy liberation support plans to open the Arctic National Wildlife Refuge and other off-limits areas to oil drilling—despite the fact that such moves would, at best, cut imports by a few percentage points. In the doublespeak of today's energy lexicon, says Julia Bovey of the Natural Resources Defense Council, " 'energy independence' has become code for 'drill it all.' "

Yet it isn't only the hacks for old energy and Archer Daniels Midland who are to blame. Some proponents of good alternatives like solar and wind have also harped on fears of foreign oil to advance their own sectors—even though many of these technologies are decades away from being meaningful oil replacements.

Put another way, the "debate" over energy independence is not only disingenuous, it's also a major distraction from the much more crucial question—namely, how we're going to build a secure and sustainable energy system. Because what America should be striving for isn't energy independence, but energy security—that is, access to energy sources that are reliable and reasonably affordable, that can be deployed quickly and easily, yet are also sale and politically and environmentally sustainable. And let's not sugarcoat it. Achieving real, lasting energy security is going to be extraordinarily hard, not only because of the scale of the endeavor, but because many of our assumptions about energy—about the speed with which new technologies can be rolled out, for example, or the role of markets—are woefully exaggerated. High oil prices alone won't cure this ill: We're burning more oil now than we were when crude sold for $25 a barrel. Nor will Silicon Valley utopianism: Thus far, most of the venture capital and innovation is flowing into status quo technologies such as biofuels. And while Americans have a proud history of inventing ourselves out of trouble, today's energy challenge is fundamentally different. Nearly every major energy innovation of the last century—from our cars to transmission lines—was itself built with cheap energy. By contrast, the next energy system will have to contend with larger populations and be constructed using far fewer resources and more expensive energy.

So it's hardly surprising that policymakers shy away from energy security and opt instead for the soothing platitudes of energy independence. But here's the rub: We don't have a choice. Energy security is non negotiable, a precondition for all security, like water or food or defense. Without it, we have no economy, no progress, no future. And to get it, we'll not only have to abandon the chimera of independence once and for all, but become the very thing that many of us have been taught to dread—unrepentant energy globalists.

MYTH #2

Ethanol Will Set Us Free

What's wrong with energy independence? Let's start with the sheer physical enormity of replacing imports. Even if we limit the discussion to oil (and America buys boatloads of foreign natural gas, electricity, and even coal), the job is far more daunting than many liberationists—or environmentalists—want to believe.

If we distilled our entire corn crop into ethanol, the fuel produced would displace less than a sixth of the gasoline we currently guzzle, and other candidates, like hydrogen, are even more marginal. The challenge isn't simply quantity, but quality. Oil dominates the energy economy, and especially the transportation sector (which is 95 percent dependent on crude), in part because no other fuel offers the same combination of massive energy density and ease of handling. As author Richard Heinberg has observed, enough energy is contained in a single gallon of gasoline to replace 240 hours of human labor—considerably more than oil's likely rivals.

And because oil is relatively easy to produce, the energy "investment" needed to exploit that massive energy content is small. On average, an oil company burns the energy equivalent of 1 gallon of oil to produce 20 gallons of oil. In other words, oil's energy return on energy invested is quite high. By contrast, the return for oil's declared alternatives is quite low. For example, hydrogen, once considered a natural successor to oil, is so tricky to refine and handle that, by one study, a gallon of hydrogen contains nearly 25 percent less energy than was consumed producing it. As for ethanol's energy return, scientists are debating whether it's slightly positive or altogether negative.

Oil's qualities were unbeatable when it cost $25 a barrel, and even at $100, it still has a critical advantage. Because it was generated ages ago and left for us in deep underground reservoirs, oil exists more or less in a state of economic isolation; that is, oil can be produced—pumped from the ground and refined—without directly impinging on other pieces of the world economy. By contrast, many of oil's competitors are intimately linked to that larger economy, in the sense that to make more of an alternative (ethanol, say) is to have less of something else (food, sustainably arable land).

Granted, oil's advantages will ultimately prove illusory due to its huge environmental costs and finite supply. But oil's decline won't, by itself, make alternatives any less problematic. Higher oil prices do encourage alternatives to expand, but in a world of finite resources, these expansions can come at substantial cost. Because good U.S. farmland is already scarce, every additional acre of corn for ethanol is an acre unavailable for soybeans, or wheat, whose prices then also rise—a ripple effect that affects meat, milk, soft drinks.... And for the record, to make enough corn ethanol to replace all our gasoline, we'd need to plant 71 percent of our farmland with fuel crops.

To be fair, ethanol can be produced in a way that is less disruptive to the food economy. Cellulosic ethanol, for example, is made from wood chips, crop detritus, and other organic waste. And in Brazil they make ethanol from sugarcane—a process a third as energy intensive as corn ethanol's. But cellulosic ethanol, though quite promising, is not yet commercial, while Brazilian ethanol is, well, Brazilian: It's effectively barred from our market by a 54 cents per gallon tariff, which U.S. lawmakers defend on the grounds of energy independence, but which coincidently leaves corn ethanol, with its massive federal subsidy, as pretty much the only game in town. So much corn is now going to biofuel that the food and energy markets are effectively linked, an unprecedented coupling that not only disrupts global food security but also undermines corn ethanol's usefulness as an oil replacement.

The ripple effect of energy alternatives isn't confined to the economic sphere. As eager farmers have expanded their corn crops (U.S. farmers planted more acres in 2007 than anytime since World War II), they've tilled land not suited for intensive agriculture, exacerbating erosion and other environmental problems. Corn is also the most chemically intensive commercial grain crop; runoff attributable to the ethanol boom is causing oceanic dead zones and pesticide-laden groundwater.

Ethanol is an easy target, but the sad truth is that all of the ballyhooed alternatives carry at least some environmental or other external costs. Wind requires vast amounts of land; solar-cell manufacturing is chemically intensive. Nuclear energy is steeped in safety and security concerns. And although the United States could fuel its entire car fleet with a synthetic gasoline made from abundant coal, syngas is even more ecologically challenged than oil. Industry likes to trumpet potential technologies to capture and sequester coal's carbon dioxide, but the federal government has cut research funding. And as Severin Borenstein, an economist at the University of California-Berkeley, points out, even if we do find climate-friendly ways to turn coal into fuel, that's only one end of the process: "We're still going to be burning that fuel in cars and thus releasing all that CO_2 out the tailpipe."

Such problems drive home a critical flaw in the paradigm of energy independence—namely, that energy isn't a zero-sum game anymore. We can no longer look at the energy economy as a constellation of discrete sectors that can be manipulated separately; everything is tied together, which means that fixing a problem in one part of the system all but invariably creates a new problem, of a whole series of problems, somewhere else.

MYTH #3

Conservation Is a "Personal Virtue"

By now it should be clear not only that energy independence is prohibitively costly, but that the saner objective—energy security—won't be met through some frantic search for a fuel to replace oil, but by finding ways to do without liquid fuel, most probably through massive increases in energy efficiency.

This isn't a popular idea with Dick Cheney, who before 9/11 famously said that "conservation may be a sign of personal virtue, but it is not a sufficient basis for a sound, comprehensive energy policy." Nor among traditional energy players, who desperately want to find something to sell us if oil becomes untenable—and don't really care if that something is hydrogen of ethanol or pig manure. But for the rest of us, the logic of conservation is pretty hard to argue with. Better energy efficiency is one of the fastest ways to reduce not only energy use, but pollution and greenhouse gas emissions: According to a new study by McKinsey & Company, if the United States aggressively adopted more efficient cars, factories, homes, and other infrastructure, our CO_2 emissions could be 28 percent below 2005 levels by 2030. And saving energy is almost always cheaper than making it: There is far more oil to be "found" in Detroit by designing more fuel-efficient cars than could ever be pumped out of ANWR. And because transportation is the biggest user of oil—accounting for 7 of every 10 barrels we burn—any significant reduction in the sector's appetite has massive ramifications. Even the relatively unambitious 2007 energy bill, which raises fuel-economy standards from 25 mpg to 35 mpg by 1020, would save 3.6 million barrels a day by 2030. And if we persuaded carmakers to switch to plug-in hybrids, we could cut our oil demand by a staggering 9 million barrels a day, about 70 percent of our current imports.

Such a shift would impose massive new demand on an electric grid already struggling to meet need, but plug-in hybrids actually stretch the grid's existing capacity. Charged up at night, when power demand (and thus prices) are low, plug-in hybrids exploit the grid's large volume of unused (and, until now, unusable) capacity. Such "load balancing" would let power companies run their plants around the clock (vastly more cost-effective than idling plants at night and revving them up at dawn); as important, it would substantially boost the grid's overall output. According to the Department of Energy, with such load balancing, America's existing power system could meet current power demands and generate enough additional electricity to run almost three-quarters of its car and light-truck fleet. That alone would be enough to drop oil consumption by 6.5 million barrels a day, or nearly a third of America's current demand.

Granted, this switch to electric-powered cars wouldn't be free. Seventy percent of America's electricity is made from high-carbon fuels like natural gas and especially coal, which is why the power sector emits 40 percent of all U.S. carbon emissions. Just 8.4 percent comes from renewable sources, and most of that is environmentally dubious hydroelectric; wind, solar, geothermal, and biomass together supply 2.4 percent, and despite rapid growth, their share of the power market will remain small for decades. Even so, an electric or plug-in hybrid fleet is still probably the most environmentally plausible path away from oil. Why? Because kilowatt for kilowatt, turning fossil fuels into electricity in massive centralized power plants and then putting that juice into car batteries is more efficient than burning fossil fuels directly in internal combustion engines, and thus generates fewer CO_2 emissions per mile traveled. (Our existing fleet generates a third of America's CO_2 emissions.) The DOE found that replacing three-quarters of the U.S. fleet with plug-in hybrids would cut vehicle CO_2 emissions by 27 percent nationwide—40 percent or more if the country's power system were upgraded to match California's low-carbon grid. And once the new fleet is in place, there is nothing stopping us from upgrading our power sources to truly renewable systems.

MYTH #4

We Can Go It Alone

Given America's reliance on imported oil, it seems safe to assume that if we succeeded in getting such dramatic reductions, whatever sacrifices we'd made would be more than compensated for by our new immunity to the nastiness of world oil markets. Let Saudi Arabia cut its production. Let Hugo Chávez sell his oil to China. Such maneuvers no longer matter to Fortress America.

And yet, no country can really hope to improve its energy security by acting alone. True, cutting our own oil use would bring great things here at home, everything from cleaner air and water to lower noise pollution. But we'd be surprised by how little our domestic reductions changed the rest of the world—or improved our overall energy security.

The first problem, once again, is the small-planet nature of energy. America may be the biggest user of oil, but the price we pay is determined by global demand, and demand is being driven largely by booming Asia, which is only too happy to bum any barrel we manage to conserve or replace. Second, any shift to alternatives or better efficiency will take years and perhaps decades to implement. The U.S. car fleet, for example, turns over at a rate of just eight percent a year. That's as fast as consumers can afford to buy new cars and manufacturers can afford to make them, which means that—even in a fantasy scenario where the cars were already designed, the factories retooled, and the workers retrained—it would still take 12 years to deploy a greener fleet.

Most forecasts fail to acknowledge how slowly such changes could actually occur. Sure, if the United States could cut its oil consumption overnight by 9 million barrels, or 6.5 million barrels, or even 3.6 million barrels, it would have a staggering impact on oil prices. But barring a global depression, demand won't ever drop so rapidly; instead, our demand reductions will be incremental and thus effectively canceled out by the expected demand growth in other, less efficiency-minded countries like China. Berkeley's Borenstein, for example, estimates that the 3.6 million barrels the United States would save by 2030 under the 2007 energy bill will be more than offset by growth in demand elsewhere. Put another way, we could all squeeze into smaller cars and still be paying $4 for a gallon of gasoline.

To be sure, energy security isn't defined solely by cheap energy, and in fact, a great many enviros and energy wonks like oil at $100 a barrel, as it seems to be the only thing keeping more of us from buying Hummers. But high prices are killing our other energy-security objectives. High prices mean that money is still flowing into rogue states. High oil prices also imply tight oil markets, prone to massive price swings that are painful for consumers and make it virtually impossible for companies and governments to forecast their future energy costs—and so correctly gauge how much to invest in next-generation energy technologies. And no matter how clean and carbon free the United States becomes, if China and India are still burning massive volumes of oil we haven't done much to improve long-term security of any kind.

The only way to achieve real energy security is to reengineer not just our energy economy but that of the entire world. Oil prices won't fall, evil regimes won't be bankrupt, and sustainability won't be possible—until global oil demand is slowed. And outside of an economic meltdown, the only way it can be is if the tools we deploy to improve our own security can be somehow exported to other countries, and especially developing countries.

Energy globalism doesn't mean that every new energy gadget or fuel we invent has to work in Beijing or Burkina Faso. It does, however, suggest that our current energy strategy, tailored primarily to our own markets and our own technical capabilities, will be next to useless in an energy economy that is increasingly global—and that at least some of our energy investments should be compatible with regions where natural resources are strained, governments are poor, and consumers don't have access to home-equity lines of credit.

MYTH #5

Some Geek in Silicon Valley
Will Fix the Problem

So, what kinds of technologies would qualify under this more global strategy? Although corn and even cane ethanol are dubious—arable land in most of the developing world is already far too scarce—cellulosic ethanol has definite potential. Plug-in hybrids are probably too expensive for most Third World consumers, but have possibilities in the megacities of Asia and Latin America.

In the near term, however, the most practical energy export will be efficiency. China is so woefully inefficient that its economy uses 4.5 times as much energy as the United States for every dollar of output. This disparity explains why China is the world's second-biggest energy guzzler, but also why selling China more efficient technologies—cars, to be sure, but also better designs for houses, buildings, and industrial processes—could have a huge impact on global energy use and emissions.

As a bonus, such exports would likely be highly profitable. Japan, whose economy is nine times as energy efficient as China's, sees enormous economic and diplomatic opportunities selling its expertise to the Chinese, and America could tap into those opportunities as well—provided technologies with export potential get the kind of R&D support they need. Yet this isn't assured. You may have read that the volume of venture capital flowing into energy-technology companies is at a record high. But much of this capital is flowing into known technologies with rapid and assured payoffs—such as corn ethanol—instead of more speculative, but potentially more useful, technologies like cellulosic ethanol.

Once upon a time, America compensated for investor reluctance with gobs of federal money. But though President Bush routinely promises to spend more on alternative energy, little new money has appeared; federal spending on solar research, for example, is well short of that in the Clinton years, and the $148 million Bush pledged for solar back in 2006 was, in inflation-adjusted terms, less than half of what we spent annually in the 1970s. Other technologies suffer as well. Senator Richard Lugar, an Indiana Republican who has long argued for a global approach to energy security, notes that despite Bush's stated support for cellulosic ethanol, the Energy Department's "glacial implementation" of R&D loan guarantees has turned off potential investors. "The project is moving forward," Lugar says, "but critical time was lost."

MYTH #6

Cut Demand and the Rest Will Follow

Given America's tectonic pace toward energy security, the time has come for tough love. Most credible proposals call for some kind of energy or carbon tax. Such a tax would have two critical effects. It would keep the cost of oil high and thus discourage demand, as it has in Europe, and it would generate substantial revenues that could be used to fund research into alternatives, for example, of tax credits and other incentives to invest in the new energy technologies.

To be sure, higher fuel taxes, never popular with voters, would be even less so with gasoline prices already so high. Indeed, many energy wonks are still bitter that President Bush didn't advocate for a fuel tax or other demand-reduction measures in the aftermath of 9/11, when oil prices were relatively low and Americans were in the mood for sacrifice. Bush "could have gotten any set of energy measures passed after 9/11 if he had had an open and honest dialogue with America about how bad things were," says Edward Morse, an energy market analyst and former State Department energy official.

Instead, Bush urged Americans to . . . go shopping. Seven years later, with oil prices soaring and the economy hurting, swaying the electorate will take a politician who is politically courageous, extraordinarily articulate—and willing to dispense with the sweet nothings of energy independence.

And higher energy taxes are just the first dose of bitter medicine America needs to swallow if it wants real energy security. For no matter how aggressively the United States cuts oil demand both at home and abroad, it will be years and perhaps decades before any meaningful decline. The 12-year fleet-replacement scenario outlined above, for example, assumes that efficient new cars are being mass-produced worldwide and that adequate new volumes of electricity can be brought online as the fleet expands—assumptions that at present are wildly invalid. A more reasonable timetable is probably on the order of 20 years.

During this transition away from oil, we will still need lots and lots (and lots) of oil to fuel what remains of the oil-burning fleet. If over those 20 years global oil demand were to fall from the current 86 million barrels a day to, say, 40 million barrels a day, we'd still need an average of 63 million barrels a day, for a total of 459 billion barrels, or almost half as much oil as we've used since the dawn of humankind.

And here we come to two key points. First, because the transition will require so much old energy, we may get only one chance: If we find ourselves in 2028 having backed the wrong clusters of technologies or policies, and are still too dependent on oil, there may not be enough crude left in the ground to fuel a second try. Second, even if we do back the right technologies, the United States and the world's other big importers will still need far too much oil to avoid dealing with countries like Iran, Saudi Arabia, and Russia—no matter how abhorrent we find their politics.

In one of the many paradoxes of the new energy order, more energy security means less energy independence.

MYTH #7

Once Bush Is Gone, Change Will Come

No presidential candidate has indicated he or she will raise energy taxes or sit down in oil talks with Tehran. All have ties to a self-interested energy sector, be it coal, ethanol, or nukes. And even after the election, energy security is so complex and requires such hard choices that any president, and most members of Congress, will be sorely tempted to skirt the issue in the tried and true manner, by pushing for a far more palatable "energy independence." As Senator Lugar so choicely put it, "The president will have advisers who will be whispering cautions about the risks of committing the prestige of any administration to aggressive energy goals. Those advisers will say with some credibility that a president can appear forward-looking on energy with a few carefully chosen initiatives and occasional optimistic rhetoric promoting alternative sources. They will say that the voting public's overwhelming energy concern is high prices for gasoline and home heating, and that as long as the president appears attentive to those concerns they can cover their political bases without asking for sacrifices or risking the possible failure of a more controversial energy policy."

Lugar, a veteran pol, is no doubt correct about the pressures the next president will face. What we can only hope is that by the time he or she is chosen, the signals from an overheating energy economy will have reached a point where platitudes no longer suffice—where it is possible to embark on a "controversial energy policy," to ask voters to make sacrifices, and above all, to push America, the champion of globalization, out of a posture of self-absorption and into a stance that is genuinely and sustainably global—at which point the Saudi ambassador really would have something to worry about.

POSTSCRIPT

Is It Realistic for the United States to Move Toward Greater Energy Independence?

Not everyone agrees that high or increasing oil imports threaten U.S. national security. Philip E. Auerswald, "The Myth of Energy Insecurity," *Issues in Science & Technology* (Summer 2006), argues that high oil prices may be hard to bear, but "in an open society with a market economy, only prices have the brute power to effect change on the scale required." We will shift to non-oil energy sources when high prices drive sufficient investment in alternatives. He does not discuss the vulnerability of oil supplies to politics or terrorism. Jane C. S. Long, "A Blind Man's Guide to Energy Policy," *Issues in Science & Technology* (Winter 2008), discusses the role of these threats, as well as that of climate change, and argues that it is time for a more deliberate approach. "We must become the makers of our energy, climate, economic, and security fate." Waiting for markets to solve the problem is an example of the kind of thinking (focused on economics) that got us into this mess.

As of mid-2008, oil prices have never been higher. It is thus no surprise to see many discussions of alternative approaches to meeting U.S. energy needs. Ken Zweibel, James Mason, and Vasilis Fthenakis, "Solar Grand Plan," *Scientific American* (January 2008), offer one of the most grandiose—and perhaps promising—schemes in their proposal to spend $420 billion from 2011 to 2050 to construct a vast array of photovoltaic cells and solar concentrator power plants in the American Southwest. By 2050, this array would be able to supply two-thirds of the nation's electricity and a third of its total energy requirements. By 2100, it would supply 100 percent of U.S. electricity and 90 percent of total energy. Transportation needs would be met by using electricity to generate hydrogen. Given that some very promising work on improved batteries and related devices is now under way, hydrogen may not be needed. For more on solar concentrators, see Susan Moran and J. Thomas McKinnon, "Hot Times for Solar Energy," *World Watch* (March/April 2008).

Jon Birger, "Oil from a Stone," *Fortune* (November 12, 2007), reminds us of oil shale, which three decades ago was being examined as a possible oil source. The United States has large amounts of this hydrocarbon-rich sedimentary rock, and new technology may allow large amounts of oil to reach the market for centuries to come. Marianne Lavelle, "Power Revolution," *U.S. News & World Report* (November 5, 2007), discusses progress in solar, wind, and geothermal energy. Joe Castaldo, et al., "The Power of

Being Green," *Canadian Business* (March 17, 2008), discuss several innovative approaches including that of Magenn Power, which plans to mount wind turbines on blimps floating at high altitude.

Replacing an infrastructure built to handle one kind of energy source (oil) with another will of course take time and money. Some people argue that we are capable of making such a change in remarkably little time; they recall how quickly the United States shifted its industry to war production in World War II. Will we do so? That answer must come from politicians, and it will be shaped by how the costs of oil compare with those of deploying alternatives.

ISSUE 3

Should Cars Be More Efficient?

YES: David Friedman, from "CAFE Standards," Testimony before Committee on Senate Commerce, Science and Transportation (March 6, 2007)

NO: Charli E. Coon, from "Why the Government's CAFE Standards for Fuel Efficiency Should Be Repealed, Not Increased," Heritage Foundation Backgrounder #1458 (July 11, 2001)

ISSUE SUMMARY

YES: David Friedman, research director at the Union of Concerned Scientists, argues that the technology exists to improve fuel efficiency for new cars and trucks and requiring improved efficiency can cut oil imports, save money, create jobs, and help with global warming.

NO: Charli E. Coon, senior policy analyst with the Heritage Foundation, argues that the 1975 Corporate Average Fuel Economy (CAFE) program failed to meet its goals of reducing oil imports and gasoline consumption and has endangered human lives. It needs to be abolished and replaced with market-based solutions.

Automobiles have been a much-beloved feature of modern technology for over a century. Their advent increased mobility, made it possible for city workers to live outside the city, enabled goods to reach stores near almost everyone, and solved a growing environmental problem. Few realize how dirty the streets can be, how smelly cities can be, or how many flies can fill the air when transportation relies on horses! Ralph Turvey, "Horse Traction in Victorian London," *Journal of Transport History* (September 2005), says that these problems drew little mention at the time, but neither did most people mention the noisiness and smokiness (and poor gas mileage) of cars and trucks through the first half of the twentieth century. Still, most people thought cars and trucks were a vast improvement over horses. Those who had made millions in the oil business—beginning in Texas, Oklahoma, California, and some other states, and later in the Middle East and elsewhere—were also quite happy with the change. See Leonardo Maugeri, *The Age of Oil: The Mythology, History, and Future of the World's Most Controversial Resource* (Praeger, 2006), and Lisa Margonelli, *Oil on the Brain: Adventures from the Pump to the Pipeline* (Nan A. Talese, 2007).

By the 1970s, there were a great many cars and trucks on the road. Local railways were extinct, and horses were no longer bred in the large numbers of the past. There really was no substitute for gasoline-powered transportation, even though it consumed large amounts of oil imported from distant parts of the world. American dependence on these imports was highlighted when the Organization of Petroleum-Exporting Countries (OPEC) cut supplies and raised prices in the Oil Crisis of 1973. In the wake of the crisis, sales of foreign cars with better gas mileage increased at the expense of American-made cars, highway speed limits were reduced, and the U.S. Congress passed the Energy Policy and Conservation Act of 1975, which included the Corporate Average Fuel Economy (CAFE) program. The goal was to double average fuel efficiency by 1985. Fuel efficiency standards for passenger cars started at 18 mpg in 1978 and rose to 27.5 mpg for 1985; these standards were lowered in the late 1980s, but rose again to 27.5 mpg in 1990, where they have remained ever since. Light trucks had lower standards; in 2007, the standard was 22.2 mpg for light trucks.

Prompted by these requirements, as well as by foreign competition for the U.S. market, manufacturers successfully improved the performance of drive trains and engines and developed lighter materials for bodies. But as oil supplies became ample, even though the price of gasoline continued to rise, manufacturers also converted light truck designs to passenger versions, now known as sports utility vehicles (SUVs), and sold them as roomier, more powerful, and safer (largely because of size and weight) automobiles. SUVs are infamous for poor gasoline mileage, compared to passenger cars, but they are still classified as light trucks and held only to that standard. Improving their performance offers "the greatest potential to reduce fuel consumption on a total-gallons-saved basis" (*Effectiveness and Impact of Corporate Average Fuel Economy [CAFE] Standards,* National Academy Press, 2002).

In the following selections, David Friedman, research director at the Union of Concerned Scientists, argues that the technology exists to improve fuel efficiency for new cars and trucks and requiring improved efficiency can cut oil imports, save money, create jobs, and help with global warming. In addition, more fuel-efficient vehicles are actually safer to drive. Charli E. Coon, senior policy analyst with the Heritage Foundation, argues that the CAFE program failed to meet its goals of reducing oil imports and gasoline consumption and has endangered human lives. It needs to be abolished and replaced with market-based solutions.

YES

David Friedman

CAFE Standards

. . . I think we have reached an important milestone on fuel economy. It would appear that some leaders in Congress, including members of this committee, and the president are basically in agreement on how far we should increase fuel economy standards in about a ten year period.

In the president's state of the union speech, he set a goal for America to conserve up to 8.5 billion gallons of gasoline by 2017. To do so, we would need to increase fuel economy standards for cars and trucks to about 34 miles per gallon by 2017, or about 4 percent per year. At the same time, the bill recently introduced by the chairman and many members of this committee establishes a fuel economy target of 35 mpg by 2019. . . . The oil savings benefits of S. 357 are almost the same as the president's goal. Other members of the Senate and House have put forth bills with similar requirements in this and recent years.

In addition, Senator Stevens has introduced a bill to raise fuel economy standards for passenger cars to 40 mpg by 2017, or about a 39 percent increase compared to the average fuel economy of cars today. If Senator Stevens applied the same improvement to the rest of the fleet, it would average just over 34 mpg by 2017. As it stands, the oil savings from S. 183 are half of the others since only half the fleet is included.

I consider this a milestone because this significant agreement on fuel economy goals means that we can focus now on how best to reach them. By reforming and strengthening fuel economy standards for cars and trucks, this committee has a significant opportunity to help cut our oil addiction, save consumers money, create new jobs, and tackle the largest long term environmental threat facing the country and the world today, global warming.

Global Warming

Carbon dioxide, the main heat trapping gas blanketing our planet and warming the earth, has reached a concentration of about 380 parts per million. That is higher than the globe has experienced in the past 650,000 years. We are already seeing the impacts of these elevated concentrations as eleven of the last 12 years rank among the 12 hottest on record.

From FDCH Congressional Testimony by David Friedman (Union of Concerned Scientists), (March 6, 2007).

The worldwide costs of global warming could reach at least five percent of global GDP each year if we fail to take steps to cut emissions. These costs would come in lives and resources as tropical diseases and agricultural pests move north due to our warming continent. These costs could also come from losing 60–80 percent of the snow cover in the Sierras by the end of the century and the resulting impacts on agriculture in California and similar states that rely on snow melt for water. We will also see increased asthma and lung disease because higher temperatures will make urban smog worse than it is today.

Global warming is a worldwide problem and our cars and trucks have impacts that are worldwide in scale. Only the entire economies of the United States, China, and Russia exceed the global warming pollution resulting from our cars and trucks alone. It is clear that the scope of pollution from our cars and trucks requires special attention as we begin to address climate change.

Oil Addiction

In addition to the costs created by the pollution from our cars and trucks, our vehicles also contribute to 40 percent of our oil addiction. Overall, data from the Energy Information Administration indicates that we imported about sixty percent of our oil and other petroleum products in 2006. Last year alone, our net imports were more than 12 million barrels per day. When oil is at $60 per barrel, every minute that passes means over $500,000 that could have been spent creating U.S. jobs and strengthening our economy instead leaves this country. At the end of the day, high oil and gasoline prices and continued increases in our oil addiction represent one of the single biggest threats to U.S. auto jobs today.

Fuel Economy Background

One of the main reasons our vehicles contribute so much to U.S. oil dependence and global warming is that the average fuel economy of the fleet of new cars and trucks sold in the U.S. in 2006 was lower than it was in 1986. And while automakers note the number of models on the market that get more than 30 miles per gallon on the highway, a look at EPA's 2007 fuel economy guide shows that there are more than 300 car and truck configurations that get 15 mpg or less in the city. Even if you exclude pickups and work vans, automakers still flood the market with nearly 200 car, minivan, and SUV configurations that get 15 mpg or less in the city. Consumers simply do not have enough high fuel economy choices when it comes to cars, minivans, SUVs and pickups.

Fuel economy standards were created to solve this exact problem. Just as we see today, automakers were not ready for the problems created in part by our gas guzzling in the early 1970s. As a result consumers jumped on the only option they had at the time, relatively poorly designed smaller cars. However, as fuel economy standards were fully phased in automakers switched from giving consumers poor choices to putting technology in all cars and trucks so car buyers could have options in the showroom with 70% higher fuel economy than they had in 1975 (*2006 EPA Fuel Economy Trends Report*). If the fuel economy of today's cars and trucks was at the level the fleet experienced in 1975 instead of today's 25 miles per gallon, we would be using an additional 80 billion gallons of gasoline on top of the 140 billion gallons we will use this year. That would represent an increase in oil demand by 5.2 million barrels of oil per day, or a 25 percent increase in our oil addiction. At [2007's] average price for regular gasoline, about $2.50 per gallon, that represents $200 billion dollars saved. That number could have been much better, however, if fuel economy standards had not remained essentially unchanged for the past two decades.

Technology to Create Consumer Choice

Driving in America has become a necessity. Because of this and a lack of options, even the spikes in gasoline prices over the past five years have not been enough to push consumers to significantly reduce their gasoline consumption. Better fuels and more alternatives to driving are important to helping consumers and cutting pollution, but the quickest route to reduced gasoline consumption and saving consumers money is put to more high fuel economy choices in the showroom.

The automobile industry has been developing technologies that can safely and economically allow consumers to get more miles to the gallon in cars, minivans, pickups and SUVs of all shapes and sizes. . . . These technologies [can] dramatically increase the fuel economy of an SUV with the size and acceleration of a Ford Explorer. This could be achieved using direct injection gasoline engines, high efficiency automatic manual transmissions, engines that shut off instead of wasting fuel while idling, improved aerodynamics, better tires and other existing efficiency technologies. These technologies have no influence on the safety of the vehicle. Others, such as high-strength steel and aluminum and unibody construction could actually help make highways safer.

For just over $2,500 a consumer could have the choice of an SUV that gets more than 35 mpg. This is an SUV that alone could meet the fuel economy targets laid out by members of this committee and the president. At $2.50 per gallon, this SUV would save consumers over $7,800 on fuel costs during the vehicle's lifetime. The technologies needed for this better SUV would even pay for themselves in about three years. Automakers do already have vehicles on the road that can match this fuel economy, but most are compact cars. That leaves a mother with three children in car-seats or a farmer who needs a work truck with few vehicle choices until these technologies are packaged into higher fuel economy minivans, SUVs, pickups and other vehicles.

The technologies in this better SUV could be used across the fleet to reach more than 40 miles per gallon over the next ten years. The 2002 study by the National Academies on CAFE showed similar results. Data in the report indicate that the technology exists to reach 37 mpg in a fleet of the same make-up as the NAS analyzed, even ignoring hybrids and cleaner diesels.

The question now is whether automakers will use these tools to increase fuel economy. Automakers have spent the past twenty years using similar technologies to nearly double power and increase weight by twenty-five percent instead of increasing fuel economy (*EPA Fuel Economy Trends Report, 2006*). As a result, consumers today have cars and trucks with race-car like acceleration and plenty of room for children, pets and weekend projects. What consumers need now is to keep the size and performance they have today, while getting higher fuel economy. Without increased fuel economy standards, however, this future is unlikely. We are already seeing automakers market muscle hybrids, vehicles that use hybrid technology for increased power instead of increased fuel economy. And technologies such as cylinder cut-off, which increases fuel economy by shutting off engine cylinders when drivers need less power, are being used to offset increased engine power rather than increased fleetwide fuel economy.

This committee is in a position to ensure that consumers can keep the power, size and safety they have in their vehicles today, and save thousands of dollars while cutting both global warming pollution and our oil addiction through deployment of technology aimed at better fuel economy across the vehicle fleet.

Economic and Employment Impacts of Setting Fuel Economy Targets

Contrary to claims by the auto industry, investments in fuel economy technology, just like other investments in the economy, will lead to prosperity. No automaker would simply shut down a plant if it was making gas guzzlers that don't meet national fuel economy targets. Instead, they would make investments to upgrade their tooling to build more fuel efficient vehicles. A 2006 study from Walter McManus at the University of Michigan shows that automakers that invest in fuel economy, even as early as 2010, will improve their competitive position (*Can Proactive Fuel Economy Strategies Help Automakers Mitigate Fuel-Price Risks?*). According to the study, Detroit's Big Three could increase profits by $1.3 billion if they invest in fuel economy, even if gasoline costs only $2 per gallon. However, if they follow a business-as-usual approach their lost profits could be as large as $3.6 billion if gasoline costs $3.10 a gallon.

UCS has also sought to quantify the benefits of increased fuel economy (Friedman, 2004, *Creating Jobs, Saving Energy and Protecting the Environment*). We estimated the effect of moving existing technologies into cars and trucks over 10 years to reach an average of 40 miles per gallon (mpg). We found that:

In 10 years, the benefits resulting from investments in fuel economy would lead to 161,000 more jobs throughout the country, with California, Michigan, New York, Florida, Ohio, and Illinois topping the list.

In the automotive sector, projected jobs would grow by 40,800 in 10 years. A similar analysis done by the economic-research firm Management Information Services (MIS) evaluated the potential job impacts of increasing fuel economy to about 35–36 mpg by 2015 and found even greater growth at more than 350,000 new jobs in 2015 (Bezdek, 2005, *Fuel Efficiency and the Economy*). This job growth included all of the major auto industry states.

In both the UCS and the MIS studies these new jobs would be created both because of investments in new technologies by the automakers and because consumers would shift spending away from gasoline to more productive products and services.

Requiring all automakers to improve fuel economy will increase the health of the industry. Companies like Ford, General Motors and the Chrysler division are currently in bad financial condition due to poor management decisions and elevated gas prices, not fuel economy standards, which have been stagnant for the past two decades. Those poor decisions have put them in a place where, just as in the 1970s, they do not have the products consumers need at a time of increased gasoline prices, and they are continuing the slide in market share that began the first time they made this mistake.

By requiring Ford, GM, Chrysler and all automakers [to] give consumers the choices they need, Congress can ensure automaker jobs stay in the U.S. and models like the Ford Explorer and Chevrolet Tahoe are still on the market ten years from now though they will go farther on a gallon of gas.

Safety Impacts of Setting Fuel Economy Targets

While the NAS study clearly states that fuel economy can be increased with no impact on the safety of our cars and trucks, critics of fuel economy standards often point to the chapter, which takes a retrospective look at safety. Despite the fact that this chapter did not represent a consensus of the committee (a dissenting opinion from two panel members was included in the appendices) and the fact that three major analyses have since shown that fuel economy and safety are not inherently linked, claims are still made to the contrary.

First, David Greene (one of the NAS panel members) produced a report with Sanjana Ahmad in 2004 (*The Effect of Fuel Economy on Automobile Safety: A Reexamination*), which demonstrates that fuel economy is not linked with increased fatalities. In fact, the report notes that, "higher mpg is significantly correlated with fewer fatalities." In other words, a thorough analysis of data from 1966 to 2002 indicates that Congress can likely increase fuel economy without harming safety if the past is precept.

Second, Marc Ross and Tom Wenzel produced a report in 2002 (*An Analysis of Traffic Deaths by Vehicle Type and Model*), which demonstrates that large vehicles do not have lower fatality rates when compared to smaller vehicles. Ross and Wenzel analyzed federal accident data between 1995 and 1999 and showed that, for example, the Honda Civic and VW Jetta both had lower fatality rates for the driver than the Ford Explorer, the Dodge Ram, or the Toyota 4Runner. Even the largest vehicles, the Chevrolet Tahoe and Suburban had fatality rates that were no better than the VW Jetta or the Nissan Maxima. In other words, a well-designed compact car can be safer than an SUV or a pickup. Design, rather than weight, is the key to safe vehicles.

Finally, a study by Van Auken and Zellner in 2003 (*A Further Assessment of the Effects of Vehicle Weight and Size Parameters on Fatality Risk in Model Year 1985–98 Passenger Cars and 1985–97 Light Trucks*) indicates that increased weight is associated with increased fatalities, while increased size is associated with decreased fatalities. While this study was not able to bring in the impacts of design as well as size, it helped inform NHTSA as they rejected weight-based standards in favor of size-based standards based on the vehicle footprint.

These studies further back up Congress' ability to set fuel economy targets as high as 40 mpg for the fleet in the next ten years without impacting highway safety.

Getting Fuel Economy Policy Right

Given broader agreement on how far fuel economy must increase, we now need policies to lay out how to get there. Congress should follow four key steps to ensure that the country gets the benefits of existing fuel economy technology:

Establish a concrete fuel economy goal

Provide NHTSA with additional flexibility to establish size based standards

Institute a backstop to ensure that the fuel savings benefits are realized

Provide consumers and/or automakers with economic incentives to invest in technology for increased fuel economy, Set a target of 34–35 mpg

Congress can set a standard either meeting the president's goals of 34 mpg by 2017 or 35 mpg by 2019 as in S. 357. Both of these fuel economy levels are supported by the guidance requested and received from the NAS and UCS analysis. By adopting S. 357, Congress would cut global warming pollution by more than 230 million metric tons 2020, the equivalent of taking more than 30 million of today`s automobiles off the road. The bill would also cut oil dependency by 2.3 million barrels of oil per day in 2027, as much oil as we currently import from the Persian Gulf.

The key to reaching these goals, however, is that Congress must set these targets and not leave it up to NHTSA. NHTSA has proven to have a poor track record when setting fuel economy standards so far. Their recent rulemaking on light trucks will save less than two weeks of gasoline each year for the next two decades. This happened in part because they did not value the important benefits of cutting oil dependence and reducing global warming pollution from cars and trucks. By setting specific standards based on where technology can take us, Congress can make clear the importance of tackling these important problems which are hard to quantify analytically, but easy to qualify based on consumer discontent with gasoline prices last summer, political instability from dependence on oil from the Persian Gulf, and the surge in concern over global warming.

Congress should not defer its regulatory authority to the Administration and it need not as it can base such standards on the scientific research it requested. Congress can be confident that the goals are technically feasible, cost effective, and safe.

Provide NHTSA Authority to Establish Size-Based Standards

The bills in the Senate and the president's plans include the ability for NHTSA to set car and light truck standards based on vehicle attributes such as vehicle size. These size-based standards give manufacturers who make everything from compact cars to minivans to large pickups the flexibility they have been asking for and eliminate any arguments automakers have made about CAFE standards treating them inequitably.

Size-based standards designed to increase fleet fuel economy to 35 mpg might require a family car to reach 40 mpg, but a pickup would only have to reach about 28 mpg because it is larger. This is good news for farmers and contractors who rely on these vehicles. With existing technology, pickups could readily reach 28 mpg and would save their owners over $6,000 on gasoline during the life of the vehicle. The pickup would have the same power, performance, size and safety it has today, and would cost an additional $1,500. However, the added fuel economy technology would pay for itself in less than two years with gasoline at $2.50 per gallon. Higher fuel economy standards will help farmers and small businesses who rely on trucks as much or even more than the average consumer.

Ensure No Backsliding

The one challenge with size-based standards is that automakers can game the system and drive down fuel economy. Much as automakers switched to marketing SUVs because of the lower standards required of light trucks to date, automakers may also upsize their vehicles to classes with lower fuel economy targets when they redesign their vehicles every four to seven years. Our analysis of NHTSA's most recent light truck rule shows that we could lose as much as half of the promised fuel economy gains, as small as they are, if the fleet of light trucks increased in size by just 10 percent over ten years. Congress must require a backstop to ensure that fuel savings that would be generated from a 10 mpg fuel economy increase are not lost due to automakers who game the system.

Provide Incentives

Because increased fuel economy will provide a wide variety of benefits for the nation, it is in the nation's interest to help automakers and suppliers who make cars and trucks in the U.S. that go farther on a gallon of gasoline. One way to help the auto industry is to provide tax credits, loan guarantees, or grants to companies that guarantee fuel economy improvements by investing in the equipment and people who will be needed to make these more efficient vehicles. This policy could be further supported by a set of charges and rebates applied to vehicles based on their fuel economy. These "feebates" will send market signals to producers and consumers in support of higher fuel economy standards and can even be made revenue neutral.

Conclusions

Climate change represents the largest long term environmental threat facing our country and the world today and the costs of our oil addiction continue to grow. Setting a fleet-wide target sufficient to meet the president's goal and guarantee fuel economy improvements of at least 10 mpg over the next decade while giving the president the authority to reach that target through size-based standards will save consumers money, stimulate the economy, create and protect jobs and preserve the safety of our vehicles. All of these benefits will come in addition to cutting our oil dependence and emissions of global warming pollutants from our cars and trucks.

Consumers are clearly happy with the size and acceleration of their vehicles today. We don't have to change that. But consumers are clearly unhappy with the growing impacts of global warming and the high cost of gasoline and the pumps and on our economy and security.

Congress has the opportunity to ensure that automakers spend the next decade or more using technology to curb our oil addiction. This is not a surprising role for Congress, the Federal government has helped drive every major transportation revolution this country has seen, whether it was trains, planes, or automobiles. The next transition will be no different.

Charli E. Coon  **NO**

Why the Government's CAFE Standards for Fuel Efficiency Should Be Repealed, Not Increased

Congress may soon decide to increase the standards for fuel economy imposed on manufacturers of vehicles sold in the United States. This would be a mistake.

In 1975, Congress reacted to the 1973 oil embargo imposed by the Organization of Petroleum Exporting Countries (OPEC) by establishing the Corporate Average Fuel Economy (CAFE) Program as part of the Energy Policy and Conservation Act. The goal of the program was to reduce U.S. dependence on imported oil and consumption of gasoline. Advocates also hoped it would improve air quality. But the evidence shows that it has failed to meet its goals; worse, it has had unintended consequences that increase the risk of injury to Americans. Instead of perpetuating such a program, Congress should consider repealing the CAFE standards and finding new market-based solutions to reduce high gasoline consumption and rising prices.

There is significant pressure on Members of Congress, however, not only to continue this failed program, but also to raise fuel efficiency standards even higher. The current CAFE standards require auto manufacturers selling in the United States to meet certain fuel economy levels for their fleets of new cars and light trucks (pickups, minivans, and sport utility vehicles, or SUVs). The standard for passenger cars is currently 27.5 miles per gallon; for light trucks, it is 20.7 mpg.

Manufacturers face stiff fines for failing to meet these standards based on the total number of vehicles in each class sold, but compliance is taken out of their hands. The government measures compliance by calculating a sales-weighted mean of the fuel economies for the fleets of new cars and light trucks a manufacturer sells each year, and it measures domestically produced and imported vehicles separately.

Clearly, the CAFE program has failed to accomplish its purposes. Oil imports have not decreased. In fact, they have increased from about 35 percent of supply in the mid-1970s to 52 percent today. Likewise, consumption has not decreased. As fuel efficiency improves, consumers have generally increased their driving, offsetting nearly all the gains in fuel efficiency. Not only has the CAFE program failed to meet its goals; it has had tragic even if unintended consequences. As vehicles were being made lighter to achieve more miles per gallon and meet the standards, the number of fatalities from crashes rose.

Politicians should stop distorting the marketplace with unwise policies and convoluted regulations and allow the market to respond to consumer demand for passenger vehicles. In addition to free-market considerations, there are other compelling reasons to reject the CAFE standards. For example:

- CAFE standards endanger human lives;
- CAFE standards fail to reduce consumption; and
- CAFE standards do not improve the environment.

How CAFE Increases Risks to Motorists

The evidence is overwhelming that CAFE standards result in more highway deaths. A 1999 USA TODAY analysis of crash data and estimates from the National Highway Traffic Safety Administration and the Insurance Institute for Highway Safety found that, in the years since CAFE standards were mandated under the Energy Policy and Conservation Act of 1975, about 46,000 people have died in crashes that they would have survived if they had been traveling in bigger, heavier cars. This translates into 7,700 deaths for every mile per gallon gained by the standards.

While CAFE standards do not mandate that manufacturers make small cars, they have had a significant effect on the designs manufacturers adopt—generally, the weights of passenger vehicles have been falling. Producing smaller, lightweight vehicles that can perform satisfactorily using low-power, fuel-efficient engines is the most affordable way for automakers to meet the CAFE standards.

More than 25 years ago, research established that drivers of larger, heavier cars have lower risks in crashes than do drivers of smaller, lighter cars. A 2000 study by Leonard Evans, now the president of the Science Serving Society in Michigan, found that adding a passenger to one of two identical cars involved in a two-car frontal crash reduces the driver fatality risk by 7.5 percent. If the cars differ in mass by more than a passenger's weight, adding a passenger to the lighter car will reduce total risk.

The Evans findings reinforce a 1989 study by economists Robert Crandall of the Brookings Institution and John Graham of the Harvard School of Public Health, who found that the weight of the average American automobile has been reduced 23 percent since 1974, much of this reduction a result of CAFE regulations. Crandall and Graham stated that "the negative relationship between weight and occupant fatality risk is one of the most secure findings in the safety literature."

Harvard University's John Graham reiterated the safety risks of weight reduction in correspondence with then-U.S. Senator John Ashcroft (R-MO) in June 2000. Graham was responding to a May 2000 letter distributed to Members of the House from the American Council for an Energy-Efficient Economy (ACEEE) and the Center for Auto Safety. Graham sought to correct its misleading statements, such as its discussion of weight reduction as a compliance strategy without reference to the safety risks associated with the use of lighter steel. For example, an SUV may be more likely to roll over if it is constructed with lighter materials, and drivers of vehicles that crash into guardrails are generally safer when their vehicle contains more mass rather than less. Further, according to Graham, government studies have found that making small cars heavier has seven times the safety benefit than making light trucks lighter.

The evidence clearly shows that smaller cars have significant disadvantages in crashes. They have less space to absorb crash forces. The less the car absorbs, the more people inside the vehicle must absorb. Consequently, the weight and size reductions resulting from the CAFE standards are linked with the 46,000 deaths through 1998 mentioned above, as well as thousands of injuries. It is time that policymakers stop defending the failed CAFE program and start valuing human lives by repealing the standards.

Why CAFE Fails to Reduce Consumption

Advocates of higher CAFE standards argue that increasing miles per gallon will reduce gas consumption. What they fail to mention is the well-known "rebound effect"—greater energy efficiency leads to greater energy consumption. A recent article in *The Wall Street Journal* noted that in the 19th century, British economist Stanley Jevons found that coal consumption initially decreased by one-third after James Watt's new, efficient steam engine began replacing older, more energy-hungry engines. But in the ensuing years (1830 to 1863), consumption increased tenfold—the engines were cheaper to run and thus were used more often than the older, less efficient models. In short, greater efficiency produced more energy use, not less.

The same principle applies to CAFE standards. A more fuel-efficient vehicle costs less to drive per mile, so vehicle mileage increases. As the author of *The Wall Street Journal* article notes, "[s]ince 1970, the United States has made cars almost 50% more efficient; in that period of time, the average number of miles a person drives has doubled." This increase certainly offsets a portion of the gains made in fuel efficiency from government mandated standards.

Why CAFE Standards Do Not Improve the Environment

Proponents of higher CAFE standards contend that increasing fuel economy requirements for new cars and trucks will improve the environment by causing less pollution. This is incorrect.

Federal regulations impose emissions standards for cars and light trucks, respectively. These standards are identical for every car or light truck in those two classes regardless of their fuel economy. These limits are stated in grams per mile of acceptable pollution, not in grams per gallon of fuel burned. Accordingly, a Lincoln Town Car with a V-8 engine may not by law emit more emissions in a mile, or 10 miles, or 1,000 miles, than a Chevrolet Metro with a three-cylinder engine.

As noted by the National Research Council (NRC) in a 1992 report on automobile fuel economy, "Fuel economy improvements will not directly affect vehicle emissions." In fact, the NRC found that higher fuel economy standards could actually have a negative effect on the environment:

Improvements in vehicle fuel economy will have indirect environmental impacts. For example, replacing the cast iron and steel components of vehicles with lighter weight materials (e.g., aluminum, plastics, or composites) may reduce fuel consumption but would generate a different set of environmental impacts, as well as result in different kinds of indirect energy consumption.

Nor will increasing CAFE standards halt the alleged problem of "global warming." Cars and light trucks subject to fuel economy standards make up only 1.5 percent of all global man-made greenhouse gas emissions. According to data published in 1991 by the Office of Technology Assessment, a 40 percent increase in fuel economy standards would reduce greenhouse emissions by only about 0.5 percent, even under the most optimistic assumptions.

The NRC additionally noted that "greenhouse gas emissions from the production of substitute materials, such as aluminum, could substantially offset decreases of those emissions achieved through improved fuel economy."

Conclusion

The CAFE program has failed to achieve its goals. Since its inception, both oil imports and vehicle miles driven have increased while the standards have led to reduced consumer choice and lives lost that could have survived car crashes in heavier vehicles.

The CAFE standards should not be increased. They should be repealed and replaced with free market strategies. Consumers respond to market signals. As past experience shows, competition can lead to a market that makes gas guzzlers less attractive than safer and more fuel-efficient vehicles. That is the right way to foster energy conservation.

POSTSCRIPT

Should Cars Be More Efficient?

In December 2007, U.S. President George W. Bush signed into law an energy bill that, among other things, requires a 10-mpg improvement in motor vehicle fuel-economy standards by 2020; see "Energy Bill Boosting CAFE Standards Approved," *Issues in Science & Technology* (Spring 2008). Debate over whether the new standards will work quickly ensued, with Robert W. Crandall, "Are Higher Vehicle Fuel-Economy Standards Good Energy Policy? No" opposing Michelle Robinson, "Are Higher Vehicle Fuel-Economy Standards Good Energy Policy? Yes," in *CQ Researcher* (January 4, 2008). Bruce Geiselman and Elizabeth McGowan, "Feds Hike CAFÉ Standards 25%," *Waste News* (April 28, 2008) note that the increase in efficiency will be phased in gradually between 2011 and 2015.

Despite the continuing debate, this bill clearly reinforces the title of Mark Clayton's and Mark Trumbull's "Fuel Economy Back on US Agenda," *Christian Science Monitor* (May 10, 2007). Whether its goals can be achieved depends on a number of factors. *Effectiveness and Impact of Corporate Average Fuel Economy (CAFE) Standards* (National Academy Press, 2002) says that while the technology exists to improve gasoline mileage by 20–40 percent or more, consumers may have to pay more, and if gasoline prices drop, they may refuse (bear in mind that gas prices show no sign of dropping). In addition, CAFE standards apply to vehicles sold in a particular year, not to all the vehicles on the road in that year. It can take a decade or more (depending on the economy) to replace all the vehicles on the road. Thus efficiency of fuel use cannot possibly rise as rapidly as the standards for new cars.

Some of the technologies that can improve fuel efficiency are still in the research and development stage. Some, however, are well established. In Europe, the Smart Car (developed by Daimler-Benz engineers; see http://www.smartusa.com/) is very common on the streets; using a diesel engine, it gets about 70 mpg. The gasoline-powered version introduced in California in June 2007 (see Robert Salonga, "Car Small in Size, Big on Fuel Mileage," *Salinas Californian,* June 25, 2007) gets about 50 mpg. The secret is in part size: The Smart Car is a small car designed for commuters and others who do not have to haul much cargo. It carries two people, plus a bag or two of groceries.

Mark Clayton, "Safe Cars versus Fuel Efficiency? Not So Fast," *Christian Science Monitor* (June 12, 2007), notes that some automakers are insisting that raising fuel efficiency requires reducing vehicle size, which then reduces safety (see also Moira Herbst, "Fighting for the Right to Make Big Cars," *Business Week Online,* May 30, 2007). But good design can change that. The Smart Car, as just one example, has an egg-shaped frame that holds up very well in crashes despite its size.

ISSUE 4

Should the Arctic National Wildlife Refuge Be Opened to Oil Drilling?

YES: Dwight R. Lee, from "To Drill or Not to Drill?" *Independent Review* (Fall 2001)

NO: Jeff Bingaman et al., from ANWR Minority Views from Senate Energy Committee (October 24th, 2005)

ISSUE SUMMARY

YES: Dwight R. Lee argues that the economic and other benefits of Arctic National Wildlife Refuge (ANWR) oil are so great that even environmentalists should agree to permit drilling.

NO: The minority members of the Senate Energy Committee objected when the Committee approved a bill that would authorize oil and gas development in the ANWR. They argued that though the bill contained serious legal and environmental flaws, the greatest flaw lay in its choice of priorities: Wilderness is to be preserved, not exploited.

According to Matthew J. Kotchen and Nicholas E. Burger, "Should We Drill in the Arctic National Wildlife Refuge? An Economic Perspective," *Energy Policy* (September 2007), Alaska's Arctic National Wildlife Refuge (ANWR) contains over 7 billion barrels of oil, about enough to satisfy U.S. demand for four months. "The oil is worth $374 billion ($2005), but would cost $123 billion to extract and bring to market. The difference, $251 billion, would generate social benefits through industry rents of $90 billion as well as state and federal tax revenues of $37 billion and $124 billion, respectively. . . . But drilling and development in ANWR would also bring about environmental costs."

The debate over whether to extract the ANWR oil has been going on for years, and in 2008, with gasoline and oil prices rising rapidly, it gained new urgency, with President George W. Bush once more urging Congress to allow drilling. So far, the environmentalists have won.

The first national parks date to the 1870s. Parks and the national forests are managed for "multiple use," on the premise that wildlife protection, recreation, timber-cutting, and even oil drilling and mining can coexist. The first "primitive areas," where all development was barred, were created by the U.S. Forest Service in the 1920s. However, pressure from commercial interests led to the reclassification of many such areas and their opening to exploitation. In 1964, the Federal Wilderness Act provided a mechanism for designating "wilderness" areas, defined as areas "where the earth and its community of life are untrammeled by man, where man himself is a visitor who does not remain." Since then it has become clear that pesticides and other chemicals are found everywhere on Earth, drifting on winds and ocean currents and travelling in migrant birds even to areas without obvious human presence in the form of buildings, towns, roads, and industry. "Man" may not be present, but his effects are. And commercial interests are just as interested in the wealth that may be extracted from these areas as they ever were. There is continual pressure to expand commercial use of national forests and parks.

The ANWR provides a good illustration. It is not a "wilderness" area, for it was designated a wildlife preserve in 1960 and enlarged and renamed in 1980 with the proviso that its "Coastal Plain" portion be evaluated for its potential value for oil and gas production. In 1987, the Department of the Interior recommended that the Coastal Plain be opened for oil and gas exploration. In 1995, Congress approved doing so, but President Clinton vetoed the legislation. After California experienced electrical blackouts in 2001, President George Bush declared opening the ANWR to oil exploitation essential to national energy security but could not muster enough votes in Congress to make it happen. In 2004, the Bush administration proposed once more to open the ANWR to oil drilling, and in December 2005, the House of Representatives approved a defense bill with a provision approving ANWR drilling. The Senate immediately blocked the provision, but with gasoline prices soaring, in March 2006 Bush renewed his call for approval to exploit the ANWR for oil. In May 2006, the House provided that approval.

The debate over protecting wilderness areas generally centers on economic arguments. In the following selections, Dwight R. Lee argues that the economic and other benefits of ANWR oil are so great that even environmentalists—if only they stood to benefit directly—should agree to permit drilling. Where environmental groups own suitable land and can collect the drilling fees, they already have shown themselves willing to permit drilling. In addition, ANWR oil could save lives by permitting more people to drive larger (and therefore safer) vehicles. When in October 2005 the Senate Energy Committee approved a bill that would authorize oil and gas development in the ANWR, the Committee's minority members argued that the bill contained serious legal and environmental flaws, but its greatest flaw lay in its choice of priorities: Wilderness is to be preserved, not exploited for its energy resources.

YES

Dwight R. Lee

To Drill or Not to Drill

High prices of gasoline and heating oil have made drilling for oil in Alaska's Arctic National Wildlife Refuge (ANWR) an important issue. ANWR is the largest of Alaska's sixteen national wildlife refuges, containing 19.6 million acres. It also contains significant deposits of petroleum. The question is, Should oil companies be allowed to drill for that petroleum?

The case for drilling is straightforward. Alaskan oil would help to reduce U.S. dependence on foreign sources subject to disruptions caused by the volatile politics of the Middle East. Also, most of the infrastructure necessary for transporting the oil from nearby Prudhoe Bay to major U.S. markets is already in place. Furthermore, because of the experience gained at Prudhoe Bay, much has already been learned about how to mitigate the risks of recovering oil in the Arctic environment.

No one denies the environmental risks of drilling for oil in ANWR. No matter how careful the oil companies are, accidents that damage the environment at least temporarily might happen. Environmental groups consider such risks unacceptable; they argue that the value of the wilderness and natural beauty that would be spoiled by drilling in ANWR far exceeds the value of the oil that would be recovered. For example, the National Audubon Society characterizes opening ANWR to oil drilling as a threat "that will destroy the integrity" of the refuge (see statement at . . .).

So, which is more valuable, drilling for oil in ANWR or protecting it as an untouched wilderness and wildlife refuge? Are the benefits of the additional oil really less than the costs of bearing the environmental risks of recovering that oil? Obviously, answering this question with great confidence is difficult because the answer depends on subjective values. Just how do we compare the convenience value of using more petroleum with the almost spiritual value of maintaining the "integrity" of a remote and pristine wilderness area? Although such comparisons are difficult, we should recognize that they can be made. Indeed, we make them all the time.

We constantly make decisions that sacrifice environmental values for what many consider more mundane values, such as comfort, convenience, and material well-being. There is nothing wrong with making such sacrifices because up to some point the additional benefits we realize from

This article is reprinted with permission from the publisher of *The Independent Review: A Journal of Political Economy* (vol. VI, no. 2, Fall 2001, pp. 217–226). Copyright © 2001 by The Independent Institute, 100 Swan Way, Oakland, CA 94621-1428. info@independent.org; www.independent.org.

sacrificing a little more environmental "integrity" are worth more than the necessary sacrifice. Ideally, we would somehow acquire the information necessary to determine where that point is and then motivate people with different perspectives and preferences to respond appropriately to that information.

Achieving this ideal is not as utopian as it might seem; in fact, such an achievement has been reached in situations very similar to the one at issue in ANWR. In this article, I discuss cases in which the appropriate sacrifice of wilderness protection for petroleum production has been responsibly determined and harmoniously implemented. Based on this discussion, I conclude that we should let the Audubon Society decide whether to allow drilling in ANWR. That conclusion may seem to recommend a foregone decision on the issue because the society has already said that drilling for oil in ANWR is unacceptable. But actions speak louder than words, and under certain conditions I am willing to accept the actions of environmental groups such as the Audubon Society as the best evidence of how they truly prefer to answer the question, To drill or not to drill in ANWR?

Private Property Changes One's Perspective

What a difference private property makes when it comes to managing multiuse resources. When people make decisions about the use of property they own, they take into account many more alternatives than they do when advocating decisions about the use of property owned by others. This straightforward principle explains why environmental groups' statements about oil drilling in ANWR (and in other publicly owned areas) and their actions in wildlife areas they own are two very different things.

For example, the Audubon Society owns the Rainey Wildlife Sanctuary, a 26,000-acre preserve in Louisiana that provides a home for fish, shrimp, crab, deer, ducks, and wading birds, and is a resting and feeding stopover for more than 100,000 migrating snow geese each year. By all accounts, it is a beautiful wilderness area and provides exactly the type of wildlife habitat that the Audubon Society seeks to preserve. But, as elsewhere in our world of scarcity, the use of the Rainey Sanctuary as a wildlife preserve competes with other valuable uses.

Besides being ideally suited for wildlife, the sanctuary contains commercially valuable reserves of natural gas and oil, which attracted the attention of energy companies when they were discovered in the 1940s. Clearly, the interests served by fossil fuels do not have high priority for the Audubon Society. No doubt, the society regards additional petroleum use as a social problem rather than a social benefit. Of course, most people have different priorities: they place a much higher value on keeping down the cost of energy than they do on bird-watching and on protecting what many regard as little more than mosquito-breeding swamps. One might suppose that members of the Audubon Society have no reason to consider such "anti-environmental" values when deciding how to use their own land. Because the society owns the Rainey Sanctuary, it can ignore interests antithetical to its own and refuse to allow drilling. Yet, precisely because the society owns the land, it has been willing to accommodate the interests of those whose priorities are different and has allowed thirty-seven wells to pump gas and oil from the Rainey Sanctuary. In return, it has received royalties of more than $25 million.

One should not conclude that the Audubon Society has acted hypocritically by putting crass monetary considerations above its stated concerns for protecting wilderness and wildlife. In a wider context, one sees that because of its ownership of the Rainey Sanctuary, the Audubon Society is part of an extensive network of market communication and cooperation that allows it to do a better job of promoting its objectives by helping others promote theirs. Consumers communicate the value they receive from additional gas and oil to petroleum companies through the prices they willingly pay for those products, and this communication is transmitted to owners of oil-producing land through the prices the companies are willing to pay to drill on that land. Money really does "talk" when it takes the form of market prices. The money offered for drilling rights in the Rainey Sanctuary can be viewed as the most effective way for millions of people to tell the Audubon Society how much they value the gas and oil its property can provide.

By responding to the price communication from consumers and by allowing the drilling, the Audubon Society has not sacrificed its environmental values in some debased lust for lucre. Instead, allowing the drilling has served to reaffirm and promote those values in a way that helps others, many of whom have different values, achieve their own purposes. Because of private ownership, the valuations of others for the oil and gas in the Rainey Sanctuary create an opportunity for the Audubon Society to purchase additional sanctuaries to be preserved as habitats for the wildlife it values. So the society has a strong incentive to consider the benefits as well as the costs of drilling on its property. Certainly, environmental risks exist, and the society considers them, but if also responsibly weighs the costs of those risks against the benefits as measured by the income derived from drilling. Obviously, the Audubon Society appraises the benefits from drilling as greater than the costs, and it acts in accordance with that appraisal.

Cooperation Between Bird-Watchers and Hot-Rodders

The advantage of private ownership is not just that it allows people with different interests to interact in mutually beneficial ways. It also creates harmony between those whose interests would otherwise be antagonistic. For example, most members of the Audubon Society surely see the large sport utility vehicles and high-powered cars encouraged by abundant petroleum supplies as environmentally harmful. That perception, along with the environmental risks associated with oil recovery, helps explain why the Audubon Society vehemently opposes drilling for oil in the ANWR as well as in the continental shelves in the Atlantic, the Pacific, and the

Gulf of Mexico. Although oil companies promise to take extraordinary pre-cautions to prevent oil spills when drilling in these areas, the Audubon Society's position is no off-shore drilling, none. One might expect to find Audubon Society members completely unsympathetic with hot-rodding enthusiasts, NASCAR racing fans, and drivers of Chevy Suburbans. Yet, as we have seen, by allowing drilling for gas and oil in the Rainey Sanctu-ary, the society is accommodating the interests of those with gas-guzzling lifestyles, risking the "integrity" of its prized wildlife sanctuary to make more gasoline available to those whose energy consumption it verbally condemns as excessive.

The incentives provided by private property and market prices not only motivate the Audubon Society to cooperate with NASCAR racing fans, but also motivate those racing enthusiasts to cooperate with the Audubon Society. Imagine the reaction you would get if you went to a stock-car race and tried to convince the spectators to skip the race and go bird-watching instead. Be prepared for some beer bottles tossed your way. Yet by purchas-ing tickets to their favorite sport, racing fans contribute to the purchase of gasoline that allows the Audubon Society to obtain additional wildlife habitat and to promote bird-watching. Many members of the Audubon Society may feel contempt for racing fans, and most racing fans may laugh at bird-watchers, but because of private property and market prices, they nevertheless act to promote one another's interests.

The Audubon Society is not the only environmental group that, be-cause of the incentives of private ownership, promotes its environmen-tal objectives by serving the interests of those with different objectives. The Nature Conservancy accepts land and monetary contributions for the purpose of maintaining natural areas for wildlife habitat and ecological preservation. It currently owns thousands of acres and has a well-deserved reputation for preventing development in environmentally sensitive ar-eas. Because it owns the land, it has also a strong incentive to use that land wisely to achieve its objectives, which sometimes means recognizing the value of developing the land.

For example, soon after the Wisconsin chapter received title to 40 acres of beach-front land on St. Croix in the Virgin Islands, it was offered a much larger parcel of land in northern Wisconsin in exchange for its beach land. The Wisconsin chapter made this trade (with some covenants on development of the beach land) because owning the Wisconsin land al-lowed it to protect an entire watershed containing endangered plants that it considered of greater environmental value than what was sacrificed by allowing the beach to be developed.

Thanks to a gift from the Mobil Oil Company, the Nature Conserv-ancy of Texas owns the Galveston Bay Prairie Preserve in Texas City, a 2,263-acre refuge that is home to the Attwater's prairie chicken, a highly endangered species (once numbering almost a million, its population had fallen to fewer than ten by the early 1990s). The conservancy has entered into an agreement with Galveston Bay Resources of Houston and Aspects Resources, LLC, of Denver to drill for oil and natural gas in the preserve.

Clearly some risks attend oil drilling in the habitat of a fragile endangered species, and the conservancy has considered them, but it considers the gains sufficient to justify bearing the risks. According to Ray Johnson, East County program manager for the Nature Conservancy of Texas. "We believe this could provide a tremendous opportunity to raise funds to acquire additional habitat for the Attwater's prairie chicken, one of the most threatened birds in North America." Obviously the primary concern is to protect the endangered species, but the demand for gas and oil is helping achieve that objective. Johnson is quick to point out, "We have taken every precaution to minimize the impact of the drilling on the prairie chickens and to ensure their continued health and safety."

Back to ANWR

Without private ownership, the incentive to take a balanced and accommodating view toward competing land-use values disappears. So, it is hardly surprising that the Audubon Society and other major environmental groups categorically oppose drilling in ANWR. Because ANWR is publicly owned, the environmental groups have no incentive to take into account the benefits of drilling. The Audubon Society does not capture any of the benefits if drilling is allowed, as it does at the Rainey Sanctuary; in ANWR, it sacrifices nothing if drilling is prevented. In opposing drilling in ANWR, despite the fact that the precautions to be taken there would be greater than those required of companies operating in the Rainey Sanctuary, the Audubon Society is completely unaccountable for the sacrificed value of the recoverable petroleum.

Obviously, my recommendation to "let the environmentalists decide" whether to allow oil to be recovered from ANWR makes no sense if they are not accountable for any of the costs (sacrificed benefits) of preventing drilling. I am confident, however, that environmentalists would immediately see the advantages of drilling in ANWR if they were responsible for both the costs and the benefits of that drilling. As a thought experiment about how incentives work, imagine that a consortium of environmental organizations is given veto power over drilling, but is also given a portion (say, 10 percent) of what energy companies are willing to pay for the right to recover oil in ANWR. These organizations could capture tens of millions of dollars by giving their permission to drill. Suddenly the opportunity to realize important environmental objectives by favorably considering the benefits others gain from more energy consumption would come into sharp focus. The environmentalists might easily conclude that although ANWR is an "environmental treasure," other environmental treasures in other parts of the country (or the world) are even more valuable; moreover, with just a portion of the petroleum value of the ANWR, efforts might be made to reduce the risks to other natural habitats, more than compensating for the risks to the Arctic wilderness associated with recovering that value.

Some people who are deeply concerned with protecting the environment see the concentration on "saving" ANWR from any development as misguided even without a vested claim on the oil wealth it contains. For example, according to Craig Medred, the outdoor writer for the *Anchorage Daily News* and a self-described "development-phobic wilderness lover,"

> That people would fight to keep the scar of clearcut logging from the spectacular and productive rain-forests of Southeast Alaska is easily understandable to a shopper in Seattle or a farmer in Nebraska. That people would argue against sinking a few holes through the surface of a frozen wasteland, however, can prove more than a little baffling even to development-phobic, wilderness lovers like me. Truth be known, I'd trade the preservation rights to any 100 acres on the [ANWR] slope for similar rights to any acre of central California wetlands. . . . It would seem of far more environmental concern that Alaska's ducks and geese have a place to winter in overcrowded, overdeveloped California than that California's ducks and geese have a place to breed each summer in uncrowded and undeveloped Alaska.
>
> — (1996, CI)

Even a small share of the petroleum wealth in ANWR would dramatically reverse the trade-off Medred is willing to make because it would allow environmental groups to afford easily a hundred acres of central California wetlands in exchange for what they would receive for each acre of ANWR released to drilling.

We need not agree with Medred's characterization of the ANWR as "a frozen wasteland" to suspect that environmentalists are overstating the environmental amenities that drilling would put at risk. With the incentives provided by private property, environmental groups would quickly reevaluate the costs of drilling in wilderness refuges and soften their rhetoric about how drilling would "destroy the integrity" of these places. Such hyperbolic rhetoric is to be expected when drilling is being considered on public land because environmentalists can go to the bank with it. It is easier to get contributions by depicting decisions about oil drilling on public land as righteous crusades against evil corporations out to destroy our priceless environment for short-run profit than it is to work toward minimizing drilling costs to accommodate better the interests of others. Environmentalists are concerned about protecting wildlife and wilderness areas in which they have ownership interest, but the debate over any threat from drilling and development in those areas is far more productive and less acrimonious than in the case of ANWR and other publicly owned wilderness areas.

The evidence is overwhelming that the risks of oil drilling to the arctic environment are far less than commonly claimed. The experience gained in Prudhoe Bay has both demonstrated and increased the oil companies' ability to recover oil while leaving a "light footprint" on arctic tundra and wildlife. Oil-recovery operations are now sited on gravel pads providing foundations that protect the underlying permafrost. Instead of using pits to contain the residual mud and other waste from drilling, techniques are now available for pumping the waste back into the well in ways that help maintain well pressure and reduce the risks of spills on the tundra. Improvements in arctic road construction have eliminated the need for the gravel access roads used in the development of the Prudhoe Bay oil fields. Roads are now made from ocean water pumped onto the tundra, where it freezes to form a road surface. Such roads melt without a trace during the short summers. The oversize rubber tires used on the roads further minimize any impact on the land.

Improvements in technology now permit horizontal drilling to recover oil that is far from directly below the wellhead. This technique reduces further the already small amount of land directly affected by drilling operations. Of the more than 19 million acres contained in ANWR, almost 18 million acres have been set aside by Congress—somewhat more than 8 million as wilderness and 9.5 million as wildlife refuge. Oil companies estimate that only 2,000 acres would be needed to develop the coastal plain.

This carefully conducted and closely confined activity hardly sounds like a sufficient threat to justify the rhetoric of a righteous crusade to prevent the destruction of ANWR, so the environmentalists warn of a detrimental effect on arctic wildlife that cannot be gauged by the limited acreage directly affected. Given the experience at Prudhoe Bay, however, such warnings are difficult to take seriously. The oil companies have gone to great lengths and spent tens of millions of dollars to reduce any harm to the fish, fowl, and mammals that live and breed on Alaska's North Slope. The protections they have provided for wildlife at Prudhoe Bay have been every bit as serious and effective as those the Audubon Society and the Nature Conservancy find acceptable in the Rainey Sanctuary and the Galveston Bay Prairie Preserve. As the numbers of various wildlife species show, many have thrived better since the drilling than they did before.

Before drilling began at Prudhoe Bay, a good deal of concern was expressed about its effect on caribou herds. As with many wildlife species, the population of the caribou on Alaska's North Slope fluctuates (often substantially) from year to year for completely natural reasons, so it is difficult to determine with confidence the effect of development on the caribou population. It is noteworthy, however, that the caribou population in the area around Prudhoe Bay has increased greatly since that oil field was developed, from approximately 3,000 to a high of some 23,400. . . . Some argue that the increase has occurred because the caribou's natural predators have avoided the area—some of these predators are shot, whereas the caribou are not. But even if this argument explains some or even all of the increase in the population, the increase still casts doubt on claims that the drilling threatens the caribou. Nor has it been shown that the viability of any other species has been genuinely threatened by oil drilling at Prudhoe Bay.

Caribou Versus Humans

Although consistency in government policy may be too much to hope for, it is interesting to contrast the federal government's refusal to open ANWR with some of its other oil-related policies. While opposing drilling in ANWR, ostensibly because we should not put caribou and other Alaskan wildlife at risk for the sake of getting more petroleum, we are exposing humans to far greater risks because of federal policies motivated by concern over petroleum supplies.

For example, the United States maintains a military presence in the Middle East in large part because of the petroleum reserves there. It is doubtful that the U.S. government would have mounted a large military action and sacrificed American lives to prevent Iraq from taking over the tiny sheikdom of Kuwait except to allay the threat to a major oil supplier. Nor would the United States have lost the nineteen military personnel in the barracks blown up in Saudi Arabia in 1996 or the seventeen killed onboard the USS Cole in a Yemeni harbor in 2000. I am not arguing against maintaining a military presence in the Middle East, but if it is worthwhile to sacrifice Americans' lives to protect oil supplies in the Middle East, is it not worthwhile to take a small (perhaps nonexistent) risk of sacrificing the lives of a few caribou to recover oil in Alaska?

Domestic energy policy also entails the sacrifice of human lives for oil. To save gasoline, the federal government imposes Corporate Average Fuel Economy (CAFE) standards on automobile producers. These standards now require all new cars to average 27.5 miles per gallon and new light trucks to average 20.5 miles per gallon. The one thing that is not controversial about the CAFE standards is that they cost lives by inducing manufacturers to reduce the weight of vehicles. Even Ralph Nader has acknowledged that "larger cars are safer—there is more bulk to protect the occupant." An interesting question is, How many lives might be saved by using more (ANWR) oil and driving heavier cars rather than using less oil and driving lighter, more dangerous cars?

It has been estimated that increasing the average weight of passenger cars by 100 pounds would reduce U.S. highway fatalities by 200 a year. By determining how much additional gas would be consumed each year if all passenger cars were 100 pounds heavier, and then estimating how much gas might be recovered from ANWR oil, we can arrive at a rough estimate of how many human lives potentially might be saved by that oil. To make this estimate, I first used data for the technical specifications of fifty-four randomly selected 2001 model passenger cars to obtain a simple regression of car weight on miles per gallon. This regression equation indicates that every additional 100 pounds decreases mileage by 0.85 miles per gallon. So 200 lives a year could be saved by relaxing the CAFE standards to allow a 0.85 miles per gallon reduction in the average mileage of passenger cars. How much gasoline would be required to compensate for this decrease of average mileage? Some 135 million passenger cars are currently in use, being driven roughly 10,000 miles per year on average (1994–95 data from U.S. Bureau of the Census 1997, 843). Assuming these vehicles travel 24 miles per gallon on average, the annual consumption of gasoline by passenger cars is 56.25 billion gallons (= 135 million × 10,000/24). If instead of an average of 24 miles per gallon the average were reduced to 23.15 miles per gallon, the annual consumption of gasoline by passenger cars would be 58.32 billion gallons (= 135 million × 10,000/23.15). So, 200 lives could be saved annually by an extra 2.07 billion gallons of gas. It is estimated that ANWR contains from 3 to 16 billion barrels of recoverable petroleum. Let us take the midpoint in this estimated range, or 9.5 billion barrels. Given that on average each barrel of petroleum is refined into 19.5 gallons of gasoline, the ANWR oil could be turned into 185.25 billion additional gallons of gas, or enough to save 200 lives a year for almost ninety years (185.25/2.07 = 89.5). Hence, in total almost 18,000 lives could be saved by opening up ANWR to drilling and using the fuel made available to compensate for increasing the weight of passenger cars.

I claim no great precision for this estimate. There may be less petroleum in ANWR than the midpoint estimate indicates, and the study I have relied on may have overestimated the number of lives saved by heavier passenger cars. Still, any reasonable estimate will lead to the conclusion that preventing the recovery of ANWR oil and its use in heavier passenger cars entails the loss of thousands of lives on the highways. Are we willing to bear such a cost in order to avoid the risks, if any, to ANWR and its caribou?

Conclusion

I am not recommending that ANWR actually be given to some consortium of environmental groups. In thinking about whether to drill for oil in ANWR, however, it is instructive to consider seriously what such a group would do if it owned ANWR and therefore bore the costs as well as enjoyed the benefits of preventing drilling. Those costs are measured by what people are willing to pay for the additional comfort, convenience, and safety that could be derived from the use of ANWR oil. Unfortunately, without the price communication that is possible only by means of private property and voluntary exchange, we cannot be sure what those costs are or how private owners would evaluate either the costs or the benefits of preventing drilling in ANWR. However, the willingness of environmental groups such as the Audubon Society and the Nature Conservancy to allow drilling for oil an environmentally sensitive land they own suggests strongly that their adamant verbal opposition to drilling in ANWR is a poor reflection of what they would do if they owned even a small fraction of the ANWR territory containing oil.

Jeff Bingaman et al.

 **NO**

ANWR Minority Views

Dissenting Views of Senators Bingaman, Dorgan, Wyden, Johnson, Feinstein, Cantwell, Corzine, and Salazar

The Arctic National Wildlife Refuge has long stirred deep emotions and strong passions. To some it is the most promising place to look for oil in the [nation]. To others it is "the Last Great Wilderness," a vast and beautiful natural wonder, which deserves permanent protection for its wildlife, scenic, and recreational values. These two viewpoints are held with equal passion by roughly equal parts of the Senate and the nation as a whole. For a quarter of a century, neither side has been able to enact legislation either opening the area to oil and gas development or permanently preserving it as wilderness.

We come down squarely in favor of preserving the Arctic National Wildlife Refuge. Opening the Refuge to oil and gas development will do little to meet our energy needs and nothing to reduce our energy prices. Not one drop of oil will come from the Refuge for ten years. And even at its peak production—twenty years from now—it will reduce our reliance on imports by only 4 percent. We believe we should tap alternative sources of oil and gas and develop alternative energy technologies, rather than sacrifice the Refuge's unique wildlife and wilderness values.

Years ago, Senator Clinton P. Anderson said that our willingness to protect wilderness areas showed "that we are still a rich Nation, tending our resources as we should—not a people in despair searching every last nook and cranny of our land for . . . a barrel of oil." We believe we still are a rich Nation, rich in untapped oil and gas resources in other areas that can be developed consistent with environmental protection, and rich in the intellectual capital needed to develop new alternative energy technologies. We do not believe we need to sacrifice our wildlife refuges or other environmentally sensitive areas to fuel our cars or heat our homes.

But even if the day should come when we do need to exploit the Arctic National Wildlife Refuge for oil, we should approach the task with care. If we must open the Refuge to oil and gas development, we should do so in accordance with existing mineral leasing laws and

From Senate Energy Committee by Jeff Bingaman et al., (October 24, 2005).

regulations, existing environmental protections, and existing rules of administrative procedure and judicial review. We should, in short, afford the Arctic Refuge no less protection than current law affords any other refuge or public land that is open to oil and gas development. In addition, we should ensure that any oil that comes from the Arctic Refuge goes to Americans, and is not sold overseas; and that the Federal Treasury receives the full amount of royalties and bonus bids that we are promised. Regrettably, the legislation recommended by a majority of the Committee fails in every one of these respects.

1. The Mineral Leasing Act and rules. Oil and gas leasing on the public lands, including wildlife refuges, is currently conducted under the Mineral Leasing Act of 1920 and regulations adopted by the Bureau of Land Management under that Act. Among other things, they require minimum royalties, maximum lease sizes, and various performance standards and environmental protections. Oil and gas development on wildlife refuges can only take place with the concurrence of the Fish and Wildlife Service and subject to stipulations prescribed by the Fish and Wildlife Service that protect wildlife.

    It is unclear from the legislation recommended by the Committee whether any of the mineral leasing laws or regulations will apply to the leasing program for the Arctic Refuge. The legislation directs the Secretary to administer an "environmentally sound" leasing program in the refuge's Coastal Plain, but does not explicitly require it to be in accordance with the existing statutory and regulatory framework. The Secretary is directed to administer the program through "regulations, lease terms, conditions, restrictions, prohibitions, stipulations, and other provisions" of the Secretary's choosing that will ensure that the leasing program is "carried out in a manner that will ensure the receipt of fair market value by the public for the mineral resources to be leased." The legislation leaves it up to the Secretary, and ultimately the courts, to decide whether existing mineral leasing regulations and procedures will still apply or whether the new system is meant to supersede it.

2. The "compatibility" determination. Under current law, the Secretary of the Interior may permit oil and gas development in a national wildlife refuge if it is "compatible" with the purposes for which the refuge was established. If oil and gas development can take place in the Arctic Refuge without harm to the wildlife populations and habitats it was established to protect, as proponents believe, the Secretary should make the compatibility determination. Instead, the legislation recommended by the Committee "deems" the leasing program to be compatible and absolves the Secretary of any responsibility for determining whether it is or is not, in fact, compatible.

3. NEPA compliance. The National Environmental Policy Act of 1969 requires federal agencies contemplating a major federal action to

prepare an environmental impact statement. The requirement is a continuing one. Agencies must supplement environmental impact statements if they make substantial changes in their proposed action or if there are significant new circumstances or information bearing on the proposed action or its impacts. The Department of the Interior last prepared an environmental impact statement on oil and gas development in ANWR in 1987, 18 years ago. In 1992, a federal court held that significant new information was available that required the Department to supplement the 1987 environmental impact statement. If a court thought that a supplement was required 13 years ago, one must surely be needed today. Yet the legislation recommended by the Committee "deems" the 1987 statement to satisfy the requirements of NEPA "with respect to prelease activities," including the development of the regulations establishing the new leasing program.

NEPA also requires that environmental impact statements consider reasonable alternatives to a proposed action. Consideration of alternatives is said to be "the heart of the environmental impact statement." The courts have said this requirement is governed by a "rule of reason," and common sense, "bounded by some notion of feasibility." The legislation recommended by the Committee waives even this common sense requirement, and limits the Secretary to consideration of only her "preferred action for leasing and a single leasing alternative."

4. Judicial review. Under current law, a person harmed by agency action is entitled to judicial review. A person can bring suit either in the District of Columbia or where he resides. The reviewing court is empowered to "decide all relevant questions of law," and set aside agency actions found to be arbitrary, capricious, or unsupported by substantial evidence. Review is generally limited to the administrative record compiled by the agency when it made its decision, though the court may sometimes look beyond the record in NEPA cases to make sure the decision maker adequately considered environmental impacts and alternatives.

The legislation recommended by the Committee restricts the right of judicial review. It does so by requiring anyone seeking to challenge the Secretary's actions to file suit in the District of Columbia Circuit, by limiting judicial review of the Secretary's decision to conduct a lease sale and the environmental analysis of that decision solely to whether the Secretary has complied with the new legislation, and by strictly limiting review to the administrative record. It is unclear to what extent the narrow scope of review imposed by the new legislation will be read to preempt to the broad scope of review afforded under the Administrative Procedure Act. The Committee leaves that question to the courts.

5. Roads, pipelines, and other rights-of-way. Current law provides a comprehensive process for approving rights-of-ways for roads,

pipelines, airstrips, and other transportation and utility systems in conservation system units in Alaska. The principal purpose of this process was to provide access to and from resource development areas, but to do so in an orderly way that would avoid or minimize harm to the environment. The legislation recommended by the Committee exempts all rights-of-way for the exploration, development, production, or transportation of oil and gas on the Coastal Plain from this process.

6. 2,000-acre limitation. The legislation recommended by the Committee restricts the surface acreage covered by oil and gas production within the Arctic Refuge to a maximum of 2,000 acres on the Coastal Plain. This limitation is cited by leasing proponents as evidence that oil and gas development will occupy a tiny footprint on the Coastal Plain. This provision contains so many loopholes, however, that exploration and development activities could impact much of the Coastal Plain. There is no requirement that the developed surface lands be contiguous or even consolidated. The limitation only applies literally to the actual ground covered, ignoring the effect on nearby lands. As example of the hollowness of the limitation, it only counts the area occupied by the footings of a pipeline support structure towards the acreage limitation, even though the pipeline itself may run many miles across the Coastal Plain.

7. Alaska Native lands. Over 100,000 acres (over 150 square miles) that are within both the boundaries of the Refuge and the definition of the Coastal Plain are owned by Alaska Natives. The surface of over 90,000 of these acres is owned by the Kaktovik Inupiat Corporation, and their subsurface is owned by the Arctic Slope Regional Corporation [ASRC]. The remaining approximately 10,000 acres are owned by individual Alaska Natives. Under a 1983 agreement . . . , oil and gas development on the Arctic Slope Regional Corporation's lands is prohibited "until Congress authorizes such activities on Refuge lands within the coastal plain or on ASRC Lands, or both." Enactment of the legislation recommended by the Committee will plainly "authorize such activities on Refuge lands within the coastal plain," enabling the Arctic Slope Regional Corporation and the individual Alaska Native owners to develop oil and gas resources on their lands within the Refuge. However, the Alaska Native lands are within the defined Coastal Plain covered by the leasing program, and thus are subject to the overall 2,000 acre limitation. But including the Native lands within this limitation appears to abrogate the Arctic Slope Regional Corporation's right to develop all of its lands under its 1983 contract . . .

Moreover, it is unclear what effect the Committee recommendation will have on revenues derived from oil and gas development on Native lands within the Refuge. The legislation plainly states that all receipts derived from oil and gas development on the Coastal Plain, which is defined to include the Native lands, are to be divided equally between the State of Alaska and the U.S. Treasury, though neither would have any right to revenues derived from oil and gas development on Native lands.

8. Division of receipts. The Congressional Budget Office estimates that oil and gas leasing in the Arctic Refuge will generate $5 billion in bonus, rental, and royalty receipts. Under current law, 90 percent of those receipts ($4.5 billion) are to be paid to the State of Alaska, and the remaining 10 percent ($500 million) to the U.S. Treasury. The legislation recommended by the Committee changes the allocation in current law, to permit the Federal Government to retain 50 percent ($2.5 billion) of the receipts.

This change is necessary for the Committee to meet its reconciliation instructions. The State of Alaska contends that any such reduction of its share of receipts violates the Alaska Statehood Act and apparently intends to challenge it in court. The Committee believes that Congress has the power to reduce the State's share and that the provision will ultimately be upheld by the courts. If, however, the State should prevail, opening the Arctic Refuge to oil and gas leasing may produce only one-fifth of the receipts the Committee expects.

9. Exports. The Mineral Leasing Act of 1920 generally prohibits the export of oil transported through pipelines over rights-of-way over public lands unless the President finds the export to be in the national interest. A 1995 amendment to the Mineral Leasing Act makes an exception for oil transported through the Trans-Alaska Pipeline. Oil moved through the Trans-Alaska Pipeline can be exported unless the President finds the export to not be in the national interest. Thus, since oil produced from the Arctic Refuge is likely to be transported through the Trans-Alaska Pipeline, it can be exported rather than used here in the [U.S.].

During consideration of the Committee recommendation, Democrats offered a series of amendments to address many of the problems in the legislation. Regrettably, all of them were rejected. Although we continue to oppose oil and gas development in the Arctic National Wildlife Refuge, adoption of our amendments would have at least ensured that development would have proceeded in accordance with the laws governing oil and gas development in other wildlife refuges, ensured that the Treasury would receive 50 percent of the receipts, and ensured that the oil would be used in the United States.

Our efforts to improve the legislation were thwarted by the fact that it is being considered under the extraordinary rules for budget reconciliation measures. All of our amendments were met with the argument that they might either reduce the amount of estimated receipts or delay their collection, or that they might not have any effect on the receipts at all, and thus would be extraneous. Such arguments only serve to remind us why important policy legislation of this sort should not be considered under the strictures of the reconciliation process.

The Senate's quarter-century debate over the future of the Arctic National Wildlife Refuge has never been about money. It has been, and continues to be, about two different sets of priorities: whether we should sacrifice a pristine wilderness to exploit the energy resources it may contain; or whether we should forego a much-needed energy resource to save a remote and frigid wilderness. Such a fundamental, deep-seated, philosophical controversy requires the deliberative process of the Senate.

Many years ago, when he introduced the bill that would become the Wilderness Act of 1964, Senator Anderson compared our wilderness areas to "our museums and our art galleries." They were "part of our cultural resource as well as our natural heritage," he said. "We should regard them as such and cherish them." We would all do well to keep Senator Anderson's words in mind as we consider the future of the Arctic National Wildlife Refuge.

POSTSCRIPT

Should the Arctic National Wildlife Refuge Be Opened to Oil Drilling?

Those who see in nature only values that can be expressed in human terms are well represented by Jonah Goldberg, who in "Ugh, Wilderness! The Horror of 'ANWR,' the American Elite's Favorite Hellhole" (*National Review*, August 6, 2001), describes the ANWR as so bleak and desolate that development can only improve it. Adam Kolton, testifying before the House Committee on Resources on July 11, 2001, in opposition to the National Energy Security Act of 2001 (NESA), presented the Coastal Plain as "the site of one of our continent's most awe-inspiring wildlife spectacles" and thus deserving of protection from exploitation. Kennan Ward's *The Last Wilderness: Arctic National Wildlife Refuge* (Wildlight Press, 2001) describes a realm where human impact is still minimal and wilderness endures. John G. Mitchell, in "Oil Field or Sanctuary?" *National Geographic* (August 2001), is more balanced in his appraisal but still sides with Amory B. Lovins and L. Hunter Lovins, "Fool's Gold in Alaska," *Foreign Affairs* (July/August 2001), concluding that better alternatives to developing the ANWR exist.

The House of Representatives approved the NESA in August 2001. The bill then stalled in the Senate, with pro-drilling senators attempting to woo votes with such measures as promising to use oil revenues to pay pension benefits for steel-workers. Their efforts failed in April 2002, when the bill was defeated, and a competing bill, sponsored by Tom Daschle (D-South Dakota) and Jeff Bingaman (D-New Mexico) and lacking approval for opening the ANWR, took the lead.

Walter J. Hickle, former U.S. Secretary of the Interior and twice the governor of Alaska, writes in "ANWR Oil: An Alternative to War Over Oil" (*American Enterprise*, June 2002), that "the issue is not going to go away. Given our continuing precarious dependence on overseas oil suppliers . . ., sensible Americans will continue to press Congress in the months and years ahead to unlock America's great Arctic energy storehouse." The recent rise in the prices of oil and gasoline renews the point: The issue is not about to go away. In fact, it is gaining urgency from growing awareness that oil production may have already passed its peak, meaning that year by year the amount of oil available to the market will decline (see Issue 1). In July 2006, backers of the failed effort to approve opening the ANWR for oil drilling introduced a new bill in the U.S. House of Representatives. This bill would dedicate leasing and royalty revenues from opening the ANWR to drilling to "a trust fund to boost production of cellulosic ethanol, liquefied coal, solar and biofuel energy, among others" ("ANWR Bill Would Direct Revenue to Alternative Fuels," *CongressDaily AM,* July 27, 2006). The bill never came to a vote, but it has been called an interesting compromise. Brian Snyder, "How to Reach a Compromise on Drilling in ANWR," *Energy Policy* (March 2008), suggests that a better compromise would dedicate revenue from ANWR oil to conservation. Marianne Lavelle, "Arctic Drilling Wouldn't Cool High Oil Prices," *U.S. News and World Report* (June 16, 2008), describes a new report ("Analysis of Crude Oil Production in the Arctic National Wildlife Refuge," http://www.eia.doe.gov/oiaf/servicerpt/anwr/index.html?featureclicked=2&) from the Energy Information Administration that says opening the ANWR to oil drilling today would have no effect on oil supply or prices for 10–20 years and even then the effect would be small. Meanwhile arctic ice is melting (thanks to global warming), and oil companies are eyeing many areas off arctic shores as worth exploring for oil. See "Arctic Melting May Lead to Expanded Oil Drilling," *World Watch* (July/August 2008).

ISSUE 5

Should Utilities Burn More Coal?

YES: Nina French, from "Clean Coal," Testimony before the Senate Finance Committee (April 26, 2007)

NO: Susan Moran, from "Coal Rush!" *World Watch* (January/February 2007)

ISSUE SUMMARY

YES: Nina French argues that the continued use of coal is critical for sustainable, inexpensive, secure, and reliable power generation. Coal meets these needs, and the technology exists—and is being improved—to ensure that coal is "clean," meaning that it emits less sulfur, mercury, and carbon.

NO: Susan Moran argues that U.S. utilities are building and planning to build a great many coal-burning power plants, often hoping to get them in operation before legislation restricting carbon emissions forces them to find alternatives.

Coal is so plentiful in the United States that the nation has been called the Saudi Arabia of coal. If the world runs out of oil, the United States will still have plenty of fossil fuel for electricity generation and—because coal can be liquefied or turned into a liquid much like petroleum—for transportation. However, coal is infamous for its environmental impacts. In the past, burning coal has put clouds of smoke, soot, fly ash, and sulfur dioxide into the air. It has been responsible for the killer smogs in Donora, Pennsylvania, and London, England, as well as elsewhere, which helped spur the passage of clean air legislation and the development of technologies to make coal burning much cleaner. Coal-smog remains a problem in some parts of the world; see D. Mira-Salama, et al., "Source Attribution of Urban Smog Episodes Caused by Coal Combustion," *Atmospheric Research* (June 2008).

Burning coal also releases more carbon dioxide, the major greenhouse gas, than does burning any other fossil fuel. If society is serious about limiting or preventing global warming by controlling carbon emissions, burning coal calls for somehow capturing the carbon dioxide emitted and keeping it out of the air (see Issue 10).

But the environmental impacts do not lie only in the *use* of coal. As a solid, it cannot be pumped from beneath the surface of the Earth. It must be dug out, either through underground mines or through strip mines. Underground mines are infamous for killing miners when they collapse, polluting waterways, and draining aquifers on which people depend (see Brad Miller, "Draining the Life from the Land," *Earth Island Journal*, Autumn 2002). When they catch fire, as one did in Centralia, Pennsylvania, they may burn for decades (see Jeff Tietz, "The Great Centralia Coal Fire," *Harper's Magazine*, February 2004). Surface mining leaves great holes in the landscape; in Appalachia, it carves off mountaintops and fills valleys; see Patrick C. McGinley, "From Pick and Shovel to Mountaintop Removal: Environmental Injustice in the Appalachian Coalfields," *Environmental Law* (Winter 2004), and Jim Motavalli, "Once There Was a Mountain," *E—The Environmental Magazine* (November/December 2007).

Despite the problems, coal remains an attractive fuel because it is plentiful and relatively cheap. In China, which like the United States has extensive coal deposits, it is used in great quantity to provide the power for economic development. Chinese cities are extraordinarily smoggy, but China feels impelled to use coal despite its environmental effects. It is also developing coal as a replacement for oil as feedstock for chemical industries and as a source of liquid fuels. However, China is also developing other energy sources, including nuclear, wind, and hydropower, and planning to slow the pace of economic development; see "A Large Black Cloud, *Economist* (March 15, 2008).

In the following selections, Nina French of ADA Environmental Solutions argues that the continued use of coal is critical for sustainable, inexpensive, secure, and reliable power generation. Coal meets these needs, and the technology exists—and is being improved—to ensure that coal is "clean," meaning that it emits less sulfur, mercury, and carbon. Environmental journalist Susan Moran argues that U.S. utilities are building and planning to build a great many coal-burning power plants, often hoping to get them in operation before legislation restricting carbon emissions forces them to find alternatives. What is needed is a broad mix of energy sources.

YES

Nina French

Clean Coal

Today we would like to give you our perspective of clean coal by discussing the following points:

1. Coal is critical to our future because it is reliable (base load capacity), inexpensive, abundant, and local.
2. The industry has demonstrated the ability to meet environmental challenges involving NOx, SO_2, particulates and mercury.
3. Federal incentives, such as tax credits, have been effective in advancing technology to ensure realistic options exist and that the costs of these options are manageable.
4. Success for new technologies depends on a careful balance between:

    - Incentives for technological developments;
    - Sufficient time for risk mitigation; and
    - Regulation or tax-based market drivers (often referred to as "sticks" or "carrots").

5. CO_2 control seems to be the next concern for our nation's coal industry and the critical points are:

    - The scale is massive;
    - The timeframe is probably long—10 to 20 years;
    - Sufficient investment is critical;
    - Success is likely; and
    - Investment and incentives need to be designed to ensure that multiple technological paths are followed and that costs and risks are reduced.

Coal Is Critical to Our Future

As an environmental technology company, ADA-ES believes that the continued use of coal is critical for sustainable and reliable power generation in the U.S. America leads the way in environmentally beneficial technologies. As a result of tightened regulations, we continue to improve technology so that the air we breathe and the water we drink are cleaner. We reap these related health benefits because our nation's strong economy allows us to allocate significant resources to these efforts. Much as our country demands higher air and water quality standards, we also need power gen-

From Senate Finance Committee by Nina French, (April 26, 2007).

eration that is inexpensive, reliable, and secure. Coal meets these needs. Today, more than 1,100 coal-fired boilers produce more than 50% of our nation's electricity. . . .

Electricity is a much more valuable commodity than it has ever been. Coal plants have increased operational capacity from 59% in 1990 to between 80% and 85% in 2006. The U.S. is expected to need 50% more electrical capacity by 2030. To meet this need, the reliability of coal-fired power plants must continue to improve. Economic development requires enormous investments in all aspects of energy infrastructure and significant increases in power generation. This is the motivation that drives us to optimize our current investment. We really have no other choice, as it would take decades to replace our current infrastructure.

Any expansion of power supplies must recognize that no single energy source can meet this need—it requires a portfolio of solutions, including efficiency gains, more renewables, new nuclear power capacity and new coal-based generation. As renewables, such as solar and wind power, become a greater portion of our energy mix, it becomes more important to maintain a source of reliable power that can operate continuously in all weather conditions. Coal can also play an important role in national security by reducing our dependence on foreign energy sources. The United States has the largest coal reserve in the world, and have more coal than any nation has of any single energy resource. At current consumption rates, these coal reserves could supply our nation with 250 years of fuel. This is far greater than our reserves of natural gas and oil combined. For these reasons, coal remains an essential part of the U.S. generation mix as a secure, plentiful, and relatively inexpensive fuel source. However, we as a nation must determine how to continuously improve emissions. Our goal needs to be "clean coal."

Clean Coal Background

The emissions control industry has made huge advancements in technology to improve emissions from coal-fired power plants. Collaboration among research organizations, universities, and power generation partners has enabled emissions of criteria pollutants sulfur dioxide (SO_2), nitrogen oxides (NOx), and particulates from the existing fleet of coal fueled power plants to be lower today than they were in 1970, even as power produced from coal plants has increased by 173%. Reductions in NOx, SO_2, and particulate emissions were driven by a balance between technology development incentives and emissions regulations. As an example, in the early 1970's, flue gas desulfurization equipment, commonly referred to as "scrubbers," were new and suffered from poor reliability and performance. Over time, as experience was gained and equipment modified, efficiencies rose from about 70% SO_2 removal to 95% to 98% today, with similar improvements in reliability. The emissions of criteria pollutions will continue to decrease each year as emission control equipment is installed on more plants as a result of new regulations such as the Clean Air Interstate Rule.

Challenges in Developing New Emission Control Technology for the Power Industry

To understand how to make coal cleaner, it is helpful to appreciate how emissions control technology has developed for this industry. Since the first Clean Air Act of 1970, the power industry has gone through several rounds of implementing emissions control technology for NOx, SO$_2$, and particulates. In each case, there were very similar experiences as new technology was applied in an industry where reliability and compliance are mandatory. We learned the following important lessons:

- Be prepared for unexpected reactions between flue gas constituents and chemical reagents used to control the pollutants;
- Do not underestimate the differences in coal and plant operating conditions to cause wide variations in emissions;
- Try to plan for significant O&M [operations & maintenance] problems that might not show up until after long-term operation; and
- Look for secondary effects on other components of the power plants.

In each case, new-technology challenges had a significant impact on the reliability of power generation. The plants were forced to operate at reduced loads and suffered many unplanned shutdowns for maintenance and repair. Over time, technologies were improved to an acceptable level of cost and reliability. This is the true measure of acceptance, although significant risks may remain depending on how widespread the technology was applied during the early adopter phase. For example, Hot-Side Electrostatic Precipitators (for particulate control) have cost the industry over a billion dollars. After initial successes, the technology was quickly applied to 150 power plants only to have a fatal flaw subsequently discovered. One of the challenges with implementing new emissions control technology is that the scale is massive. For example, emissions control equipment for a 500 MW plant treats two million cubic feet of flue gas every minute. Scrubbers may be as large as the power plant to which they are attached. Imagine the complications involved when we need to add new emissions control technology without taking the plant off-line.

We have learned that the best way to bring new technologies to an existing coal-fired power plant is to proceed through a carefully chartered course:

1. Laboratory testing: Provides a cost effective means to determine general feasibility and test a variety of parameters.
2. Pilot-scale: Test under actual flue gas conditions but at a reduced scale.
3. Full-scale field tests: Scale up the size of the equipment and perform tests under optimum operating conditions to define capabilities and limits of the technology.

4. Full-scale field tests at multiple sites: Each new site represents new operating conditions and new challenges.
5. Long-term demonstrations at several sites: Some problems will not show up until the first year or so of operation.
6. Widespread implementation: Problems will still be found at new sites, but most of the fatal flaws will have already been discovered and resolved.

We know from experience that trying to accelerate technology development by skipping these steps can result in large-scale operating problems and untimely and expensive plant outages. We also know that it takes ten to twenty years to successfully implement a major technology in this industry and implementation presents significant risks to the developer and user at each stage. In addition to the technology risk, there is significant financial risk to the developer. This is especially true when there is no regulation to guarantee a market will exist for a technology to control an emission that has not been previously regulated. There is often a "chicken and egg" dilemma in which there is no regulation to incentivize the development of a new technology and therefore there is no technology on which to base a regulation. Such was the case in the recent past, when the power industry was faced with reducing mercury emissions for the first time as discussed below.

ADA-ES Experience in Developing and Implementing Mercury Control Technology

It is instructive to present a case study on how Federal initiatives effectively provided incentives and risk mitigation that allowed industry to successfully develop cost-effective mercury control technologies for coal-fired power plants. Methyl mercury, which builds up in certain fish, is a neurotoxin that leads to developmental problems in fetuses of pregnant women. Mercury contained in coal represented the largest manmade source of mercury. In December 2000, the Environmental Protection Agency announced that it was beginning to consider regulating mercury emissions from the nation's coal-fired power plants.

In anticipation of future regulations, the Federal government and industry funded research to characterize the emission and control of mercury compounds from the combustion of coal. Some estimates showed that 90% mercury reduction for utilities would be expensive for the industry because of the large volumes of gas to be treated, the relatively low mercury concentrations, and the difficulty of capturing certain species of mercury in its vapor phase. With potential regulations rapidly approaching, it was important to concentrate efforts on the most mature retrofit control technologies. Injection of dry sorbents such as powdered activated carbon (PAC) into the flue gas and further collection of the sorbent by ESPs and fabric filters represented potentially the most cost-effective control technology for power plants. The Department of Energy (DOE) realized the criticality of demonstrating and optimizing scaleup of sorbent injection technology to provide performance data for regulations. The DOE National Energy Technology Laboratory cost-shared these demonstrations, with additional funding from several power companies, the Electric Power Research Institute, and private ADAES funding.

The DOE-supported field tests resulted in great advances in technologies to capture mercury emissions and decreased costs. A 2005 report by the DOE Energy Information Administration concluded that because technology for 90% mercury control from Western (Powder River Basin) coals was not available, an overall 90% mercury control rule could cost $358 billion. However, use of these new technologies later demonstrated that the 90% reduction for PRB coal could be achieved for less than $1 billion per year. This saving represents a huge return on the investment made by the Federal government in supporting early development and demonstration of mercury control technology. This success has allowed a dozen states to take mercury control into their own hands and implement stringent regulations on power plants in their respective states. This action has created the first real commercial market for the new mercury control technology.

Refined Coal Tax Credit (Section 45)

Tax incentives also play a vital role in achieving even further emission reductions. The 2004 American Jobs Creation Act included a production tax credit designed to incentivize clean coal at the front end—changing the way the coal burns—for older plants with limited resources or space to add back-end emission control. The tax credit was written with clear emissions reduction goals: 20% NOx reduction and either 20% mercury or SO_2 reduction. An additional market value test, requiring that the product result in a 50% increase in market value over the feedstock coal still needs clarification (e.g., a baseline determination), but the credit is significant in that it represents a strong goal-oriented, rather than specific technology-driven, tax incentive. ADA-ES responded to the incentive of the tax credit and assembled a team to apply mercury control expertise to invest in technology development for a refined coal product that will allow older cyclone boilers to reduce mercury emissions by 90%—enough to meet stringent state regulations—simply by burning refined coal. Clarification on the market value test will allow us to move to full-scale demonstrations to optimize and deploy our refined coal technology, and realize the goals Congress intended by the legislation.

Clean Coal: Carbon Challenges

Carbon, in the form of carbon dioxide (CO_2), is a greenhouse gas that contributes to climate changes. Our goal is to reduce CO_2 from both new and existing coal-fired power plants. This presents a number of challenges for technology development. It is not our purpose to detail the technologies being advanced to address these issues—there will be a comprehensive report issued by the National Coal Council this summer that will provide in-depth background on the various approaches. Instead, we would like to briefly note three key areas for technology development.

1. First, increased efficiency. The most effective way to quickly decrease carbon emissions is to increase efficiency of power production on new and existing boilers. Today we have more than 1,100 coal-fired boilers in the U.S. with an average age of 45 years. When many of these plants were built during the 1950's and 1960's, we did not care much about efficiency because coal was readily available, and inexpensive .... We produce 25% less CO_2 as boiler efficiency increases from 35% to 50%. That is 25% less carbon that we have to separate and seques- ter. In May 2001, the National Coal Council produced a report that identified technologies that could increase the amount of electricity from the existing fleet of coal plants by 40,000 MW in a three-year period. Those recommendations remain viable today. To increase the amount of electricity generated by the existing fleet by 40,000 MW without the need to build a single new plant of any fuel type repre- sents a tremendous greenhouse gas mitigation opportunity for this country.

   However, although increased efficiencies result in lower CO_2/ MW-hr, it also requires higher investment per mega watt-hour. At present, there is no incentive to absorb these increased costs for reducing carbon dioxide emissions.

2. Carbon separation. Nitrogen comprises 78% of the flue gas from a coal-fired power plant. We have to separate the carbon from the nitrogen. Known technologies to do so include oxygen-fired combustion and amine (MEA) scrubbing for pulverized coal (PC) boilers, or chemical separation for integrated gasification com- bined cycle (IGCC) systems. The challenges now relate to scale and cost with this technology. 3. Carbon storage and sequestra- tion. Once the carbon is separated, we must store, or sequester, it. Known technologies to do so include injection for enhanced oil recovery (representing only a small percent of CO_2), deep well injection, and deep ocean injection. The biggest challenges are the unknown long-term effects, which will determine long-term ownership and legal liabilities. Transportation of CO_2 from plants to storage sites will require large and expensive infrastructure development.

The Size of the CO_2 Problem

Carbon dioxide emissions from coal-fired power plants are bigger than anything our industry has experienced in the past. The average 500MW plant produces 900,000 lbs of CO_2 per hour, and for a typical PC boiler, this CO_2 is highly diluted in the flue gas. Compare this amount of CO_2 to about 0.01 lbs of mercury per hour for the same plant. The scale for carbon capture and storage technology is daunting and the costs will be high. Technology maturation for carbon capture and storage will take time and the technologies are in their infancy. However, based on advances to date, they should become available and less costly, within the next 20 years or sooner. Carbon capture and storage technologies can be expedited, but they cannot be willed into existence overnight by changes in policy. CO_2 emissions from the U.S. are only a fraction of the world's carbon emissions. Technology developed in the U.S. can be transferred to countries like China and India that will allow the U.S. to leverage its investment in technology development.

New Coal-Fired Generation

Utilities are designing new coal-fired power plants to incorporate carbon separation and capture technologies as they become available. New coal plants will include both supercritical and ultrasupercritical PC boilers, as well as IGCC systems. They will incorporate the same carbon separation and storage technologies described above.

The Role of Carrots and Sticks in Encouraging Investment in Technology: Not Choosing a Winning Technology

Coal-fired electricity is cleaner today as a result of a balance between "carrots" (e.g., government-funded technology development or tax incentives) and "sticks" (e.g., government regulation or restrictions). It is ineffective to impose the stick until technologies are ready, or nearly ready. Carrots, of course, will help speed up this process. In promulgating carrots and sticks, it is also important that the government defines a goal (e.g., reduced carbon emissions), but does not choose winning technologies. This notion is supported by most recent collaborative studies on reduced carbon emissions. For example, the 2007 MIT Interdisciplinary study, "The Future of Coal," suggests that the government must not select specific technologies, but rather should incentivize technology development towards a common goal.

Timing is Critical: If we impose clean coal restrictions (e.g., in the form of carbon taxes or emission limits) before separation and storage technologies are available, electricity costs will spiral, unraveling our economy and our ability to afford new technologies. However, history has demonstrated that if we first incentivize technology development, provide for risk reduction, and carefully time restrictions, the market will develop and provide winning technologies.

Summary

Clean coal is an important and viable part of our energy future. To move coal into a carbon-constrained world, we need to:

- Preserve base load electricity-generating capacity with reliable, inexpensive sources.
- Balance base-load capacity with renewable sources.
- Carefully balance timing between the carrots (e.g., tax credits and technology development funding) and the sticks (e.g., regulations).
- Incentivize the achievement of goals, not specific technologies (i.e., we should reward any carbon reduction, not just the known technologies to do so).
- Encourage more technology development (R&D tax credits, demonstration tax credits, etc., and coordination with DOE R&D funding).

We need to invest now in tax incentives and support for technology development. We do not know enough, yet, to decide which technology will be most cost-effective for each particular facility. Following multiple paths will increase the likelihood of sufficient successful options for application in the future, and will not preclude out-of-the-box technologies that have not yet been envisioned. . . .

Susan Moran  **NO**

Coal Rush!

For all the talk about renewable energy, the extraction industry is alive and well in the United States. In Texas, utility company TXU Energy has proposed building 11 new coal-fired power plants. American Electric Power, of Columbus, Ohio, is also seeking approval for several new coal plants. In the interior West, Minnesota-based Xcel Energy is building one of the nation's largest coal plants in Pueblo, Colorado, while planning for others in the next few years.

These are but a sampling of the 150-plus new coal-fired plants being proposed throughout the United States, according to the Department of Energy's National Technology Laboratory. The vast majority of them will use conventional coal burning technology. (Elsewhere in the world, hundreds of new coal-fired plants are planned or under construction, some 550 of them in China alone. Of the 2004 U.S. total emissions of 5.9 billion metric tons of carbon dioxide (CO_2), electric power generation contributed 2.3 billion metric tons, or 39 percent, and coal-fired plants accounted for 82 percent of that. Because CO_2 is the dominant human-caused greenhouse gas, that unheralded feat makes power plants among the biggest culprits behind climate change. And while power plant emissions of sulfur dioxide, nitrogen oxides, and particulates have dipped since the early 1990s, thanks to federal legislation, CO_2 emissions continue unabated. In fact, coal is making a comeback.

For nearly three decades no new U.S. coal plants came on line. But suddenly that's changed. "No question about it, this is a coal rush," says Robert McIlvaine, a coal industry consultant in Northfield, Illinois. "This is on par with the biggest expansion coal has ever seen, assuming all the ones proposed are actually built," adds Travis Madsen, a policy analyst with U.S. Public Interest Research Group (PIRG).

Nationwide support for coal dates back several decades. Between 1950 and 1997 the coal industry received more than US$70 billion in federal subsidies, or nearly $1.5 billion a year, according to a 2006 report from PIRG. In the Energy Policy Act of 2005, Congress approved an additional $7.8 billion for coal, including several billion for a "clean coal" research and development program.

But what accounts for the current feverish pace? Utilities point to all of us, our insatiable appetite for the must-have gadgets of the modern

From *World Watch* Magazine, vol. 20, no. 1, January/February 2007. Copyright © 2007 by Worldwatch Institute. Reprinted by permission. www.worldwatch.org

world, such as laptops and iPods, as well as plasma televisions, refrigerators, and other household appliances. And as the population grows, that demand—absent any serious drive for higher efficiency—will only head upward. "In the last decade our customer base has gone up 20 percent, and the amount of electricity per household is up 10 percent," says Mark Stutz, a spokesman for Xcel, which generates 66 percent of its kilowatthours of electricity from coal. "That's a lot of demand."

Coal is especially attractive now because its prices are low and stable relative to those of natural gas, which fluctuate unpredictably. But some critics of coal suspect that the current rush has more to do with fear and greed. With the specter of climate change looming ever larger in the public consciousness, utilities are anticipating that the time will soon come when legislators will slap a limit on carbon emissions from electric power generators and perhaps other industrial sources, and that the more coal-fired capacity the producers build before that day of reckoning, the higher their share of the total cap will be.

Of course, utilities have choices. Some climate change is inevitable, and it will get worse before it gets better. But utilities can still do plenty to stabilize and even reverse the course of climate change by dramatically cutting back on carbon emissions and by advancing solar, wind, and other renewable energy sources. "We're at a really interesting fork in the road," says Jim White, a paleoclimatologist at the University of Colorado in Boulder. "Do we recognize that continuing to burn these fuels will cause a lot more problems than they solve, and therefore do we promote alternative energy supplies? Or are we going to go down the road of coal?"

Gambles

Many utilities are hedging their bets by investing to some degree in renewables and even nuclear power, and a few have even asked the federal government for uniform, nationwide carbon restrictions now. But the industry in general is choosing the coal road for the time being. Charlotte, North Carolina-based Duke Energy, which generates 54 percent of its electricity from coal and 46 percent from nuclear power, in September appealed to state utility regulators to construct two coal-fired plants totaling 1,600 megawatts of generation capacity. "Abandoning coal and moving to another source, such as natural gas, is not a viable economic option for our company or its customers," James Rogers, Duke Energy's chief executive officer, wrote in an article published in July for the American Air & Waste Management Association. He said the company's views on climate change "reflect the need to ensure a future role for coal in our nation's electricity generation portfolio."

Ohio-based American Electric Power is about as coal dependent as they come; its coal-fired plants account for 73 percent of its capacity. The company plans to build several new coal plants, including some with cleaner-burning coal (called integrated gasification combined cycle, or IGCC) technology that can be equipped to capture and sequester carbon.

"Coal is a domestic source and there's a vast amount of it now," says Melissa Henry, a spokeswoman for American Electric, which owns units in coal-rich West Virginia, as well as in Tennessee, Indiana, Kentucky, and other states. She said the company's reliance on coal will likely continue at the same level in the future, but that investments in IGCC and other "clean" coal technologies will help mitigate the company's carbon footprint. "The reality is that we will have to continue to use coal to generate electricity to meet demand in the U.S.," she says.

Perhaps the most brazen example of the current rush to coal is TXU Energy, which boasts it is planning "a Texas-sized $10 billion investment" in 11 conventional coal-fired power plants across Texas. Collectively, they would emit 78 million metric tons of CO_2 per year, doubling the utility's emissions. Those 78 million tons are more than the total 2001 emissions of 21 different U.S. states or many countries, including Sweden, Denmark, and Portugal. While several utilities are introducing cleaner, advanced technologies, TXU's proposed power plants are to be pulverized coal-fired generators—old technology that is difficult and expensive to retrofit later to capture carbon.

(In late summer, the company hit a speed bump, however, when judges in Texas ruled that the proposed pollution controls of one of TXU's proposed plants—a 1,720-megawatt generator—weren't proven and that the plant's emissions could harm downwind cities. That ruling was heralded by environmentalists as it suggests that utilities may be under increasing scrutiny in their push to build more coal plants nationwide.)

TXU and other companies generally point to steep natural gas prices and customers' rabid demand for more electricity as the incentives for their coal plant buildup. But some analysts question whether this strategy even makes sense economically, much less politically and morally. "A lot of utilities are ignoring the whole issue. They're pretending there's not going to be a climate policy" says Bruce Biewald, president of Synapse Energy Economics, a research and policy organization in Cambridge, Massachusetts. "We're saying, 'get your heads out of the sand.' Your particular decision, say, to build out fossil-fuel plants in Texas while pretending there'll be no costs to carbon emissions is simply imprudent."

While there is no mandated nationwide emission limit for carbon dioxide, thanks largely to the fact that the Bush administration wouldn't ratify the Kyoto Protocol, several bills being mulled in Washington call for a cap and various forms of carbon trading programs to help reward cleaner emitters and punish the dirtier ones. In Europe such a market, called the European Trading System, already exists, and California and other individual states, as well as a group of northeastern states, are already setting themselves up for a cap-and-trade system. In essence, such a system could allocate to utilities and other emitters allowances based on their emissions levels, or the caps could be auctioned, as many economists prefer.

Synapse estimates that if U.S. companies had to comply now with the Kyoto Protocol the cost of emitting carbon would be $20 to $50 a ton of carbon dioxide. (TXU's proposed new coal plants' emissions, therefore, might cost the utility up to $3.9 billion every year if it had to pay out-right for them.) Biewald says companies that try to "grandfather" in new coal plants so they can get free allowances are banking on a "highly risky strategy." The key precedent in the United States that Biewald and others point to is the successful sulfur dioxide cap-and-trade program spurred by the 1990 Clean Air Act. It allocated allowances to polluters based on their emissions levels from several years prior to the ruling. Another model is the California Climate Registry, which allows utilities and other companies to claim credit for acting early. The message is, do good now and you'll be rewarded once a cap-and-trade system is in place. . . .

Energy Costs

Whatever kind of emissions mandates the courts or politicians may im-pose, many utilities (backed by Department of Energy incentives and re-search projects) are developing "cleaner" coal burning technologies. The most conservative form applies to conventional pulverized-coal plants—making them burn more efficiently and creating higher steam tempera-tures and water pressures, for instance. These are called "supercritical" and "ultra-supercritical" steam boiler technologies. At best, such plants, intended to operate for at least 50 years, would make coal combustion at least 46 percent efficient, compared with an average 30 percent ef-ficiency rate of conventional pulverized plants. But critics view these plants as a mere band-aid approach to carbon emission reduction and, more important, a diversion from investing in much cleaner coal tech-nology and renewable energy sources. These plants would also require as much water for cooling as conventional generators.

IGCC, mentioned above, is the least polluting coal burning technol-ogy being developed today. The advantages of IGCC over pulverized coal technology are that it is more efficient (using less coal to produce each kilowatt-hour of electricity), uses much less water, and emits much less SO_2, particulates, and mercury. Most important, carbon capture can be integrated into an IGCC plant much more easily and cheaply than into a pulverized coal plant. Jana Milford, a senior scientist with the U.S. NGO Environmental Defense, says that IGCC combined with sequestration can cut CO_2 emissions by 90 percent compared with conventional plants.

Sequestration will not be cheap, however. In fact, Environmental Defense, along with Western Resource Advocates (WRA), another envi-ronmental research and policy organization, took the unusual step last summer of publicly praising Xcel Energy for proposing the nation's first IGCC plant designed from the beginning to capture and sequester carbon. That is critical, because without capturing and sequestering carbon, IGCC plants do little to reduce carbon emissions beyond their higher efficiency (i.e., slightly lower kilograms of CO_2 per kilowatt-hour produced). (Xcel isn't off the hook, however. Some environmentalists continue opposing the company's ongoing construction of a 750 megawatt supercritical pul-verized coal plant in Pueblo, Colorado, next to two existing facilities it operates there.) Currently two other commercial-scale IGCC plants are operating in the United States, one in Indiana and one in Florida, but neither entails capture and sequestration. Several other companies, including Duke Energy, American Electric Power, and TXU, have proposed IGCC plants, but they won't necessarily incorporate capture and sequestration of carbon emissions either.

Utilities often cite the high capital costs of IGCC plants. According to WRA, however, electricity produced with current IGCC technology is estimated to be only 5 to 10 percent more costly than that from a new pulverized coal plant if no carbon capture is included. If carbon capture is considered across all plant types, electricity generated with IGCC will cost 18–32 percent less than pulverized coal technologies, WRA asserts. Retrofitting old-technology power plants to capture carbon is extremely difficult because the entire fluegas stream must be processed to remove the CO_2. With IGCC, the carbon removal occurs early in the generation cycle and involves processing much lower gas volumes.

Many environmentalists are skeptical of IGCC and all other "clean" coal technologies. Perhaps the most vocal and influential of them is former U.S. vice president Al Gore. "It is time to recognize that the phrase 'clean coal technology' is devoid of meaning unless it means 'zero carbon emissions' technology," he said in an address to students at New York University in September. Others, like WRA energy project director John Nielsen, argue that cleaner coal technologies will help some but are not enough by themselves. "We're looking at emissions trajectories over time still going up. They need to go down," says Nielsen. "But eventually we'll need some federal limits on overall CO_2 emissions to bring them down."

True Prices

Whether they dig in their heels or willingly leap forward, utilities will probably face some kind of carbon constraints in the future. The sooner they clean up their act, the lower their future costs will likely be. For many, even politicians, the question is not should we put a price on carbon, but what kind of price, and who pays.

In September the Congressional Budget Office (CBO) published a report on the role of CO_2 pricing. The report notes that human activities are increasing the concentrations of CO_2 and other greenhouse gases in the atmosphere and acknowledges that energy markets fail to capture the "external effects" of emissions from fossil fuel combustion, that is, the costs that are imposed on society by the use of fossil fuels but are not reflected in the prices paid for them. Setting a price (i.e., tax) on carbon emissions would help change industry and consumer behavior, the report says, suggesting that carbon emissions could be assigned prices by taxing fossil fuels in proportion to their carbon content or by establishing a cap-and-trade program. Under such a program, policymakers would set an overall cap on emissions but leave it to carbon emitters to trade rights (called allowances) to those capped emissions.

So far the carbon taxing approach has gained little traction among politicians. Some call it political suicide to even mention the word "tax." But cap-and-trade bills proposed by various politicians are gaining momentum. The one that has enjoyed the most bipartisan support in the US. Senate was introduced in mid-2005 by Jeff Bingaman, a Democrat from New Mexico and a member of the Energy and Natural Resources Committee. Bingaman's proposal called for a cap-and-trade system that would require emitters to gradually stop the growth of their emissions by 2020 but not actually reduce emissions from today's levels. Further, the legislation would place an upper limit for pollution credits of $7 per metric ton of emissions—a modest ceiling aimed at keeping polluters' costs relatively low and predictable. By contrast, carbon credits in the European market, called the European Trading System, have to date traded at substantially higher prices. Some environmentalists have called Bingaman's proposal too soft on businesses.

Although utility executives have been reluctant to publicly endorse any one piece of legislation, as noted above some are increasingly showing support for some form of federally mandated cap on carbon emissions. Executives from Exelon Corporation of Chicago, American Electric Power, Duke Energy, General Electric, and PNM Resources all testified last spring before the Energy and Natural Resources Committee that indeed they want and are ready for carbon regulations. More recently, Xcel Energy chief Richard Kelly voiced his desire for mandatory limits on carbon emissions.

Most utilities that do support federal mandates want any caps to apply to all sectors across the economy rather than just their own, and they prefer waiting for nationwide limits rather than supporting or joining a patchwork of state or regional initiatives. "We believe the science of climate change is real, and we recognize that our industry, the electric sector, contributes roughly one-third of CO_2 emissions in the U.S.," says Helen Howes, vice president of environmental health and safety at Exelon. "But the transportation sector also is a big producer."

As the power companies wait for federal legislation (which few expect to pass before the 2008 elections), they are keeping a close watch on the various state and regional carbon-trading initiatives as well as the privately run and voluntary Chicago Climate Exchange, which now has more than 100 members spanning many industries. Although members' commitments to reduce their greenhouse gas emissions are not enforced, members and industry analysts say the exchange will likely be a model for any federal legislation. The biggest and most-watched regional carbon trading system yet to be crafted is the Regional Greenhouse Gas Initiative. It began in 2005 when seven northeastern states reached an agreement to cap carbon dioxide emissions from their power plants at current levels and to cut those emissions by 10 percent by 2019. The system is slated to go into effect in 2009. (Maryland has since joined the group as well.)

Meanwhile, California has taken the lead among individual states on the climate change front. The state's Democrat-controlled legislature and the Republican governor, Arnold Schwarzenegger, agreed last August on sweeping legislation aimed at reducing CO_2 emissions by 25 percent by 2020. Although this pledge doesn't meet the Kyoto Protocol's mandate to cut carbon emissions to 7 percent below 1990 levels, it is the strongest pledge yet by any state. Further, California has ruled that its electricity distributors will not purchase power unless it meets the lowest possible greenhouse gas emission standards. That ruling will force producers outside the state to accommodate, or lose a huge chunk of their revenues. Pacific Gas and Electric, one of California's regulated electric utilities, already has phased out much of its fossil fuel sources. Forty-six percent of the electricity it delivers to customers comes from fossil fuels, primarily natural gas. Only 1 percent comes from coal, according to utility spokeswoman Darlene Chiu.

Clearly, state and region-wide efforts to cut carbon emissions are grabbing the attention of utilities and the public alike. "What this means is that states are not willing to wait for the Bush administration to catch on," says Dale Bryk, an attorney with the Natural Resources Defense Council, which helped design the northeastern states' program.

Ultimately, many scientists, economists, environmentalists, legislators, and a growing number of utility executives agree that a multi-pronged approach—technology, carbon markets, and public policy—will be necessary to attack global warming. "A responsible approach to solutions would avoid the mistake of trying to find a single magic 'silver bullet'," Gore said in his NYU speech in September. The answer, he added, quoting environmental writer Bill McKibben, lies in a "silver buckshot" approach—an effective blend of several solutions.

POSTSCRIPT

Should Utilities Burn More Coal?

A great deal of work has gone into finding ways to control the pollutants, including carbon dioxide, emitted by coal-burning power plants. Much of that work has been funded by the U.S. Department of Energy (DOE). However, in January 2008, the DOE announced that it was "restructuring" its FutureGen program, among the projects described in Eli Kintisch's "Making Dirty Coal Plants Cleaner," *Science* (July 13, 2007). According to *New Scientist* ("US Government Pulls the Plug on Flagship Clean Coal Project," February 9, 2008), the restructuring "decision was based on rising costs of the project and notes that money will continue to be contributed to CCS [carbon capture and storage] development. Some scientists believe the move has set back CCS technology by three to five years."

On April 15, 2008, the House Science and Technology Committee held a hearing on DOE's restructuring plans. According to Paul Thompson, chairman of the FutureGen Alliance, "The FutureGen program is a global public-private partnership formed to design, build, and operate the world's first near-zero emission coal-fueled power plant with 90 percent capture and storage of carbon dioxide (CO_2). It will determine the technical and economic feasibility of generating electricity from coal with near-zero emission technology. FutureGen has five years of progress behind it. More than fifty-million dollars have been obligated to the effort with the majority spent. It is positioned to advance integrated gasification combined cycle (IGCC) and carbon capture and storage (CCS) technology faster and further than any other program in the world."

Such developments raise questions about the commitment of the U.S. government to clean dirty energy technologies. Jeff Goodell, *Big Coal: The Dirty Secret Behind America's Energy Future* (Houghton Mifflin, 2006), says that our reliance on coal is so great that it is difficult to fund work that will lead to change. However, there will be a new administration in Washington, D.C., in 2009, and that may not remain true. Meanwhile construction of coal-burning power plants continues and environmentalists continue to try to stop them; see Glenn Unterberger, Brendan Collins, and Sabrina Mizrachi, "Litigation Challenging Coal Plants, One Permit at a Time," *Natural Resources & Environment* (Spring 2008). Yet there is a need for energy, and some parts of the world are far more dependent on coal than the United States. Seyward Darby, "Clearing the Air," *Transitions Online* (April 14, 2008), notes that the Czech Republic generates 60 percent and Poland 90 percent of its electricity with coal, and coal emissions cause serious environmental problems in these countries. There is a real need for clean coal technologies. If the United States adds as many coal-burning power plants as Susan Moran says have been proposed (over 150), U.S. need will be even greater than it is today. Perhaps DOE is betting that U.S. electricity generation will shift toward nuclear power, as discussed in Issue 12. There are other options as well; James Ridgeway, "Scrubbing King Coal," *Mother* Jones (May/June 2008), says they include nuclear power and wind, geothermal, and solar power; see also Unit 4 of this book.

Internet References . . .

Intergovernmental Panel on Climate Change (IPCC)

The IPCC was formed by the World Meteorological Organization (WMO) and the United Nations Environment Programme (UNEP) to assess the scientific, technical, and socio-economic information relevant for understanding whether the climate is changing, humans have a role in causing the change, and what the consequences are likely to be.

http://www.ipcc.ch/

Climate Change

The United Nations Environmental Program maintains this site as a central source for substantive work and information resources with regard to climate change.

http://climatechange.unep.net/

International Emissions Trading Association (IETA)

The IETA works to develop an active, flexible, global greenhouse gas market, consistent across national boundaries.

http://www.ieta.org/ieta/www/pages/index.php

The U.S. Department of Energy—Carbon Capture

The DOE's Carbon Capture page provides information on current research in this area.

http://www.fossil.energy.gov/programs/sequestration/capture/

Weather Modification Association

The Weather Modification Association promotes research and development of technologies such as cloud seeding for increasing rainfall.

http://www.weathermodification.org/

University Corporation for Atmospheric Research

The University Corporation for Atmospheric Research and the National Center for Atmospheric Research are part of a collaborative community dedicated to understanding the atmosphere—the air around us—and the interconnected processes that make up the Earth system, from the ocean floor to the Sun's core.

http://www.ucar.edu/

Global Warming

*W*hatever you call it—the greenhouse effect, global warming, or climate change—it is a major topic of concern and debate around the world today. It is a consequence of the way human activities have added large amounts of carbon dioxide and other "greenhouse gases" to the atmosphere, and among its likely future impacts are rising average temperatures, rising sea level, and spreading disease. Understanding the issues in this unit of the book is essential to understanding what is happening and what society can do about it.

- Are Global Warming Facts Too Uncertain to Guide Government Policy?

- Is Global Warming Skepticism Just Smoke and Mirrors?

- Are the Potential Costs of Global Warming Too High to Ignore?

- Can Carbon Trading Help Control Carbon Emissions?

- Is Carbon Capture Technology Ready to Limit Carbon Emissions?

- Is "Geoengineering" a Possible Answer to Global Warming?

ISSUE 6

Are Global Warming Facts Too Uncertain to Guide Government Policy?

YES: Roy W. Spencer, from "How Serious Is the Global Warming Threat?" *Society* (September 2007)

NO: Ralph J. Cicerone, from Testimony on "Questions Surrounding the 'Hockey Stick' Temperature Studies: Implications for Climate Change Assessments," before the Committee on Energy and Commerce, Subcommittee on Oversight and Investigations, U.S. House of Representatives (July 27, 2006)

ISSUE SUMMARY

YES: Roy W. Spencer argues that the science of global warming is not as certain as the public is told, but even if predictions of strong global warming are correct, it is not at all clear what the best policy reaction to that threat should be.

NO: Ralph J. Cicerone argues that though it may be hard to pinpoint the magnitude of future climate changes, there are multiple lines of evidence supporting the reality of and human roles in global climate change. We must decide how best to respond to climate change and associated global changes.

Scientists have known for more than a century that carbon dioxide and other "greenhouse gases" (including water vapor, methane, and chlorofluorocarbons) help prevent heat from escaping the Earth's atmosphere. In fact, it is this "greenhouse effect" that keeps the Earth warm enough to support life. Yet there can be too much of a good thing. Ever since the dawn of the industrial age, humans have been burning vast quantities of fossil fuels, releasing the carbon they contain as carbon dioxide. Because of this, scientists estimate that by the year 2050, the amount of carbon dioxide in the air will be double what it was in 1850. By 1982 an increase was apparent. Less than a decade later, many researchers were saying that the climate had already begun to warm.

Debate over the reality of the warming trend and its significance for humanity and the environment has been vigorous. Much of this debate has been over the validity of the "hockey-stick" graph alluded to in the title of the "Questions Surrounding the 'Hockey Stick' Temperature Studies: Implications for Climate Change Assessments" hearing held on July 27, 2006, before the Committee on Energy and Commerce, Subcommittee on Oversight and Investigations, U.S. House of Representatives. The graph presents estimates of Northern Hemisphere temperatures over the past thousand years. Some years, the temperatures are relatively high; some years, they are relatively low. There is a lot of "jitter" in the graph. But the trend is fairly clear: Temperatures are more or less stable over most of the millennium but shoot upward in recent years. The overall shape of the graph is that of a hockey stick. Critics have insisted the shape was a statistical artifact. One of the researchers responsible for the original "hockey stick" reports, Michael E. Mann, associate professor, Departments of Meteorology and Geosciences, Penn State University, and director, Penn State Earth System Science Center, defended it at the House hearing, saying that not only has the claim that the graph's shape is a statistical artifact been rejected multiple times, but the same graph is produced when the data are analyzed by other methods. "The 'hockey stick' is not simply an isolated or aberrational finding my co-authors and I reached only once, in one study. On the contrary, it is a finding that every climate scientist who has performed a detailed examination of the available data has reached, because the hockey stick figure is driven by the data." One of the chief critics of the "hockey stick" graph, Edward J. Wegman, director of the Center for Computational Statistics at George Mason University in Fairfax, Virginia, also testified at the hearing.

The quality of the data and of the conclusions drawn from the data are crucial in any discussion of global warming (and other issues). If the data and conclusions are not solid, they cannot be used to go further, as in forming public policy designed to ward off disaster that people think the data allow us to predict. If the data *are* solid, however, then moving from the data to public policy may be urgent. In the following selections, Roy W. Spencer argues that the science of global warming is not as certain as the public is told, but even if predictions of strong global warming are correct, it is not at all clear what the best policy reaction to that threat should be. Massive reductions in greenhouse gas emissions will require new energy technologies, which are most likely to be developed in the countries that can afford massive energy R&D efforts. Therefore, draconian, government-mandated controls on emissions could very well hurt, rather than help, efforts to develop those new technologies. Ralph J. Cicerone, president of the National Academy of Sciences, argues that though it may be hard to pinpoint the magnitude of future climate changes, there are multiple lines of evidence supporting the reality of and human roles in global climate change. We can and must decide how best to respond to climate change and associated global changes.

YES

Roy W. Spencer

How Serious Is the Global Warming Threat?

Global warming is the quintessential environmental issue. While the local effects of litter, chemical contamination, and aerosol pollution dominated our environmental concerns in the 1970s and 1980s, we are now faced with a threat that is global in extent and predicted to be long-lasting. The culprit is humanity's use of fossil fuels, which release carbon dioxide into the atmosphere when burned. Because carbon dioxide is a "greenhouse gas," it affects the radiative energy budget of the Earth. Though carbon dioxide is a relatively minor atmospheric constituent, with a concentration now approaching 400 ppm (pre-industrial levels were about 280 ppm), it acts like a "blanket" for infrared (heat) radiation, warming the lower atmosphere, and cooling the upper atmosphere.

The direct warming effect of a doubling of carbon dioxide concentrations (doubling is predicted to occur late in this century) has been estimated to be only about 1°C. While this is not a very worrisome level of warming, many computer climate models suggest warming levels of three or four times this magnitude. This extra warming is due to "positive feedback" in the models. Positive feedbacks occur when the direct warming tendency of the carbon dioxide is amplified by changes in clouds, water vapor, snow cover, and sea ice in the models. The existence and magnitude of these positive feedbacks are at the heart of scientific arguments over how much of the current global warmth is due to mankind's activities, and, therefore, how much global warming we can expect in the future.

But even if predictions of strong warming—say 10°F by the end of this century—are correct, it is not at all clear what the best policy reaction to that threat should be. Because of the necessity of inexpensive energy sources for the health and well-being of humans, it will be impossible to achieve substantial reductions in energy use through conservation. Instead, massive reductions in greenhouse gas emissions will require new energy technologies. Those technologies will likely be developed in the countries that can afford massive energy R&D efforts. Therefore, draconian, government-mandated punishment of fossil fuel use through carbon taxes or caps on greenhouse gases (GHGs) could very well hurt, rather than help, efforts to develop those new technologies.

From *Society*, vol. 44, no. 5, September 2007, pp. 45–50. Copyright © 2007 by Springer Science and Business Media. Reprinted by permission via Rightslink.

Global Warming to Date

Globally averaged temperatures as measured by surface thermometers have warmed by about 0.6°C (about 1°F) over the last 100 years. Three major features are evident in this temperature record. The first is a warming trend up until 1940, which is believed by many to represent the end of the "Little Ice Age." Then, a gradual cooling trend is seen from the 1940s to the 1970s. This cooling could have been due to man-made aerosol pollution, which reflects sunlight, but this explanation is somewhat speculative. Finally, stronger warming has occurred since the 1970s up to the present. This warming is widely attributed to man-made greenhouse gases.

This recent warming trend is what worries many scientists, and has led to considerable media hysteria. Some believe that global temperatures are now warmer than they have been anytime in the last 1,000 years.

The claims that current temperatures are warmer than anytime in the last 1,000 years depend critically on proxy measurements—primarily tree ring data from a handful of locations that have long-lived species of trees. No doubt, most of the paleoclimate experts that perform this kind of research are fully convinced of the accuracy of these proxy estimates; however, many of the assumptions involved can never be tested and verified. Therefore, conclusions based upon proxy data are very suspect.

A central question is, "How much of the present warmth is due to mankind's activities?" While several climate modelers have indeed come up with assumed magnitudes for aerosol cooling and greenhouse gas warming effects that explain the current warming trend, these are by no means the only possible explanations. Because we really do not understand, and thus are unable to model, the decadal-scale natural variability of the climate system, we really cannot know with any certainty how much of the present warming is due to burning fossil fuels. For instance, due to a lack of sufficient observational data, changes in ocean circulation or cloud amounts could have occurred without being detected. But science can only deal with what is understood, not with what is unknown. As a result, science has fallen into the bad habit of attributing most climate changes to human activities.

Anecdotal evidence such as melting sea ice and retreating glaciers would seem to provide convincing evidence. But thermometer measurements suggest that the Arctic region was at least as warm in the late 1930s as it is now. We only have reliable sea ice measurements since about 1979, when satellite measurements first began, thus, we really do not know whether recent sea ice trends are outside the realm of natural variability.

Similar points can be made about receding glaciers. Glaciers respond to a variety of influences, especially precipitation. Only a handful of the thousands of the world's glaciers have been measured for decades, let alone for centuries. Some of the glaciers that are receding are uncovering tree stumps, indicating previous times when natural climate fluctuations were responsible for a restricted extent of the ice fields.

The bottom line is that, while we are indeed in a period of unusual warmth, it is not at all clear whether it is either unprecedented, or directly attributable to man-made greenhouse warming. Though scientists have suggested explanations for current warming that involve only man-made aerosols and greenhouse gas emissions, these are by no means the only possible explanations.

The Earth's Greenhouse Effect

The term "greenhouse effect" really has two meanings. The Earth has a natural greenhouse effect that is mostly due to water vapor (about 90% of the effect), as well as carbon dioxide and methane. It has been pointed out many times that the Earth's natural greenhouse effect (again, primarily due to water vapor) keeps the Earth habitably warm. Indeed, were it not for this warming effect, life as we know it might not exist on Earth, as the surface would be too cold.

But the term "greenhouse effect" is also used to refer to the man-made "enhancement" of the Earth's natural greenhouse effect due to extra carbon dioxide produced by burning fossil fuels. "Global warming" usually refers to this man-made enhancement of the Earth's natural greenhouse effect.

A useful analogy for the Earth's natural greenhouse effect is that of a blanket. The blanket of water vapor, carbon dioxide, and methane traps infrared radiation and warms the lower atmosphere, while at the same time cooling the upper atmosphere. This effect is somewhat analogous to that of a blanket keeping warm air close to your body, while at the same time keeping cooler air away from your body. The thicker the blanket, the warmer it stays under the blanket, and the cooler it remains outside of the blanket.

While sunlight ultimately drives the climate system, infrared radiation is an equally important player. For the temperature of the Earth to remain roughly constant, the amount of sunlight absorbed by the entire Earth must equal the amount of infrared radiation lost to outer space. This is called radiative energy balance. Adding carbon dioxide, a greenhouse gas, changes the radiative balance of the Earth by not allowing as much infrared cooling to occur to balance the solar heating. The result is presumed to be a warming that proceeds until the higher temperatures push the outgoing infrared radiation intensity back up to where it, once again, balances the incoming sunlight.

This radiative balance (or the presumed imbalance) has not, however, actually been measured; it has only been inferred. NASA flies Earth-orbiting instruments that measure these radiative components, but the instruments are not accurate enough to reliably measure the expected imbalance between incoming sunlight and outgoing infrared energy. For all we know, the oceans may be giving up large amounts of heat that had been stored in centuries past, or clouds may have undergone recent changes, leading to natural radiative imbalances in the system. Because we do not have enough information to conclude otherwise, most scientists simply assume that balance exists.

Global Warming Theory

The fundamentals of global warming theory have a sound physical basis. We know that carbon dioxide is a greenhouse gas, and that atmospheric concentrations of CO_2 are increasing. . . . The atmospheric concentration is still relatively small as of 2005, only about 380 ppm by volume. Based upon theoretical calculations, and assuming that no natural radiative imbalance exists, one study infers a current man-made imbalance of about 0.85 W/m^2. For reference, this can be compared to an estimated average value of about 240 W/m^2 for both incoming and outgoing levels of radiation at the top of the atmosphere (globally averaged). If not for the current global warmth, the calculated imbalance would be even larger since some of the imbalance has presumably been alleviated by increased global temperatures.

The accuracy of the 0.85 W calculation, however, depends upon assumptions about many variables, such as global water vapor and cloud distributions, that are really not measured accurately enough to give this level of precision. In other words, this small imbalance assumes all the natural forcings in the climate system are stable. This is unlikely to be true. The oceans can store or release huge amounts of heat without large temperature changes. Indeed, we already know that large radiative imbalances exist locally and regionally, for this is what drives much of our weather.

My focus on these potential natural sources of global imbalances does not by itself prove that the man-made portion of any imbalance is unimportant. I only point them out as an example of how we assume climate stability is tied to radiative balance, when in fact climate stability (say, as measured by the average surface temperature of the Earth) might well exist even in the face of substantial radiative imbalances—imbalances that climate models have not been built to deal with.

Despite all of these uncertainties, we do know that the extra carbon dioxide does cause an extra trapping of infrared radiation, resulting in a warming tendency in the lower atmosphere (and presumably in the oceans). Doubling of CO_2 concentrations is expected to occur late in this century. The warming due to a doubling of carbon dioxide alone, without any other changes in the atmosphere (an unlikely scenario), would amount to only about 1–2°F. If this was the expected level of warming during this century, there would be relatively little worry.

Instead, the concern over how much warming will occur in the future is not so much because of the direct warming effects of the extra CO_2. Instead, the worry is that various weather processes might change in response to the warming tendency from the extra carbon dioxide in such a way that amplifies that response (positive feedback). For instance, a decrease in low clouds in response to the warming tendency would be a positive feedback, since it amplifies the warming by letting more sunlight reach the surface.

Similarly, an increase in water vapor (the Earth's dominant greenhouse gas) would also amplify the warming. Indeed, water vapor is believed by many climate scientists to be the dominant positive feedback in the climate system. A warming tendency should evaporate more water from the surface, which by itself would cause further warming, which causes more evaporation, etc. This is why water vapor feedback is generally believed to amplify the warming due to carbon dioxide alone, by at least a factor of two.

In computer model simulations of the climate system, which are simplified mathematical representations of the most important weather processes, the net feedback is usually found to be positive. In a few models, it is strongly positive. This is why some climate experts talk about a potential threat of temperature rises of 10°F or more in response to a doubling of carbon dioxide. These large values occur because positive feedbacks combine in such a way that they tend to amplify each other.

But are these feedbacks really understood well enough to believe the predictions of climate models that include those feedbacks? Is our climate system really that sensitive to a small increase in greenhouse gases? At some point, climate modelers must depend upon faith . . . faith that they know the sign and magnitude of these feedbacks, and that the model forced by these feedbacks is behaving in a realistic manner.

Clearly, global warming theory depends upon assumptions as much as it does on scientific observations. How much of the current (or predicted) warming a scientist believes is due to mankind ultimately comes down to how much faith that person has in our present understanding of what drives climate fluctuations, the computer climate models that contain that understanding, and ultimately, faith in how fragile or resilient the Earth is.

The Earth's Thermostat

There is a yet another simple aspect of the climate system that argues against substantial future warming. It has been computed that, even though the natural greenhouse effect "tries" to increase the surface temperature of the Earth to about 140°F, 75% of that warming is prevented from ever occurring. Weather—clouds, rain, wind—is the result of the atmosphere's response to the warming rays of the Sun, short-circuiting the Earth's natural greenhouse effect and greatly limiting surface warming.

Thus, even though water vapor (through its greenhouse effect) keeps the Earth habitably warm, the same water vapor also represents heat removal processes that also keep the Earth habitably cool. In other words, the characteristics of water moderate and stabilize the climate against large temperature fluctuations.

The heat absorbed by the water vapor is carried by convective air currents that transport the extra heat and water vapor upward, eventually causing clouds to form. This further cools the climate by shading some of the Earth from the sun. Some of the condensed water in the clouds returns to the Earth as precipitation, replenishing the surface water so that the whole process, called the hydrologic cycle, can start all over again. As a result of all of the cooling processes associated with weather systems, the average surface temperature of the Earth is about 55°F, rather than a scorching 140°F.

These processes are, however crudely, included in climate models. The point is that the net effect of clouds, water vapor, precipitation—in short, weather and the global hydrologic cycle—is to substantially cool the surface of the Earth below what the natural greenhouse effect would cause it to be for a given amount of incoming sunlight. So, without firm evidence that the net atmospheric feedbacks are indeed positive, there is still substantial uncertainty about mankind's influence on global temperatures. But how could climate models that predict large amounts of warming all be wrong? First, let us look at a feedback that is believed to be well understood: positive water vapor feedback.

It is true that if the surface warms, there will be more water evaporated from the surface, and water vapor is the Earth's dominant greenhouse gas. But the average amount of water vapor in the atmosphere is not simply due to how much water is evaporated from the surface . . . that is only half of the story. If evaporation was to occur unchecked, the global atmosphere would become totally saturated with water within a matter of days or weeks. This does not happen. Instead, the average amount of vapor in the atmosphere is the result of a balance between the vapor source (evaporation) and the vapor sink (precipitation). Therefore, one cannot determine how atmospheric water vapor will change with warming without understanding precipitation systems and their response to warming.

And how will precipitation systems change in response to warming? No one knows. A minority of scientists (myself included) contend that, until we understand how precipitation processes respond to warming, we really do not know whether water vapor feedback is strongly positive, weakly positive, or zero. Yet water vapor feedback is considered by many scientists to be a "solved" problem. Clouds, in contrast, represent a feedback that everyone agrees is uncertain. It has been calculated that only a couple percent increase in low clouds would offset the warming effects of a doubling of atmospheric carbon dioxide from fossil fuel use. Because all of these processes (evaporation, clouds, precipitation) are interconnected, it really is misleading to treat them as separate feedbacks. They are all so intimately tied together, that climate models should treat them as a system, not individually.

Global Warming Prdictions as Faith

Hopefully the foregoing discussion makes it clear just how much faith is required to extrapolate our current level of climate understanding to predictions of future climate change. Climate models are, their creators will admit, relatively crude representations of how the atmosphere works. Just because the models do a reasonably good job of replicating the seasons (which are forced by huge variations in the energy source, sunlight) does not mean that they respond properly to the warming tendency of a minor greenhouse gas, carbon dioxide.

Nevertheless, a majority of climate modelers and climate scientists have sufficient faith in the models to argue for their use as predictive tools. Unfortunately, the track record of scientific predictions of massive environmental changes of any kind has been poor. This has led to a public distrust, mostly deserved, of scientific predictions of catastrophe. Of course, substantial global warming is not out of the question. Nevertheless, both in terms of threats to humanity as well as to the Earth, there are usually unforeseen checks and balances in place that prevent predicted climate calamities from ever materializing. This statement involves faith, as well, but it is grounded in past experience, whereas catastrophic global warming beliefs are founded more in fear, conjecture, and a myriad of assumptions (both explicit and implicit).

Benefits from Warming

Suppose future warming is relatively modest, due to stabilizing mechanisms within the climate system. If this is the case, global warming could actually produce substantial net benefits. These benefits are seldom discussed in scientific circles. Comparatively little government research money is available to investigate possible benefits, and the media prefer to report predictions of gloom and doom.

The largest positive impact could be to agriculture. Based upon estimates of global energy use, the current rate of rise in atmospheric carbon dioxide concentration . . . is only 50% of what it should be. The other 50% is apparently being absorbed by the biosphere, which uses it for food. This fact alone has led some plant physiologists to conclude that some of the increase in agricultural productivity in recent decades is likely due to the increased fertilization of crops from higher carbon dioxide levels. Of course, most of the vegetation on Earth is non-agricultural, and it, too, is being increasingly fertilized. Much research has been performed examining the combined effects of extra warmth and extra CO_2 on various kinds of plants. The bulk of the results show net benefits to plant health, growth, and sensitivity to drought.

Policy Implications

Even if global warming proves to be a serious problem, it is not at all clear what should (or even can) be done about it. If it was easy to switch to fuels which produce little or no carbon dioxide, it would be foolish not to do so, given the potential risks of a 10°F rise in global temperatures by the end of this century. But policy choices invariably involve weighing costs and benefits. They also necessarily involve assumptions about where our future sources of energy will come from, and whether there will be any countries wealthy enough to fund new energy technology R&D if we mandate CO_2 reductions by fiat.

The main difficulty in "doing something" about global warming is the fact that inexpensive energy helps drive economic growth, human health and well-being. Historically, those countries that build wealth through efficient use of natural resources have the lowest levels of pollution and population growth. The poorest countries have the worst environmental problems, and their high rates of population growth put additional pressures on the environment.

The concern that the richest countries of the world have the least sustainable environmental practices is contrary to the evidence. The relationship between an Environmental Sustainability Index and per capita gross domestic product for 117 nations of the world shows a statistically significant positive relationship between the two variables. Thus, on average, the wealthier the country, the more sustainable are its environmental practices.

Because alternative fuels are, at least for now, more expensive than fossil fuels, mandating their use through governmental controls will come at the expense of other portions of the economy. If there were alternative sources of energy that were cost-competitive with petroleum and coal, they would already be in widespread use, at least in those economies that, like the USA, have free markets. Any economic downturn resulting from punishing fossil fuel use will affect the poor first and foremost. They can ill afford high heat and light bills and high transportation costs. While the wealthy can absorb the extra cost of, say, a $2 increase in the cost of gasoline, many of the poor cannot. Moreover unskilled workers are more likely to become unemployed due to economic contractions.

Even if global warming ends up being a serious problem, it is not at all clear what should be done about it right now. Environmental activists today seem only interested in reducing fossil fuel use immediately. They appear unwilling to consider other approaches (e.g. intensive research into new energy technologies) that might actually accomplish the greatest reductions in the long term.

Summary

While catastrophic global warming is theoretically possible, such a conclusion depends critically upon a myriad of assumptions contained in computer climate models being substantially correct. These assumptions, taken together, represent faith on the part of many climate modelers. A basic tenet of that faith is that the climate system is fragile, and very sensitive to small perturbations, particularly our production of carbon dioxide, a relatively minor atmospheric greenhouse gas. I have argued that there is just as much reason to have faith that the climate system is relatively insensitive to a doubling of carbon dioxide, which is expected to occur later in this century.

But even if predictions of strong global warming are correct, it is not clear what policies to employ to avoid this eventuality. Inexpensive energy is necessary for human health and well-being. Punishing the use of fossil fuel through CO_2 emission caps or taxation will be unpopular and relatively ineffective. Technological solutions to the problem seem to be the only long-term option. Because only the wealthy countries of the world can afford the R&D to bring this about, hurting those economies with carbon caps and taxes would likely prove to be counter-productive to finding those solutions.

Ralph J. Cicerone

NO

Climate Change: Evidence and Future Projections

The greenhouse effect is a natural phenomenon. Without greenhouse gases, the surface of the Earth would be about 60°F (33°C) colder than it is today. Now, humans are amplifying the greenhouse effect by increasing the concentrations of many greenhouse gases (carbon dioxide, methane, nitrous oxide, synthetic chlorofluorocarbons and other fluorocarbons, and tropospheric ozone) in the atmosphere. The extra energy trapped near Earth's surface by the human-amplified greenhouse effect is presently about 2.5 Watts per square meter, which is about 100 times larger than all human energy usage.

There is no doubt that the Earth is warming. Weather-station records and ship-based observations show that global average surface air temperature has increased by about 1.2°F (0.7°C) since the beginning of the 20th century, more than half of it since 1975. Scientists have also measured upward temperature trends in the lower atmosphere and in the upper oceans, and this continuing warming has been accompanied by world-wide changes in many other indicators, such as shifts in ecosystems and decreases in Arctic sea ice thickness and extent.

Last week you heard testimony from Dr. Gerald North, chair of the National Research Council committee that examined surface temperature reconstructions for the last 2,000 years derived from tree rings, boreholes, ice cores, glacier length records, and other types of proxy evidence. The committee concluded that the Earth was warmer during the last few decades of the 20th century than at any other time during at least the last 400 years, and potentially the last several thousand years. These temperature reconstructions provide a useful context for evaluating late 20th century warming. However, they are not the primary evidence for the widely accepted view that global warming is occurring, that human beings are responsible, at least in part, for this warming, and that the Earth's climate will continue to change during the next century.

Many additional lines of evidence demonstrate that climate is changing:

- Measurements show large increases in carbon dioxide and other greenhouse gases (methane and nitrous oxide, for example)

Committee on Energy and Commerce, Subcommittee on Oversight and Investigations, U.S. House of Representatives, Ralph J. Cicerone (July 27, 2006).

beginning in the middle of the 19th century. These increases in greenhouse gases are due to human activities such as burning fossil fuel for energy, industrial processes, and transportation. The concentration of carbon dioxide in the atmosphere is now at its highest level in 650,000 years and continues to rise.

- We understand how carbon dioxide and other greenhouse gases affect global temperature. Rigorous radiative transfer calculations of the temperature changes associated with increasing greenhouse gas concentrations, together with reasonable assumptions about climate feedbacks, provide a physically based theoretical explanation for the observed warming.

- State-of-the-art mathematical climate models are able to reproduce the warming of the past century only if human-caused greenhouse gases are included.

- Analysis of high-quality, precise measurements of the Sun's total brightness over the past 25 years shows that there has been little if any change in the long-term average of solar output over this time period. Thus, changes in the Sun can not explain the warming observed over the past 25 years.

- The oceans have warmed in recent decades and the stratosphere has cooled. Extratropical land masses in the Northern Hemisphere have warmed even more than the oceans. These large-scale changes are consistent with the predicted spatial and temporal pattern of greenhouse surface warming.

- Ice covered regions of the Earth have experienced significant melting. For example, the annual average sea-ice extent in the Artic has decreased by about 8%, or nearly one million square kilometers, over the past 30 years. Measurements from Earth-orbiting satellites (from synthetic aperture radars and from Earth's gravity sensors) over the last few years have shown that both the Greenland and West Antarctic Ice Sheets are losing ice.

- Several publications in 2005 and 2006 show that hurricane intensities have increased in some parts of the world, in lock step with oceanic warming.

While we are quite certain that the Earth's surface has warmed rapidly during the last 30 years and that it is warmer now than at any other time during at least the last 400 years, projecting what will happen to important climate variables in the future is more difficult. As stated in the 2001 NRC report, "climate change simulations . . . yield a globally averaged surface temperature increase by the end of the century of 2.5 to 10.4°F (1.4 to 5.8°C) relative to 1990." Since 2001, we have continued to make advances in our knowledge of the climate system and in our ability to model it mathematically. Yet, pinpointing the magnitude of future climate changes is hindered both by remaining gaps in our ability to simulate scientific phenomena, and by the fact that it is difficult to predict society's future actions, particularly in the areas of population growth, energy consumption, and energy technologies. In general, temperature is easier to predict than changes such as rainfall, storm patterns, and ecosystems.

While future climate change and its impacts are inherently uncertain, they are far from unknown. A broad-brush picture of how global warming may affect certain regions of the world is starting to emerge from climate modeling efforts. Models generally project more warming in continental regions than over the oceans and in polar regions than near the equator. Precipitation is expected to increase in the tropics, decrease in the subtropics, and increase in the midlatitudes. Rainfall is also expected to increase in the monsoon regimes in South Asia, West Africa, and South America; these changes may create the potential for stronger El Niño events. Some models indicate that midlatitude continents will likely be drier during the summer in a warmer climate, leading to an increased chance for summer drought conditions.

Even if no further increases in the atmospheric concentrations of greenhouse gases occur, we are very likely to experience additional warming of 0.7°F (0.4°C). In colder climates, such warming could bring less severe winters and longer growing seasons (if soil moisture is adequate). Several studies have projected that summertime ice in the Arctic could disappear by A.D. 2100. The combined effects of ice melting and sea water expansion from ocean warming will likely cause the global average sea level to rise by between 0.1 and 0.9 meters between 1990 and 2100. Those in coastal communities, many in developing nations, will experience increased flooding due to sea level rise and are likely to experience more severe storms and surges. Increasing acidification of the surface ocean (due to added carbon dioxide from the atmosphere) will harm marine organisms such as corals and some plankton species.

In summary, there are multiple lines of evidence supporting the reality of and human roles in global climate change. The task of mitigating and preparing for the impacts of climate change will require worldwide collaborative inputs from a wide range of experts, including natural scientists, engineers, social scientists, medical scientists, those in government at all levels, business leaders and economists. For example, researchers and resource managers have only begun to address how climate change will impact future demands for electricity and water. Society faces increasing pressure to decide how best to respond to climate change and associated global changes, and applied research in direct support of decision making is needed.

POSTSCRIPT

Are Global Warming Facts Too Uncertain to Guide Government Policy?

On May 29, 2008, the Bush administration finally released the long-awaited report of the U.S. Climate Change Science Program (CCSP). The last such report appeared in 2000. The law requires new reports every four years, and the 2008 report appeared only after a federal district court judge demanded it. The current report, "Scientific Assessment of the Effects of Global Change on the United States, A Report of the Committee on Environment and Natural Resources, National Science and Technology Council" (available at http://www.ostp.gov/cs/nstc), describes the current and potential impacts of climate change. In sum, it says that the evidence is clear and getting clearer that global warming is "very likely" due to greenhouse gases largely released by human activity and there will be consequent changes in precipitation, storms, droughts, sea level, food production, fisheries, and more. Globally, "poor communities can be especially vulnerable, particularly those concentrated in high-risk areas." Dealing with these effects may require changes in many areas, particularly relating to energy use, but "significant uncertainty exists about the potential impacts of climate change on energy production and distribution, in part because the timing and magnitude of climate impacts are uncertain." See Susan Milius, "Already Feeling the Heat," *Science News* Web edition (May 29, 2008).

Consonant with the Bush administration's previous position that imposing restrictions on fossil fuel use or carbon emissions is a bad idea both because of uncertainty about global warming and because it would harm the economy, mitigation of the risks—which the report says are likely or very likely—is barely mentioned. U.S. goals should be limited to reducing uncertainty in projections of how the Earth's climate and related systems may change in the future. "Reducing uncertainty is crucial to providing decision makers with tools for assessing strategies for adaptation, mitigation, and other forms of risk reduction." Richard Moss of the World Wildlife Foundation, a past director of the CCSP, says that because of its shortcomings, the report fails to meet the needs of the public.

In April 2008, President Bush said in a speech (http://www.whitehouse.gov/news/releases/2008/04/20080416-6.html) that there are wrong ways and right ways to go about solving the global warming problem. The wrong way is raising energy taxes and prices (which hurts consumers and business), imposing restrictions, and abandoning the use of nuclear power and coal. The right way is setting realistic goals, adopting policies that spur investment in new technologies, encouraging the use of nuclear power (see Issue 12) and "clean" coal (see Issue 5), and enhancing international cooperation through free trade in clean energy technologies. Such measures rely on the market to stimulate voluntary reductions in emissions. It's possible that increasing funding for alternative energy technologies would lead to solutions that greatly ease the problem, but many observers think it folly to rely on future breakthroughs. The new administration that moves into the White House in 2009 may be less optimistic and more inclined to impose restrictions.

ISSUE 7

Is Global Warming Skepticism Just Smoke and Mirrors?

YES: Union of Concerned Scientists, from "Smoke, Mirrors & Hot Air: How ExxonMobil Uses Big Tobacco's Tactics to Manufacture Uncertainty on Climate Science," http://www.ucsusa.org/global_warming/science/exxonmobil-smoke-mirrors-hot.html (January 2007)

NO: Ivan Osorio, Iain Murray, and Myron Ebell, from "Liberal 'Scientists' Lead Jihad Against Global-Warming Skeptics," *Human Events*, http://www.cei.org/gencon/019,05908.cfm or http://www.humanevents.com/article.php?id=20573 (May 8, 2007)

ISSUE SUMMARY

YES: The Union of Concerned Scientists argues that opposition to the idea that global warming is real, is due to human activities, and is a threat to human well-being has been orchestrated by ExxonMobil in a disinformation campaign very similar to the tobacco industry's efforts to convince the public that tobacco was not bad for health.

NO: Ivan Osorio, Iain Murray, and Myron Ebell, all of the Competitive Enterprise Institute, argue that the Union of Concerned Scientists is a liberal-funded partisan organization that distorts facts and attempts to discredit opponents with innuendo.

Debate over the reality of the global warming trend and its significance for humanity and the environment has been vigorous. But the data are now very clear. See Richard A. Kerr, "A Worrying Trend of Less Ice, Higher Seas," *Science* (March 24, 2006), and Jeffrey Kluger, "By Any Measure, Earth Is at the Tipping Point," *Time* (April 3, 2006). In 2007, the Intergovernmental Panel on Climate Change (IPCC; http://www.ipcc.ch/) issued its Fourth Assessment Report, saying in no uncertain terms that "Warming of the climate system is unequivocal, as is now evident from observations of increases in global average air and ocean temperatures, widespread melting of snow and ice, and rising global average sea level." The impacts on ecosystems and human well-being (especially in developing nations) will be serious. The report also outlines the steps that must be taken to prevent, ease, or cope with these impacts. The importance of early action is stressed in "Confronting Climate Change: Avoiding the Unmanageable and Managing the Unavoidable," a Scientific Expert Group Report on Climate Change and Sustainable Development, sponsored by Sigma Xi and the United Nations Foundation, prepared for the 15th Session of the U.N.'s Commission on Sustainable Development and presented on February 27, 2007 (available at http://www.sigmaxi.org/about/news/UNSEGonline.pdf). See also William Collins, et al., "The Physical Science Behind Climate Change," *Scientific American* (August 2007).

Critics continue to stress uncertainties in the data, as well as in projections of how severe global warming will be and how severe the impact will be on human (and other) life. See Michael Shnayerson, "A Convenient Untruth," *Vanity Fair* (May 2007). Before 2007, the Bush administration showed little interest in addressing the issue. Its plan for dealing with global warming insisted that short-term economic benefits must come first. Stuart Jordan, "The Global Warming Crisis," *The Humanist* (November/December 2005), wrote that "I see little evidence that the Bush Administration has given more than lip service to the problem. . . . There are . . . things that can be done [and] the important thing is to get started doing some of these things in earnest, and not for us to stick our heads in the sand doing business as usual until the water comes in over our eyelids. If we wait long enough, it will."

In the following selections, the Union of Concerned Scientists argues that opposition to the idea that global warming is real, is due to human activities, and is a threat to human well-being has been orchestrated by ExxonMobil in a disinformation campaign very similar to the tobacco industry's efforts to convince the public that tobacco was not bad for health. It has funded groups such as the Competitive Enterprise Institute (which was founded to fight government regulation of business), funded and orchestrated "climate contrarians" whose research lacks credibility, and lobbied government to block federal action and weaken government reports on the problem. Ivan Osorio, Iain Murray, and Myron Ebell, all of the Competitive Enterprise Institute, argue that the Union of Concerned Scientists is a liberal-funded partisan organization that distorts facts and attempts to discredit opponents with innuendo.

YES

Seth Schulman et al.

Smoke, Mirrors & Hot Air

Executive Summary

In an effort to deceive the public about the reality of global warming, ExxonMobil has underwritten the most sophisticated and most successful disinformation campaign since the tobacco industry misled the public about the scientific evidence linking smoking to lung cancer and heart disease. As this report documents, the two disinformation campaigns are strikingly similar. ExxonMobil has drawn upon the tactics and even some of the organizations and actors involved in the callous disinformation campaign the tobacco industry waged for 40 years. Like the tobacco industry, ExxonMobil has:

- *Manufactured uncertainty* by raising doubts about even the most indisputable scientific evidence.
- Adopted a strategy of *information laundering* by using seemingly independent front organizations to publicly further its desired message and thereby confuse the public.
- *Promoted scientific spokespeople* who misrepresent peer-reviewed scientific findings or cherry-pick facts in their attempts to persuade the media and the public that there is still serious debate among scientists that burning fossil fuels has contributed to global warming and that human-caused warming will have serious consequences.
- *Attempted to shift the focus* away from meaningful action on global warming with misleading charges about the need for "sound science."
- *Used its extraordinary access to the Bush administration* to block federal policies and shape government communications on global warming.

The report documents that, despite the scientific consensus about the fundamental understanding that global warming is caused by carbon dioxide and other heat-trapping emissions, ExxonMobil has funneled about $16 million between 1998 and 2005 to a network of ideological and advocacy organizations that manufacture uncertainty on the issue. Many of these organizations have an overlapping—sometimes identical—collection of spokespeople serving as staff, board members, and scientific advisors. By publishing and republishing the non-peer-reviewed works of a small group of scientific spokespeople, ExxonMobil-funded organizations have propped up and amplified work that has been discredited by reputable climate scientists.

ExxonMobil's funding of established research institutions that seek to better understand science, policies, and technologies to address global warming has given the corporation "cover," while its funding of ideological and advocacy organizations to conduct a disinformation campaign works to confuse that understanding. This seemingly inconsistent activity makes sense when looked at through a broader lens. Like the tobacco companies in previous decades, this strategy provides a positive "pro-science" public stance for ExxonMobil that masks their activity to delay meaningful action on global warming and helps keep the public debate stalled on the science rather than focused on policy options to address the problem.

In addition, like Big Tobacco before it, ExxonMobil has been enormously successful at influencing the current administration and key members of Congress. Documents highlighted in this report, coupled with subsequent events, provide evidence of ExxonMobil's cozy relationship with government officials, which enables the corporation to work behind the scenes to gain access to key decision makers. In some cases, the company's proxies have directly shaped the global warming message put forth by federal agencies. . . .

Background the Facts about ExxonMobil

ExxonMobil is a powerful player on the world stage. It is the world's largest publicly traded company: at $339 billion, its 2005 revenues exceeded the gross domestic products of most of the world's nations. It is the most profitable corporation in history. In 2005, the company netted $36 billion—nearly $100 million in profit *each day*.

As the biggest player in the world's gas and oil business, ExxonMobil is also one of the world's largest producers of global warming pollution. Company operations alone pumped the equivalent of 138 million metric tons of carbon dioxide into the atmosphere in 2004 and roughly the same level of emissions in 2005, according to company reporting. In 2005, the end use combustion of ExxonMobil's products—gasoline, heating oil, kerosene, diesel products, aviation fuels, and heavy fuels—resulted in 1,047 million metric tons of carbon dioxide–equivalent emissions. If it was a country, ExxonMobil would rank sixth in emissions.

While some oil companies like BP, Occidental Petroleum, and Shell have begun to invest in clean energy technologies and publicly committed to reduce their heat-trapping emissions, ExxonMobil has made no such commitment.

Lee Raymond, ExxonMobil's chief executive officer (CEO) until 2006, set a brazenly unapologetic corporate tone on global warming. During his nearly 13 years as ExxonMobil's leader, Raymond unabashedly opposed caps on carbon dioxide emissions and refused to acknowledge the scientific consensus on global warming. Under Raymond's direction, ExxonMobil positioned itself, as Paul Krugman of the *New York Times* recently put it, as "an enemy of the planet." Not only did he do nothing to curb his company's global warming emissions, during his tenure Raymond divested the company of nearly all its alternative energy holdings. During his time as CEO, ExxonMobil's board lavishly rewarded him with compensation amounting to more than $686 million. When Raymond retired at the end of 2005, he received an exorbitant retirement package worth nearly $400 million, prompting sharp criticism from shareholders. ExxonMobil is now headed by CEO Rex Tillerson, but the corporate policies Raymond forged so far remain largely intact.

ExxonMobil has played the world's most active corporate role in underwriting efforts to thwart and undermine climate change regulation. For instance, according to the Center for Responsive Politics, ExxonMobil's PAC—its political action committee—and individuals affiliated with the company made more than $4 million in political contributions throughout the 2000 to 2006 election cycles. It was consistently among the top four energy sector contributors. In the 2004 election cycle alone, ExxonMobil's PAC and individuals affiliated with the company gave $935,000 in political contributions, more than any other energy company. Much of that money went in turn to President Bush's election campaign. In addition, ExxonMobil paid lobbyists more than $61 million between 1998 and 2005 to help gain access to key decision makers.

This report does not attempt to shed light on all ExxonMobil activities related to global warming. Instead, it takes an in-depth look at how the relatively modest investment of about $16 million between 1998 and 2004 to select political organizations has been remarkably effective at manufacturing uncertainty about the scientific consensus on global warming. It offers examples to illustrate how ExxonMobil's influence over key administration officials and members of Congress has fueled the disinformation campaign and helped forestall federal action to reduce global warming emissions. And this report identifies how strategies and tactics used by ExxonMobil mirror the well-documented campaign by the tobacco industry to prevent government regulation by creating public confusion about the link between smoking and disease.

The Origins of a Strategy

In its campaign to sow uncertainty about the scientific evidence on global warming, ExxonMobil has followed a corporate strategy pioneered by the tobacco industry. Because ExxonMobil's strategy, tactics, and even some personnel draw heavily from the tobacco industry's playbook, it is useful to look briefly at this earlier campaign. The settlement of the lawsuit brought by the attorneys general of 46 states forced the major tobacco companies to place their enormous caches of internal documents online. Thanks to these archives, the details of the tobacco industry's covert strategy are now clear.

The story begins in the mid-1950s when scientific evidence began to emerge linking smoking to cancer. The tobacco industry's initial response was to fund a research consortium, initially called the Tobacco Industry Research Committee and later known as the U.S. Tobacco Institute, to "study the issue." In 1954, Big Tobacco released a seminal public document called the "Frank Statement to Cigarette Smokers," which set the industry's tone for the coming decades. This document questioned the emerging scientific evidence of the harm caused by smoking but tried to appear concerned about the issue, pledging to the public that the industry would look closely at the scientific evidence and study it themselves.

As we now know, tobacco industry lawyers advised the companies early on that they could never admit they were selling a hazardous product without opening themselves to potentially crippling liability claims. So, rather than studying the health hazards posed by their products, the tobacco industry hired Hill & Knowlton, a leading public relations firm of the day to mount a public relations campaign on their behalf. In a key memo, Hill & Knowlton framed the issue this way: "There is only one problem—confidence and how to establish it; public assurance, and how to create it." In other words, the tobacco companies should ignore the deadly health effects of smoking and focus instead on maintaining the public's confidence in their products.

As time went on, a scientific consensus emerged about a multitude of serious dangers from smoking—and the tobacco manufacturers knew it. Despite the evidence, the industry developed a sophisticated disinformation campaign—one they knew to be misleading—to deceive the public about the hazards of smoking and to forestall governmental controls on tobacco consumption.

How Big Tobacco's Campaign Worked

In executing their calculated strategy over the course of decades, tobacco industry executives employed five main tactics:

- They sought to *manufacture uncertainty* by raising doubts about even the most indisputable scientific evidence showing their products to be hazardous to human health.
- They pioneered a strategy of *"information laundering"* in which they used—and even covertly established—seemingly independent front organizations to make the industry's own case and confuse the public.
- They *promoted scientific spokespeople* and invested in scientific research in an attempt to lend legitimacy to their public relations efforts.

- They attempted to *recast the debate* by charging that the wholly legitimate health concerns raised about smoking were not based upon "sound science."
- Finally, they *cultivated close ties with government officials* and members of Congress. While many corporations and institutions seek access to government, Tobacco's size and power gave it enormous leverage.

In reviewing the tobacco industry's disinformation campaign, the first thing to note is that the tobacco companies quickly realized they did not need to prove their products were safe. Rather, as internal documents have long since revealed, they had only to "maintain doubt" on the scientific front as a calculated strategy. As one famous internal memo from the Brown & Williamson tobacco company put it: "Doubt is our product, since it is the best means of competing with the 'body of fact' that exists in the minds of the general public. It is also the means of establishing a controversy." David Michaels, professor of occupational and environmental health at George Washington University School of Public heath and former assistant secretary for the environment, safety and health at the Department of Energy during the Clinton administration, has dubbed the strategy one of "manufacturing uncertainty." As Michaels has documented, Big Tobacco pioneered the strategy and many opponents of public health and environmental regulations have emulated it. . . .

ExxonMobil's Disinformation Campaign

In the late 1980s, when the public first began to hear about global warming, scientists had already conducted more than a century of research on the impact of carbon dioxide on earth's climate. As the science matured in the late 1980s, debate, a key component of the scientific process, surfaced among reputable scientists about the scope of the problem and the extent to which human activity was responsible. Much like the status of scientific knowledge about the health effects of smoking in the early 1950s, emerging studies suggested cause for concern but many scientists justifiably argued that more research needed to be done.

Exxon (and later ExxonMobil), concerned about potential repercussions for its business, argued from the start that no global warming trend existed and that a link between human activity and climate change could not be established. Just as the tobacco companies initially responded with a coalition to address the health effects of smoking, Exxon and the American Petroleum Institute (an organization twice chaired by former Exxon CEO Lee Raymond) joined with other energy, automotive, and industrial companies in 1989 to form the Global Climate Coalition. The coalition responded aggressively to the emerging scientific studies about global warming by opposing governmental action designed to address the problem.

Drawing on a handful of scientific spokespeople during the early and mid-1990s, the Global Climate Coalition emphasized the remaining uncertainties in climate science. Exxon and other members of the coalition challenged the need for action on global warming by denying its existence as well as characterizing global warming as a natural phenomenon. As Exxon and its proxies mobilized forces to cast doubt on global warming, however, a scientific consensus was emerging that put their arguments on exceptionally shaky scientific ground.

Manufacturing Uncertainty

By 1997, scientific understanding that human-caused emissions of heat-trapping gases were causing global warming led to the Kyoto Protocol, in which the majority of the world's industrialized nations committed to begin reducing their global warming emissions on a specified timetable. In response to both the strength of the scientific evidence on global warming and the governmental action pledged to address it, leading oil companies such as British Petroleum, Shell, and Texaco changed their stance on climate science and abandoned the Global Climate Coalition.

ExxonMobil chose a different path.

In 1998, ExxonMobil helped create a small task force calling itself the "Global Climate Science Team" (GCST). Members included Randy Randol, ExxonMobil's senior environmental lobbyist at the time, and Joe Walker, the public relations representative of the American Petroleum Institute. One member of the GCST task force, Steven Milloy, headed a nonprofit organization called the Advancement of Sound Science Coalition, which had been covertly created by the tobacco company Philip Morris in 1993 to manufacture uncertainty about the health hazards posed by second-hand smoke.

A 1998 GCST task force memo outlined an explicit strategy to invest millions of dollars to manufacture uncertainty on the issue of global warming—a strategy that directly emulated Big Tobacco's disinformation campaign. Despite mounting scientific evidence of the changing climate, the goal the team outlined was simple and familiar. As the memo put it, "Victory will be achieved when average citizens understand (recognize) uncertainties in climate science" and when public "recognition of uncertainty becomes part of the 'conventional wisdom.'"

Regardless of the mounting scientific evidence, the 1998 GCST memo contended that "if we can show that science does not support the Kyoto treaty . . . this puts the United States in a stronger moral position and frees its negotiators from the need to make concessions as a defense against perceived selfish economic concerns."

ExxonMobil and its partners no doubt understood that, with the scientific evidence against them, they would not be able to influence reputable scientists. The 1998 memo proposed that ExxonMobil and its public relations partners "develop and implement a national media relations program to inform the media about uncertainties in climate science." In the years that followed, ExxonMobil executed the strategy as planned underwriting a wide array of front organizations to publish in-house articles by select scientists and other like-minded individuals to raise objections about legitimate climate science research that has withstood rigorous peer review and has been replicated in multiple independent peer-reviewed studies—in other words, to attack research findings that were well established in the scientific community. The network ExxonMobil created masqueraded as a credible scientific alternative, but it publicized discredited studies and cherry-picked information to present misleading conclusions.

Information Laundering

A close review reveals the company's effort at what some have called "information laundering": projecting the company's desired message through ostensibly independent nonprofit organizations. First, ExxonMobil underwrites well-established groups such as the American Enterprise Institute, the Competitive Enterprise Institute, and the Cato Institute that actively oppose mandatory action on global warming as well as many other environmental standards. But the funding doesn't stop there. ExxonMobil also supports a number of lesser-known organizations that help to market and distribute global warming disinformation. Few of these are household names. For instance, most people are probably not familiar with the American Council for Capital Formation Center for Policy Research, the American Legislative Exchange Council, the Committee for a Constructive Tomorrow, or the International Policy Network, to name just a few. Yet these organizations—and many others like them—have received sizable donations from ExxonMobil for their climate change activities.

Between 1998 and 2005 (the most recent year for which company figures are publicly available), ExxonMobil has funneled approximately $16 million to carefully chosen organizations that promote disinformation on global warming. As the *New York Times* has reported, ExxonMobil is often the single largest corporate donor to many of these nonprofit organizations, frequently accounting for more than 10 percent of their annual budgets.

A close look at the work of these organizations exposes ExxonMobil's strategy. Virtually all of them publish and publicize the work of a nearly identical group of spokespeople, including scientists who misrepresent peer-reviewed climate findings and confuse the public's understanding of global warming. Most of these organizations also include these same individuals as board members or scientific advisers.

Why would ExxonMobil opt to fund so many groups with overlapping spokespeople and programs? By generously funding a web of organizations with redundant personnel, advisors, or spokespeople, ExxonMobil can quietly and effectively provide the appearance of a broad platform for a tight-knit group of vocal climate science contrarians. The seeming diversity of the organizations creates an "echo chamber" that amplifies and sustains scientific disinformation even though many of the assertions have been repeatedly debunked by the scientific community.

Take, for example, ExxonMobil's funding of a Washington, DC-based organization called Frontiers of Freedom. Begun in 1996 by former Senator Malcolm Wallop, Frontiers of Freedom was founded to promote property rights and critique environmental regulations like the Endangered Species Act. One of the group's staff members, an economist named Myron Ebell, later served as a member of the Global Climate Science Team, the small task force that laid out ExxonMobil's 1998 message strategy on global warming. Following the outline of the task force's plan in 1998, ExxonMobil began funding Frontiers of Freedom—a group that Vice President Dick Cheney recently called "an active, intelligent, and needed presence in the national debate."

Since 1998, ExxonMobil has spent $857,000 to underwrite the Frontiers of Freedom's climate change efforts. In 2002, for example, ExxonMobil made a grant to Frontiers of Freedom of $232,000 (nearly a third of the organization's annual budget) to help launch a new branch of the organization called the Center for Science and Public Policy, which would focus primarily on climate change.

A recent visit to the organization's website finds little information about the background or work of the Center for Science and Public Policy. The website offers no mention of its staff or board members other than its current executive director Robert Ferguson, for whom it offers no biographical information. As of September 2006, however, the website did prominently feature a 38-page nonpeer-reviewed report by Ferguson on climate science, heavily laden with maps, graphs, and charts, entitled "Issues in the Current State of Climate Science: A Guide for Policy Makers and Opinion Leaders." The document offers a hodgepodge of distortions and distractions posing as a serious scientific review. Ferguson questions the clear data showing that the majority of the globe's glaciers are in retreat by feebly arguing that not all glaciers have been inventoried, despite the monitoring of thousands of glaciers worldwide. And, in an attempt to dispute solid scientific evidence that climate change is causing extinctions of animal species, Ferguson offers the non sequitur that several new butterfly and frog species were recently discovered in New Guinea.

Perhaps most notable are Ferguson's references, citing a familiar collection of climate science contrarians such as Willie Soon. In fact, although his title is not listed on the organization's website, Soon is the Center for Science and Public Policy's "chief science researcher," according to a biographical note accompanying a 2005 *Wall Street Journal* op-ed co-authored by Ferguson and Soon. Ferguson's report was not subject to peer review, but it is nonetheless presented under the auspices of the authoritative-sounding Center for Science and Public Policy.

Another organization used to launder information is the George C. Marshall Institute. During the 1990s, the Marshall Institute had been known primarily for its work advocating a "Star Wars" missile defense program. However, it soon became an important home for industry-financed "climate contrarians," thanks in part to ExxonMobil's financial backing. Since 1998, ExxonMobil has paid $630,000 primarily to underwrite the

Marshall Institute's climate change effort. William O'Keefe, CEO of the Marshall Institute, formerly worked as executive vice president and chief operating officer of the American Petroleum Institute, served on the board of directors of the Competitive Enterprise Institute, and is chairman emeritus of the Global Climate Coalition.

Since ExxonMobil began to support its efforts, the Marshall Institute has served as a clearinghouse for global warming contrarians, conducting round-table events and producing frequent publications. Most recently, the Marshall Institute has been touting its new book, *Shattered Consensus: The True State of Global Warming,* edited by longtime climate contrarian Patrick Michaels (a meteorologist). Michaels has, over the past several years, been affiliated with at least ten organizations funded by ExxonMobil. Contributors to the book include others with similar affiliations with Exxon-funded groups: Sallie Baliunas, Robert Balling, John Christy, Ross McKitrick, and Willie Soon.

The pattern of information laundering is repeated at virtually all the private, nonprofit climate change programs ExxonMobil funds. The website of the Chicago-based Heartland Institute, which received $119,000 from ExxonMobil in 2005, offers recent articles by the same set of scientists. A visit to the climate section of the website of the American Legislative Exchange Council, which received $241,500 from ExxonMobil in 2005, turns up yet another nonpeer-reviewed paper by Patrick Michaels. The Committee for a Constructive Tomorrow, which received $215,000 from Exxon-Mobil over the past two funding cycles of 2004 and 2005, boasts a similar lineup of articles and a scientific advisory panel that includes Sallie Baliunas, Robert Balling, Roger Bate, Sherwood Idso, Patrick Michaels, and Frederick Seitz—all affiliated with other ExxonMobil-funded organizations.

A more prominent organization funded by ExxonMobil is the Washington, DC-based Competitive Enterprise Institute (CEI). Founded in 1984 to fight government regulation on business, CEI started to attract significant ExxonMobil funding when Myron Ebell moved there from Frontiers of Freedom in 1999. Since then, CEI has not only produced a steady flow of vituperative articles and commentaries attacking global warming science, often using the same set of global warming contrarians; it has also sued the federal government to stop the dissemination of a National Assessment Synthesis Team report extensively documenting the region-by-region impacts of climate change in the United States. For its efforts, CEI has received more than $2 million in funding from ExxonMobil from 1998 through 2005.

The irony of all these efforts is that ExxonMobil, a company that claims it is dedicated to supporting organizations favoring "free market solutions to public policy problems," is actively propping up discredited studies and misleading information that would otherwise never thrive in the scientific marketplace of ideas. . . .

Confounding the matter further is ExxonMobil's funding of established research institutions that seek to better understand science, policies, and technologies to address global warming. . . .

The funding of academic research activity has provided the corporation legitimacy, while it actively funds ideological and advocacy organizations to conduct a disinformation campaign.

Promoting Scientific Spokespeople

Inextricably intertwined with ExxonMobil's information laundering strategy of underwriting multiple organizations with overlapping staff is the corporation's promotion of a small handful of scientific spokespeople. Scientists are trusted messengers among the American public. Scientists can and do play an important and legitimate role in educating the public and policymakers about issues that have a scientific component, including global warming. Early on, Exxon (and later ExxonMobil) sought to support groups that worked with the handful of scientists, such as Frederick Singer (a physicist), John Christy (an atmospheric scientist), and Patrick Michaels, who had persistently voiced doubt about humancaused global warming and its consequences, despite mounting evidence.

However, to pull off the disinformation campaign outlined in the 1998 GCST task force memo, ExxonMobil and its public relations partners recognized they would need to cultivate new scientific spokespeople to create a sense among the public that there was still serious debate among scientists. Toward that end, the memo suggested that the team "identify, recruit and train a team of five independent scientists to participate in media outreach. These will be individuals who do not have a long history of visibility and/or participation in the climate change debate. Rather, this team will consist of new faces who will add their voices to those recognized scientists who already are vocal."

By the late 1990s, the scientific evidence on global warming was so strong that it became difficult to find scientists who disputed the reality of human-caused climate change. But ExxonMobil and its public relations partners persevered. The case of scientists Willie Soon and Sallie Baliunas is illustrative.

Soon and Baliunas are astrophysicists affiliated with the Harvard-Smithsonian Center for Astrophysics who study solar variation (i.e., changes in the amount of energy emitted by the Sun). Solar variation is one of the many factors influencing Earth's climate, although according to the IPCC it is one of the minor influences over the last century. In the mid-1990s, ExxonMobil-funded groups had already begun to spotlight the work of Soon and Baliunas to raise doubts about the human causes of global warming. To accomplish this, Baliunas was initially commissioned to write several articles for the Marshall Institute positing that solar activity might be responsible for global warming. With the Baliunas articles, the Marshall Institute skillfully amplified an issue of minor scientific importance and implied that it was a major driver of recent warming trends.

In 2003, Baliunas and Soon were catapulted into a higher profile debate when they published a controversial review article about global warming in the peer-reviewed scientific literature. Writing in the journal *Climate*

Research, the two contrarians reviewed the work of a number of previous scientists and alleged that the twentieth century was not the warmest century of the past 1,000 years and that the climate had not changed significantly over that period. The Soon-Baliunas paper was trumpeted widely by organizations and individuals funded by ExxonMobil. It was also seized upon by like-minded politicians, most notably James Inhofe (R-OK), chair (until January 2007) of the Senate Environment and Public Works Committee, who has repeatedly asserted that global warming is a hoax. Inhofe cited the Soon-Baliunas review as proof that natural variability, not human activity, was the "overwhelming factor" influencing climate change.

Less widely publicized was the fact that three of the editors of *Climate Research*—including incoming editor-in-chief Hans von Storch—resigned in protest over the Soon-Baliunas paper. Storch stated that he suspected that "some of the skeptics had identified *Climate Research* as a journal where some editors were not as rigorous in the review process as is otherwise common" and described the manuscript as "flawed." In addition, thirteen of the scientists cited in the paper published a rebuttal explaining that Soon and Baliunas had seriously misinterpreted their research.

The National Research Council recently examined the large body of published research on this topic and concluded that, "It can be said with a high level of confidence that global mean surface temperature was higher during the last few decades of the 20th century than during any comparable period during the preceding four centuries. . . . Presently available proxy evidence indicates that temperatures at many, but not all, individual locations were higher in the past 25 years than during any period of comparable length since A.D. 900." The brouhaha in the scientific community had little public impact. The echo chamber had already been set in motion reverberating among the mainstream media, while the correction became merely a footnote buried in the science sections of a few media outlets.

This controversy did not stop Soon and Baliunas from becoming central "new voices" in ExxonMobil's effort to manufacture uncertainty about global warming. Both scientists quickly established relationships with a network of organizations underwritten by the corporation. Over the past several years, for example, Baliunas has been formally affiliated with no fewer than nine organizations receiving funding from ExxonMobil. Among her other affiliations, she is now a board member and senior scientist at the Marshall Institute, a scientific advisor to the Annapolis Center for Science-Based Public Policy, an advisory board member of the Committee for a Constructive Tomorrow, and a contributing scientist to the online forum Tech Central Station, all of which are underwritten by ExxonMobil.

Another notable case is that of Frederick Seitz, who has ties to both Big Tobacco and ExxonMobil. Seitz is the emeritus chair of the Marshall Institute. He is also a prominent solid state physicist who was president of the National Academy of Sciences (NAS) from 1962 to 1969.

In an example of the tobacco industry's efforts to buy legitimacy, the cigarette company R.J. Reynolds hired Seitz in 1979. His role was to oversee a tobacco industry–sponsored medical research program in the 1970s and 1980s.

"They didn't want us looking at the health effects of cigarette smoking," Seitz, who is now 95, admitted recently in an article in *Vanity Fair,* but he said he felt no compunction about dispensing the tobacco company's money.

While working for R.J. Reynolds, Seitz oversaw the funding of tens of millions of dollars worth of research. Most of this research was legitimate. For instance, his team looked at the way stress, genetics, and lifestyle issues can contribute to disease. But the program Seitz oversaw served an important dual purpose for R.J. Reynolds. It allowed the company to tout the fact that it was funding health research (even if it specifically proscribed research on the health effects of smoking) and it helped generate a steady collection of ideas and hypotheses that provided "red herrings" the company could use to disingenuously suggest that factors other than tobacco might be causing smokers' cancers and heart disease.

Aside from giving the tobacco companies' disinformation campaign an aura of scientific credibility, Seitz is also notable because he has returned from retirement to play a prominent role as a global warming contrarian involved in organizations funded by ExxonMobil. Consider, for instance, one of Seitz's most controversial efforts. In 1998, he wrote and circulated a letter asking scientists to sign a petition from a virtually unheard-of group called the Oregon Institute of Science and Medicine calling upon the U.S. government to reject the Kyoto Protocol. Seitz signed the letter identifying himself as a former NAS president. He also enclosed with his letter a report co-authored by a team including Soon and Baliunas asserting that carbon dioxide emissions pose no warming threat. The report was not peer reviewed. But it was formatted to look like an article from *The Proceedings of the National Academy of Sciences* (PNAS), a leading scientific journal.

The petition's organizers publicly claimed that the effort had attracted the signatures of some 17,000 scientists. But it was soon discovered that the list contained few credentialed climate scientists. For example, the list was riddled with the names of numerous fictional characters. Likewise, after investigating a random sample of the small number of signers who claimed to have a Ph.D. in a climate-related field, *Scientific American* estimated that approximately one percent of the petition signatories might actually have a Ph.D. in a field related to climate science. In a highly unusual response, NAS issued a statement disavowing Seitz's petition and disassociating the academy from the PNAS-formatted paper. None of these facts, however, have stopped organizations, including those funded by ExxonMobil, from touting the petition as evidence of widespread disagreement over the issue of global warming. For instance, in the spring of 2006, the discredited petition surfaced again when it was cited in a letter to California legislators by a group calling itself "Doctors for Disaster Preparedness," a project of the Oregon Institute of Science and Medicine.

Shifting the Focus of the Debate

One prominent component of ExxonMobil's disinformation campaign on global warming is the almost unanimous call for "sound science" by the organizations it funds. Like the Bush administration's "Healthy Forests" program, which masks a plan to augment logging, the rallying call for "sound science" by ExxonMobil-funded organizations is a clever and manipulative cover. It shifts the focus of the debate away from ExxonMobil's irresponsible behavior regarding global warming toward a positive concept of "sound science." By keeping the discussion focused on refining scientific understanding, ExxonMobil helps delay action to reduce heat-trapping emissions from its company and products indefinitely. For example, like the company itself, ExxonMobil-funded organizations routinely contend, despite all the solid evidence to the contrary, that scientists don't know enough about global warming to justify substantial reductions in heat-trapping emissions. As ExxonMobil explains prominently on the company's website:

> *While assessments such as those of the IPCC [Intergovernmental Panel on Climate Change] have expressed growing confidence that recent warming can be attributed to increases in greenhouse gases, these conclusions rely on expert judgment rather than objective, reproducible statistical methods. Taken together, gaps in the scientific basis for theoretical climate models and the interplay of significant natural variability make it very difficult to determine objectively the extent to which recent climate changes might be the result of human actions.*

In contrast, 11 of the world's major national scientific academies issued a joint statement in 2005 that declared, "The scientific understanding of climate change is now sufficiently clear to justify nations taking prompt action. It is vital that all nations identify cost-effective steps that they can take now to contribute to substantial and long-term reduction in net global greenhouse gas emissions."

There is no denying that the tactic of demanding "certainty" in every aspect of our scientific understanding of global warming is a rhetorically effective one. If manufactured uncertainty and governmental inaction is the goal, science will arguably never be "sound enough," or 100 percent certain, to justify action to protect public health or the environment.

Again, the tobacco industry paved the way. The calculated call for "sound science" was successfully used by tobacco firms as an integral part of a tobacco company's pioneering "information laundering" scheme. As we now know from internal tobacco industry documents, a campaign to demand "sound science" was a key part of a strategy by the cigarette manufacturer Philip Morris to create uncertainty about the scientific evidence linking disease to "secondhand" tobacco smoke, known in the industry as "environmental tobacco smoke" or ETS. Toward this end, in 1993, Philip Morris covertly created a front organization called "The Advancement of Sound Science Coalition" or TASSC.

In setting up the organization, Philip Morris took every precaution. The company opted not to use its regular public relations firm, Burson-Marsteller, choosing instead APCO Associates, a subsidiary of the international advertising and PR firm of GCI/Grey Associates. For a sizable retainer, APCO agreed to handle every aspect of the front organization. . . .

The public relations firm introduced TASSC to the public through a decentralized launch outside the large markets of Washington, DC, and New York in order to "avoid cynical reporters from major media" who might discover the truth that the organization was nothing more than a front group created by Philip Morris. Top Philip Morris media managers compiled lists of reporters they deemed most sympathetic to TASSC's message. But they left all press relations to APCO so as to, in the words of one internal memo, "remove any possible link to PM."

The TASSC campaign was a particularly obvious example of information laundering. But it also represented an important messaging strategy by using the concept of "sound science" to attach Philip Morris's disinformation about second-hand smoke to a host of other antiregulation battles. Philip Morris sought to foil any effort by the Environmental Protection Agency (EPA) to promulgate regulations to protect the public from the dangers of ETS. But the company realized that it could build more support for its discredited position that ETS was safe by raising the broader "sound science" banner. As a result, it took stands against government efforts to set safety regulations on everything from asbestos to radon. "The credibility of EPA is defeatable," one Philip Morris strategy document explained, "but not on the basis of ETS alone. It must be part of a large mosaic that concentrates all of the EPA's enemies against it at one time."

The important point in reviewing this history is that it is not a coincidence that ExxonMobil and its surrogates have adopted the mantle of "sound science." In so doing, the company is simply emulating a proven corporate strategy for successfully deflecting attention when one's cause lacks credible scientific evidence. From the start in 1993, in TASSC's search for other antiregulation efforts to provide political cover, the organization actively welcomed global warming contrarians like Frederick Seitz, Fred Singer, and Patrick Michaels to its scientific board of advisors. Thanks to the online archive of tobacco documents, we know that in 1994, when Philip Morris developed plans with APCO to launch a TASSC-like group in Europe, "global warming" was listed first among suggested topics with which the tobacco firm's cynical "sound science" campaign could profitably ally itself.

Given these historical connections, it is disturbing that ExxonMobil would continue to associate with some of the very same TASSC personnel who had overseen such a blatant and shameful disinformation campaign for Big Tobacco. The most glaring of ExxonMobil's associations in this regard is with Steven Milloy, the former executive director of TASSC. Milloy's involvement with ExxonMobil is more than casual. He served as a member of the small 1998 Global Climate Science Team task force that mapped out ExxonMobil's disinformation strategy on global warming.

Milloy officially closed TASSC's offices in 1998 as evidence of its role as a front organization began to surface in the discovery process of litigation against Big Tobacco. Thanks in part to ExxonMobil, however, the "sound science" disinformation campaign continued unabated. Resuscitating TASSC under the slightly altered name The Advancement of Sound Science Center (rather than Coalition), Milloy continues to operate out of his home in Maryland. Between 2000 and 2004, ExxonMobil gave $50,000 to Milloy's Advancement of Sound Science Center, and another $60,000 to an organization called the Free Enterprise Education Institute (a.k.a. Free Enterprise Action Institute), which is also registered to Milloy's home address. According to its 2004 tax return, this group was founded to "educate the public about the American system of free enterprise," employed no staff, and incurred approximately $48,000 in expenses categorized as "professional services."

In addition to serving as a columnist on *FoxNews.com,* Milloy is also a contributor to Tech Central Station and an adjunct scholar at the Competitive Enterprise Institute, both funded by ExxonMobil.

The irony of the involvement of tobacco disinformation veterans like Milloy in the current campaign against global warming science is not lost on close watchers. Representative Henry Waxman (D-CA), for instance, chaired the 1994 hearings where tobacco executives unanimously declared under oath that cigarettes were not addictive. As Waxman marveled recently about the vocal contrarians like Milloy on global warming science: "Not only are we seeing the same tactics the tobacco industry used, we're seeing some of the same groups." Of course, unlike the tobacco companies, ExxonMobil has yet to receive a court order to force to light internal documents pertaining to its climate change activities. Nonetheless, even absent this information, the case could hardly be clearer: ExxonMobil is waging a calculated and familiar disinformation campaign to mislead the public and forestall government action on global warming.

Buying Government Access

Tobacco companies have historically been very successful at cultivating close ties in government and hiring former government officials to lobby on their behalf. This list includes, among others, Craig Fuller, who served in the Reagan and Bush administrations, and former GOP chair Haley Barbour as well as former Senate majority leader George Mitchell, who was recruited in 1997 by the tobacco industry firm Verner, Liipfert, Bernhard, McPherson, and Hand to help negotiate a settlement.

When it comes to exerting influence over government policy, however, ExxonMobil, in its global warming disinformation campaign, may have even surpassed the tobacco industry it so clearly emulates. During the 2000 to 2006 election cycles, ExxonMobil's PAC and individuals affiliated with the company gave more than $4 million to federal candidates and parties. Shortly after President Bush's inauguration, ExxonMobil, like other large corporate backers in the energy sector, participated in Vice President Dick Cheney's "Energy Task Force" to set the administration's goals for a national energy plan. ExxonMobil successfully urged the Bush administration to renege on the commitments to the Kyoto Protocol made by previous administrations. Paula Dobriansky, who currently serves as undersecretary for global affairs in the State Department and who has headed U.S. delegations negotiating follow-ons to the Kyoto Protocol in Buenos Aires and Montreal, explicitly said as much in 2001. Just months after she had been confirmed by the U.S. Senate, Dobriansky met with ExxonMobil lobbyist Randy Randol and other members of the Global Climate Coalition. Her prepared talking points, un- covered through a Freedom of Information Act request, reveal that Dobrian- sky thanked the group for their input on global warming policy. One of her notes reads: "POTUS [the President of the United States] rejected Kyoto, in part, based on input from you."

A Freedom of Information Act request also revealed that in February 2001, immediately following the release of the authoritative 2001 report on global warming from the Intergovernmental Panel on Climate Change (IPCC), ExxonMobil successfully lobbied the Bush administration to try to oust the chair of the IPCC. In a memo sent to the White House, Randol complained that Robert Watson, who had chaired the IPCC since 1996, had been "hand- picked by Al Gore." Watson is an internationally respected scientist who has served as the director of the science division at NASA and as chief scientist at the World Bank. His work at the IPCC had met with widespread inter- national approval and acclaim. Nonetheless, the ExxonMobil memo urged: "Can Watson be replaced now at the request of the U.S.?" At its next oppor- tunity, the Bush administration's State Department refused to re-nominate Dr. Watson for a second five-year term as head of the IPCC, instead backing an Indian engineer-economist for the post. In April 2002, lacking U.S. sup- port, Dr. Watson lost his position as chair. The Bush administration's move outraged many in the scientific community who saw it as a blatantly political attempt to undermine an international scientific effort. At the time, however, ExxonMobil's behind-the-scenes role in the incident remained secret.

Meanwhile, in an equally consequential recommendation, the 2001 ExxonMobil memo suggested that President Bush's climate team hire Har- lan Watson (no relation), a staff member on the House Science Committee who had served as a climate negotiator at the 1992 Rio Earth Summit for the administration of George Bush Senior and had worked closely with members of Congress who opposed action on global warming. Shortly thereafter, the Bush administration announced Harlan Watson's appoint- ment as its chief climate negotiator. He has steadfastly opposed any U.S. engagement in the Kyoto process.

As successful as ExxonMobil's efforts to lobby the Bush administra- tion have been, perhaps even more striking is the way the company's disinformation campaign on global warming science has managed to per- meate the highest echelons of the federal government. Between 2001 and 2005, the nerve center for much of this censorship and control resided in the office of Philip Cooney, who served during this time as chief of staff in the White House Council on Environmental Quality. Thanks to a whistle-blowing researcher named Rick Piltz in the U.S. government's in- teragency Climate Change Science Program who resigned in protest over the practice, we now know that Cooney spent a significant amount of time censoring and distorting government reports so as to exaggerate scientific uncertainty about global warming.

Cooney, a lawyer with an undergraduate degree in economics, had no scientific credentials that might qualify him to rewrite the findings of top government scientists. Rather, before coming to the Bush administration in 2001, Cooney had spent roughly a decade as a lawyer for the American Petroleum Institute, the oil industry lobby that worked with ExxonMobil in 1998 to develop a global warming disinformation campaign. In that capacity, Cooney served as a "climate team leader" seeking to prevent the U.S. government from entering into any kind of international agreement or enacting any domestic legislation that might lead to mandatory limits on global warming emissions. After joining the White House staff in 2001, Cooney furthered much the same work agenda from the top ranks of the Bush administration.

During his tenure, Cooney altered and compromised the accuracy of numerous official scientific reports on climate change issued by agencies of the federal government. For instance, in 2002, as U.S. government scientists struggled to finalize the Climate Change Science Program's strategic plan, Cooney dramatically altered the document, editing it heavily and repeatedly inserting qualifying words to create an unwarranted aura of scientific uncertainty about global warming and its implications.

As Rick Piltz explained in his resignation letter when he exposed Cooney's efforts, the government agencies had adapted to the environment created within the Bush administration by "engaging in a kind of anticipatory self-censorship on this and various other matters seen as politically sensitive under this administration." Even beyond the outright suppression and distortion by Cooney and others, according to Piltz, this self-censorship on the part of career professionals marked one of the most insidious and "deleterious influences of the administration" on climate research efforts within the government.

On June 10, 2005, Cooney resigned, two days after the *New York Times* first reported Piltz's revelations. Despite the suspicious timing, the White House claimed that Cooney's resignation was unrelated to Piltz's disclosures. But it was not surprising when Cooney announced, one week after he left the White House, that he was accepting a high-ranking public relations position at ExxonMobil.

One of the most damning incidents involving Cooney also illustrates the extent of ExxonMobil's influence over the Bush administration policy on global warming. In May 2002, the administration issued the "U.S. Climate Action Report," which the U.S. State Department was obligated by treaty to file with the United Nations. Major elements of the report were based on an in-depth, peer-reviewed government research report analyzing the potential effects of global warming in the United States. That report, titled "U.S. National Assessment of the Potential Consequences of Climate Variability and Change," predates the Bush administration and had already been attacked by ExxonMobil. The report generated widespread headlines such as one in the *New York Times* proclaiming: "Climate Changing, US Says in Report."

Not surprisingly, ExxonMobil vociferously objected to the conclusion of the multiagency "Climate Action Report" that climate change posed a significant risk and was caused by humanmade emissions. Concerned about the matter, Cooney contacted Myron Ebell at the ExxonMobil-funded Competitive Enterprise Institute. "Thanks for calling and asking for our help," Ebell responded in a June 3, 2002, email to Cooney that surfaced as a result of a Freedom of Information Act request. Ebell urged that the President distance himself from the report. Within days, President Bush did exactly that, denigrating the report in question as having been "put out by the bureaucracy."

In the June 3 email, Ebell explicitly suggests the ouster of then-EPA head Christine Todd Whitman. "It seems to me that the folks at the EPA are the obvious fall guys and we would only hope that the fall guy (or gal) should be as high up as possible," Ebell wrote. "Perhaps tomorrow we will call for Whitman to be fired." Sure enough, Whitman would last for less than a year in her post, resigning in May 2003. Finally, Ebell pledged he would do what he could to respond to the White House's request to "clean up this mess."

A major piece of Ebell's "clean-up" effort presumably came on August 6, 2003, when the Competitive Enterprise Institute filed the second of two lawsuits calling for the Bush administration to invalidate the National Assessment (a peer-reviewed synthesis report upon which the U.S. Climate Action Report was based). The CEI lawsuit called for it to be withdrawn because it was not based upon "sound science."

Given the close, conspiratorial communication between Ebell and Cooney that had come to light, the lawsuit prompted the attorneys general of Maine and Connecticut to call upon the U.S. Justice Department to investigate the matter. However, the Bush administration Justice Department, then led by John Ashcroft, refused to launch such an investigation, despite the fact that the Maine and Connecticut attorneys general stated forcefully that the evidence suggested that Cooney had conspired with Ebell to cause the Competitive Enterprise Institute to sue the federal government. As Maine Attorney General Steven Rowe noted: "The idea that the Bush administration may have invited a lawsuit from a special interest group in order to undermine the federal government's own work under an international treaty is very troubling."

A key piece of evidence, unnoticed at the time, strongly suggests just how the scheme fit together. In 2002, in a move virtually unprecedented in its corporate giving program, ExxonMobil offered an additional $60,000 in support for the Competitive Enterprise Institute—specifically earmarked to cover the organization's unspecified "legal activities."

In addition to a high level of administration access, ExxonMobil has cultivated close relationships with members of Congress. In July 2005, ExxonMobil's generous campaign contributions paid off when Congress passed the Energy Policy Act of 2005. This bill, modeled on the President's 2001 energy plan, provides more than $7.4 billion in tax breaks and subsidies to the oil and gas industry over 10 years and excludes any provisions that would mandate reductions in U.S. global warming emissions.

Joe Barton (R-TX), chair of the house Energy and Commerce Committee from 2004 through 2006 and the lead author of the 2005 energy bill, has received more than $1 million from the oil and gas industry over the course of his career, including $22,000 in PAC contributions from ExxonMobil between 2000 and 2006. In addition to shepherding through the massive oil and gas subsidies in that bill, Representative Barton has played a key role in elevating misleading information and delaying congressional action on global warming. Before he became chair of the full committee in 2004, Barton chaired the Energy and Air Quality Subcommittee. In that capacity, he stated at a March 2001 hearing that as long as he was the subcommittee chair, regulation of global warming emissions would be "off the table indefinitely." As Barton put it: "I don't want there to be any uncertainty about that." In his capacity as chair of the full committee, Barton has held true to his word, holding only two climate-related hearings, both aimed at attacking reputable climate scientists.

Meanwhile, the most vocal opponent to climate action in the Senate is James Inhofe (R-OK), chair—until January 2007—of the Environment and Public Works Committee. He adamantly denies the reality of global warming and has prevented consideration of climate bills by his committee during his tenure as chair from 2003 to 2006. In September 2005, he went so far as to invite Michael Crichton, a science fiction writer, to testify at a hearing on climate science and policy. Despite Crichton's lack of expertise, he attempted to undermine peer-reviewed climate science in his testimony. Inhofe was also a coplaintiff in the first Competitive Enterprise Institute lawsuit, filed in 2000, which attempted to bar the distribution or use of the National Assessment. Senator Inhofe has received a total of $847,123 from ExxonMobil and others in the oil and gas industry over the course of his career.

Like Big Tobacco before it, ExxonMobil has been enormously successful at influencing the current administration and key members of Congress. From successfully recommending the appointment of key personnel in the Bush administration, to coordinating its disinformation tactics on global warming with high-ranking Bush administration personnel, to funding climate change contrarians in Congress, ExxonMobil and its proxies have exerted extraordinary influence over the policies of the U.S. government during the Bush administration. The cozy relationship ExxonMobil enjoys with government officials has enabled the corporation to work effectively behind the scenes to block federal policies and shape government communications on global warming.

Ivan Osorio, Iain Murray,
and Myron Ebell

 **NO**

Liberal "Scientists" Lead Jihad against Global-Warming Skeptics

On Oct. 30, 2006, Senators John D. Rockefeller (D.-W.Va.) and Olympia Snowe (R.-Maine) wrote an extraordinary open letter to ExxonMobil CEO Rex Tillerson urging him to end his company's support of "climate-change-denial front groups." The only organization mentioned by name is the one that the authors of this article work for—the Competitive Enterprise Institute (CEI). The senators' letter then goes on to announce: "A study to be released in November by an American scientific group will expose ExxonMobil as the primary funder of no fewer than 29 climate-change-denial front groups in 2004 alone."

The letter brought a strong reaction from the *Wall Street Journal* editorial page: "[I]f the senators are so afraid that a handful of policy wonks at a single small think tank are in danger of winning this debate, they must not have much confidence in their own case." Home state newspapers also chided the senators. In West Virginia, the *Charleston Daily Mail* called the letter "an intemperate attempt to squelch debate," while in Maine, an editor at the *Portland Press Herald* wrote that a spokeswoman for Snowe told him that "the senator is greatly worried that the average moke on the street can't figure all this out on his own. So she and her colleague were just trying to clarify the issue, that is, by telling someone they disagreed with to shut up." The accompanying news release from Snowe's office was headlined: "Rockefeller and Snowe demand that ExxonMobil end funding of campaign that denies global climate change."

Be a Concerned Scientist for $35

It's astonishing that elected officials would use their taxpayer-funded offices to bully a company's president into changing his corporation's philanthropic giving practices. And it's deplorable that in trying to discredit critics of catastrophic global warming, Rockefeller and Snowe would stoop to using smear rhetoric that alludes to "Holocaust denial"—and is inaccurate to boot. No one seriously denies that the Earth is warming. The debate is over the extent and consequences of such warming. Remarkable, too, is

As seen in *Human Events,* May 8, 2007, by Ivan Osorio, Iain Murray, and Myron Ebell, original to *Organization Trends,* March 2007. Copyright © 2007 by Capital Research Center. Reprinted by permission. www.capitalresearch.org

the senators' cryptic reference to a "scientific group" that would soon issue its "findings," words that bestow authority on what, as we expected, would turn out to be no more than a political attack.

It didn't take us long to figure out what this "scientific group" might be and who is behind it: For almost four decades, the Union of Concerned Scientists (UCS) has manipulated the high reputation of "science" to serve the low ends of politics. It has done a good job of cherry-picking scientific facts to stir up public fears to advance its agenda. This time it is promoting alarmist claims about global warming by leveraging the prestige of the "concerned scientist."

The credulous media usually fall all over themselves to defer to UCS every time the group takes a political position. For instance, when it issued a report in 2004 criticizing President George W. Bush's handling of science policy, the union was described as "a scientific advocacy group" (*New York Times*), "a group of scientists" (Reuters), "an independent Cambridge-based organization" (*Boston Globe*), and a "nonprofit . . . advocacy group in Cambridge, Mass." (*Newsday*). After all, who but concerned scientists would pass judgment on President Bush and conclude that he was a scientific ignoramus manipulating science in order to advance a partisan agenda?

That UCS is a highly partisan operation—well funded by left-leaning foundations and Hollywood celebrities and happy to ignore established scientific methodologies for its own purposes—is apparently not newsworthy. The group has a long history of being just plain wrong on many scientific issues, and its current agenda conforms to the extremes of environmentalist ideology. Moreover, UCS is neither representative of the scientific community at large nor is it a gathering of top scientists. Instead, a cadre of senior staff whose credentials are steeped more in Washington policy-making than in scientific research rides herd over a grassroots membership from all walks of life. You too can be a Concerned Scientist for a new member fee of $35!

In 2006, UCS decided to attack ExxonMobil, the world's largest private energy company, over the issue of global warming. It also decided on its tactics: It would demonize the oil company by comparing it to cigarette companies. ExxonMobil, said UCS, was "adopt[ing] the tobacco industry's disinformation tactics . . . to cloud the scientific understanding of climate change and delay action on the issue."

In a paper issued Jan. 3, 2007, UCS accuses ExxonMobil of funding "front groups" opposed to the climate-alarmist agenda of groups such as UCS and of former Vice President Al Gore. The company, said the UCS report, had distributed $16 million to 43 advocacy groups from 1998 to 2005 "to confuse the public on global-warming science."

Let's leave aside the fact that $16 million over eight years can't match the $2 billion that the federally funded Climate Change Science Program spends each year on global warming, or even the $4 million annual budget of just one of the many well-funded global-warming advocacy groups, Strategies for the Global Environment (the umbrella organization for the

Pew Center on Global Climate Change). Moreover, the UCS document is hardly an investigative breakthrough. ExxonMobil itself publishes its philanthropic contributions to nonprofit organizations online.

Most interesting, however, about the UCS report are its distortions of fact and what they reveal about UCS political tactics. These should have undermined the group's credibility long ago were it not for that high-minded name: Union of Concerned Scientists.

Conspiracy? No.

UCS plays the game of Washington politics using hardball tactics, including innuendo, and its report on ExxonMobil epitomizes this approach. The UCS document cites what it terms a "conspiratorial communication" between one of the authors of this article, Myron Ebell of the Competitive Enterprise Institute, and Phil Cooney, then-chief of staff to the chairman of the White House Council on Environmental Quality (CEQ). In 2002, Ebell sent Cooney an e-mail expressing his distress over the Bush Administration's handling of the global-warming issue.

A front-page *New York Times* story had reported that the Bush Administration was conceding that global warming was a big problem. According to *Times* reporter Andrew Revkin, the administration had quietly sent a document titled "Climate Action Report 2002" (CAR) to the United Nations Framework Convention on Climate Change. CAR contained extremely inaccurate materials from the "National Assessment," an overview of the climate-change issue produced by the Clinton Administration. The Bush Administration had disavowed the "National Assessment" as a result of a lawsuit filed by CEI. But Revkin reported that CAR used a big chunk of the "National Assessment." As soon as this story broke, CEI sent out a press release sharply criticizing the Environmental Protection Agency (EPA) and then-Administrator Christine Todd Whitman for sending the report to the UN.

At that point, Phil Cooney left a message on Ebell's answering machine asking Ebell to call him, saying that he needed his help. Soon after, Ebell left a message on Cooney's answering machine. After not hearing back from him for several hours, Ebell sent him an e-mail saying that CEI would be glad to help. This e-mail is described in the UCS report as a "conspiratorial communication." If anyone from the Union of Concerned Scientists had bothered to ask Ebell, they could have gotten the facts straight.

When Phil Cooney called Ebell back, he explained that he wanted CEI to stop attacking EPA and refrain from calling on President Bush to fire Whitman, because she had nothing to do with the report. Cooney said EPA was not ultimately responsible for what was an interagency document on an environmental issue. Cooney further told Ebell that CEQ was in charge of conducting the interagency review and producing the final version of the report. As CEQ chief of staff, Cooney had directed the review and made the final edits. Cooney said that if Ebell wanted anyone fired, it should be him. Ebell replied that CEI would stop attacking Whitman but would not attack Cooney because he was not an appointee nominated by the President and confirmed by the Senate. So much for this "conspiracy."

The story doesn't end there. CEI unsuccessfully petitioned President Bush to rescind his submission of the flawed CAR to the UN and subsequently filed a second lawsuit in federal court against the "National Assessment" on the grounds that it did not meet the minimal requirements of the Federal Data Quality Act. CEI dropped the suit after the White House Office of Science and Technology Policy agreed to put a disclaimer on the "National Assessment" website that states that the document had not been subjected to the Federal Data Quality guidelines. That caused some of the report's authors to claim that the Bush Administration was suppressing scientific research. But if administration officials are burying research, they're not doing a very good job. The "National Assessment" is still available on more than one federal website.

A subsequent *New York Times* front-page story further fueled the controversy. While one *Times* story claimed that "Climate Action Report 2002" constituted an admission by the Bush Administration that global warming is real and serious, another story claimed that, in producing CAR, the White House had doctored the science because Phil Cooney had edited the text. Yet, since CAR is not a scientific report but an official U.S. government policy document, editing the text to reflect accurately the administration's official policies should be obligatory. Rather than doing anything wrong, Cooney was doing his job.

And rather than suppress science, Cooney was trying to get the science right in the document he was editing. What Cooney was trying to do was correct the "National Assessment" text by replacing the most obvious junk science claims with information and conclusions taken from the UN Intergovernmental Panel on Climate Change Third Assessment Report.

UCS doesn't focus its attacks on the actual work produced by the organizations it targets. Instead, it tries to discredit its opponents by using *ad hominem* innuendo. And that's what gets the attention of the media. For instance, when astrophysicist Sallie Baliunas determined that the Earth's temperature had actually been warmer at earlier times in history—a premise endorsed by a National Academy of Sciences (NAS) panel—UCS ignored the research but attacked the researcher personally, noting that Baliunas was affiliated with the George C. Marshall Institute, which UCS said had received $630,000 in ExxonMobil grants for its climate-science program.

Politics before Science

The UCS track record is bursting with examples of how it puts politics ahead of science. Founded in 1969 by a group of Massachusetts Institute of Technology (MIT) scientists concerned about the threat of nuclear war, the group currently claims a membership base of more than 100,000 "citizens and scientists" and an annual budget of more than $10 million.

True to its peacenik roots, UCS organized opposition to President Ronald Reagan's Strategic Defense Initiative (SDI) in the 1980s, fearing that it would push the world to war. But history showed otherwise. British Prime

Minister Margaret Thatcher would call Reagan's decision to go ahead with SDI the "one vital factor in the ending of the Cold War." UCS continues its anti-nuclear activism today.

The 1980s were not a good decade for the union's predictive powers in other ways. In 1980, UCS claimed that "it is now abundantly clear that the world has entered a period of chronic energy shortages." As is now abundantly clear, known energy reserves are higher than ever. Middle East oil reserves alone are estimated to have increased from 431 billion barrels in 1985 to 742 billion in 2005. Of course, if UCS achieved its stated aim of capping energy production from fossil fuel sources and closing down nuclear plants, then the world most certainly would face a major energy shortage today.

More recently, UCS has been consistently wrong in its stated concerns about genetically modified crops. In 1999, it publicized reports that corn modified with the natural pesticide Bacillus thuringiensis (Bt) is harmful to the monarch butterfly, findings that were subsequently rejected by NAS.

Another NAS report found that increasing CAFE (corporate average fuel economy) standards contributed to between 1,300 and 2,600 additional traffic deaths per year because manufacturers downsize cars to increase their fuel economy and comply with the regulation. Yet the UCS website still says, "To reduce fuel consumption and address global warming, CAFE standards must increase."

UCS helped coordinate a campaign to attempt to discredit Danish statistician Bjørn Lomborg, whose 2001 best-selling book, *The Skeptical Environmentalist,* presents compelling statistical evidence refuting many of the modern environmental movement's alarmist claims.

In other matters—abortion, suburban "sprawl" and the war in Iraq—UCS stakes out policy positions that are predictably those of a far-left pressure group.

Funding Sources

The database of campaign contributions assembled by the Center for Responsive Politics contains abundant evidence of the partisan political leanings of UCS officials. For instance, UCS Chairman Cornell physicist Kurt Gottfried has donated more than $10,000 to Democratic Party organizations since 1990, mostly to the Democratic National Committee.

Signatories to a 2004 statement attacking President Bush over alleged manipulation of science donated more than $300,000 to Democratic candidates and liberal organizations since 1990—long before the supposed Bush "assault on science." In contrast, they donated only $5,050 to Republicans—the majority of that to liberal Sen. Arlen Specter (Pa.). The signatories donated $28,000 to the presidential campaign funds of Democratic Senators John Kerry (Mass.) and John Edwards (N.C.). Nobel laureates affiliated with UCS have contributed $97,000 to Democrats.

All of this undermines the credibility of UCS President Kevin Knobloch, who claimed in the 2003 UCS annual report: "Several key principles and beliefs will guide my leadership. Nonpartisanship is one." Knobloch, an environmental activist, spent six years on Capitol Hill, where he worked for Sen. Tim Wirth (D.-Colo.) and Rep. Ted Weiss (D.-N.Y.).

UCS Director of Strategy and Policy Alden Meyer is also a longtime environmental activist. Prior to joining the UCS staff in 1989, Meyer worked as executive director at a series of green groups: League of Conservation Voters, Americans for the Environment, and Environmental Action. Meyer's academic background isn't in the natural sciences. His biography on the UCS website notes that he received an undergraduate degree from Yale in 1975 "concentrating in political science and economics" and that "he received a Master of Science degree in human resource and organization development from American University in 1990."

UCS likes to attack free-market groups for accepting corporate donations, but much of its own funding comes from foundations established by conservative businessmen but subsequently hijacked by left-wing partisans. Unlike the leftists on many foundation boards, companies like ExxonMobil make grants from money that they actually earned.

The John D. and Catherine T. MacArthur Foundation has given the Union of Concerned Scientists $3.09 million since 2000. Long a major funder of leftist peace and environmental causes, the foundation owes its independence and generosity to its careless founder, John D. MacArthur, who neither formulated a mission for his foundation nor provided clear instructions as to how its money should be spent. In 1987, the foundation's then-president admitted to *USA Today* that if MacArthur were alive to see how his money was spent, "I think a lot of it would just make him furious." And how! In a 1974 interview, MacArthur, an insurance entrepreneur, denounced environmentalists as "bearded jerks and little old ladies" who "are obstructionists and just throw rocks in your path."

Other prominent businessmen whose name-bearing foundations fund UCS include Henry Ford ($950,000 from the Ford Foundation since 2000), *Time* magazine founder Henry Luce ($400,000 from the Henry Luce Foundation during 2001–2002), and J. Howard Pew ($1 million from the Pew Memorial Trust during 2002–2003). In a 1957 deed establishing the J. Howard Pew Freedom Trust, he wrote that the trust's mission was "to acquaint the American public" with "the evils of bureaucracy" and "the values of a free market."

UCS also receives funding from Hollywood celebrities and explicitly activist leftist foundations such as the Barbra Streisand Foundation ($10,000 for "general use" in 2004), the [Ted] Turner Foundation (nearly $500,000 since 2000), and the Energy Foundation, which states on its website that its "mission is to advance energy efficiency and renewable energy" ($5.08 million since 1999).

Indeed, UCS took in more money from 1998 to 2005 than ExxonMobil contributed to global-warming skeptics during the same period. In that seven-year span, ExxonMobil contributed $16 million in grants to groups that combat climate-change alarmism, while UCS alone received nearly $24 million in foundation grants.

UCS Political Circus

The Union of Concerned Scientists has powerful allies in Congress. Recently, UCS took advantage of a congressional hearing to publicize yet another report smearing its political opponents. On Jan. 30, 2007, House Oversight and Government Reform Chairman Henry Waxman (D.-Calif.) held a hearing on "Political Interference on Government Climate Change-Scientists." Waxman, a member of the radical Congressional Progressive Caucus [See "Fringe-Left Democrats Wield New Influence," by Cheryl Chumley, *Human Events,* February 26.] and other Democrats took the opportunity to once again pillory former CEQ chief of staff Phil Cooney over his editing of "Climate Action Report 2002" and his allegedly conspiratorial e-mail exchange with CEI's Myron Ebell. Rep. Darrell Issa (R.-Calif.) commented that the committee has "been trashing a lawyer we've never met."

One of the witnesses, UCS spokeswoman Francesca Grifo, announced a new UCS survey that allegedly showed political interference by the Bush Administration into climate science. But, as Issa noted, this survey was hardly representative, since only 19% of the 1,600 scientists polled responded—a response rate so low that it suggests bias in favor of a self-selected minority with a political axe to grind. Grifo had no response to this criticism.

Media Allies

UCS also has powerful allies in the media. On Jan. 31, 2007, CNN's "Larry King Live" hosted a debate on global warming featuring Bill Nye, best known for his television appearances as "The Science Guy." On the show, Nye boasted about being "a member of the advisory board of the Union of Concerned Scientists." He also warned that fresh water from melting ice caps flowing into the sea would upset "the salt-heat driven ocean currents," which are "what makes the Gulf Stream go . . . and if the Gulf Stream stops. . . ."

MIT professor of atmospheric science Richard Lindzen, a highly respected scientist, responded on air that there is no danger of the Gulf Stream's stopping, since it would require one of two physical impossibilities. "The Gulf Stream is driven by wind," he said. "To shut it down, you'd have to stop the rotation of the Earth or shut off the wind." After further debate, Lindzen noted, "I was saying textbook material. And if the textbooks are out-voiced by environmental advocacy groups like the Union of Concerned Scientists by 100,000 to one, that would be bizarre. We should close down our schools."

The Union of Concerned Scientists is not about to relent in its green climate crusade. Yet UCS does not speak for the scientific community. Instead, it is a well-funded, left-wing pressure group, which politicizes science while claiming to be its true guardian. A partisan is no less a partisan because he has won the Nobel Prize, but a scientist is less of a scientist if he allows ideology to color his research.

POSTSCRIPT

Is Global Warming Skepticism Just Smoke and Mirrors?

The United Nations Conference on Environment and Development in Rio de Janeiro, Brazil, took place in 1992. High on the agenda was the problem of global warming, but despite widespread concern and calls for reductions in carbon dioxide releases, the United States refused to consider rigid deadlines or set quotas. The uncertainties seemed too great, and some thought the economic costs of cutting back on carbon dioxide might be greater than the costs of letting the climate warm.

The nations that signed the UN Framework Convention on Climate Change in Rio de Janeiro in 1992 met again in Kyoto, Japan, in December 1997 to set carbon emission limits for the industrial nations. The United States agreed to reduce its annual greenhouse gas emissions 7 percent below the 1990 level between 2008 and 2012 "but still has not ratified the Kyoto Treaty. In November 2005, [the same nations] met in Montreal, Canada, and decided to begin formal talks on mandatory post–2012 reductions in greenhouse gases. The U.S. agreed to talk but ruled out any future commitments." Ross Gelbspan, in "Rx for a Planetary Fever," *American Prospect* (May 8, 2000), blames much of the opposition to commitments on "big oil and big coal [which] have relentlessly obstructed the best-faith efforts of government negotiators." See also Fred Pearce, "State of Denial," *New Scientist* (November 4, 2006). At the most recent meeting of the nations that signed the Kyoto Protocol, held in Nairobi, Kenya, in November 2006, Kofi Annan, Secretary-General of the UN, said that the facts are so clear that skeptics about global warming are "out of step, out of arguments, and out of time." James Lovelock, creator of the Gaia metaphor for the living Earth beloved by many environmental activists, warns in *The Revenge of Gaia: Earth's Climate in Crisis and the Fate of Humanity* (Basic Books, 2006) that global warming may prove catastrophic. Tim Appenzeller, "The Big Thaw," *National Geographic* (June 2007), discusses the rapid loss of ice from ice caps and glaciers, with serious impacts expected on economies dependent on winter sports and—much more ominously—on the summertime flow of water from melting snow and ice in nearby mountains. According to Richard A. Kerr, "Pushing the Scary Side of Global Warming," *Science* (June 8, 2007), some climate researchers are concerned that we are seriously underestimating how disastrous global warming will be.

In June 2006, the National Academy of Sciences reported that the Earth is now warmer than it has been in the last 400 years, and perhaps in the last 1,000 (*Surface Temperature Reconstructions for the Last 2,000 Years,*

National Academies Press, 2006). Concerns have been raised about the risks to coastal populations from rising seas and changes in storm patterns; see John Young, "Black Water Rising," *World Watch* (September/October 2006). States and environmental groups brought before the U.S. Supreme Court a case demanding that the U.S. Environmental Protection Agency regulate carbon dioxide as a threat to public health. In April 2007 the Court ruled against the EPA, saying that carbon dioxide is an air pollutant that the EPA can regulate under the Clean Air Act. No one yet knows what form regulations (if any) will take, but requirements for better automobile fuel efficiency seem likely. See Charles Q. Choi, "Warming to Law: After the U.S. Supreme Court Ruling, How Stiff Will Greenhouse Gas Regulations Be?" *Scientific American* (July 2007).

The price tag for immediate action to prevent or—with luck—reduce the negative impacts of global warming will not be small (see Issue 8), but it should be worth it in many ways. Gregg Easterbrook, "Global Warming: Who Loses—and Who Wins?" *The Atlantic* (April 2007), concludes that "Keeping the world economic system and the global balance of power the way they are seems very strongly in the U.S. national interest—and keeping things the way they are requires prevention of significant climate change. That, in the end, is what's in it for us."

ISSUE 8

Are the Potential Costs of Global Warming Too High to Ignore?

YES: Nicholas Stern, from "Stern Review: The Economics of Climate Change, Executive Summary," http://www.hm-treasury. gov.uk/independent_reviews/stern_review_economics_climate_change/ sternreview_index.cfm (October 30, 2006)

NO: John Stone, from "'Global Warming' Scare-Mongering Revisited," *National Observer* (Autumn 2007)

ISSUE SUMMARY

YES: Sir Nicholas Stern, head of the British Government Economics Service, reports that although taking steps now to limit future impacts of global warming would be very expensive, the economic and social impacts of not doing so will be much more expensive.

NO: John Stone finds the Stern report deeply flawed and argues that it would be unforgivable to destroy the world's economic welfare in accord with its charlatanism.

$\mathbf{A}$s Issues 6 and 7 make clear, global warming is real, and its impacts on ecosystems and human well-being (especially in developing nations) will be serious. But there are steps that society can take to prevent, ease, or cope with those impacts. Not surprisingly, the earlier those steps are taken, the more likely it is that they will work as intended. See "Confronting Climate Change: Avoiding the Unmanageable and Managing the Unavoidable," a Scientific Expert Group Report on Climate Change and Sustainable Development, sponsored by Sigma Xi and the United Nations Foundation, prepared for the 15th Session of the U.N.'s Commission on Sustainable Development and presented on February 27, 2007 (available at http://www.sigmaxi.org/about/news/UNSEGonline.pdf), and William Collins, et al., "The Physical Science Behind Climate Change," *Scientific American* (August 2007).

Is "impact on ecosystems and human well-being" something we should worry about? Environmental activists find that it is often difficult to convince people to change their activities (such as building houses and highways and exploring wilderness preserves for oil) just because those activities might harm the environment. Human well-being might seem an easier sell, but the humans whose well-being is affected are often poor people in lands far away; their misery is not visible to American or European politicians (for instance) and they don't vote for those politicians. It is much easier to convince politicians to take action if you can show them how something like global warming will affect them, their wallets, or their voters. It is perhaps easiest if you can put the damage in monetary terms.

The Bush administration has insisted that taking specific steps to deal with global warming will cost too much. It will be bad for business and therefore bad for jobs, incomes, and the economy as a whole. However, others have begun to consider not only the amount of damage to coastal nations, farmers, ecosystems, and others, but also its monetary value, and then to compare that figure to the cost of preventing that damage. Sir Nicholas Stern, head of the British Government Economics Service, reports that although taking steps now to limit future impacts of global warming would be very expensive, "the benefits of strong, early action considerably outweigh the costs. . . . Ignoring climate change will eventually damage economic growth. . . . Tackling climate change is the pro-growth strategy for the longer term, and it can be done in a way that does not cap the aspirations for growth of rich or poor countries. The earlier effective action is taken, the less costly it will be." The Stern report argues that we should begin now to spend $68–170 billion per year—less than one percent of global GDP—to implement new technologies to reduce carbon emissions. Other expenditures could more than double the bill. Australian John Stone, a former Treasury Secretary and senator, finds the Stern report deeply flawed and argues that it would be unforgivable to destroy the world's economic welfare in accord with its charlatanism.

YES

Nicholas Stern

Stern Review: The Economics of Climate Change, Executive Summary

The scientific evidence is now overwhelming: climate change presents very serious global risks, and it demands an urgent global response.

This independent Review was commissioned by the Chancellor of the Exchequer, reporting to both the Chancellor and to the Prime Minister, as a contribution to assessing the evidence and building understanding of the economics of climate change. ...

The Review takes an international perspective. Climate change is global in its causes and consequences, and international collective action will be critical in driving an effective, efficient and equitable response on the scale required. This response will require deeper international co-operation in many areas—most notably in creating price signals and markets for carbon, spurring technology research, development and deployment, and promoting adaptation, particularly for developing countries.

Climate change presents a unique challenge for economics: it is the greatest and widest-ranging market failure ever seen. The economic analysis must therefore be global, deal with long time horizons, have the economics of risk and uncertainty at centre stage, and examine the possibility of major, non-marginal change. To meet these requirements, the Review draws on ideas and techniques from most of the important areas of economics, including many recent advances.

The Benefits of Strong, Early Action on Climate Change Outweigh the Costs

The effects of our actions now on future changes in the climate have long lead times. What we do now can have only a limited effect on the climate over the next 40 or 50 years. On the other hand what we do in the next 10 or 20 years can have a profound effect on the climate in the second half of this century and in the next.

No one can predict the consequences of climate change with complete certainty; but we now know enough to understand the risks. Mitigation—taking strong action to reduce emissions—must be viewed as an investment, a cost incurred now and in the coming few decades to avoid the risks of very severe consequences in the future. If these investments are made wisely, the costs will be manageable, and there will be a wide range of opportunities for growth and development along the way. For this to work well, policy must promote sound market signals, overcome market failures and have equity and risk mitigation at its core. That essentially is the conceptual framework of this Review.

The Review considers the economic costs of the impacts of climate change, and the costs and benefits of action to reduce the emissions of greenhouse gases (GHGs) that cause it, in three different ways:

- Using disaggregated techniques, in other words considering the physical impacts of climate change on the economy, on human life and on the environment, and examining the resource costs of different technologies and strategies to reduce greenhouse gas emissions;
- Using economic models, including integrated assessment models that estimate the economic impacts of climate change, and macro-economic models that represent the costs and effects of the transition to low-carbon energy systems for the economy as a whole;
- Using comparisons of the current level and future trajectories of the 'social cost of carbon' (the cost of impacts associated with an additional unit of greenhouse gas emissions) with the marginal abatement cost (the costs associated with incremental reductions in units of emissions).

From all of these perspectives, the evidence gathered by the Review leads to a simple conclusion: the benefits of strong, early action considerably outweigh the costs.

The evidence shows that ignoring climate change will eventually damage economic growth. Our actions over the coming few decades could create risks of major disruption to economic and social activity, later in this century and in the next, on a scale similar to those associated with the great wars and the economic depression of the first half of the 20th century. And it will be difficult or impossible to reverse these changes. Tackling climate change is the pro-growth strategy for the longer term, and it can be done in a way that does not cap the aspirations for growth of rich or poor countries. The earlier effective action is taken, the less costly it will be.

At the same time, given that climate change is happening, measures to help people adapt to it are essential. And the less mitigation we do now, the greater the difficulty of continuing to adapt in future.

The Scientific Evidence Points to Increasing Risks of Serious, Irreversible Impacts from Climate Change Associated with Business-as-Usual (BAU) Paths for Emissions

The scientific evidence on the causes and future paths of climate change is strengthening all the time. In particular, scientists are now able to attach probabilities to the temperature outcomes and impacts on the natural environment associated with different levels of stabilisation of greenhouse gases in the atmosphere. Scientists also now understand much more about the potential for dynamic feedbacks that have, in previous times of climate change, strongly amplified the underlying physical processes.

The stocks of greenhouse gases in the atmosphere (including carbon dioxide, methane, nitrous oxides and a number of gases that arise from industrial processes) are rising, as a result of human activity. . . .

The current level or stock of greenhouse gases in the atmosphere is equivalent to around 430 parts per million (ppm) CO_2, compared with only 280ppm before the Industrial Revolution. These concentrations have already caused the world to warm by more than half a degree Celsius and will lead to at least a further half degree warming over the next few decades, because of the inertia in the climate system.

Even if the annual flow of emissions did not increase beyond today's rate, the stock of greenhouse gases in the atmosphere would reach double pre-industrial levels by 2050—that is 550ppm CO_2-equivalent—and would continue growing thereafter. But the annual flow of emissions is accelerating, as fast-growing economies invest in high-carbon infrastructure and as demand for energy and transport increases around the world. The level of 550ppm CO_2-equivalent could be reached as early as 2035. At this level there is at least a 77% chance—and perhaps up to a 99% chance, depending on the climate model used—of a global average temperature rise exceeding 2°C.

Under a BAU scenario, the stock of greenhouse gases could more than treble by the end of the century, giving at least a 50% risk of exceeding 5°C global average temperature change during the following decades. This would take humans into unknown territory. An illustration of the scale of such an increase is that we are now only around 5°C warmer than in the last ice age.

Such changes would transform the physical geography of the world. A radical change in the physical geography of the world must have powerful implications for the human geography—where people live, and how they live their lives. . . .

Climate Change Threatens the Basic Elements of Life for People Around the World—Access to Water, Food Production, Health, and Use of Land and the Environment

. . . On current trends, average global temperatures will rise by 2–3°C within the next fifty years or so. The Earth will be committed to several degrees more warming if emissions continue to grow.

Warming will have many severe impacts, often mediated through water:

- Melting glaciers will initially increase flood risk and then strongly reduce water supplies, eventually threatening one-sixth of the world's population, predominantly in the Indian sub-continent, parts of China, and the Andes in South America.

- Declining crop yields, especially in Africa, could leave hundreds of millions without the ability to produce or purchase sufficient food. At mid to high latitudes, crop yields may increase for moderate temperature rises (2–3°C), but then decline with greater amounts of warming. At 4°C and above, global food production is likely to be seriously affected.
- In higher latitudes, cold-related deaths will decrease. But climate change will increase worldwide deaths from malnutrition and heat stress. Vector-borne diseases such as malaria and dengue fever could become more widespread if effective control measures are not in place.
- Rising sea levels will result in tens to hundreds of millions more people flooded each year with warming of 3 or 4°C. There will be serious risks and increasing pressures for coastal protection in South East Asia (Bangladesh and Vietnam), small islands in the Caribbean and the Pacific, and large coastal cities, such as Tokyo, New York, Cairo and London. According to one estimate, by the middle of the century, 200 million people may become permanently displaced due to rising sea levels, heavier floods, and more intense droughts.
- Ecosystems will be particularly vulnerable to climate change, with around 15–40% of species potentially facing extinction after only 2°C of warming. And ocean acidification, a direct result of rising carbon dioxide levels, will have major effects on marine ecosystems, with possible adverse consequences on fish stocks.

The Damages from Climate Change Will Accelerate as the World Gets Warmer

Higher temperatures will increase the chance of triggering abrupt and large-scale changes.

- Warming may induce sudden shifts in regional weather patterns such as the monsoon rains in South Asia or the El Niño phenomenon—changes that would have severe consequences for water availability and flooding in tropical regions and threaten the livelihoods of millions of people.
- A number of studies suggest that the Amazon rainforest could be vulnerable to climate change, with models projecting significant drying in this region. One model, for example, finds that the Amazon rainforest could be significantly, and possibly irrevocably, damaged by a warming of 2–3°C.
- The melting or collapse of ice sheets would eventually threaten land which today is home to 1 in every 20 people.

While there is much to learn about these risks, the temperatures that may result from unabated climate change will take the world outside the range of human experience. This points to the possibility of very damaging consequences.

The Impacts of Climate Change Are Not Evenly Distributed—the Poorest Countries and People Will Suffer Earliest and Most. And If and When the Damages Appear It Will Be Too Late to Reverse the Process. Thus We Are Forced to Look a Long Way Ahead

Climate change is a grave threat to the developing world and a major obstacle to continued poverty reduction across its many dimensions. First, developing regions are at a geographic disadvantage: they are already warmer, on average, than developed regions, and they also suffer from high rainfall variability. As a result, further warming will bring poor countries high costs and few benefits. Second, developing countries—in particular the poorest—are heavily dependent on agriculture, the most climate-sensitive of all economic sectors, and suffer from inadequate health provision and low-quality public services. Third, their low incomes and vulnerabilities make adaptation to climate change particularly difficult.

Because of these vulnerabilities, climate change is likely to reduce further already low incomes and increase illness and death rates in developing countries. Falling farm incomes will increase poverty and reduce the ability of households to invest in a better future, forcing them to use up meagre savings just to survive. At a national level, climate change will cut revenues and raise spending needs, worsening public finances.

Many developing countries are already struggling to cope with their current climate. Climatic shocks cause setbacks to economic and social development in developing countries today even with temperature increases of less than 1°C. The impacts of unabated climate change—that is, increases of 3 or 4°C and upwards—will be to increase the risks and costs of these events very powerfully.

Impacts on this scale could spill over national borders, exacerbating the damage further. Rising sea levels and other climate-driven changes could drive millions of people to migrate: more than a fifth of Bangladesh could be under water with a 1m rise in sea levels, which is a possibility by the end of the century. Climate-related shocks have sparked violent conflict in the past, and conflict is a serious risk in areas such as West Africa, the Nile Basin and Central Asia.

Climate Change May Initially Have Small Positive Effects for a Few Developed Countries, But Is Likely to Be Very Damaging for the Much Higher Temperature Increases Expected by Mid- to Late-Century under BAU Scenarios

In higher latitude regions, such as Canada, Russia and Scandinavia, climate change may lead to net benefits for temperature increases of 2 or 3°C, through higher agricultural yields, lower winter mortality, lower heating requirements, and a possible boost to tourism. But these regions will also experience the most rapid rates of warming, damaging infrastructure, human health, local livelihoods and biodiversity.

Developed countries in lower latitudes will be more vulnerable—for example, water availability and crop yields in southern Europe are expected to decline by 20% with a 2°C increase in global temperatures. Regions where water is already scarce will face serious difficulties and growing costs.

The increased costs of damage from extreme weather (storms, hurricanes, typhoons, floods, droughts, and heat waves) counteract some early benefits of climate change and will increase rapidly at higher temperatures. Based on simple extrapolations, costs of extreme weather alone could reach 0.5–1% of world GDP per annum by the middle of the century, and will keep rising if the world continues to warm.

- A 5 or 10% increase in hurricane wind speed, linked to rising sea temperatures, is predicted approximately to double annual damage costs, in the USA.
- In the UK, annual flood losses alone could increase from 0.1% of GDP today to 0.2–0.4% of GDP once the increase in global average temperatures reaches 3 or 4°C.
- Heat waves like that experienced in 2003 in Europe, when 35,000 people died and agricultural losses reached $15 billion, will be commonplace by the middle of the century.

At higher temperatures, developed economies face a growing risk of large-scale shocks—for example, the rising costs of extreme weather events could affect global financial markets through higher and more volatile costs of insurance.

Integrated Assessment Models Provide a Tool for Estimating the Total Impact on the Economy; Our Estimates Suggest That This Is Likely to Be Higher Than Previously Suggested

. . . Formal modelling of the overall impact of climate change in monetary terms is a formidable challenge, and the limitations to modelling the world over two centuries or more demand great caution in interpreting results. However, as we have explained, the lags from action to effect are very long and the quantitative analysis needed to inform action will depend on such long-range modelling exercises. The monetary impacts of climate change are now expected to be more serious than many earlier studies suggested, not least because those studies tended to exclude some of the most uncertain but potentially most damaging impacts. Thanks to recent advances in the science, it is now possible to examine these risks more directly, using probabilities.

Most formal modelling in the past has used as a starting point a scenario of 2–3°C warming. In this temperature range, the cost of climate change could be equivalent to a permanent loss of around 0–3% in global world output compared with what could have been achieved in a world without climate change. Developing countries will suffer even higher costs.

However, those earlier models were too optimistic about warming: more recent evidence indicates that temperature changes resulting from BAU trends in emissions may exceed 2–3°C by the end of this century. This increases the likelihood of a wider range of impacts than previously considered. Many of these impacts, such as abrupt and large-scale climate change, are more difficult to quantify. With 5–6°C warming—which is a real possibility for the next century—existing models that include the risk of abrupt and large-scale climate change estimate an average 5–10% loss in global GDP, with poor countries suffering costs in excess of 10% of GDP. Further, there is some evidence of small but significant risks of temperature rises even above this range. Such temperature increases would take us into territory unknown to human experience and involve radical changes in the world around us. . . .

[W]e estimate the total cost over the next two centuries of climate change associated under BAU emissions involves impacts and risks that are equivalent to an average reduction in global per-capita consumption of at least 5%, now and forever. While this cost estimate is already strikingly high, it also leaves out much that is important.

The cost of BAU would increase still further, were the model systematically to take account of three important factors:

- First, including direct impacts on the environment and human health (sometimes called 'non-market' impacts) increases our estimate of the total cost of climate change on this path from 5% to 11% of global per-capita consumption. There are difficult analytical and ethical issues of measurement here. The methods used in this model are fairly conservative in the value they assign to these impacts.

- Second, some recent scientific evidence indicates that the climate system may be more responsive to greenhouse-gas emissions than previously thought, for example because of the existence of amplifying feedbacks such as the release of methane and weakening of carbon sinks. Our estimates, based on modelling a limited increase in this responsiveness, indicate that the potential scale of the climate response could increase the cost of climate change on the BAU path from 5% to 7% of global consumption, or from 11% to 14% if the non-market impacts described above are included.

- Third, a disproportionate share of the climate-change burden falls on poor regions of the world. If we weight this unequal burden appropriately, the estimated global cost of climate change at 5–6°C warming could be more than one-quarter higher than without such weights.

Putting these additional factors together would increase the total cost of BAU climate change to the equivalent of around a 20% reduction in consumption per head, now and into the future.

In summary, analyses that take into account the full ranges of both impacts and possible outcomes—that is, that employ the basic economics of risk—suggest that BAU climate change will reduce welfare by an amount equivalent to a reduction in consumption per head of between 5 and 20%. Taking account of the increasing scientific evidence of greater risks, of aversion to the possibilities of catastrophe, and of a broader approach to the consequences than implied by narrow output measures, the appropriate estimate is likely to be in the upper part of this range. . . .

Emissions Have Been, and Continue to Be, Driven by Economic Growth; yet Stabilisation of Greenhouse-Gas Concentrations in the Atmosphere Is Feasible and Consistent with Continued Growth

CO_2 emissions per head have been strongly correlated with GDP per head. As a result, since 1850, North America and Europe have produced around 70% of all the CO_2 emissions due to energy production, while developing countries have accounted for less than one quarter. Most future emissions growth will come from today's developing countries, because of their more rapid population and GDP growth and their increasing share of energy-intensive industries.

Yet despite the historical pattern and the BAU projections, the world does not need to choose between averting climate change and promoting growth and development. Changes in energy technologies and the structure of economies have reduced the responsiveness of emissions to income growth, particularly in some of the richest countries. With strong, deliberate policy choices, it is possible to 'decarbonise' both developed and developing economies on the scale required for climate stabilisation, while maintaining economic growth in both.

Stabilisation—at whatever level—requires that annual emissions be brought down to the level that balances the Earth's natural capacity to remove greenhouse gases from the atmosphere. The longer emissions remain above this level, the higher the final stabilisation level. In the long term, annual global emissions will need to be reduced to below 5 $GtCO_2$-equivalent, the level that the earth can absorb without adding to the concentration of GHGs in the atmosphere. This is more than 80% below the absolute level of current annual emissions. . . .

Stabilising at or below 550ppm CO_2-equivalent would require global emissions to peak in the next 10–20 years, and then fall at a rate of at least 1–3% per year. . . . By 2050, global emissions would need to be around 25% below current levels. These cuts will have to be made in the context of a world economy in 2050 that may be 3–4 times larger than today—so emissions per unit of GDP would need to be just one quarter of current levels by 2050.

To stabilise at 450ppm CO_2-equivalent, without overshooting, global emissions would need to peak in the next 10 years and then fall at more than 5% per year, reaching 70% below current levels by 2050. . . .

Achieving These Deep Cuts in Emissions Will Have a Cost. The Review Estimates the Annual Costs of Stabilisation at 500–550ppm CO_2-Equivalent to Be around 1% of GDP by 2050—A Level That Is Significant but Manageable

Reversing the historical trend in emissions growth, and achieving cuts of 25% or more against today's levels is a major challenge. Costs will be incurred as the world shifts from a high-carbon to a low-carbon trajectory. But there will also be business opportunities as the markets for low-carbon, high-efficiency goods and services expand.

Greenhouse-gas emissions can be cut in four ways. Costs will differ considerably depending on which combination of these methods is used, and in which sector:

- Reducing demand for emissions-intensive goods and services
- Increased efficiency, which can save both money and emissions
- Action on non-energy emissions, such as avoiding deforestation
- Switching to lower-carbon technologies for power, heat and transport

Estimating the costs of these changes can be done in two ways. One is to look at the resource costs of measures, including the introduction of low-carbon technologies and changes in land use, compared with the costs of the BAU alternative. This provides an upper bound on costs, as it does not take account of opportunities to respond involving reductions in demand for high-carbon goods and services.

The second is to use macroeconomic models to explore the system-wide effects of the transition to a low-carbon energy economy. These can be useful in tracking the dynamic interactions of different factors over time, including the response of economies to changes in prices. But they can be complex, with their results affected by a whole range of assumptions.

On the basis of these two methods, central estimate is that stabilisation of greenhouse gases at levels of 500–550ppm CO_2-equivalent will cost, on average, around 1% of annual global GDP by 2050. This is significant, but is fully consistent with continued growth and development, in contrast with unabated climate change, which will eventually pose significant threats to growth.

Resource Cost Estimates Suggest That an Upper Bound for the Expected Annual Cost of Emissions Reductions Consistent with a Trajectory Leading to Stabilisation at 550ppm CO_2-Equivalent Is Likely to Be around 1% of GDP by 2050

This Review has considered in detail the potential for, and costs of, technologies and measures to cut emissions across different sectors. As with the impacts of climate change, this is subject to important uncertainties. These include the difficulties of estimating the costs of technologies several decades into the future, as well as the way in which fossil-fuel prices evolve in the future. It is also hard to know how people will respond to price changes.

The precise evolution of the mitigation effort, and the composition across sectors of emissions reductions, will therefore depend on all these factors. But it is possible to make a central projection of costs across a portfolio of likely options, subject to a range.

The technical potential for efficiency improvements to reduce emissions and costs is substantial. Over the past century, efficiency in energy supply improved ten-fold or more in developed countries, and the possibilities for further gains are far from being exhausted. Studies by the International Energy Agency show that, by 2050, energy efficiency has the potential to be the biggest single source of emissions savings in the energy sector. This would have both environmental and economic benefits: energy-efficiency measures cut waste and often save money.

Non-energy emissions make up one-third of total greenhouse-gas emissions; action here will make an important contribution. A substantial body of evidence suggests that action to prevent further deforestation would be relatively cheap compared with other types of mitigation, if the right policies and institutional structures are put in place.

Large-scale uptake of a range of clean power, heat, and transport technologies is required for radical emission cuts in the medium to long term. The power sector around the world will have to be least 60%, and perhaps as much as 75%, decarbonised by 2050 to stabilise at or below 550ppm CO_2-equivalent. Deep cuts in the transport sector are likely to be more difficult in the shorter term, but will ultimately be needed. While many of the technologies to achieve this already exist, the priority is to bring down their costs so that they are competitive with fossil-fuel alternatives under a carbon-pricing policy regime.

A portfolio of technologies will be required to stabilise emissions. It is highly unlikely that any single technology will deliver all the necessary emission savings, because all technologies are subject to constraints of some kind, and because of the wide range of activities and sectors that generate greenhouse-gas emissions. It is also uncertain which technologies will turn out to be cheapest. Hence a portfolio will be required for low-cost abatement.

The shift to a low-carbon global economy will take place against the background of an abundant supply of fossil fuels. That is to say, the stocks of hydrocarbons that are profitable to extract (under current policies) are more (than enough to take the world to levels of greenhouse-gas concentrations well beyond 750ppm CO_2-equivalent, with very dangerous consequences. Indeed, under BAU, energy users are likely to switch towards more carbon-intensive coal and oil shales, increasing rates of emissions growth.

Even with very strong expansion of the use of renewable energy and other low-carbon energy sources, hydrocarbons may still make over half of global energy supply in 2050. Extensive carbon capture and storage would allow this continued use of fossil fuels without damage to the atmosphere, and also guard against the danger of strong climate-change policy being undermined at some stage by falls in fossil-fuel prices.

Estimates based on the likely costs of these methods of emissions reduction show that the annual costs of stabilising at around 550ppm CO_2-equivalent are likely to be around 1% of global GDP by 2050, with a range from –1% (net gains) to +3.5% of GDP. . . .

Reducing the Expected Adverse Impacts of Climate Change Is Therefore Both Highly Desirable and Feasible

This conclusion follows from a comparison of . . . estimates of the costs of mitigation with the high costs of inaction. . . .

Preliminary calculations adopting the approach to valuation taken in this Review suggest that the social cost of carbon today, if we remain on a BAU trajectory, is of the order of $85 per tonne of CO_2—higher than typical numbers in the literature, largely because we treat risk explicitly and incorporate recent evidence on the risks, but nevertheless well within the range of published estimates. This number is well above marginal abatement costs in many sectors. Comparing the social costs of carbon on a BAU trajectory and on a path towards stabilisation at 550ppm CO_2-equivalent, we estimate the excess of benefits over costs, in net present value terms, from implementing strong mitigation policies this year, shifting the world onto the better path: the net benefits would be of the order of $2.5 trillion. This figure will increase over time. This is not an estimate of net benefits occurring in this year, but a measure of the benefits that could flow from actions taken this year; many of the costs and benefits would be in the medium to long term. . . .

Greater International Co-operation to Accelerate Technological Innovation and Diffusion Will Reduce the Costs of Mitigation

The private sector is the major driver of innovation and the diffusion of technologies around the world. But governments can help to promote international collaboration to overcome barriers in this area, including through formal arrangements and through arrangements that promote public-private co-operation such as the Asia Pacific Partnership. Technology co-operation enables the sharing of risks, rewards and progress of technology development and enables co-ordination of priorities. . . .

Curbing Deforestation Is a Highly Cost-Effective Way of Reducing Greenhouse Gas Emissions

Emissions from deforestation are very significant—they are estimated to represent more than 18% of global emissions, a share greater than is produced by the global transport sector.

Action to preserve the remaining areas of natural forest is needed urgently. Large-scale pilot schemes are required to explore effective approaches to combining national action and international support.

Policies on deforestation should be shaped and led by the nation where the particular forest stands. But those countries should receive strong help from the international community, which benefits from their actions to reduce deforestation. At a national level, defining property rights to forestland, and determining the rights and responsibilities of landowners, communities and loggers, is key to effective forest management. This should involve local communities, respect informal rights and social structures, work with development goals and reinforce the process of protecting the forests.

Research carried out for this report indicates that the opportunity cost of forest protection in 8 countries responsible for 70 per cent of emissions from land use could be around $5 billion per annum initially, although over time marginal costs would rise.

Compensation from the international community should take account of the opportunity costs of alternative uses of the land, the costs of administering and enforcing protection, and the challenges of managing the political transition as established interests are displaced.

Carbon markets could play an important role in providing such incentives in the longer term. But there are short-term risks of destabilising the crucial process of strengthening existing strong carbon markets if deforestation is integrated without agreements that strongly increase demand for emissions reductions. These agreements must be based on an understanding of the scale of transfers likely to be involved.

Adaptation Efforts in Developing Countries Must Be Accelerated and Supported, Including through International Development Assistance

The poorest developing countries will be hit earliest and hardest by climate change, even though they have contributed little to causing the problem. Their low incomes make it difficult to finance adaptation. The international community has an obligation to support them in adapting to climate change. Without such support there is a serious risk that development progress will be undermined. . . .

Strong and early mitigation has a key role to play in limiting the long-run costs of adaptation. Without this, the costs of adaptation will rise dramatically.

Building and Sustaining Collective Action Is Now an Urgent Challenge

The key building blocks for any collective action include developing a shared Understanding of the long-term goals for climate policy, building effective institutions for co-operation, and demonstrating leadership and working to build trust with others.

Without a clear perspective on the long-term goals for stabilisation of greenhouse gas concentrations in the atmosphere, it is unlikely that action will be sufficient to meet the objective.

Action must include mitigation, innovation and adaptation. There are many opportunities to start now, including where there are immediate benefits and where large-scale pilot programmes will generate valuable experience. And we have already begun to create the institutions to underpin co-operation.

The challenge is to broaden and deepen participation across all the relevant dimensions of action—including co-operation to create carbon prices and markets, to accelerate innovation and deployment of low-carbon technologies, to reverse emissions from land-use change and to help poor countries adapt to the worst impacts of climate change.

There Is Still Time to Avoid the Worst Impacts of Climate Change if Strong Collective Action Starts Now

This Review has focused on the economics of risk and uncertainty, using a wide range of economic tools to tackle the challenges of a global problem which has profound long-term implications. Much more work is required, by scientists and economists, to tackle the analytical challenges and resolve some of the uncertainties across a broad front. But it is already very clear that the economic risks of inaction in the face of climate change are very severe.

There are ways to reduce the risks of climate change. With the right incentives, the private sector will respond and can deliver solutions. The stabilisation of greenhouse gas concentrations in the atmosphere is feasible, at significant but manageable costs.

The policy tools exist to create the incentives required to change investment patterns and move the global economy onto a low-carbon path. This must go hand-in-hand with increased action to adapt to the impacts of the climate change that can no longer be avoided.

Above all, reducing the risks of climate change requires collective action. It requires co-operation between countries, through international frameworks that support the achievement of shared goals. It requires a partnership between the public and private sector, working with civil society and with individuals. It is still possible to avoid the worst impacts of climate change; but it requires strong and urgent collective action. Delay would be costly and dangerous.

"Global Warming" Scare-Mongering Revisited

. . . In 1992, the so-called Rio Earth Summit resulted in the *UN Framework Convention on Climate Change*. Subsequent meetings of the contracting parties to that convention, including Australia, led to the 1997 negotiation of the Kyoto Protocol, whereby those developed nations ratifying it agreed to reduce their emissions of greenhouse gases, and carbon dioxide (CO_2) in particular. In 2005 this treaty, signed by Australia but not ratified either by it or, more importantly, by the United States, came into force when finally ratified by Russia.

Meanwhile, in 1990, 1995 and 2001 the IPCC had issued its First, Second and Third Assessment Reports. These advanced its thesis that global temperatures were rising steadily, and that this was due principally to anthropogenic (i.e., man-made) causes—notably the growing use of fossil fuels (coal, oil and natural gas). These Assessment Reports claimed, increasingly shrilly, that the rising concentration of atmospheric CO_2 was directly responsible for rising global temperatures. Using highly complex computer models of the atmospheric and other processes involved, projections (which however were increasingly treated as *predictions*) were also made of the likely future consequences if effective action were not taken to rein in the growth of, and stabilise, the atmospheric concentration of CO_2.

These likely consequences ranged widely. They included melting of the Antarctic and Greenland ice caps (which between them contain about 95 per cent of the world's frozen water); melting of the (floating) Arctic sea-ice; "shutting down" of the Gulf Stream; growing frequency of extreme weather events, such as hurricanes and floods; disruption of world food supplies; spread of "tropical" (*sic.*) diseases such as malaria; rising sea-levels as the ice caps melt, with inundation of low-lying areas; displacement of people living in such areas; destruction of animal habitat (those cuddly-looking polar bears again!); and so on.

Because projections of future CO_2 emissions depend, *inter alia,* on projections of world economic growth, the IPCC Assessment Reports involved not only the work of climatologists to underpin the basic "science", but also of economists to undertake those economic growth projections.

For many years, some prominent economists, such as Professor William Nordhaus, have extensively researched the potential costs *and benefits*

From *National Observer,* No. 72, Autumn 2007, pp. 19–32 (notes omitted). Copyright © 2007 by National Observer. Reprinted by permission of Council for the National Interest, Melbourne, Australia.

that might arise from a world warming in line with IPCC projections/predictions. In doing so they have accepted, at least for purposes of their calculations, the underlying "science".

In July 2005, the (UK) House of Lords Select Committee on Economic Affairs issued an impressive report on these topics. It too largely accepted the IPCC-determined "science". However, its conclusions about the risk-assessment processes involved, particularly the relative costs of abatement versus mitigation measures, were significantly at odds with the rising tide of IPCC-inspired opinion. It expressed concern "that UK energy and climate policy appears to rest on a very debatable model of the energy-economic systems and on dubious assumptions about the costs of meeting the long-run target of 60 per cent reduction in CO_2 emissions". It called on the government "to improve substantially (a) the cost estimates being conveyed to the public and (b) the manner of their presentation". It urged, further, "that explicit comparisons be made between the monetary cost of adaptation measures and their benefits", and considered that "the Treasury should become directly involved itself, making its own economic assessment of the issue".

Without acknowledging that call, the UK government, in July 2005, did institute what looked like such an assessment under the direction of Sir Nicholas Stern. His report was formally submitted on 30 October 2006. However, in keeping with the Blair Government's *modus operandi*, its conclusions had been widely disseminated to appropriately compliant journalists before publication. To say that those conclusions were alarming would be a huge understatement. Yet, as I hope to show, this is an essentially fraudulent document.

Nevertheless, the Stern Report provided both a dramatic and timely stage setting for the release in February, 2007 of the IPCC's next instalment. So let us now examine what it said.

The Stern Report

The four key elements of the Report were:

- Its wholehearted acceptance of the IPCC's "science" on global warming.
- Its apocalyptic predictions as to the consequences for the human race if effective action were not taken to halt the otherwise "inevitable" soaring temperatures resulting from economic-growth-related CO_2 emissions.
- Its striking assertion that, without preventive action, the economic costs "will be equivalent to losing at least 5 per cent of global Gross Domestic Product (GDP) each year, now and forever" (with the effects falling disproportionately more heavily on the world's poor).
- Its comforting (*sic.*) assertion that these predicted dangers could however be averted by measures that would "only" reduce world growth by about one per cent per annum.

As to the "science", there is no trace of skepticism in the Report. In one sense, that was reasonable for a report by economists, who simply accepted the IPCC thesis as their starting point. Even so, it was strange then that the UK government chose to undertake the inquiry, and Stern to rush it through to publication, while the IPCC's Fourth Assessment Report (4AR) was still in train. As noted below, the conclusions of 4AR—to the extent that they have so far been revealed—differ appreciably from their 3AR predecessor. Stern was thus basing his report on "science" that the IPCC itself was changing even as he wrote. And that leaves aside other recent scientific developments which, to any intelligent layman, appear worth considering but which the IPCC itself has also chosen to ignore.

It might not be going too far to say that the Stern Report has produced a fifth Horseman of the Apocalypse. To Pestilence, War, Famine and Death it has added Carbon Dioxide Emissions. If not checked, Stern says, they will produce economic and social disruption "on a scale similar to those associated with the great wars and the economic depression of the first half of the 20th century".

These assertions derive from the Report's calculations that, without preventive action, the world will suffer huge economic damage. This will stem from rising sea-levels, increasingly frequent extreme weather events, and so on. Totting them all up, Stern suggests that if such "a wider range of risks and impacts is taken into account, the estimate of damage could rise to 20 per cent of GDP or more" within about two centuries from now.

Having posed this dire threat, Stern then holds out the hope that, if we sinners can only agree to mend our ways, salvation can after all be had at what he sees as a modest cost. If we are willing to sacrifice (although he does not use that word) about one percentage point per annum from the growth rate of global GDP, all will be well. Emissions of CO_2 will be reduced, the growth of CO_2 concentrations in the atmosphere will taper off, and Planet Earth, along with those who dwell on it, will be saved.

There's just one problem: the quality of Sir Nicholas's Report itself, on which this Doomsday scenario is based.

In my earlier article I noted that, even then, the Report had already "been subjected to utter ridicule—criticism of the most damaging, authoritative and immediate kind, such as I cannot ever recall of any document of such allegedly high level provenance". For example:

- On 1 November 2006, Nigel Lawson attacked the Report's economics in trenchant terms as "scare-mongering". The Report, he said, "adds disappointingly little . . . apart from a battery of essentially spurious statistics based on theoretical models and conjectural worst cases". It "is clearly no basis for policy decisions which would have the most profound adverse effect on people's lives, and at a cost which Stern almost certainly underestimates".
- On 2 November, world-renowned Danish statistician Bjorn Lomborg focused on "Mr Stern's core argument that the price of inaction would be extraordinary and the cost of action modest". Lomborg's

review, all the more damaging because it does not challenge either the underlying "science" or the claim that global warming/climate change is anthropogenically induced, describes the Report as seeming "hastily put together, with many sloppy errors". Its argument is "selective" and "its conclusion flawed". Stern, he says, is guilty of "cherry-picking statistics to fit an argument". Whereas "the most well-recognized climate economist in the world", Professor William Nordhaus, estimates that "3 per cent will be wiped off global GDP if nothing is done", Stern, by not one but a whole series of statistical fudges, purports to derive a damage assessment of 20 per cent of GDP. There is more, but you get the picture.

- On 3 November, Max Wilkinson, a former natural resources editor and chief leader writer of *The Financial Times,* excoriated the Report even more harshly. First, and of crucial importance, nowhere does Stern "reveal what discount rate he assumes to estimate the present value of future disasters". Anyone with the slightest knowledge of cost-benefit analysis knows that the discount rate is central to such analysis. So by any professional economists' standards, Stern's omission is extraordinary. It becomes all the more so when examination of the Report's calculations reveals that "the actual figure used by Sir Nicholas seems to have been between 2 and 3 per cent". This ridiculously low rate is "less than half the rate that the [British] Treasury now uses for assessing large capital projects, and much lower than the private sector would expect". Obviously, a discount rate "more in line with commercial realities . . . would make the costs of global warming in 100 years' time appear small or even negligible in present day terms". Moreover, Sir Nicholas cannot have it both ways (despite, I should add, apparently trying hard to do so). If he is to assume a very low discount rate for computing the present value of his distant future damage bill, he cannot (legitimately) use a different discount rate when calculating the costs of his present proposed mitigation and abatement measures. In short, "a new economic framework based on a vision of Armageddon" is unlikely to make any sense.

- Even Martin Wolf, who clearly regards "Nick" as a personal friend, offered only half-hearted support. He too did not question the underlying "science", nor (very surprisingly for such a normally distinguished economic journalist) did he even mention the extraordinary matter of the discount rate. Yet the best he could say of Stern's proposals was that, while "in principle" they would be feasible, "in practice" they are not. "The difficulties to be overcome in creating an effective global regime [including all the big developing countries such as China, India and Brazil] that constrains greenhouse gas emissions over a century are gigantic. . .".

What is striking about these (and other such) criticisms is that they appeared so quickly. In other words, the Stern Report is so transparently in error (some would say "rigged") that it took no time at all for the gaping analytical holes in it to be exposed by competent economic journalists.

Still, you might say, these are but journalists: what about the professional economists themselves? Again, there has been no lack of criticism from that quarter, including from Professor William Nordhaus, referred to earlier. On 17 November 2006, he posted a major assessment of the Stern Report. It represents, he said, "a radical revision of global warming economics". However, it "should be viewed as a political document", whose "radical revision arises because of an extreme assumption about discounting". Noting that discounting for these purposes "involves a concept called the pure rate of social time preference" (referred to by economists as "the social discount rate"), Nordhaus points out that the Report "proposes using a social discount rate that is essentially zero" (to be precise, 0.1 per cent per annum). By contrast, his own DICE model assumes a social discount rate "starting at 3 per cent per year and declining slowly to about 1 per cent in 300 years".

Such key differences aside, Nordhaus shows that Stern's own modelling leads to conclusions that he rightly describes as "bizarre". For example, it implies (though it does not state) that if Stern's recommendations were accepted, "global consumption would be reduced by about 14 per cent, requiring a reduction of US$6 trillion per year in current consumption". Where, he not unreasonably asks, would the consumption cuts come from? Moreover, the Report is implicitly advocating (although again, it does not say so) "reducing current consumption to prevent the decline in consumption of future generations that it projects to be much richer than today". As Nordhaus dryly observes, "while this might be worth contemplating, it hardly seems ethically compelling".

Finally, "a most unattractive feature" of the Report, in Nordhaus's view, is that "it puts present decisions on a hair-trigger in response to far-future contingencies". Consider, he says, the military analogy. "Countries might start wars today because of the possibility of nuclear proliferation ahead. . . . It is not clear how long the globe could survive the calculations and machinations of zero-discount-rate military powers". President Truman, he recalls, complaining that his economists were given to saying "on the one hand, but on the other hand", once famously said that "he wanted a one-handed economist". In that sense, "the Stern Report is a Prime Minister's dream come true".

After that demolition job from such a highly respected quarter, one might have thought that not much more needed to be said. Nevertheless, the most definitive professional critique of the Report was published early this year in a major article in *World Economics*. Despite its formally polite language, it is utterly damning. First, the economist authors note and agree with the main conclusions "reached by our scientific colleagues" in Part I of the article. "Like them, we would emphasise" that the Report "greatly underestimates the extent of uncertainty as to possible developments", and that "its treatment of sources and evidence is persistently selective and biased". These twin features have combined to make it "a vehicle for speculative alarmism".

Warming to their work, the economists note that, "among other weak-nesses", the Report "systematically overstates projected costs of climate change, partly . . . [through] its failure to acknowledge the scope for long-term adaptation to possible global warming". It also "underestimates the likely cost—including to the world's poor—of the drastic global mitigation programme that it calls for". To sum up, "so far from being an authoritative guide to the economics of climate change", the Report "is deeply flawed. It does not provide a basis for informed and responsible policies".

Be that as it may, what the Stern Report did provide was a dramatically alarmist made-to-measure backdrop for the unveiling of the IPCC's next installment.

IPCC Developments

Before describing the recent IPCC publication processes it is necessary to outline that body's framework. According to its website, the IPCC "has three Working Groups and a Task Force". Leaving the latter aside, the Working Groups are, respectively:

- "Working Group I assesses the scientific aspects of the climate system and climate change".
- "Working Group II assesses the vulnerability of socio-economic and natural systems to climate change, negative and positive consequences of climate change, and options for adapting to it".
- "Working Group III assesses options for limiting greenhouse gas emissions and otherwise mitigating climate change".

The much-publicised document produced by the IPCC last February was treated by most of the media as being its long awaited Fourth Assessment Report. In fact, it was nothing of the kind. Indeed, it was not even the report of one of the three Working Groups, let alone all three of them. Rather, it consisted of a 21-page *Summary for Policymakers* entitled *Climate Change 2007: The Physical Science Basis*. This document, which purported to be an "executive summary" of the then still *draft* report of Working Group I (WGI), was formally approved by governmental representatives meeting in Paris and issued on 2 February. WGI's final report will not be issued until after this article is completed, by which time its conclusions will, apparently, have been brought into line with the already published *Summary for Policymakers*.

Again, while WGII's report, *Impacts, Adaptation and Vulnerability,* has not yet been finalised, a much less highly publicised *Summary for Policymakers* has already been issued in its case also on 6 April following a meeting of governmental representatives in Brussels.

WGIII's still draft report, *Mitigation of Climate Change,* will be considered at a meeting in Bangkok on 30 April–3 May. We are told that all three Working Group reports will then be issued.

Even that, however, will not be the end of the matter. The 4AR *Synthesis Report,* which "integrates the information [in the Working Group reports] around six topic areas", will be reviewed at a seven-week-long meeting of "governments and experts" beginning on 21 May. It is then scheduled for "adoption and approval" at the 27th Session of the IPCC in Valencia, Spain, on 12–16 November 2007.

So there you have it. If you ask members of the lay public, or almost any of our politicians or journalists, whether the IPCC's Fourth Assessment Report has yet been published, you will almost certainly be told by everyone that indeed it has, on 2 February last, and that (of course!) it confirmed that the outlook for the world was even more serious than had been thought. Taken in conjunction with the ostensibly alarming imperatives of the Stern Report, the requirements for policy action are now clear. The scientific debate is now "over".

Since the Stern Report has been convincingly shown to be intellectually fraudulent; since none of the IPCC Working Groups (at the time of writing) has yet issued its report; since the 4AR *Synthesis Report* will not be available until mid-November; and since, meanwhile, a vigorous debate about the science is still proceeding (see below), that conclusion could hardly be further from the truth.

Nevertheless, with all its deficiencies, it is still worth noting some interesting aspects of that 2 February *Summary for Policymakers.* For example:

- Equilibrium global average warming if CO2 is stabilised at 550 ppmv is *very likely* to be between 1.5°C and 4.5°C, and *likely* to be at least 2°C above 1750 values. (My italics) These figures, which all incorporate the warming that has already occurred between 1750 and today, are lower than their equivalent 3AR predecessors published in 2001, although for technical reasons direct comparisons are difficult.
- By contrast with 3AR, the IPCC is no longer claiming significant melting of the Antarctic or Greenland ice caps.
- Largely as a consequence, the projected range of sea-level rise over the period to 2100 is now only 18–38 cm. This compares with a range of 9–88 cm projected/predicted in 3AR.
- Essentially, the tendency of the Global Circulation Models to "over-predict" increases in temperatures and sea levels, with those projections not being borne out by subsequent observations, has produced what seems to be a significant re-think within WGI since 3AR.

The Global Circulation Models (GCM)

At this point, a short comment on those GCMs may be appropriate. Since I first started looking into these matters in 1990 (visiting the then Atmospheric Research Division of the CSIRO to do so), the size, complexity and above all computing power of these models has increased considerably.

Moreover, whereas the earlier GCMs purported to model relatively few variables, such as CO_2 concentrations and temperatures at the Earth's surface, their successors have become more complex. Ironically, in some respects these added sophistications have resulted from the modeller's own need to "explain" why their earlier model projections failed, time and again, to be verified by later observations. To take but one example, the IPCC now "explains" why there was no warming between 1940 and 1975 (indeed, there was a cooling) by pointing to the cooling effect of the sulphates emitted during those years from power station chimneys—a phenomenon first noted, incidentally, by Professor Lindzen. So current GCMs now incorporate a "sulphates emissions" variable.

This is one example of a more general feature of the GCMs. Again and again, they are having to be "tuned" to make their projected versions of climatic change consistent with actual observations. Most recently, the models have been confounded by the fact that, since 1998 (an El Nino "high") there has been no further increase in global temperature. The modellers' response is not to concede that their models are regularly producing inaccurate forecasts of the future, but simply to incorporate an "El Niño" variable in their models.

All this illustrates George Orwell's famous remark that "one has to belong to the intelligentsia to believe things like that: no ordinary man could be such a fool". Climatologists' computer models for predicting our *weekly* weather patterns regularly fail to do so, despite their much enhanced size, complexity and power. Yet these people continue to press their intellectually arrogant claim that they can provide useful results from models purporting to project the weather decades, or even hundreds of years, into the future. It is one thing to play around with such fascinating toys (at taxpayers' expense) and write learned papers about the results for audiences of your fellow academics. It is altogether another thing to pretend that your GCMs provide a genuinely realistic picture of future climate. And it is surely unforgivable to argue that we should set about destroying our economic welfare, now and in the future, to accord with your charlatanism.

The Science

All of this would be bad enough if the "science" involved in climate projection/prediction were being conducted on a genuinely scientific basis. In fact, it is not. The climatologists principally involved in the IPCC seem determined to ignore all scientific research but their own, unless (as in the case of Professor Lindzen's work on sulphates) they subsequently find it convenient to incorporate such work as a kind of computer "patch" to "tune" their own earlier faulty models.

There is no space to go into this aspect thoroughly. However, the more one reads the contributions to the scientific debate, the more I, at any rate, become convinced that the IPCC climatological framework is seriously deficient. Among others, two deficiencies in particular are evident: its attempted denial of the historical geological evidence, and its virtual ignoring of the work of the astrophysicists.

In the latter area, one recent development must be mentioned. Remarkable recent work by a group of Danish scientists has shown experimentally that, when cosmic radiation from outer space enters the Earth's atmosphere, the electrons then released can produce cloud condensation nuclei in the lower troposphere that then come together to form low-level clouds. Such clouds are very important in cooling us. (The IPCC climatologists themselves acknowledge—nowadays, though not originally—the importance of clouds, and have sought to incorporate a "clouds" variable into their GCMs; but even they, so far as I know, don't claim to have done so in any convincing manner).

Why is this important? Because it seems to provide *experimental* evidence for a phenomenon long known to astronomers, namely that sunspot cycles, which have been observed and recorded for many centuries, appear to be closely correlated with our weather.

Solar radiation is of course being emitted constantly from our Sun's surface, but sunspots involve a stepping-up of such radiation. Coming within the path of that radiation, the Earth's electro-magnetic field (or "shield") is affected. In layman's terms, a strengthened Earth electro-magnetic "shield" can be seen as deterring more of the cosmic radiation from coming in from outer space. So if those Danish astrophysicists are right (and my gut feeling is that probably they are), then the relative intensity of sunspots will affect the relative extent of cloud formation on Earth. In broad terms, the Earth will get warmer if less cosmic radiation is getting through its electro-magnetic "shield" to form those cloud condensation nuclei which go to form clouds; and it will get cooler if the opposite is the case.

Of course, no real scientist would claim that the work of Dr Svensmark and his colleagues constitutes the definitive answer to our climatic puzzles—still less that, even if it does, it will allow us to make realistic projections of our climate for centuries into the future. Its importance lies in the fact that, whereas the *anthropogenic* warming thesis is becoming less and less convincing as the years go by, the Svensmark thesis looks highly plausible. And, *mirabile dictu,* **the level of CO_2 emissions plays no role in it whatsoever.**

Political Developments

During recent months, political developments on these climate change issues, both internationally and within Australia, have come thick and fast. Internationally, for example:

- The UK Government has announced two "targets" for reducing Britain's CO_2 emissions—a reduction, from levels in the year 2000, of 20 per cent by 2020 (or 30 per cent if the rest of the world joins in), and of 60 per cent by 2050.

- The European Union, while not committing itself in the nearer-term, has also announced a 60 per cent reduction target by 2050.

In Australia, pressures have been mounting for us to take similar leave of our senses. Thus:

- The Labor Party has announced that, if elected federally later this year, it will commit to a programme to reduce CO_2 emissions by 60 per cent, from their 2000 levels, by 2050.
- The Greens have gone further, advocating a reduction of 80 per cent by 2050. Predictably, this is supported by a gaggle of environmental activist groups, such as the Australian Conservation Foundation and the Wilderness Society.
- The Coalition Government, while not (at the time of writing) committing to any target, has said that it accepts that the threat from climate change is real, and that it will shortly announce measures to address it. Some of those measures may be contained in the 2007–08 Budget on 8 May. Others may follow the government's receipt, by 31 May, of the Report of its Task Group on Emissions Trading. . . .

POSTSCRIPT

Are the Potential Costs of Global Warming Too High to Ignore?

John Broome, "The Ethics of Climate Change," *Scientific American* (June 2008), explains that many factors go into comparing present costs to control global warming with the future costs of the damage done by global warming. These factors include the discount rate (the value of tomorrow's money today), confidence that the economy will (or will not) continue to grow, and choice of moral philosophy. William Nordhaus, "Critical Assumptions in the Stern Review on Climate Change," *Science* (July 13, 2007), calls Stern's choice of discount rate "extreme." Nicholas Stern and Chris Taylor, "Climate Change: Risk, Ethics, and the Stern Review," *Science* (July 13, 2007), emphasize the role of value judgments. S. Niggol Seo, "Is Stern Review on Climate Change Alarmist?" *Energy & Environment* (July 2007), finds Stern's estimates of future costs to be worst-case costs; costs are likely to be less. Yet Stern is by no means alone in estimating high costs. In June 2008, the International Energy Agency released *Energy Technology Perspectives 2008* (http://www.iea.org/Textbase/techno/etp/index.asp). Among its points is that in our use of energy, we are not living sustainably. In order to reduce carbon emissions by 50 percent and avoid harmful climate change while still having sufficient energy for human needs, the world will need to spend $45 trillion on technology and deployment by 2050.

Other studies suggest that the Stern report and other estimates of the costs of global warming may be low. Tim Appenzeller, "The Big Thaw," *National Geographic* (June 2007), discusses the rapid loss of ice from ice caps and glaciers, with serious impacts expected on economies dependent on winter sports and—much more ominously—on the summertime flow of water from melting snow and ice in nearby mountains. According to Richard A. Kerr, "Pushing the Scary Side of Global Warming," *Science* (June 8, 2007), some climate researchers are concerned that we are seriously underestimating how disastrous global warming will be. Indeed, recent projections suggest sea level may rise as much as 1.5 meters (5 feet) by 2100 (see "Global Sea Levels Set to Rise above IPCC Forecast," *Geographical,* June 2008).

In January 2006, the U.K.'s Department for Environment, Food and Rural Affairs (DEFRA) published "Avoiding Dangerous Climate Change" (http://www.defra.gov.uk/environment/climatechange/research/dangerous-cc/index. htm), warning that immediate and expensive action is essential if catastrophe is to be avoided. Necessary action may be expensive, but studies do suggest it will be affordable. For instance, when the National Commission on Energy Policy published its report, *Ending the Energy Stalemate: A Bipartisan Strategy to Meet America's Energy Challenges* in December 2004, the Energy Information Administration promptly analyzed its economic impact in *Impacts of Modeled Recommendations of the National Commission on Energy Policy* (April 2005) (http://www.eia.doe.gov/oiaf/servicerpt/bingaman/index.html) and concluded that increasing automobile fuel efficiency, encouraging alternate energy sources, and increasing oil production and clean coal technology would cost the "U.S. economy . . . no more than 0.15% of GDP or about $78 per household per year, while overall GDP is projected to grow by 87%." (See http://www.energycommission.org/ for the latest recommendations and analysis.)

ISSUE 9

Can Carbon Trading Help Control Carbon Emissions?

YES: James Allen and Anthony White, from "Carbon Trading," *Electric Perspectives* (September/October 2005)

NO: Brian Tokar, from "Trading Away the Earth: Pollution Credits and the Perils of 'Free Market Environmentalism,'" *Dollars & Sense* (March/April 1996)

ISSUE SUMMARY

YES: James Allen and Anthony White describe the European Union's Greenhouse Gas Emissions Trading Scheme and argue that it encourages investment in carbon-abatement technologies and depends on governmental commitments to reducing emissions despite possible adverse economic effects.

NO: Brian Tokar, recalling the application of pollution credit trading to sulfur dioxide, not carbon dioxide, argues that such "free-market environmentalism" tactics fail to reduce pollution while turning environmental protection into a commodity that corporate powers can manipulate for private profit.

The Environmental Protection Agency (EPA) was established in 1970 in response to concerns about air and water pollution. During the next two decades, an unprecedented series of legislative acts and administrative rules were promulgated, placing numerous restrictions on industrial and commercial activities that might result in the pollution, degradation, or contamination of land, air, water, food, and the workplace.

Such forms of regulatory control have always been opposed by the affected industrial corporations and developers as well as by advocates of a free-market policy. More moderate critics of the government's regulatory program recognize that adequate environmental protection will not result from completely voluntary policies. They suggest that a new set of strategies is needed. Arguing that "top down, federal, command and control legislation" is not an appropriate or effective means of preventing environmental degradation, they propose a wide range of alternative tactics, many of which are designed to operate through the economic marketplace. The first significant congressional response to these proposals was the incorporation of tradable pollution emission rights into the 1990 Clean Air Act amendments as a means for reducing acid rain–causing sulfur dioxide emissions. More recently, the 1997 international negotiations on controlling global warming, held in Kyoto, Japan, resulted in a protocol that includes emissions trading as one of the key elements in the plan to limit the atmospheric buildup of greenhouse gases.

Charles W. Schmidt, "The Market for Pollution," *Environmental Health Perspectives* (August 2001), argues that emissions trading schemes represent "the most significant developments" in the use of economic incentives to motivate corporations to reduce pollution. However, many environmentalists oppose the idea of allowing anyone to pay to pollute, either on moral grounds or because they doubt that these tactics will actually achieve the goal of controlling pollution. Diminishment of the acid rain problem is often cited as an example of how well emission rights trading can work, but in "Dispelling the Myths of the Acid Rain Story," *Environment* (July–August 1998), Don Munton argues that other control measures, such as switching to low-sulfur fuels, deserve much more of the credit for reducing sulfur dioxide emissions.

In "A Low-Cost Way to Control Climate Change," *Issues in Science and Technology* (Spring 1998), Byron Swift argues that the "cap-and-trade" feature of the U.S. Acid Rain Program has been so successful that a similar system for implementing the Kyoto Protocol's emissions trading mandate as a cost-effective means of controlling greenhouse gases should work. In March 2001, the U.S. Senate Committee on Agriculture, Nutrition, and Forestry held a "Hearing on Biomass and Environmental Trading Opportunities for Agriculture and Forestry," in which witnesses urged Congress to encourage trading for both its economic and its environmental benefits. Richard L. Sandor, chairman and chief executive officer of Environmental Financial Products LLC, said that "200 million tons of CO_2 could be sequestered through soils and forestry in the United States per year. At the most conservative prices of \$20–\$30 per ton, this could potentially generate \$4–\$6 billion in additional agricultural income."

According to Bret Schulte, "Putting a Price on Pollution," *U.S. News and World Report* (May 14, 2007), the Bush administration continues to oppose emissions trading, but support in the United States is growing. The European Union has actually established a Greenhouse Gas Emissions Trading Scheme, which James Allen and Anthony White describe in the following selections, arguing that it encourages investment in carbon-abatement technologies and depends on governmental commitments to reducing emissions despite possible adverse economic effects. "The carbon market in Europe is here to stay," they say. Brian Tokar, recalling the application of pollution credit trading to sulfur dioxide, not carbon dioxide, argues that such "free-market environmentalism" tactics fail to reduce pollution while turning environmental protection into a commodity that corporate powers can manipulate for private profit.

YES  James Allen and Anthony White

Carbon Trading

The European Union Greenhouse Gas Emissions Trading Scheme (EUETS) rests on a simple concept: The right to emit greenhouse gases (GHGs) can be allocated and traded. The scheme's purpose is relatively straightforward, as well: to help the 25 member states of the European Union achieve an 8-percent collective reduction below 1990 levels of six greenhouse gases by 2008–12.

More than 12,000 installations, totaling nearly half of all emissions in the European Union, must retire these rights (EU emissions allowances, or EUAs) corresponding to their actual emissions over the compliance period. Failure to do so will result in a fine of €40 (around $48) per ton of CO_2 in excess during Phase I (2005–07), rising to €100 ($120) per ton (equivalent) in Phase II (2008–12). And paying the fine does not remove the obligation to retire the missing certificates.

Also, the European Commission environmental directorate designed EUETS with the Kyoto Protocol in mind. In place of EUAs, installations can retire "clean development mechanism" [CDM] credits (generated through GHG reduction projects in developing countries) in Phase I and, in Phase II, CDM and joint implementation (JI) credits (the latter being credits generated in developed countries that have ratified the protocol). Companies may trade all these credits among themselves—the market mechanism is to ensure that abatement be achieved more efficiently than through a command-and-control regime. Trading is currently limited primarily to futures contracts, traded over-the-counter, but increasingly it is mediated via exchanges, such as the European Climate Exchange. EUETS provides a price signal to companies that operate and own emissions-intensive installations, which encourages investment in carbon-abatement technologies, as well as measures to increase efficiency. This kind of cap-and-trade system is fundamentally policy-driven—that is, it depends entirely on the will of governments to impose emission reduction obligations, despite the possibility that these may create adverse economic effects.

The European carbon market is in a critical phase. Already, fundamental changes in the European economy—particularly a switch from coal- to gas-fired power generation—are taking place. Carbon funds are beginning to attract private capital to invest in renewable technologies,

From *Electric Perspectives*, September/October 2005, pp. 50–59. Copyright © 2005 by Edison Electric Institute. Reprinted by permission.

often in developing countries. And even at this early stage, when only half of all installations have received allowances, fully 1 million tons of CO_2 are traded each day.

Still, the price of emitting CO_2 has risen beyond many predictions, mostly due to unexpected growth in natural gas prices. Meanwhile, member states are debating whether to expand EUETS to gases other than CO_2 and to additional sectors of the economy, such as transportation, responsible for a great deal of all EU emissions. Moreover, bureaucracy at the United Nations (which oversees Kyoto and the CDM and JI credits) and a lack of experience in this new market are limiting investment opportunities for carbon speculators.

But benefits and challenges aside, one thing is clear: The world's largest emissions trading scheme has arrived.

Long-Term Commitment or Unstable Pact?

From a European perspective, policy on climate change in the United States is uneven, though certainly there are efforts to push markets. The federal government is investing large sums of money to promote new renewable energy, nuclear, and clean coal technologies; at the same time the Bush administration, opposed to mandatory CO_2 emission reductions, has focused on voluntary efforts. Meanwhile at the state and regional levels, efforts are moving forward—but they face many hurdles.

In contrast, European governments have settled on a long-term course of action. And, in addition to the targets agreed at Kyoto and implemented via the EUETS, some EU nations have set mandatory emission targets for dates beyond 2012. Some of these targets may be aspirational, but the United Kingdom, for example, has set a long-term target for a 60-percent reduction of CO_2 emissions of 1990 levels by 2050. In any event, it is likely that EUETS will be the linchpin for all efforts to reduce European emissions. Successful implementation of the scheme, along with a demonstration of minimal cost and competitiveness effects, will fortify efforts within the European Union (and possibly abroad) to guarantee a long-term continuation of the current arrangements.

Still, people compare EUETS with the European Stability and Growth Pact, which was negotiated in 1997 by members of the economic and monetary union (the pact included adoption of the euro) within the European Union. Among other things, the pact limits a nation's annual budget deficit to lower than 3 percent of GDP, and a public debt lower than 60 percent of GDP. Several member states have flouted these rules (France and Germany, in particular) but faced little punishment from the European Commission.

Regarding EUETS, the argument goes something like this: If France and Germany could not adhere to their commitment to a fundamental economic component of European monetary union, what is to keep them from doing the same thing with EUETS? Actually, several things, first, the attempt to reduce global GHG emissions does not derive from an arbitrary line drawn in the macro-economic sand—the member states accept the fundamental proposition in the Kyoto Protocol about climate change and its scientific underpinnings. The recent pronouncement by the scientific academies of the G8 nations (together with those of China, Brazil, and India) regarding the validity of the problem, highlights the necessity for addressing it.

There are economic incentives, as well. One way for member states to weaken the scheme would be to issue more allowances. But, since each state has passed national legislation creating the allowances, such action would damage the "property rights" of the various plant operators. Moreover, member states could also be held liable to compensate for economic losses associated with a collapsed market.

And, after 2012 (under the Kyoto Protocol), member states in noncompliance will have to retire allowances corresponding to any excess over their target level, plus an additional 30 percent. (It may be that a larger international trading scheme may not come to fruition, thereby making Kyoto compliance measures after 2012 problematic. But most observers expect such a scheme to be established.) The strength of the legislation agreed to by European governments is therefore a more onerous constraint on their behavior than the debt limits implied by the Stability and Growth Pact. In short, countries should not fail to fulfil their obligations under the EUETS directive. But, because an international emissions trading scheme inevitably creates competitive effects on industries covered by it, any scheme will likely result in protectionist measures. Therefore, the commitment of individual countries, the strength of legislation, and the effectiveness of noncompliance procedures will all be important determinants of its eventual success.

National Plans

For Phase I of EUETS, the member states have set targets, defined right down to the plant level for 2007, in National Allocation Plans (NAPs). (Nations must submit Phase II allocations plans for approval by the end of June in 2006.) In Phase I, each plant will know, from the moment of its allocation, precisely how much it may emit during the period 2005–07. If it needs to emit more than allocated, the company must purchase the right to do so from other installations within the scheme, or from CDM projects in developing countries. The carbon-intensity of an installation within the European Union is now an asset or a liability that can be monetized. It is equal to the value of allowances that must be bought to offset . . . emissions above the allocated level.

The level of allocation, also, defines the scale of potential asset or liability. EUETS prevents member states from auctioning more than 5 percent of EUAs in Phase I and 10 percent in Phase II. Allowances have so far been grandfathered to installations based on historical projections and the "business as usual" case, with a little bit subtracted. It is possible that the allocation methodology will be revised in Phase II to allow for "benchmarking," which defines "standard" levels of emissions for different sectors based on both historical trends and newly available technologies. The benchmark provides the level of emissions the regulator thinks [is] necessary (or appropriate) for a sector or installation.

Many debate whether allocation or auction of allowances is most efficient in a new market. Some see allocations as a market-creation strategy that has a proven track record in other cap-and-trade regimes; and auctions as a way to make a company pay twice for compliance (that is, for compliance technology and the allowance). On the other hand, many consider grandfathering and benchmarking as attempts to "predict" the market, with government allocating allowances where it thinks they are most needed. Historical and benchmarked emissions may not reflect technological feasibility but rather the amount of effort invested in reducing emissions from a particular sector. Allocating rather than auctioning allowances may therefore impose minimal requirements on inefficient (or high-emissions-intensity) economic sectors while punishing efficient ones.

Perhaps changes will take place in the post-2012, Phase III EUETS, but it will likely depend on the structure of the post-2012 international trading scheme.

Another issue is the harmonization of NAPs across the European Union. Member states have the flexibility to implement several aspects of the EUETS Directive in their own ways. Clearly this is important, due to different conditions in different nations. A country with low capacity margin, for example, may wish to allocate more allowances to its power sector (and less elsewhere) than another country, in order to protect domestic consumers against high electricity prices.

Decisions to include or exclude some plants (based on the definition of "small" and "combustion"), and the treatment of new entrants to the scheme during 2005–07, have also varied among states. Whether this is related to economics or simply politics (probably both), such decisions will have an impact on domestic competitiveness and may therefore put some companies at a disadvantage. But other issues, such as the scope of the scheme (relating both to gases—only CO_2 thus far—and sectors—currently excluding transportation), have fallen evenly across member states. Harmonization across the European Union is necessary, because no country wishes to move first and risk being left alone to the detriment of its domestic industry. Because such unanimity is difficult to achieve, no substantial changes appear likely before 2012 (with the possible exception of the inclusion of the aviation sector).

Like aviation, many sectors (transportation, most significantly) that contribute large amounts of GHGs are not included in EUETS. Still, these areas will face measures to reduce emissions in line with the overall national targets. The Directive on Renewable Transport Fuels, for example, obliges member states to devise plans to meet (nonbinding) targets to replace a proportion of gasoline and diesel with ethanol and biodiesel. Other measures include a directive on energy performance of buildings; and a directive that sets targets for the reduction of biodegradable waste sent to landfill. None of these measures has the strength of EUETS, but for all these sectors, there are efforts to create markets to provide reduction incentives.

Business as Usual—Except Power

Let's look at the "business-as-usual" (BAU) allocations. In total they have equaled roughly 97 percent of covered entities projected emissions in a BAU scenario. That makes a shortfall of 200 million tons (plus or minus 50 million tons) of CO_2 during Phase I. The sector that has taken the biggest hit is the power sector. In the United Kingdom, powerplants have received, on average, 72 percent of reference emissions. (These are the emissions upon which allocations are based. The "reference" is the average of the five highest annual emissions totals from 1998–2003.)

For example, AES Kilroot, a coal-fired power station in Northern Ireland with 520 megawatts of capacity, received allowances corresponding to 2.05 million tons of CO_2 emissions per year during Phase I. This is 25 percent below Kilroot's 2.71 million tons of actual emissions in 2003. In comparison, cement manufacturers received 96.5 percent of reference emissions, while chemicals plants received 88.0 percent of theirs. Moreover, a company loses remaining allocations if a plant is closed during the commitment period, a fact that serves to ensure that aging capacity remains available, even if does not operate for much of that time.

All this means that operating costs for coal plants have risen sufficiently to induce coal generators to switch from operating at their traditional baseload or midpeak load to move to the margin, displacing existing marginal gas capacity.

From that method of abatement, approximately 120 million EUAs per year are available within EUETS. In fact, the "switch" from coal to gas is the cheapest form of abatement. Hence the cost of the coal-gas switch drives the cost of EUAs. And what drives the cost of the coal-gas switch? The relative cost of coal and gas within the European Union.

Many analysts have been surprised by the levels EUA prices have reached. Indeed, our own estimates were of the range €5–10 ($6–12) per ton of CO_2 for Phase I and €10–15 ($12–18) for Phase II. But this was based on costs of coal and natural gas at the time, which were in line with the long-run marginal cost of production. Since then gas prices have doubled. Our models show that current prices (as of July) imply a price of roughly €20–25 ($24–30) per ton of CO_2. In both cases, the coal-gas differential provides the best estimate of allowance prices in EUETS. Volumes have reached an all-time high, with 1 million tons of CO_2 being traded per day, on average. But liquidity is still low, given that less than half of all installations have actually received their allowances. A cold winter and hot, dry summer have also helped to drive prices upward.

There should also be a change in allowance prices between Phases I and II because of the tighter allocations expected in the latter. All but two member states restrict the banking of allowances from one period to the other (though EUETS allows banking of CDM credits). Banking, however, would have reduced the volatility in allowance prices by placing an option value on Phase I allowances. It would also have rewarded early abatement in the first phase. However, governments were reluctant to permit banking because they worried it would result in unacceptably high allowance prices during Phase I and give states less control over Phase II allocations.

The Next Phase and the United Nations

As June 30, 2006, approaches, the focus turns to Phase II NAPs. Broadly speaking, if the European Union wants to reach the Kyoto targets, allocations must be far stricter in this phase than the previous one. Current targets put EU emissions at 2 percent below their 1990 levels by the end of 2007; by 2010, this will need to be 8 percent below, requiring roughly 100 million tons of abatement each year (compared to 70 million tons from 2005–07). As for the NAPs, it is unlikely that the member states will add other gases to the trading list or include other sectors in EUETS. The European Commission recently announced that it will not seek to make any changes to the scheme until 2012. While it is possible for governments to agree to changes without Commission involvement, the time this would normally take seems prohibitive given the deadline for Phase II NAPs.

Clouding the picture are difficulties with the CDM mechanism and a lack of visibility over the JI mechanism. The CDM Executive Board, a United Nations institution, oversees the CDM process and registers emission reduction projects in developing countries as being able to generate CDM allowances, known as certified emissions reductions, or CERs. But, so far in Phase I, a lack of adequate funding and an overly bureaucratic registration process have seriously affected the volume of authorized projects. Currently, in fact, only 11 projects are capable of generating CERs. Just 60 million CERs are expected by the end of 2007, compared to a total EU shortfall of roughly 200 million. Volumes up to 2012 are very uncertain but may not reach the originally predicted 500 million.

The JI mechanism is uncertain because it depends heavily on the governments of developed countries, which must create the procedures by which a project can claim JI allowances (known as emission reduction units, or ERUs). ERUs cannot be used for compliance in EUETS until 2008, so there has been little movement. Russia, the last Kyoto signatory, recently created the first JI project, although it awaits government approval, procedures for which are not yet in place.

Russia is, in a sense, the OPEC of Kyoto. In addition to allowances at the installation level, the Kyoto Protocol established "assigned amount units" (AAUs) for national governments. One allowance for each ton of CO_2 equivalent corresponding to the total amount of emissions permitted between 2008 and 2012. And Russia has significantly more allowances than required to meet its Kyoto obligations—due to the collapse of the Soviet Union, emissions have dropped since 1990, the reference year for Kyoto targets. With all that so-called extra hot air, Russia and other former Soviet Union states could probably supply the entire demand for allowances in EUETS Phase II. They can't due to Kyoto's supplementarity principle, which will probably require a 50-percent limit on the use of foreign-sourced AAUs. (The principle was included in the protocol at the behest of environmental groups, which sought to encourage abatement in the industrialized world and let developed nations show leadership in "cleaning up their own backyards.") But, just as the Organization of Petroleum Exporting Countries restricts its supply of oil, Russia may restrict its supply of allowances to keep prices high and to maintain a competitive position for a post-2012 system.

Would Governments Limit the Price of Carbon?

But back to fossil fuels. Driving the current high prices of natural gas in the European Union is the soaring cost of oil, which has recently reached historic highs. What if oil prices were to climb even higher? Under these circumstances, allowance prices could reach sufficient levels to prompt coal plants to close in 2007 or perhaps for carbon capture and sequestration to become economical.

One can reasonably expect governments not to allow prices in EUETS to go too high; and prices in excess of €20–30 ($12–36) per ton of CO_2 sustained over the Phase I period could force governments to limit the reductions for coal plants in Phase II. Governments are likely to be unwilling to let plants close when there are decreasing capacity margins across the European Union and a policy objective to maintain diversity in energy supplies. Also, many coal plants have installed or are in the process of installing flue-gas desulphurization equipment (typically costing €45 million, or $54 million) to comply with the EU directive on large combustion plants. Sectors under EUETS that are most exposed to international competitors (such as the aluminum sector) face potentially damaging competitive effects. Recently, for example, the owners of the HAW aluminum mill in Hamburg, Germany, said high EUA prices contributed to the decision to shut the facility. But most important is the political fall-out that would result from high electricity prices when the full costs of carbon are passed through.

To keep plants in operation and electricity prices down, governments might allocate to them sufficient allowances over Phase II and apply the hit in another industry sector. Indeed, governments could avoid EUETS entirely by purchasing CDMs, JIs, and AAUs. There are currently more than 20 European government procurement funds (including investments in World Bank and other multilateral funds) with a total committed capital of over €1 billion—at a final purchase price of €6 per ton of CO_2, this would yield 170 million allowances. The value of such emission reduction purchase agreements actually signed, however, is unknown, given a lack of market data. But is likely to be less than €1 billion.

The fact that this is a policy-driven market means that governments will take whatever action necessary to minimize impacts on domestic industry and consumers—that is, voters. But because European governments have also shown a willingness to use EUETS to achieve their policy goals, it is likely they will allocate few enough allowances to guarantee a minimum price in Phase II (say, €10 per ton), but not too few to make prices spiral out of control.

After Kyoto

And what about post-2012? These discussions continue. At the G8 summit in Scotland last July, the participants agreed to an ongoing dialogue on climate change, as well as on action to develop low-carbon technologies. But there was no progress about binding emission reduction targets outside the Kyoto Protocol. In December 2005, the members of the United Nations Foundation on Climate Change will meet in Montreal. The best estimate is that the "Conference of the Parties" will hold to the status quo and not wrangle over the future course of international policy.

A recent study published by Climate Change Capital suggests that an agreement may be possible that would incorporate the United States and China, India, and Brazil in emission reduction efforts. The study finds that price caps (to limit abatement costs) and flexible targets (such as emissions-intensity targets, linking reductions to the rate of GDP growth) would be attractive to governments concerned about the economic impacts of reducing GHG emissions. Other mechanisms that could prompt agreement include positively-binding targets on developing countries and an expanded CDM. The positively-binding target in an international emissions trading scheme would reward over-achievement of a target with tradable credits, but would not impose a penalty for under-achievement. The expanded CDM would let companies in developed countries buy a greater number of less expensive credits generated in developing countries, where abatement costs are lower.

Of course, if nations reach an international agreement beyond the Kyoto Protocol, European efforts to reduce GHG emissions will not occur alone. To many, the signs for wider participation are favorable. Recent developments in the United States, for example, seem to make an enhancement of its emissions trading scheme a possibility in the future. Whatever the outcome, the political climate in Europe is currently widely supportive of EUETS; for the most part, skepticism exists not about scientific basis but about competitiveness with nonparticipating countries. In the main, the carbon market in Europe is here to stay.

Brian Tokar  **NO**

Trading Away the Earth: Pollution Credits and the Perils of "Free Market Environmentalism"

The Republican takeover of Congress has unleashed an unprecedented assault on all forms of environmental regulation. From the Endangered Species Act to the Clean Water Act and the Superfund for toxic waste cleanup, laws that may need to be strengthened and expanded to meet the environmental challenges of the next century are instead being targeted for complete evisceration.

For some activists, this is a time to renew the grassroots focus of environmental activism, even to adopt a more aggressively anti-corporate approach that exposes the political and ideological agendas underlying the current backlash. But for many, the current impasse suggests that the movement must adapt to the dominant ideological currents of the time. Some environmentalists have thus shifted their focus toward voluntary programs, economic incentives and the mechanisms of the "free market" as means to advance the cause of environmental protection. Among the most controversial, and widespread, of these proposals are tradeable credits for the right to emit pollutants. These became enshrined in national legislation in 1990 with President George Bush's amendments to the 1970 Clean Air Act.

Even in 1990, "free market environmentalism" was not a new phenomenon. In the closing years of the 1980s, an odd alliance had developed among corporate public relations departments, conservative think tanks such as the American Enterprise Institute, Bill Clinton's Democratic Leadership Council (DLC), and mainstream environmental groups such as the Environmental Defense Fund. The market-oriented environmental policies promoted by this eclectic coalition have received little public attention, but have nonetheless significantly influenced debates over national policy.

Glossy catalogs of "environmental products," television commercials featuring environmental themes, and high profile initiatives to give corporate officials a "greener" image are the hallmarks of corporate environmentalism in the 1990s. But the new market environmentalism goes much further than these showcase efforts. It represents a wholesale effort

From *Dollars & Sense*, March/April 1996, pp. 24–29. Reprinted by permission of Dollars & Sense, a progressive economics magazine. www.dollarsandsense.org.

to recast environmental protection based on a model of commercial transactions within the marketplace. "A new environmentalism has emerged," writes economist Robert Stavins, who has been associated with both the Environmental Defense Fund and the DLC's Progressive Policy Institute, "that embraces . . . market-oriented environmental protection policies."

Today, aided by the anti-regulatory climate in Congress, market schemes such as trading pollution credits are granting corporations new ways to circumvent environmental concerns, even as the same firms try to pose as champions of the environment. While tradeable credits are sometimes presented as a solution to environmental problems, in reality they do nothing to reduce pollution—at best they help businesses reduce the costs of complying with limits on toxic emissions. Ultimately, such schemes abdicate control over critical environmental decisions to the very same corporations that are responsible for the greatest environmental abuses.

How It Works, and Doesn't

A close look at the scheme for nationwide emissions trading reveals a particular cleverness; for true believers in the invisible hand of the market, it may seem positively ingenious. Here is how it works: The 1990 Clean Air Act amendments were designed to halt the spread of acid rain, which has threatened lakes, rivers and forests across the country. The amendments required a reduction in the total sulfur dioxide emissions from fossil fuel burning power plants, from 19 to just under 9 million tons per year by the year 2000. These facilities were targeted as the largest contributors to acid rain, and participation by other industries remains optional. To achieve this relatively modest goal for pollution reduction, utilities were granted transferable allowances to emit sulfur dioxide in proportion to their current emissions. For the first time, the ability of companies to buy and sell the "right" to pollute was enshrined in U.S. law.

Any facility that continued to pollute more than its allocated amount (roughly half of its 1990 rate) would then have to buy allowances from someone who is polluting less. The 110 most polluting facilities (mostly coal burners) were given five years to comply, while all the others would have until the year 2000. Emissions allowances were expected to begin selling for around $500 per ton of sulfur dioxide, and have a theoretical ceiling of $2000 per ton, which is the legal penalty for violating the new rules. Companies that could reduce emissions for less than their credits are worth would be able to sell them at a profit, while those that lag behind would have to keep buying credits at a steadily rising price. For example, before pollution trading, every company had to comply with environmental regulations, even if it cost one firm twice as much as another to do so. Under the new system, a firm could instead choose to exceed the mandated levels, purchasing credits from the second firm instead of implementing costly controls. This exchange would save money, but in principle yield the same overall level of pollution as if both companies had complied equally. Thus, it is argued, market forces will assure that the most cost-effective means of reducing acid rain will be implemented first, saving the economy billions of dollars in "excess" pollution control costs.

Defenders of the Bush plan claimed that the ability to profit from pollution credits would encourage companies to invest more in new environmental technologies than before. Innovation in environmental technology, they argued, was being stifled by regulations mandating specific pollution control methods. With the added flexibility of tradeable credits, companies could postpone costly controls—through the purchase of some other company's credits—until new technologies became available. Proponents argued that, as pollution standards are tightened over time, the credits would become more valuable and their owners could reap large profits while fighting pollution.

Yet the program also included many pages of rules for extensions and substitutions. The plan eliminated requirements for backup systems on smokestack scrubbers, and then eased the rules for estimating how much pollution is emitted when monitoring systems fail. With reduced emissions now a marketable commodity, the range of possible abuses may grow considerably, as utilities will have a direct financial incentive to manipulate reporting of their emissions to improve their position in the pollution credits market.

Once the EPA actually began auctioning pollution credits in 1993, it became clear that virtually nothing was going according to their projections. The first pollution credits sold for between $122 and $310, significantly less than the agency's estimated minimum price, and by 1995, bids at the EPA's annual auction of sulfur dioxide allowances averaged around $130 per ton of emissions. As an artificial mechanism superimposed on existing regulatory structures, emissions allowances have failed to reflect the true cost of pollution controls. So, as the value of the credits has fallen, it has become increasingly attractive to buy credits rather than invest in pollution controls. And, in problem areas air quality can continue to decline, as companies in some parts of the country simply buy their way out of pollution reductions.

At least one company has tried to cash in on the confusion by assembling packages of "multi-year streams of pollution rights" specifically designed to defer or supplant purchases of new pollution control technologies. "What a scrubber really is, is a decision to buy a 30-year stream of allowances," John B. Henry of Clean Air Capital Markets told the *New York Times,* with impeccable financial logic. "If the price of allowances declines in future years," paraphrased the *Times,* "the scrubber would look like a bad buy."

Where pollution credits have been traded between companies, the results have often run counter to the program's stated intentions. One of the first highly publicized deals was a sale of credits by the Long Island Lighting Company to an unidentified company located in the Midwest, where much of the pollution that causes acid rain originates. This raised concerns that places suffering from the effects of acid rain were shifting "pollution rights" to the very region it was coming from. One of the first companies to bid for additional credits, the Illinois Power Company, canceled construction of a $350 million scrubber system in the city of Decatur, Illinois. "Our compliance plan is based almost totally on purchase of credits," an Illinois Power spokesperson told the *Wall Street Journal*. The comparison with more traditional forms of commodity trading came full circle in 1991, when the government announced that the entire system for trading and auctioning emissions allowances would be administered by the Chicago Board of Trade, long famous for its ever-frantic markets in everything from grain futures and pork bellies to foreign currencies.

Some companies have chosen not to engage in trading pollution credits, proceeding with pollution control projects, such as the installation of new scrubbers, that were planned before the credits became available. Others have switched to low-sulfur coal and increased their use of natural gas. If the 1990 Clean Air Act amendments are to be credited for any overall improvement in the air quality, it is clearly the result of these efforts and not the market in tradeable allowances.

Yet while some firms opt not to purchase the credits, others, most notably North Carolina-based Duke Power, are aggressively buying allowances. At the 1995 EPA auction, Duke Power alone bought 35% of the short-term "spot" allowances for sulfur dioxide emissions, and 60% of the long-term allowances redeemable in the years 2001 and 2002. Seven companies, including five utilities and two brokerage firms, bought 97% of the short-term allowances that were auctioned in 1995, and 92% of the longer-term allowances, which are redeemable in 2001 and 2002. This gives these companies significant leverage over the future shape of the allowances market.

The remaining credits were purchased by a wide variety of people and organizations, including some who sincerely wished to take pollution allowances out of circulation. Students at several law schools raised hundreds of dollars, and a group at the Glens Falls Middle School on Long Island raised $3,171 to purchase 21 allowances, equivalent to 21 tons of sulfur dioxide emissions over the course of a year. Unfortunately, this represented less than a tenth of one percent of the allowances auctioned off in 1995.

Some of these trends were predicted at the outset. "With a tradeable permit system, technological improvement will normally result in lower control costs and falling permit prices, rather than declining emissions levels," wrote Robert Stavins and Brad Whitehead (a Cleveland-based management consultant with ties to the Rockefeller Foundation) in a 1992 policy paper published by the Progressive Policy Institute. Despite their belief that market-based environmental policies "lead automatically to the cost-effective allocation of the pollution control burden among firms," they are quite willing to concede that a tradeable permit system will not in itself reduce pollution. As the actual pollution levels still need to be set by some form of regulatory mandate, the market in tradeable allowances merely gives some companies greater leverage over how pollution standards are to be implemented.

Without admitting the underlying irrationality of a futures market in pollution, Stavins and Whitehead do acknowledge (albeit in a footnote to an Appendix) that the system can quite easily be compromised by large companies' "strategic behavior." Control of 10% of the market, they suggest, might be enough to allow firms to engage in "price-setting behavior," a goal apparently sought by companies such as Duke Power. To the rest of us, it should be clear that if pollution credits are like any other commodity that can be bought, sold and traded, then the largest "players" will have substantial control over the entire "game." Emissions trading becomes yet another way to assure that large corporate interests will remain free to threaten public health and ecological survival in their unchallenged pursuit of profit.

Trading the Future

Mainstream groups like the Environmental Defense Fund (EDF) continue to throw their full support behind the trading of emissions allowances, including the establishment of a futures market in Chicago. EDF senior economist Daniel Dudek described the trading of acid rain emissions as a "scale model" for a much more ambitious plan to trade emissions of carbon dioxide and other gases responsible for global warming. This plan was unveiled shortly after the passage of the 1990 Clean Air Act amendments, and was endorsed by then-Senator Al Gore as a way to "rationalize investments" in alternatives to carbon dioxide-producing activities.

International emissions trading gained further support via a U.N. Conference on Trade and Development study issued in 1992. The report was coauthored by Kidder and Peabody executive and Chicago Board of Trade director Richard Sandor, who told the *Wall Street Journal,* "Air and water are simply no longer the 'free goods' that economists once assumed. They must be redefined as property rights so that they can be efficiently allocated."

Radical ecologists have long decried the inherent tendency of capitalism to turn everything into a commodity; here we have a rare instance in which the system fully reveals its intentions. There is little doubt that an international market in "pollution rights" would widen existing inequalities among nations. Even within the United States, a single large investor in pollution credits would be able to control the future development of many different industries. Expanded to an international scale, the potential for unaccountable manipulation of industrial policy by a few corporations would easily compound the disruptions already caused by often reckless international traders in stocks, bonds and currencies.

However, as long as public regulation of industry remains under attack, tradeable credits and other such schemes will continue to be promoted as market-savvy alternatives. Along with an acceptance of pollution as "a by-product of modern civilization that can be regulated and reduced, but not eliminated," to quote another Progressive Policy Institute paper, self-proclaimed environmentalists will call for an end to "widespread antagonism toward corporations and a suspicion that anything supported by business was bad for the environment." Market solutions are offered as the only alternative to the "inefficient," "centralized," "command-and-control" regulations of the past, in language closely mirroring the rhetoric of Cold War anti-communism.

While specific technology-based standards can be criticized as inflexible and sometimes even archaic, critics choose to forget that in many cases, they were instituted by Congress as a safeguard against the widespread abuses of the Reagan-era EPA. During the Reagan years, "flexible" regulations opened the door to widely criticized—and often illegal—bending of the rules for the benefit of politically favored corporations, leading to the resignation of EPA administrator Anne Gorsuch Burford and a brief jail sentence for one of her more vocal legal assistants.

The anti-regulatory fervor of the present Congress is bringing a variety of other market-oriented proposals to the fore. Some are genuinely offered to further environmental protection, while others are far more cynical attempts to replace public regulations with virtual blank checks for polluters. Some have proposed a direct charge for pollution, modeled after the comprehensive pollution taxes that have proved popular in Western Europe. Writers as diverse as Supreme Court Justice Stephen Breyer, American Enterprise Institute economist Robert Hahn and environmental business guru Paul Hawken have defended pollution taxes as an ideal market-oriented approach to controlling pollution. Indeed, unlike tradeable credits, taxes might help reduce pollution beyond regulatory levels, as they encourage firms to control emissions as much as possible. With credits, there is no reduction in pollution below the threshold established in legislation. (If many companies were to opt for substantial new emissions controls, the market would soon be glutted and the allowances would rapidly become valueless.) And taxes would work best if combined with vigilant grassroots activism that makes industries accountable to the communities in which they operate. However, given the rapid dismissal of Bill Clinton's early plan for an energy tax, it is most likely that any pollution tax proposal would be immediately dismissed by Congressional ideologues as an outrageous new government intervention into the marketplace.

Air pollution is not the only environmental problem that free marketeers are proposing to solve with the invisible hand. Pro-development interests in Congress have floated various schemes to replace the Endangered Species Act with a system of voluntary incentives, conservation easements and other schemes through which landowners would be compensated by the government to protect critical habitat. While these proposals are being debated in Congress, the Clinton administration has quietly changed the rules for administering the Act in a manner that encourages voluntary compliance and offers some of the very same loopholes that anti-environmental advocates have sought. This, too, is being offered in the name of cooperation and "market environmentalism."

Debates over the management of publicly-owned lands have inspired far more outlandish "free market" schemes. "Nearly all environmental problems are rooted in society's failure to adequately define property rights for some resource," economist Randal O'Toole has written, suggesting a need for "property rights for owls and salmon" developed to "protect them from pollution." O'Toole initially gained the attention of environmentalists in the Pacific Northwest for his detailed studies of the inequities of the U.S. Forest Service's long-term subsidy programs for logging on public lands. Now he has proposed dividing the National Forest system into individual units, each governed by its users and operated on a for-profit basis, with a portion of user fees allocated for such needs as the protection of biological diversity. Environmental values, from clean water to recreation to scenic views, should simply be allocated their proper value in the marketplace, it is argued, and allowed to out-compete unsustainable resource extraction. Other market advocates have suggested far more sweeping transfers of federal lands to the states, an idea seen by many in the West as a first step toward complete privatization.

Market enthusiasts like O'Toole repeatedly overlook the fact that ecological values are far more subjective than the market value of timber and minerals removed from public lands. Efforts to quantify these values are based on various sociological methods, market analysis and psychological studies. People are asked how much they would pay to protect a resource, or how much money they would accept to live without it, and their answers are compared with the prices of everything from wilderness expeditions to vacation homes. Results vary widely depending on how questions are asked, how knowledgeable respondents are, and what assumptions are made in the analysis. Environmentalists are rightfully appalled by such efforts as a recent Resources for the Future study designed to calculate the value of human lives lost due to future toxic exposures. Outlandish absurdities like property rights for owls arouse similar skepticism.

The proliferation of such proposals—and their increasing credibility in Washington—suggest the need for a renewed debate over the relationship between ecological values and those of the free market. For many environmental economists, the processes of capitalism, with a little fine tuning, can be made to serve the needs of environmental protection. For many activists, however, there is a fundamental contradiction between the interconnected nature of ecological processes and an economic system which not only reduces everything to isolated commodities, but seeks to manipulate those commodities to further the single, immutable goal of maximizing individual gain. An ecological economy may need to more closely mirror natural processes in their stability, diversity, long time frame, and the prevalence of cooperative, symbiotic interactions over the more extreme forms of competition that thoroughly dominate today's economy. Ultimately, communities of people need to reestablish social control over economic markets and relationships, restoring an economy which, rather than being seen as the engine of social progress, is instead, in the words of economic historian Karl Polanyi, entirely "submerged in social relationships."

Whatever economic model one proposes for the long-term future, it is clear that the current phase of corporate consolidation is threatening the integrity of the earth's living ecosystems—and communities of people who depend on those ecosystems—as never before. There is little room for consideration of ecological integrity in a global economy where a few ambitious currency traders can trigger the collapse of a nation's currency, its food supply, or a centuries-old forest ecosystem before anyone can even begin to discuss the consequences. In this kind of world, replacing our society's meager attempts to restrain and regulate corporate excesses with market mechanisms can only further the degradation of the natural world and threaten the health and well-being of all the earth's inhabitants.

POSTSCRIPT

Can Carbon Trading Help Control Carbon Emissions?

Does carbon trading give major corporate polluters too much power to control and manipulate the market for emissions credits? This is one of the key issues that continues to inspire developing countries to withhold their endorsements of the greenhouse gas emissions trading provisions of the Kyoto Protocol. The evidence that Tokar cites, which is primarily based on short-term experience with trading in sulfur dioxide pollution credits, does not appear to fully justify the broad generalizations he makes about the inherent perils of market-based regulatory plans. Recent assessments of the Acid Rain Program by the EPA and such organizations as the Environmental Defense Fund are more positive. So is the corporate world: In "Economic Man, Cleaner Planet," *The Economist* (September 29, 2001), it is asserted that economic incentives have proved very useful and that "market forces are only just beginning to make inroads into green policy-making." T. H. Tietenberg, *Emissions Trading: Principles and Practice,* 2nd ed. (RFF Press, 2006), notes that emissions trading has a definite niche in pollution control policies. On the other hand, Ruth Greenspan Bell, "The Kyoto Placebo, " *Issues in Science and Technology* (Winter 2006), notes that "Though heavily promoted by the World Bank, U.S.-style environmental trading has yet to be tested on a global scale and has never been successfully deployed on a national level in the developing world." There is more to be gained by helping developing nations gain regulatory skills ("What to Do about Climate Change," *Foreign Affairs,* May/June 2006).

The position of those who are ideologically opposed to pollution rights is concisely stated in Michael J. Sandel's op-ed piece, "It's Immoral to Buy the Right to Pollute," *The New York Times* (December 15, 1997). In "Selling Air Pollution," *Reason* (May 1996), Brian Doherty supports the concept of pollution rights trading but argues that the kind of emission cap imposed in the case of sulfur dioxide is an inappropriate constraint on what he believes should be a completely free-market program. Richard A. Kerr, in "Acid Rain Control: Success on the Cheap," *Science* (November 6, 1998), contends that emissions trading has greatly reduced acid rain and that the annual cost has been about a tenth of the $10 billion initially forecast. According to Barry D. Solomon and Russell Lee, "Emission Trading Systems and Environmental Justice," *Environment* (October 2000), "a significant part of the opposition to emissions trading programs is a perception that they do little to reduce environmental injustice and can even make it worse."

The threat of global warming from continuing emissions of greenhouse gases has prompted the extension of emissions trading to carbon dioxide. Europe is implementing its Greenhouse Gas Emissions Trading Scheme, although so far its effectiveness is in doubt; Marianne Lavelle, "The Carbon Market Has a Dirty Little Secret," *U.S. News and World Report* (May 14, 2007), reports that in Europe the value of tradable emissions allowances has fallen so low, partly because too many allowances were issued, that it has become cheaper to burn more fossil fuel and emit more carbon than to burn and emit less. Future trading schemes will need to be designed to avoid the problem, and there are several bills before Congress that address the issue (see "Support Grows for Capping and Trading Carbon Emissions," *Issues in Science and Technology,* Summer 2007). David G. Victor and Danny Cullenward, "Making Carbon Markets Work," *Scientific American* (December 2007), argue that what is needed is to combine a trading program with limits on emissions and careful management. Bill McKibben, "The Greenback Effect," *Mother Jones* (May/June 2008), agrees, noting that though markets may not be perfect, when they work, they work fast.

Meanwhile, there is great interest in what is known as "carbon offsets," by which corporations, governments, and even individuals compensate for carbon dioxide emissions by investing in activities that remove carbon dioxide from the air or reduce emissions from a different source. See Anja Kollmuss, "Carbon Offsets 101," *World Watch* (July/August 2007). On the other hand, Kevin Smith, "Offsetting Democracy," *Resurgence Magazine* (March/April 2008), argues that carbon trading and offsets distract from the need to move away from free-market dogma, the false economy of supposed quick fixes, and the short-term self-interest of big business.

ISSUE 10

Is Carbon Capture Technology Ready to Limit Carbon Emissions?

YES: David G. Hawkins, from "Carbon Capture and Sequestration," Testimony before the Committee on House Energy and Commerce, Subcommittee on Energy and Air Quality (March 6, 2007)

NO: Charles W. Schmidt, from "Carbon Capture & Storage: Blue-Sky Technology or Just Blowing Smoke?" *Environmental Health Perspectives* (November 2007)

ISSUE SUMMARY

YES: David G. Hawkins, director of the Climate Center of the Natural Resources Defense Council, argues that we know enough to implement large-scale carbon capture and sequestration for new coal plants. The technology is ready to do so safely and effectively.

NO: Charles W. Schmidt argues that the technology is not yet technically and financially feasible, research is stuck in low gear, and the political commitment to reducing carbon emissions is lacking.

It is now well established that burning fossil fuels is a major contributor to global warming, and thus a hazard to the future well-being of human beings and ecosystems around the world. The reason lies in the release of carbon dioxide, a major "greenhouse gas." It follows logically that if we reduce the amount of carbon dioxide we release to the atmosphere, we must prevent or ease global warming. Such a reduction would of course follow if we shifted away from fossil fuels as an energy source. Another option is to capture the carbon dioxide before it reaches the atmosphere and put it somewhere else.

The question is: Where? Lal Rattan, "Carbon Sequestration," *Philosophical Transactions: Biological Sciences* (February 2008), describes a number of techniques and notes that all are expensive and have leakage risks. One proposal is that supplying nutrients to ocean waters could stimulate the growth of algae, which removes carbon dioxide from the air; when the algae die, the carbon should settle to the ocean floor. The few experiments that have been done so far indicate that though fertilization does in fact stimulate algae growth, carbon does not always settle deep enough to keep it out of the air for long. The experiments also fail to say whether the procedure would damage marine ecosystems. See Eli Kintisch, "Should Oceanographers Pump Iron?" *Science* (November 30, 2007), and Sandra Upson, "Algae Bloom Climate-Change Scheme Doomed," *IEEE Spectrum* (January 2008). Another proposal is that carbon dioxide be concentrated from power plant exhaust streams, liquefied, and pumped to the deep ocean, where it would remain for thousands of years. Concern that that storage time is not long enough helped shift most attention to underground storage. Carbon dioxide, in either gas or liquid form, can be pumped into porous rock layers deep beneath the surface. Such layers are accessible in the form of depleted oil deposits, and in fact carbon dioxide injection can be used to force residual oil out of the deposits. See Robert H. Sokolow, "Can We Bury Global Warming?" *Scientific American* (July 2005), and Valerie Brown, "A Climate Change Solution?" *High Country News* (September 3, 2007). Jennie C. Stephens and Bob Van Der Zwann, "The Case for Carbon Capture and Storage," *Issues in Science and Technology* (Fall 2005), note that the technology exists but that industry lacks incentives to implement it; such incentives could be supplied if the federal government established limits for carbon emissions. Additional research is also needed to determine the long-term stability of carbon storage.

In the following selections, David G. Hawkins, director of the Climate Center of the Natural Resources Defense Council, argues that we know enough to implement large-scale carbon capture and sequestration for new coal plants. The technology is ready to do so safely and effectively. Charles W. Schmidt argues that the technology is not yet technically and financially feasible, research is stuck in low gear, and the political commitment to reducing carbon emissions is lacking. In addition, it has not been shown that carbon dioxide stored in underground reservoirs will stay in place indefinitely, and it has not been decided who will monitor such storage and take responsibility if it fails.

YES

David G. Hawkins

Carbon Capture and Sequestration

Today, the U.S. and other developed nations around the world run their economies largely with industrial sources powered by fossil fuel and those sources release billions of tons of carbon dioxide (CO_2) into the atmosphere every year. There is national and global interest today in capturing that CO_2 for disposal or sequestration to prevent its release to the atmosphere. To distinguish this industrial capture system from removal of atmospheric CO_2 by soils and vegetation, I will refer to the industrial system as carbon capture and disposal or CCD.

The interest in CCD stems from a few basic facts. We now recognize that CO_2 emissions from use of fossil fuel result in increased atmospheric concentrations of CO_2, which along with other so-called greenhouse gases, trap heat, leading to an increase in temperatures, regionally and globally. These increased temperatures alter the energy balance of the planet and thus our climate, which is simply nature's way of managing energy flows. Documented changes in climate today along with those forecasted for the next decades, are predicted to inflict large and growing damage to human health, economic well-being, and natural ecosystems.

Coal is the most abundant fossil fuel and is distributed broadly across the world. It has fueled the rise of industrial economies in Europe and the U.S. in the past two centuries and is fueling the rise of Asian economies today. Because of its abundance, coal is cheap and that makes it attractive to use in large quantities if we ignore the harm it causes. However, per unit of energy delivered, coal today is a bigger global warming polluter than any other fuel: double that of natural gas; 50 per cent more than oil; and, of course, enormously more polluting than renewable energy, energy efficiency, and, more controversially, nuclear power. To reduce coal's contribution to global warming, we must deploy and improve systems that will keep the carbon in coal out of the atmosphere, specifically systems that capture carbon dioxide (CO_2) from coal-fired power plants and other industrial sources for safe and effective disposal in geologic formations. . . .

The Need for CCD

Turning to CCD, my organization supports rapid deployment of such capture and disposal systems for sources using coal. Such support is not a statement

From U.S. House of Representatives Committee on House Energy and Commerce by David G. Hawkins, (March 6, 2007).

about how dependent the U.S. or the world should be on coal and for how long. Any significant additional use of coal that vents its CO_2 to the air is fundamentally in conflict with the need to keep atmospheric concentrations of CO_2 from rising to levels that will produce dangerous disruption of the climate system. Given that an immediate world-wide halt to coal use is not plausible, analysts and advocates with a broad range of views on coal's role should be able to agree that, if it is safe and effective, CCD should be rapidly deployed to minimize CO_2 emissions from the coal that we do use.

Today coal use and climate protection are on a collision course. Without rapid deployment of CCD systems, that collision will occur quickly and with spectacularly bad results. The very attribute of coal that has made it so attractive—its abundance—magnifies the problem we face and requires us to act now, not a decade from now. Until now, coal's abundance has been an economic boon. But today, coal's abundance, absent corrective action, is more bane than boon.

Since the dawn of the industrial age, human use of coal has released about 150 billion metric tons of carbon into the atmosphere—about half the total carbon emissions due to fossil fuel use in human history. But that contribution is the tip of the carbon iceberg. Another 4 *trillion* metric tons of carbon are contained in the remaining global coal resources. That is a carbon pool nearly seven times greater than the amount in our pre-industrial atmosphere. Using that coal without capturing and disposing of its carbon means a climate catastrophe. And the die is being cast for that catastrophe today, not decades from now. Decisions being made today in corporate board rooms, government ministries, and congressional hearing rooms are determining how the next coal-fired power plants will be designed and operated. Power plant investments are enormous in scale, more than $1 billion per plant, and plants built today will operate for 60 years or more. The International Energy Agency (IEA) forecasts that more than $5 trillion will be spent globally on new power plants in the next 25 years. Under IEA's forecasts, over 1800 gigawatts (GW) of new coal plants will be built between now and 2030—capacity equivalent to 3000 large coal plants, or an average of ten new coal plants every month for the next quarter century. This new capacity amounts to 1.5 times the total of all the coal plants operating in the world today.

The astounding fact is that under IEA's forecast, 7 out of every 10 coal plants that will be operating in 2030 don't exist today. That fact presents a huge opportunity—many of these coal plants will not need to be built if we invest more in efficiency; additional numbers of these coal plants can be replaced with clean, renewable alternative power sources; and for the remainder, we can build them to capture their CO_2, instead of building them the way our grandfathers built them.

If we decide to do it, the world could build and operate new coal plants so that their CO_2 is returned to the ground rather than polluting the atmosphere. But we are losing that opportunity with every month of delay—10 coal plants were built the old-fashioned way last month somewhere in the world and 10 more old-style plants will be built this month, and the next and the next. Worse still, with current policies in place, none of the 3000 new plants projected by IEA are likely to capture their CO_2.

Each new coal plant that is built carries with it a huge stream of CO_2 emissions that will likely flow for the life of the plant—60 years or more. Suggestions that such plants might be equipped with CO_2 capture devices later in life might come true but there is little reason to count on it. As I will discuss further in a moment, while commercial technologies exist for pre-combustion capture from gasification-based power plants, most new plants are not using gasification designs and the few that are, are not incorporating capture systems. Installing capture equipment at these new plants after the fact is implausible for traditional coal plant designs and expensive for gasification processes.

If all 3000 of the next wave of coal plants are built with no CO_2 controls, their lifetime emissions will impose an enormous pollution lien on our children and grandchildren. Over a projected 60-year life these plants would likely emit 750 billion tons of CO_2, a total, from just 25 years of investment decisions, that is 30% greater than the total CO_2 emissions from all previous human use of coal. Once emitted, this CO_2 pollution load remains in the atmosphere for centuries. Half of the CO_2 emitted during World War I remains in the atmosphere today. In short, we face an onrushing train of new coal plants with impacts that must be diverted without delay. What can the U.S. do to help? The U.S. is forecasted to build nearly 300 of these coal plants, according to reports and forecasts published by the U.S. EIA. By taking action ourselves, we can speed the deployment of CO_2 capture here at home and set an example of leadership. That leadership will bring us economic rewards in the new business opportunities it creates here and abroad and it will speed engagement by critical countries like China and India.

To date our efforts have been limited to funding research, development, and limited demonstrations. Such funding can help in this effort if it is wisely invested. But government subsidies—which are what we are talking about—cannot substitute for the driver that a real market for low-carbon goods and services provides. That market will be created only when requirements to limit CO_2 emissions are adopted. This year in Congress serious attention is finally being directed to enactment of such measures and we welcome your announcement that you intend to play a leadership role in this effort.

Key Questions about CCD

I started studying CCD in detail ten years ago and the questions I had then are those asked today by people new to the subject. Do reliable systems exist to capture CO_2 from power plants and other industrial sources? Where can we put CO_2 after we have captured it? Will the CO_2 stay where we put it or will it leak? How much disposal capacity is there? Are CCD systems "affordable"? To answer these questions, the Intergovernmental Panel on

Climate Change (IPCC) decided four years ago to prepare a special report on the subject. That report was issued in September, 2005 as the IPCC Special Report on Carbon Dioxide Capture and Storage. I was privileged to serve as a review editor for the report's chapter on geologic storage of CO_2.

CO_2 Capture

The IPCC special report groups capture or separation of CO_2 from industrial gases into four categories: post-combustion; pre-combustion; oxyfuel combustion; and industrial separation. I will say a few words about the basics and status of each of these approaches. In a conventional pulverized coal power plant, the coal is combusted using normal air at atmospheric pressures. This combustion process produces a large volume of exhaust gas that contains CO_2 in large amounts but in low concentrations and low pressures. Commercial post-combustion systems exist to capture CO_2 from such exhaust gases using chemical "stripping" compounds and they have been applied to very small portions of flue gases (tens of thousands of tons from plants that emit several million tons of CO_2 annually) from a few coal-fired power plants in the U.S. that sell the captured CO_2 to the food and beverage industry. However, industry analysts state that today's systems, based on publicly available information, involve much higher costs and energy penalties than the principal demonstrated alternative, pre-combustion capture.

New and potentially less expensive post-combustion concepts have been evaluated in laboratory tests and some, like ammonia-based capture systems, are scheduled for small pilot-scale tests in the next few years. Under normal industrial development scenarios, if successful such pilot tests would be followed by larger demonstration tests and then by commercial-scale tests. These and other approaches should continue to be explored. However, unless accelerated by a combination of policies, subsidies, and willingness to take increased technical risks, such a development program could take one or two decades before post-combustion systems would be accepted for broad commercial application.

Pre-combustion capture is applied to coal conversion processes that gasify coal rather than combust it in air. In the oxygen-blown gasification process coal is heated under pressure with a mixture of pure oxygen, producing an energy-rich gas stream consisting mostly of hydrogen and carbon monoxide. Coal gasification is widely used in industrial processes, such as ammonia and fertilizer production around the world. Hundreds of such industrial gasifiers are in operation today. In power generation applications as practiced today this "syngas" stream is cleaned of impurities and then burned in a combustion turbine to make electricity in a process known as Integrated Gasification Combined Cycle or IGCC. In the power generation business, IGCC is a relatively recent development—about two decades old and is still not widely deployed. There are two IGCC power-only plants operating in the U.S. today and about 14 commercial IGCC plants are operating, with most of the capacity in Europe. In early years of operation for power applications a number of IGCC projects encountered availability problems but those issues appear to be resolved today, with Tampa Electric Company reporting that its IGCC plant in Florida is the most dispatched and most economic unit in its generating system.

Commercially demonstrated systems for pre-combustion capture from the coal gasification process involve treating the syngas to form a mixture of hydrogen and CO_2 and then separating the CO_2, primarily through the use of solvents. These same techniques are used in industrial plants to separate CO_2 from natural gas and to make chemicals such as ammonia out of gasified coal. However, because CO_2 can be released to the air in unlimited amounts under today's laws, except in niche applications, even plants that separate CO_2 do not capture it; rather they release it to the atmosphere. Notable exceptions include the Dakota Gasification Company plant in Beulah, North Dakota, which captures and pipelines more than one million tons of CO_2 per year from its lignite gasification plant to an oil field in Saskatchewan, and ExxonMobil's Shute Creek natural gas processing plant in Wyoming, which strips CO_2 from sour gas and pipelines several million tons per year to oil fields in Colorado and Wyoming.

Today's pre-combustion capture approach is not applicable to the installed base of conventional pulverized coal in the U.S. and elsewhere. However, it is ready today for use with IGCC power plants. The oil giant BP has announced an IGCC project with pre-combustion CO_2 capture at its refinery in Carson, California. When operational the project will gasify petroleum coke, a solid fuel that resembles coal more than petroleum to make electricity for sale to the grid. The captured CO_2 will be sold to an oil field operator in California to enhance oil recovery. The principal obstacle for broad application of pre-combustion capture to new power plants is not technical, it is economic: under today's laws it is cheaper to release CO_2 to the air rather than capturing it. Enacting laws to limit CO_2 can change this situation, as I discuss later.

While pre-combustion capture from IGCC plants is the approach that is ready today for commercial application, it is not the only method for CO_2 capture that may emerge if laws creating a market for CO_2 capture are adopted. I have previously mentioned post-combustion techniques now being explored. Another approach, known as oxyfuel combustion, is also in the early stages of research and development. In the oxyfuel process, coal is burned in oxygen rather than air and the exhaust gases are recycled to build up CO_2 concentrations to a point where separation at reasonable cost and energy penalties may be feasible. Small scale pilot studies for oxyfuel processes have been announced. As with post-combustion processes, absent an accelerated effort to leapfrog the normal commercialization process, it could be one or two decades before such systems might begin to be deployed broadly in commercial application.

Given, the massive amount of new coal capacity scheduled for construction in the next two decades, we cannot afford to wait until we see if these alternative capture systems prove out, nor do we need to. Coal plants in the design process today can employ proven IGCC and pre-combustion capture systems to reduce their CO_2 emissions by about 90 percent. Adoption of policies that set a CO_2 performance standard now for such new plants will not anoint IGCC as the technological winner since alternative approaches can be employed when they are ready. If the alternatives prove superior to IGCC and pre-combustion capture, the market will reward them accordingly. As I will discuss later, adoption of CO_2 performance standards is a critical step to improve today's capture methods and to stimulate development of competing systems.

I would like to say a few words about so-called "capture-ready" or "capture-capable" coal plants. I will admit that some years ago I was under the impression that some technologies like IGCC, initially built without capture equipment could be properly called "capture-ready." However, the implications of the rapid build-out of new coal plants for global warming and many conversations with engineers since then have educated me to a different view. An IGCC unit built without capture equipment can be equipped later with such equipment and at much lower cost than attempting to retrofit a conventional pulverized coal plant with today's demonstrated post-combustion systems. However, the costs and engineering reconfigurations of such an approach are substantial. More importantly, we need to begin capturing CO_2 from new coal plants without delay in order to keep global warming from becoming a potentially runaway problem. Given the pace of new coal investments in the U.S. and globally, we simply do not have the time to build a coal plant today and think about capturing its CO_2 down the road.

Implementation of the Energy Policy Act of 2005 approach to this topic needs a review in my opinion. The Act provides significant subsidies for coal plants that do not actually capture their CO_2 but rather merely have carbon "capture capability." While the Act limits this term to plants using gasification processes, it is not being implemented in a manner that provides a meaningful substantive difference between an ordinary IGCC unit and one that genuinely has been designed with early integration of CO_2 capture in mind. Further, in its FY2008 budget request, the administration seeks appropriations allowing it to provide $9 billion in loan guarantees under Title XVII of the Act, including as much as $4 billion in loans for "carbon sequestration optimized coal power plants." The administration request does not define a "carbon sequestration optimized" coal power plant and it could mean almost anything, including, according to some industry representatives, a plant that simply leaves physical space for an unidentified black box. If that makes a power plant "capture-ready" Mr. Chairman, then my driveway is "Ferrari-ready." We should not be investing today in coal plants at more than a billion dollars apiece with nothing more than a hope that some kind of capture system will turn up. We would not get on a plane to a destination if the pilot told us there was no landing site but options were being researched.

Geologic Disposal

We have a significant experience base for injecting large amounts of CO_2 into geologic formations. For several decades oil field operators have received high pressure CO_2 for injection into fields to enhance oil recovery, delivered by pipelines spanning as much as several hundred miles. Today in the U.S. a total of more than 35 million tons of CO_2 are injected annually in more than 70 projects. (Unfortunately, due to the lack of any controls on CO_2 emissions, about 80 per cent of that CO_2 is sources from natural CO_2 formations rather than captured from industrial sources. Historians will marvel that we persisted so long in pulling CO_2 out of holes in the ground in order to move it hundreds of miles and stick in back in holes at the same time we were recognizing the harm being caused by emissions of the same molecule from nearby large industrial sources.) In addition to this enhanced oil recovery experience, there are several other large injection projects in operation or announced. The longest running of these, the Sleipner project, began in 1996.

But the largest of these projects injects on the order of one million tons per year of CO_2, while a single large coal power plant can produce about five million tons per year. And of course, our experience with man-made injection projects does not extend for the thousand year or more period that we would need to keep CO_2 in place underground for it to be effective in helping to avoid dangerous global warming. Accordingly, the public and interested members of the environmental, industry and policy communities rightly ask whether we can carry out a large scale injection program safely and assure that the injected CO_2 will stay where we put it.

. . . In its 2005 report the IPCC concluded the following with respect to the question of whether we can safely carry out carbon injection operations on the required scale:

> "With appropriate site selection based on available subsurface information, a monitoring programme to detect problems, a regulatory system and the appropriate use of remediation methods to stop or control CO_2 releases if they arise, the local health, safety and environment risks of geological storage would be comparable to the risks of current activities such as natural gas storage, EOR and deep underground disposal of acid gas."

The knowledge exists to fulfill all of the conditions the IPCC identifies as needed to assure safety. While EPA has authority regulate large scale CO_2 injection projects its current underground injection control regulations are not designed to require the appropriate showings for permitting a facility intended for long-term retention of large amounts of CO_2. With adequate resources applied, EPA should be able to make the necessary revisions to its rules in two to three years. We urge this Committee to act to require EPA to undertake this effort this year.

Do we have a basis today for concluding that injected CO_2 will stay in place for the long periods required to prevent its contributing to global warming? The IPCC report concluded that we do, stating:

"Observations from engineered and natural analogues as well as models suggest that the fraction retained in appropriately selected and managed geological reservoirs is very likely to exceed 99% over 100 years and is likely to exceed 99% over 1,000 years."

Despite this conclusion by recognized experts there is still reason to ask what are the implications of imperfect execution of large scale injection projects, especially in the early years before we have amassed more experience? Is this reason enough to delay application of CO_2 capture systems to new power plants until we gain such experience from an initial round of multi-million ton "demonstration" projects? To sketch an answer to this question, my colleague Stefan Bachu, a geologist with the Alberta Energy and Utilities Board, and I wrote a paper for the Eighth International Conference on Greenhouse Gas Control Technologies in June 2006. The obvious and fundamental point we made is that without CO_2 capture, new coal plants built during any "delay and research" period will put 100 per cent of their CO_2 into the air and may do so for their operating life if they were "grandfathered" from retrofit requirements. Those releases need to be compared to hypothetical leaks from early injection sites.

Our conclusions were that even with extreme, unrealistically high hypothetical leakage rates from early injection sites (10% per year), a long period to leak detection (5 years) and a prolonged period to correct the leak (1 year), a policy that delayed installation of CO_2 capture at new coal plants to await further research would result in cumulative CO_2 releases twenty times greater than from the hypothetical faulty injection sites, if power plants built during the research period were "grandfathered" from retrofit requirements. If this wave of new coal plants were all required to retrofit CO_2 capture by no later than 2030, the cumulative emissions would still be four times greater than under the no delay scenario. I believe that any objective assessment will conclude that allowing new coal plants to be built without CO_2 capture equipment on the ground that we need more large scale injection experience will always result in significantly greater CO_2 releases than starting CO_2 capture without delay for new coal plants now being designed.

The IPCC also made estimates about global storage capacity for CO_2 in geologic formations. It concluded as follows:

"Available evidence suggests that, worldwide, it is likely that there is a technical potential of at least about 2,000 $GtCO_2$ (545 GtC) of storage capacity in geological formations. There could be a much larger potential for geological storage in saline formations, but the upper limit estimates are uncertain due to lack of information and an agreed methodology."

Current CO_2 emissions from the world's power plants are about 10 Gt (billion metric tons) per year, so the IPCC estimate indicates 200 years of capacity if power plant emissions did not increase and 100 years capacity if annual emissions doubled.

Policy Actions to Speed CCD

As I stated earlier, research and development funding is useful but it cannot substitute for the incentive that a genuine commercial market for CO_2 capture and disposal systems will provide to the private sector. The amounts of capital that the private sector can spend to optimize CCD methods will almost certainly always dwarf what Congress will provide with taxpayer dollars. To mobilize those private sector dollars, Congress needs a stimulus more compelling than the offer of modest handouts for research. Congress has a model that works: intelligently designed policies to limit emissions cause firms to spend money finding better and less expensive ways to prevent or capture emissions.

Where a technology is already competitive with other emission control techniques, for example, sulfur dioxide scrubbers, a cap and trade program like that enacted by Congress in 1990, can result in more rapid deployment, improvements in performance, and reductions in costs. Today's scrubbers are much more effective and much less costly than those built in the 1980s. However, a CO_2 cap and trade program by itself may not result in deployment of CCD systems as rapidly as we need. Many new coal plant design decisions are being made literally today. Depending on the pace of required reductions under a global warming bill, a firm may decide to build a conventional coal plant and purchase credits from the cap and trade market rather than applying CCD systems to the plant. While this may appear to be economically rational in the short term, it is likely to lead to higher costs of CO_2 control in the mid and longer term if substantial amounts of new conventional coal construction leads to ballooning demand for CO_2 credits. Recall that in the late 1990's and the first few years of this century, individual firms thought it made economic sense to build large numbers of new gas-fired power plants. The problem is too many of them had the same idea and the resulting increase in demand for natural gas increased both the price and volatility of natural gas to the point where many of these investments are idle today.

Moreover, delaying the start of CCD until a cap and trade system price is high enough to produce these investments delays the broad demonstration of the technology that the U.S. and other countries will need if we continue substantial use of coal as seem likely. The more affordable CCD becomes, the more widespread its use will be throughout the world, including in rapidly growing economies like China and India. But the learning and cost reductions for CCD that are desirable will come only from the experience gained by building and operating the initial commercial plants. The longer we wait to ramp up this experience, the longer we will wait to see CCD deployed here and in countries like China.

Accordingly, we believe the best policy package is a hybrid program that combines the breadth and flexibility of a cap and trade program with well-designed performance measures focused on key technologies like CCD. One such performance measure is a CO_2 emissions standard that applies to new power investments. California enacted such a measure in SB1368 last year. It requires new investments for sale of power in California to meet a performance standard that is achievable by coal with a moderate amount of CO_2 capture.

Another approach is a low-carbon generation obligation for coal-based power. Similar in concept to a renewable performance standard, the low-carbon generation obligation requires an initially small fraction of sales from coal-based power to meet a CO_2 performance standard that is achievable with CCD. The required fraction of sales would increase gradually over time and the obligation would be tradable. Thus, a coal-based generating firm could meet the requirement by building a plant with CCD, by purchasing power generated by another source that meets the standard, or by purchasing credits from those who build such plants. This approach has the advantage of speeding the deployment of CCD while avoiding the "first mover penalty." Instead of causing the first builder of a commercial coal plant with CCD to bear all of the incremental costs, the tradable low-carbon generation obligation would spread those costs over the entire coal-based generation system. The builder of the first unit would achieve far more hours of low-carbon generation than required and would sell the credits to other firms that needed credits to comply. These credit sales would finance the incremental costs of these early units. This approach provides the coal-based power industry with the experience with a technology that it knows is needed to reconcile coal use and climate protection and does it without sticker shock.

A bill introduced in the other body, S. 309, contains such a provision. It begins with a requirement that one-half of one per cent of coal-based power sales must meet the low-carbon performance standard starting in 2015 and the required percentage increases over time according to a statutory minimum schedule that can be increased in specified amounts by additional regulatory action.

A word about costs is in order. With today's off the shelf systems, estimates are that the production cost of electricity at a coal plant with CCD could be as much as 40% higher than at a conventional plant that emits its CO_2. But the impact on average electricity prices of introducing CCD now will be very much smaller due to several factors. First, power production costs represent about 60% of the price you and I pay for electricity; the rest comes from transmission and distribution costs. Second, coal-based power represents just over half of U.S. power consumption. Third, and most important, even if we start now, CCD would be applied to only a small fraction of U.S. coal capacity for some time. Thus, with the trading approach I have outlined, the incremental costs on the units equipped with CCD would be spread over the entire coal-based power sector or possibly across all fossil capacity depending on the choices made by

Congress. Based on CCD costs available in 2005 we estimate that a low-carbon generation obligation large enough to cover all forecasted new U.S. coal capacity through 2020 could be implemented for about a two per cent increase in average U.S. retail electricity rates.

Conclusions

To sum up, since we will almost certainly continue using large amounts of coal in the U.S. and globally in the coming decades, it is imperative that we act now to deploy CCD systems. Commercially demonstrated CO_2 capture systems exist today and competing systems are being researched. Improvements in current systems and emergence of new approaches will be accelerated by requirements to limit CO_2 emissions. Geologic disposal of large amounts of CO_2 is viable and we know enough today to conclude that it can be done safely and effectively. EPA must act without delay to revise its regulations to provide the necessary framework for efficient permitting, monitoring and operational practices for large scale permanent CO_2 repositories.

Finally CCD is an important strategy to reduce CO_2 emissions from fossil fuel use but it is not the basis for a climate protection program by itself. Increased reliance on low-carbon energy resources is the key to protecting the climate. The lowest carbon resource of all is smarter use of energy; energy efficiency investments will be the backbone of any sensible climate protection strategy. Renewable energy will need to assume a much greater role than it does today. With today's use of solar, wind and biomass energy, we tap only a tiny fraction of the energy the sun provides every day. There is enormous potential to expand our reliance on these resources.

We have no time to lose to begin cutting global warming emissions. Fortunately, we have technologies ready for use today that can get us started.

Charles W. Schmidt

NO

Carbon Capture & Storage: Blue-Sky Technology or Just Blowing Smoke?

Towering 650 feet over the sea surface and spouting an impressive burning flare, it would be easy to mistake the Sleipner West gas platform for an environmental nightmare. Its eight-story upper deck houses 200 workers and supports drilling equipment weighing 40,000 tons. Located off the Norwegian coast, it ranks among Europe's largest natural gas producers, delivering more than 12 billion cubic feet of the fuel annually to onshore terminals by pipeline. Roughly 9% of the natural gas extracted here is carbon dioxide (CO_2), the main culprit behind global warming. But far from a nightmare, Sleipner West is actually a bellwether for environmental innovation. Since 1996, the plant's operators have stripped CO_2 out of the gas on-site and buried it 3,000 feet below the sea floor, where they anticipate it will remain for at least 10,000 years.

Operated by StatoilHydro, Norway's largest company, Sleipner is among the few commercial-scale facilities in the world today that capture and bury CO_2 underground. Many experts believe this practice, dubbed carbon capture and storage (sometimes known as carbon capture and sequestration, but in either case abbreviated CCS), could be crucial for keeping industrial CO_2 emissions out of the atmosphere. Sleipner injects 1 million tons of CO_2 annually into the Utsira Formation, a saline aquifer big enough to store 600 years' worth of emissions from all European power plants, company representatives say.

With mounting evidence of climate change—and predictions that fossil fuels could supply 80% of global energy needs indefinitely—the spotlight on CCS is shining as brightly as the Sleipner flare. A panel of experts from the Massachusetts Institute of Technology (MIT) recently concluded that CCS is "the critical enabling technology to reduce CO_2 emissions significantly while allowing fossil fuels to meet growing energy needs." The panel's views were presented in *The Future of Coal*, a report issued by MIT on 14 March 2007.

Environmental groups are split on the issue. Speaking for the Natural Resources Defense Council (NRDC), David Hawkins, director of the council's Climate Center and a member of the MIT panel's external advisory commit-

From *Environmental Health Perspectives*, 115(11), November 2007, pp. A538–A545. Copyright © 2007 by National Institute of Environmental Health Sciences. Reprinted by permission.

tee, says, "We believe [CCS] is a viable way to cut global warming pollution
. . . . We have the knowledge we need to start moving forward." Other environmental groups, including the World Resources Institute, Environmental
Defense, and the Pew Center on Global Climate Change, have also come out
in support of CCS. These groups view CCS as one among many alternatives
(including renewable energy) for reducing CO_2 emissions.

Greenpeace is perhaps the most vocal critic of CCS. Truls Gulowsen,
Greenpeace's Nordic climate campaigner, stresses that CCS deflects attention from renewable energy and efficiency improvements, which, he says,
offer the best solutions to the problem of global warming. "Companies are
doing a lot of talking about CCS, but they're doing little to actually put it
into place," he says. "So, they're talking about a possible solution that they
don't really want to implement now, and at the same time, they're trying
to push for more coal, oil, and gas development instead of renewables,
which we already know can deliver climate benefits."

Coal Use Drives CCS Adoption

The pressure to advance on CCS has been fueled by soaring coal use worldwide. China, which is building coal-fired power plants at the rate of two
per week, surpassed the United States as the world's largest producer of
greenhouse gases in June 2007, years earlier than predicted. Coal use in
India and other developing nations is also on the rise, while the United
States sits on the largest coal reserves in the world, enough to supply domestic energy needs for 300 years, states the MIT report. Coal already supplies more than 50% of U.S. electricity demand and could supply 70%
by 2025, according to the International Energy Agency. Meanwhile, coal-fired power plants already account for nearly 40% of CO_2 emissions worldwide, a figure that—barring some dramatic advance in renewable energy
technology—seems poised to rise dramatically. During a 6 September 2007
hearing of the House Select Committee on Energy Independence and Global Warming, Chairman Edward Markey (D–MA) noted that more than
150 new coal plants are being planned in the United States alone, with
another 3,000 likely to be built worldwide by 2030.

A mature CCS system would capture, transport, and inject those emissions underground to depths of at least 1 km, where porous rock formations in geologically favorable locations absorb CO_2 like a sponge. At those
depths, high pressures and temperatures compress the gas into a dense,
liquid-like "supercritical" state that displaces brine and fills the tiny pores
between rock grains. Three types of geological formations appear especially
promising for sequestration: saline (and therefore nonpotable) aquifers located beneath freshwater deposits; coal seams that are too deep or thin
to be extracted economically; and oil and gas fields, where CO_2 stripped
from fuels on-site can be injected back underground to force dwindling reserves to the surface, a process called "enhanced recovery." Using CO_2 for
enhanced recovery has a long history, particularly in southwestern Texas,
where oil yields have been declining for decades.

Of these three options, saline aquifers—with their large storage capacity and broad global distribution—are considered the most attractive. Thomas Sarkus, director of the Applied Science and Energy Technology Division of the DOE National Energy Technology Laboratory (NETL), suggests saline aquifers in the central United States could conceivably store 2,000 years' worth of domestic CO_2 emissions.

Apart from Sleipner, only two other industrial-scale CCS projects are in operation today. In Algeria, a joint venture involving three energy companies—Statoil-Hydro, BP, and Sonatrach—stores more than 1 million tons of CO_2 annually under a natural gas platform near In Salah, an oasis town in the desert. And in Weyburn, Canada, comparable volumes are being used by EnCana Corporation, a Canadian energy company, for enhanced recovery at an aging oil field. The CO_2 sequestered at Weyburn comes by pipeline from a coal gasification plant in Beulah, North Dakota, 200 miles away. Unlike other enhanced recovery projects—wherein the ultimate fate of CO_2 is not the primary concern—Weyburn combines fossil fuel recovery with research to study sequestration on a large scale.

What's needed now, says Jim Katzer, a visiting scholar at MIT's Laboratory for Energy and the Environment, are more large-scale demonstrations of CCS in multiple geologies, integrated with policies that address site selection, licensing, liability, and other issues. Katzer says there are a number of investigations that are investigating storage in the 5,000- to 20,000-ton-capacity range, and they're generating some useful information. "But," he says, "none of them are getting us to the answer we really need: how are we going to manage storage in the millions of tons over long periods of time?"

Paying for Storage

The task of managing carbon storage is nothing if not daunting: in the United States alone, coal plants produce more than 1.5 billion tons of CO_2 every year. Sequestering that amount of gas will require not only a vast new infrastructure of pipelines and storage sites but also that the country's coal plants adopt costly technologies for carbon capture. Most existing U.S. plants—indeed, most of the world's 5,000 coal-fired power plants, including the ones now being built in China—burn pulverized coal (PC) using technologies essentially unchanged since the Industrial Revolution. CO_2 can be extracted from PC plants only after the fuel has been burned, which is inefficient because the combustion emissions are highly diluted with air.

A more efficient approach is to capture highly concentrated streams of CO_2 from coal before it's burned. Precombustion capture is usually applied at integrated gasification combined cycle (IGCC) coal plants, which are extremely rare, numbering just five worldwide, according to Sarkus. IGCC plants cost roughly 20% more to operate because the gasification process requires additional power, which explains why there are so few of them.

Although they don't rule out the possibility, none of the industry sources interviewed for this article welcome the prospect of retrofitting traditional PC plants for carbon capture. That would require major plant modifications and could potentially double the cost of electricity to consumers, they say. But by ignoring existing facilities, industry will set back CCS expansion by decades—most PC plants in use today have been designed for lifetimes of 30 to 40 years.

Whatever path it takes, the transition to CCS will require enormous sums of money. When used for enhanced recovery, CO_2 is a commodity that pays for its own burial. But only a small fraction of the CO_2 generated by coal plants and other industrial processes is used for that purpose. Creating a broad CCS infrastructure will ultimately require a charge on carbon emissions that, according to calculations described in *The Future of Coal*, should total at least $30 per ton—$25 per ton for CO_2 capture and pressurization and $5 per ton for transportation and storage—with this figure rising annually in accordance with inflation.

Sally Benson, a professor of energy resources engineering at Stanford University, points to different ways to pay that charge. One is a tax on CO_2 emissions, an option she concedes has little political support. Funds could also be raised with a "cap-and-trade" system, which sets area-wide limits on CO_2 emissions that industries can meet by trading carbon credits on the open market. A cap-and-trade system for CO_2 has already been established by the European Union, which regulates the greenhouse gas to meet obligations under the Kyoto Protocol. Jeff Chapman, chief executive officer of the Carbon Capture and Storage Association, a trade group based in London, suggests the European cap-and-trade system could ultimately raise €62 billion.

In the United States, a national cap-and-trade system likely won't appear until the federal government regulates CO_2 as a pollutant, says Luke Popovich, vice president of external communications with the National Mining Association, a coal industry trade group in Washington, DC. In the meantime, individual states—for instance, California, which sets its own air quality standards per a waiver under the Clean Air Act—are planning for their own cap-and-trade systems. California regulates CO_2 under a state law called AB32, which directs industries to reduce all greenhouse gas emissions by 25% over the next 13 years. CCS may ultimately emerge on a state-by-state basis in this country, where charges on carbon emissions allow it, Benson suggests.

Technical Questions Remain

Until the early 1990s, most researchers involved in CCS worked in isolation. But in March 1992, more than 250 gathered for the first International Conference on Carbon Dioxide Removal in Amsterdam. Howard Herzog, a principal research engineer at the MIT Laboratory for Energy and the Environment and a leading expert on CCS, says attendees arrived as individuals but left as a research community that now includes funding agencies, industries, and nongovernmental organizations throughout the world. Unfortunately, that community doesn't have nearly the resources it needs to study CCS on a realistic scale, Katzer says. Indeed, *The Future of Coal* states emphatically that "government and private-sector programs to implement on a timely basis the large-scale integrated demonstrations needed to confirm the suitability of carbon sequestration are completely inadequate."

Absent sufficient evidence, most experts simply assume that vast amounts of sequestered CO_2 will stay in place without leaking to the atmosphere. They base that assumption on available monitoring data from the big three industrial projects—none of which have shown any evidence of CO_2 leakage from their underground storage sites, according to *The Future of Coal*—and also on expectations that buried CO_2 will behave in essentially the same way as underground fossil fuel deposits. "We're optimistic it will work," says Jeffrey Logan, a senior associate in the Climate, Energy, and Transport Program at the World Resources Institute. "The general theory is that if oil and gas resources can remain trapped for millions of years, then why not CO_2?"

Franklin Orr, director of the Global Climate and Energy Project at Stanford University, says monitoring data show that CO_2 injected underground for enhanced oil and gas recovery remains trapped there by the same geological structures that trapped the fuels for millions of years; specifically overlying shale deposits through which neither fossil fuels nor CO_2 can pass. Decades of research by the oil and gas industries, in addition to basic research in geology, have revealed the features needed for CO_2 sequestration, he says: "You're looking for deep zones with highly porous rocks—for instance, sandstone—capped by shale seals with low permeability. Sleipner and Weyburn are both good examples; both have thick shale caps that keep the CO_2 from getting out."

But Orr concedes that questions remain about how large amounts of CO_2 might behave underground. A key risk to avoid, he says, is leakage through underlying faults or abandoned wells that provide conduits to the atmosphere. Yousif Kharaka, a research hydrologist with the USGS in Menlo Park, California, says an unknown but possibly large number of orphaned or abandoned wells in the United States could pose a risk of leakage to the atmosphere. And that, he warns, would negate the climate benefits of sequestration.

The likelihood that CO_2 levels could accumulate and cause health or ecological injuries is minimal, Kharaka says, echoing the conclusions reached in *The Future of Coal*. He says CO_2 in air only becomes harmful to humans at concentrations of 3% or above, which is far higher than might be expected from slow leaks out of the ground. Nonetheless, the possibility that CO_2 leaking from underground storage sites might accumulate to harmful levels in basements or other enclosed spaces can't be discounted entirely, cautions Susan Hovorka, a senior research scientist at the Bureau of Economic Geology, a state-sponsored research unit at the University of Texas at Austin. "It's important that we manage this substance correctly," she says. "If you determine that there's a risk to confined places, then you have to provide adequate ventilation. But we have a high level of confidence that CO_2 will be retained at depth."

The greater concern says Kharaka, is that migrating CO_2 might mix with brine, forming carbonic acid that could leach metals such as iron, zinc, or lead from the underlying rock. In some cases, acidified brine alone could migrate and mix with fresh groundwater, posing health risks through drinking or irrigation water, he says. Results from an investigation conducted near Houston, Texas, led by Hovorka as principal investigator along with Kharaka and other scientists from 21 organizations, indicate that CO_2 injected into saline aquifers produced sharp drops in brine pH, from 6.5 to around 3.5. These results were published in the September 2007 report *Water–Rock Interaction: Proceedings of the 12th International Symposium on Water–Rock Interaction, Kunming, China, 31 July–5 August, 2007*. Chemical analyses showed the brine contained high concentrations of iron and manganese, which suggests toxic metal contamination can't be ruled out, Hovorka says. "I'd describe this as a nonzero concern," she adds. "It's not something we should write off, but it's not a showstopper."

Experts in this area consistently point to the need for more detailed investigations of CO_2 movements at depth and their geochemical consequences. Hovorka's investigation was among the first of this kind, but its scale—just 1,600 tons—paled in comparison to realistic demands for CO_2 mitigation to combat climate change.

Constrained by inadequate funding, the DOE has put much of its CCS investment into a project dubbed "FutureGen." This initiative seeks to build a prototype coal-fired power plant that will integrate all three features of a CCS system, namely, carbon capture (achieved with IGCC technology), CO_2 transportation, and sequestration. Supported by the DOE and an alliance of industry partners, the four-year, $1.5 billion project was announced formally by President Bush in his 2002 State of the Union Address. Once operational, the plant will supply 275 megawatts of power (compared with the 600–1,300 megawatts supplied by typical U.S. coal plants), enough for 275,000 households. Sarkus, who is also the FutureGen director, says four potential sites for the plant and its CO_2 reservoirs—including two in Illinois and two in Texas—are under consideration. Final site selection, he says, will depend on community support, adequate transportation lines, and proximity to underground storage reservoirs.

The Bush administration's stance is that FutureGen will promote CCS advancements throughout the coal and utility industries. But many stakeholders don't think it goes far enough toward meeting existing needs; the project is "too much 'future' and not enough 'generation,'" quips Hawkins. "What we need is legislation that specifies future power plants must be outfitted with CCS, period." To that, Katzer adds, "FutureGen was announced in 2002, and they still haven't settled on site selection, nor have they resolved key design issues. Operations were set to begin in 2012, and now that's slipping back even further. Assuming you start in 2012 and operate for four years, you're looking at 2016 before you complete a single demonstration project. That stretches things out too far, and speaks to the need for several demonstration projects funded now by the U.S. government so we can deal with CO_2 emissions in a timely fashion."

The Developing Country Factor

With U.S. research efforts stuck in low gear, concerns over a comparable lack of progress in the developing world are growing. China already obtains more than 80% of its domestic electricity from coal. And with a relentless push for economic growth, lowering CO_2 emissions from its coal plants is a low priority. It's likely that none of China's coal-fired plants are outfitted for carbon capture, says Richard Lester, a professor of nuclear science and engineering at MIT. "Given the scale and expansion of China's electric power sector, the eventual introduction of CCS there is going to be absolutely critical to global efforts to abate or reduce the atmospheric carbon burden," he says.

Meanwhile, India lags just a decade or less behind China in terms of its own economic growth, which is increasingly fueled by coal use, Katzer says. The key difference between the two countries, he says, has to do with planning for environmental and energy development. In China, Katzer explains, growth and environment strategies seem to be dictated at regional levels without any central coordination, which is ironic considering the country's socialist political structure. India, on the other hand, seems to have what Katzer calls a "master plan" for growth. "But they have no clue how to move forward in terms of CO_2 reductions," Katzer says. "What officials in India say to me is, 'We'll manage CO_2 if it doesn't cost too much.' That's the downside in all of this."

In the end, CCS seems to be stuck in a catch-22: In the view of the developing world, the United States and other wealthier nations should take the lead with respect to emissions reduction technology. Governments in wealthier nations, meanwhile—particularly the United States—look to industries in the free market for solutions to the problem. But U.S. industries say they can't afford large-scale research; in industry's opinion, the government should pay for additional studies that lay the groundwork for industry research and the technology's future implementation. The government, however, doesn't fund the DOE and other agencies at nearly the amounts required to achieve this. And at the same time, the two mechanisms that could possibly generate sufficient revenues for CCS—carbon taxes and cap-and-trade systems for CO_2 emissions—are trapped by perpetual political gridlock.

Leslie Harroun, a senior program officer at the Oak Foundation, a Geneva-based organization that funds social and environmental research, warns that industry might leverage the promise of CCS as a public relations strategy today while doing little to ensure its broad-based deployment tomorrow. "The coal industry's many proposals to build 'clean' coal plants that are 'capture ready' across the U.S. is a smokescreen," she asserts. "Coal companies are hoping to build new plants before cap-and-trade regulations go into effect—and they will, soon—with the idea that the plants

and their greenhouse gas emissions will be grandfathered in until sequestration is technically and financially feasible. This is an enormously risky
investment decision on their part, and morally irresponsible, but maybe
they think there is power in numbers."

In a sense, the inertia surrounding CCS might reflect a collective wilt
in the face of a seemingly overwhelming technical and social challenge. To
make a difference for climate change, a CCS infrastructure will have to capture and store many billions of tons of CO_2 throughout the world for hundreds of years. Those buried deposits will have to be monitored by unknown
entities far into the future. Many questions remain about who will "own"
these deposits and thereby assume responsibility for their long-term storage.
Meanwhile, industry and the government are at an impasse, with neither
taking a leading role toward making large-scale CCS a reality. How this state
of affairs ultimately plays out for health of the planet remains to be seen.

Whatever Happened to Deep Ocean Storage?

One CCS option that appears to have fallen by the wayside is deep ocean
storage. Scientists have long speculated that enormous volumes of CO_2
could be stored in the ocean at depths of 3 km or more. High pressure
would compress the CO_2, making it denser than seawater and thus enabling it to sink. So-called CO_2 lakes would hover over the sea floor, suggests
Ken Caldeira, a Stanford University professor of global ecology.

"A coal-fired power plant produces a little under one kilogram of CO_2
for each kilowatt-hour of electricity produced," says Caldeira. "An individual one-gigawatt coal-fired power plant, . . . if completely captured and the
CO_2 stored on the sea floor, would make a lake ten meters deep and nearly
one kilometer square—and it [would grow] by that much each year."

But Caldeira and others acknowledge that deep ocean storage doesn't
offer a permanent solution. Unless the gas is somehow physically confined, over time—perhaps 500 to 1,000 years—up to half the CO_2 would
diffuse through the ocean and be released back into the atmosphere. Moreover, most life within CO_2 lakes would be extinguished. However, Caldeira
believes this consequence would be balanced by the benefits of keeping
the greenhouse gas out of the atmosphere, where under global warming
scenarios it acidifies and endangers sea life at the surface.

No one knows precisely what would happen during deep ocean
storage because it's never been tested. A planned experiment off the
coast of Hawaii in the late 1990s, with participation of U.S., Norwegian,
Canadian, and Australian researchers, was canceled because of opposition
of local environmental activists. According to Caldeira, who previously
co-directed the DOE's now-defunct Center for Research on Ocean Carbon
Sequestration, government program managers who backed the Hawaiian
study were laterally transferred, sending a signal that advocating for this
type of research was politically dangerous for career bureaucrats. "Today,
there's zero money going into it," Caldeira says. "Right now, ocean sequestration is dead in the water."

POSTSCRIPT

Is Carbon Capture Technology Ready to Limit Carbon Emissions?

One of the great concerns about carbon capture and sequestration (CCS) is that once immense amounts of carbon dioxide have been stored underground, it will leak out again, either slowly or—perhaps after an earthquake—suddenly. Study of past eras has suggested that sudden releases of carbon dioxide from volcanoes have led to rapid greenhouse warming, which reduced oxygen levels in the ocean and caused the buildup of toxic hydrogen sulfide, which in turn reached the air and killed plants and animals on land, resulting in mass extinctions such as the one 250 million years ago. See Peter D. Ward, "Impact from the Deep," *Scientific American* (October 2006). A smaller scale threat, exemplified by Cameroon's Lake Nyos, which released so much dissolved carbon dioxide in 1986 that it flowed downhill and suffocated almost 2,000 people, along with their domestic animals, has been cited by environmental justice groups protesting CCS legislation in California. See Valerie J. Brown, "Of Two Minds: Groups Square Off on Carbon Mitigation," *Environmental Health Perspectives* (November 2007).

Such threats should concern us, but so should the threat of global warming itself. In the long run, we must move to non-fossil fuel sources of energy, because even coal, as plentiful as it is, will not last forever. In the short run, we have coal-burning power plants that continue to emit carbon dioxide, and we are planning to build more. As the Royal Society of Chemistry (RSC) notes in "Can We Bury Our Carbon Dioxide Problem?" *Bulletin 3* (Spring 2006), CCS will require the use of energy and will therefore increase the burning of fossil fuels and the price of energy to the consumer. The RSC also notes that researchers are not sure that there is enough underground capacity for all the carbon dioxide that CCS would endeavor to keep out of the atmosphere. More research is needed in this area, as well as in finding better, more efficient methods of capturing carbon dioxide, which can account for three-quarters of the cost of CCS. Fortunately, researchers are developing new materials that may lower that cost significantly. See Rahul Banerjee, et al., "High-Throughput Synthesis of Zeolitic Imidazolate Frameworks and Application to CO_2 Capture," *Science* (February 15, 2008), Kevin Bullis, "A Better Way to Capture Carbon," *Technology Review* online (February 15, 2008) (http://www.technologyreview.com/Energy/20295/?a=f), and Sid Perkins, "Down with Carbon," *Science News* (May 10, 2008).

Even with much improved technology, any CCS program will require commitment from both industry and government. In this connection, it is discouraging to note that the U.S. Department of Energy has backed out of the FutureGen project due to high costs and an inability to agree on funding with industry partners. FutureGen's objective was a clean coal–fired power plant incorporating the latest CCS technologies; it was scheduled to begin operation in 2012. See Jeff Tollefson, "Carbon Burial Buried," *Nature* (January 24, 2008).

It is worth stressing that even those who favor CCS also believe, as David G. Hawkins says in his last paragraph, that though CCS "is an important strategy to reduce CO_2 emissions from fossil fuel . . . it is not the basis for a climate protection program by itself. Increased reliance on low-carbon energy resources is the key to protecting the climate."

ISSUE 11

Is "Geoengineering" a Possible Answer to Global Warming?

YES: Roger Angel, from "Feasibility of Cooling the Earth with a Cloud of Small Spacecraft near the Inner Lagrange Point (L1)," Proceedings of the National Academy of Sciences of the United States of America (November 14, 2006)

NO: James R. Fleming, from "The Climate Engineers," *Wilson Quarterly* (Spring 2007)

ISSUE SUMMARY

YES: Professor of astronomy Roger Angel argues that if dangerous changes in global climate become inevitable, despite greenhouse gas controls, it may be possible to solve the problem by reducing the amount of solar energy that hits the Earth, using reflective spacecraft.

NO: James R. Fleming, professor of science, technology, and society, argues that climate engineers such as Roger Angel fail to consider both the risks of unintended consequences to human life and political relationships and the ethics of the human relationship to nature.

It has been known for a very long time that natural events such as volcanic eruptions can cool climate, sometimes dramatically, by injecting large quantities of dust and sulfates into the stratosphere, where they serve as a "sunshade" that reflects a portion of solar heat back into space before it can warm the Earth. In 1815, the Tambora volcano on Sumbawa Island, Indonesia, put so much material (especially sulfates) into the atmosphere that 1816 was known in the United States, Canada, and Europe as the "year without a summer." There was crop-killing frost, snow, and ice all summer long, which gave the year its other name of "eighteen-hundred-and-froze-to-death." See Clive Oppenheimer, "Climatic, Environmental and Human Consequences of the Largest Known Historic Eruption: Tambora Volcano

(Indonesia) 1815," *Progress in Physical Geography* (June 2003). In 1992, Mount Pinatubo, in the Philippines, had a similar, if smaller, effect and hid for a time the climate warming otherwise produced by increasing amounts of greenhouse gases. See Alan Robock, "The Climatic Aftermath," *Science* (February 15, 2002). Changes in solar activity can also have effects. Periods of climate chilling and climate warming have been linked to decreases and increases in the amount of energy released by the sun and reaching the Earth. See Caspar M. Ammann, et al., "Solar Influence on Climate during the Past Millennium: Results from Transient Simulations with the NCAR Climate System Model," Proceedings of the National Academy of Sciences of the United States of America (March 6, 2007).

Such effects have prompted many researchers to think that global warming is not just a matter of increased atmospheric content of green-house gases such as carbon dioxide (which slow the loss of heat to space and thus warm the planet) but also of the amount of sunlight that reaches Earth from the sun. So far, most attempts to find a solution to global warming have focused on reducing human emissions of greenhouse gases. But it does not seem unreasonable to consider the other side of the problem, the energy that reaches Earth from the sun. After all, if you are too warm in bed at night, you can remove the blanket *or* turn down the furnace.

One such researcher is Paul Crutzen, who in "Albedo Enhancement by Stratospheric Sulfur Injections: A Contribution to Resolve a Policy Dilemma?" *Climate Change* (August 2006), suggested that adding sulfur compounds to the stratosphere (as volcanoes have done) could reflect some solar energy and help relieve the problem. According to Bob Henson, "Big Fixes for Climate?" *UCAR Quarterly* (Fall 2006) (http://www.ucar.edu/communications/quarterly/fall06/bigfix.jsp), the National Center for Atmospheric Research is currently testing the idea with computer simulations; one conclusion is that a single Pinatubo-sized stratospheric injection could buy 20 years of time before we would have to cut back carbon dioxide emissions in a big way. Such measures would not be cheap, and at present there is no way to tell whether they would have undesirable side-effects. But they are being discussed.

In the following selections, professor of astronomy Roger Angel argues that if dangerous changes in global climate become inevitable, despite greenhouse gas controls, it may be possible to solve the problem by reducing the amount of solar energy that hits the Earth, using reflective spacecraft. James R. Fleming, professor of science, technology, and society, argues that climate engineers such as Roger Angel fail to consider both the risks of unintended consequences to human life and political relationships and the ethics of the human relationship to nature. They also, he says, display signs of over-confidence in technology as a solution of first resort.

YES

Roger Angel

Feasibility of Cooling the Earth with a Cloud of Small Spacecraft near the Inner Lagrange Point (L1)

Projections by the Intergovernmental Panel on Climate Change are for global temperature to rise between 1.5 and 4.5°C by 2100, but recent studies suggest a larger range of uncertainty. Increases as high as 11°C might be possible given CO_2 stabilizing at twice preindustrial content. Holding to even this level of CO_2 will require major use of alternative energy sources and improvements in efficiency. Unfortunately, global warming reasonably could be expected to take the form of abrupt and unpredictable changes, rather than a gradual increase. If it were to become apparent over the next decade or two that disastrous climate change driven by warming was in fact likely or even in progress, then a method to reduce the sun's heat input would become an emergency priority. A 1.8% reduction is projected to fully reverse the warming effect of a doubling of CO_2, although not the chemical effects.

One way known to reduce heat input, observed after volcanic eruptions, is to increase aerosol scattering in the stratosphere. Deployment of 3 to 5 million tons/year of sulfur would be needed to mitigate a doubling of CO_2. This amount is not incompatible with a major reduction in the current atmospheric sulfur pollution of 55 million tons/year that goes mostly into the troposphere. The approach we examine here to reduce solar warming is to scatter away sunlight in space before it enters the Earth's atmosphere. The preferred location is near the Earth–sun inner Lagrange point (L1) in an orbit with the same 1-year period as the Earth, in-line with the sun at a distance [from Earth] ≥1.5 million km (Gm). From this distance, the penumbra shadow covers and thus cools the entire planet.

A major technical hurdle to be overcome is the instability of the orbit, which is at a saddle point. A cloud of scattering particles introduced there would dissipate in a few months. But a cloud of spacecraft holding their orbits by active station-keeping could have a lifetime of many decades. Stabilizing forces could be obtained by modulating solar radiation pressure, with no need for expendable propellants. The same controls could be used, if desired, to stop the cooling at any time by displacing the

From *Proceedings of the National Academy of Sciences,* by Roger Angel, vol. 103, no. 46, November 14, 2006, excerpts pp. 17184–17189. Copyright © 2006 by National Academy of Sciences, USA. Reprinted by permission.

orbit slightly. In addition to longevity, space shading has the advantages that the composition of the atmosphere and ocean would not be altered further, beyond their loading with greenhouse gases, and because only a single parameter is modified, the flux of solar radiation, the results should be predictable.

Because of its enormous area and the mass required, shading from space has in the past been regarded as requiring manufacture in space from lunar or asteroid material and, thus, as rather futuristic. Here we explore quantitatively an approach aimed at a relatively near-term solution in which the sunshade would be manufactured completely and launched from Earth, and it would take the form of many small autonomous spacecraft ("flyers").

Shading Efficiency and Radiation Pressure

Early recognized that the orbit of a lightweight sunshade would be disturbed by radiation pressure. With the balance point moved farther away from L1 toward the sun, the area would need to be increased for a given flux reduction. This effect can be characterized by the blocking efficiency ε, defined as the fraction of the light blocked by a spacecraft that otherwise would have illuminated the Earth. It depends on the Earth's motion within the Earth–moon system as well as the orbital distance. Although the barycenter of the combined system and the L1 point sweep around the sun with uniform angular speed, the Earth's wobble in reaction to the moon can carry it partly out of the penumbral shadow. . . . $\varepsilon = 68\%$ for L1 at distance 1.5 Gm, and it drops to 25% at 3 Gm. To reduce the solar flux by a fraction f, the total area A of sunlight that must be blocked by the spacecraft at a given distance is given by $A = f\pi R_E^2/\varepsilon$, where R_E is the Earth's radius. The sunshade area for our goal of $f = 0.018$ varies from 3.4 million km² at 1.5 Gm distance to 9.4 million km² at 3 Gm. The total mass of the sunshade is given by $M = A\rho_s$, where ρ_s is its average areal density. . . .

In general, the total mass is reduced for sunshades with low areal density, but very low densities can be orbited near the L1 point only if they have very low reflectivity to minimize radiation pressure. For sunshades with density ≤ 40 g/m², for any given reflectivity, the total mass is minimized at a distance of ≈ 2.5 Gm. Thus, for a high reflectivity (R ~ 1), the density required at this distance is 40 g/m² and the mass is ≈ 270 million tons. Such a sunshade might be manufactured in space from an iron asteroid, which would have to be formed into ≈ 10-∞m-thick foil. An opaque sunshade could be built with lower mass if its reflectivity were reduced by applying coatings that absorb light energy on the sunward side and reemit it as heat mostly on the Earthward side. Reflectivity as low as $R = 0.3$ might be achievable, given a sun-side coating with 90% solar absorption and 10% emissivity. The corresponding minimum mass at 2.5 Gm would be 80 million tons. . . .

Further reduction of the overall mass will be crucially important for a sunshade that could be launched relatively soon from Earth. To achieve the required lower reflectivities, a transparent screen is needed that deflects the transmitted sunlight by a couple of degrees, enough to miss the Earth but not enough to transfer significant radiation pressure. Early envisaged a 10-μm-thick glass Fresnel screen with dielectric reflectivity $R = 8\%$ and areal density 25 g/m^2. Together with 5 g/m^2 of supporting structure, $\rho_s \approx 30$ g/m^2. The equilibrium distance is then 1.58 Gm, and for $f = 1.8\%$ the required area is 3.6 million km^2. But, still, the mass is high at 100 million tons. . . .

A more efficient optical design is needed to deflect the light with a screen of lower areal density. A sunshade with $R = 10\%$ and $\rho_s \approx 5.6$ g/m^2 could be orbited at 2.25 Gm distance, where it would need area 5 million km^2 and would weigh 27 million tons. A still lower mass of 11 million tons could be achieved with $R = 3.2\%$ and $\rho_s = 2.5$ g/m^2. . . .

From the Earth to L1

Is it at all realistic to transport a total payload mass of 20 million tons from Earth? If, for the sake of argument, we allow $1 trillion for the task, a transportation cost of $50/kg of payload would be needed. The present cost for multistage rocket transportation to high orbit is ≈$20,000/kg. For very high volume, it is reasonable to suppose that the cost might brought to a level approaching fuel cost, not unlike car and airline transportation. Thus, the cost to low-Earth orbit for a two-stage system using kerosene liquid oxygen fuel might approach $100/kg, with additional costs to get to L1. Here, we explore the potential for still lower costs by using electromagnetic launch followed by ion propulsion.

In electromagnetic launch, the payload is driven by a current-carrying armature in a magnetic field. From the analysis below, it seems that there is no fundamental reason why launch from Earth by linear acceleration to escape velocity of 11.2 km/sec should not be possible, even allowing for atmospheric slowing and heating. Once the launch vehicle is clear of Earth's gravity, additional propulsion will be necessary to reach L1. If auxiliary rockets were used, the potential for large savings from the initial electromagnetic launch could not be fully realized. But ion propulsion is an ideally suited, low-cost alternative that adds only a small additional mass to the vehicle and is now space-proven by the SMART1 spacecraft to the moon.

The potential for very low transportation cost can be seen by consideration of launch energy cost. Kinetic energy at escape velocity is 63 MJ/kg = 17kW · hr/kg (1kW · hr = 3.6 · 10^6 J). Taking into account the mass of the armature and the ion-propulsion fuel, and the loss in conversion from electrical to kinetic energy, the energy for launch (as shown below) will be ≈10 times this final payload energy. At the current cost to industry of 5.3¢/kW · hr, the launch energy cost would be $9/kg of payload. The additional major cost for energy storage is likely to be comparable, thus the $50/kg target for transportation is not unrealistic.

Atmospheric drag and heating.   On exiting the evacuated launch tube, the launch vehicle will be subject for about a second to strong drag and heating as it transits the atmosphere. . . . To minimize the energy loss, the launch would be vertical from a high site. A realistic goal would be an atmospheric entry point at 5.5 km elevation (18,000 feet) where [the atmospheric pressure is] half that at sea level. Setting as a goal $\Delta v/v = 1/8$, an initial velocity of 12.8 km/sec would be needed for escape velocity of 11.2 km/sec above the atmosphere, and the vehicle will need an areal density $\rho v = 4$ tons/m^2.

The drag results in loss of 25% of the initial kinetic energy. Most will go into moving and heating the displaced air, but some will heat the vehicle itself. To prevent damage, an ablative shield must be used, as for space vehicles designed for atmospheric reentry. Based on past experience, it would seem that such a shield could be designed to weigh only a small fraction of the total vehicle mass. Measurements of a test vehicle with a low-drag ($\delta = 0.06$) carbon nosecone entering the Earth's atmosphere at 6 km/sec showed an ablative loss of ≈0.1 kg, for a mass-loss to energy-loss ratio of 0.14 kg/GJ. A similar ratio of 0.25 kg/GJ was measured for the Galileo probe, which entered Jupiter's atmosphere at 47 km/sec and was brought to rest by a carbon ablation shield designed for high drag. In our case, a 4 ton/m^2 vehicle losing 77 GJ/m^2 would suffer an ablation loss of 20 kg/m^2, if the loss rate were 0.25 kg/GJ. Even if the rate were twice as much, and the ablator including safety factor weighed 100 kg/m^2, it would still make up only 2.5% of the vehicle total of 4,000 kg/m^2. Based on the above considerations, it seems reasonable to suppose that atmospheric drag should not prevent Earth launch, but clearly modeling with codes such as those used for the Galileo heat shield needs to be undertaken. A full-scale test at 12.8 km/sec could be made with a rocket-propelled reentry vehicle.

Electromagnetic launch to 12.8 km/sec.   Two types of electromagnetic launchers, rail and coil, have been studied over the years. In the rail type, the current in the armature is delivered by rails with sliding contact, and the driving magnetic field perpendicular to the armature current provided by a combination of the rail current and external coils. Laboratory experiments with rail systems have demonstrated acceleration of projectiles of a few grams to ≈8 km/sec and ≈1 kg to 2–3 km/sec. In the coil type, the armature is a cylinder with no contact, carrying a ring current maintained by magnetic induction. The magnetic field is provided by a long solenoid comprised of many short coils that are energized successively in synchronization with the armature accelerating along the axis. A 30-coil test system has been used in the laboratory to accelerate a 240-g armature to 1 km/sec with a comoving field of 30 T. The average accelerating pressure measured at 150 MPa reached nearly half the theoretical limit of $B^2/2\mu_0$. For comparison, the same pressure applied to a 1-m-diameter armature would yield a thrust of 10^8 N, four times that of the Saturn V first stage.

Designs to harness such prodigious magnetic force to deliver payloads into orbit have been worked out for both launcher types but have never been attempted. The reasons are high up-front costs, the restriction to payloads able to survive very high acceleration, and the difficulty of launch into low-Earth orbits. Such orbits can be reached only by launch at low elevation angle, which incurs substantial aerodynamic drag, and with the addition of a supplemental rocket. However, these difficulties do not apply in our case, where a high volume is to be carried to very high orbit, and there is the possibility of ruggedizing the simple payloads to withstand high g force. The coil type is the better choice to survive a very large number of launches, given active control to prevent mechanical contact during launch. (Rail launchers inevitably suffer wear from the electrical connection required between the armature and rails.) . . .

Ion propulsion.   Going from a highly eccentric orbit with 2-month period and 1.5 Gm apogee to L1 requires changes in velocity totaling $\approx$1 km/sec. Given also some margin to correct for errors in launch velocity, a total of $\Delta v = 2$ km/sec is wanted. The propulsion force of $\approx$0.2 N available from ion propulsion will be sufficient, when applied over a few months. The mass of fuel needed is relatively low, because of its high ejection velocity, $\geq$20 km/sec. Thus, the Dawn spacecraft to the asteroids will carry 30% of its mass in xenon fuel to obtain a total Δv of 11 km/sec. For our task, a mass of $\approx$5% of the launch vehicle should be sufficient. Argon, which might be stored by adsorption in carbon, would be preferred to xenon to remove fuel as a significant factor in the transportation cost.

The Sunshade as a Cloud
of Autonomous Spacecraft

Previous L1 concepts have envisaged very large space structures. The alternative described here has many free-flyers located randomly within a cloud elongated along the L1 axis. The cloud cross-section would be comparable to the size of the Earth and its length much greater, $\approx$100,000 km. This arrangement has many advantages. It would use small flyers in very large numbers, eliminating completely the need for on-orbit assembly or an unfolding mechanism. The requirements for station-keeping are reduced by removing the need for the flyers to be regularly arrayed or to transmit any signals.

The cross-sectional area of the cloud with random placement must be several times larger than the area of sunlight to be blocked, or the individual flyers will shadow one another and lose efficiency. On the other hand, if they are spread out too far off the axis, their penumbral shadows will move off the Earth. For randomly distributed flyers with the design parameters established above, namely a residual on-axis transmission of 10% and 1.85 Gm of distance, the optimum cloud cross-section size is a 6,200 · 7,200-km ellipse. For this choice, the average off-axis shadowing efficiency is 51% (compared with 54% on-axis), and the loss from shadows overlapping is 6.5%. These two losses combined result in a 13% reduction in blocking, compared with the maximum achievable for the same number of elements in a tightly controlled, close-packed array, which would have a 7.6 times smaller cross-sectional area. The additional flyers needed to make up for the losses of the random configuration result in an increase in the total mass from 20 to 23 million tons, given the same areal density. In reality, the mass penalty may be smaller or even negative because small flyers will require lighter structural supports and simpler controls for station keeping.

Position and momentum control.   The key requirements for autonomous control are to hold within the cloud envelope, to move slowly, and to keep facing the sun. The position must be actively controlled to prevent axial instability, which if left uncorrected will result in exponential increase in velocity with an *e*-folding time of 22 days. There is an independent need to control velocity, to minimize the chance of collisions between the randomly moving flyers, which even at low speed could set them spinning out of control. Control to ≤1 cm/sec, for example, will keep the collision probability to 10% per century per flyer.

To provide position and velocity information, special spacecraft with radio beacons in a global positioning system (GPS)-like system will be scattered through the cloud. Each flyer will incorporate a radio receiver to sense its velocity and position. In addition, it will carry two small tracker cameras mounted back-to-back to track the sun, Earth, and moon, to determine orientation.

Control of lateral and rotational motion will be accomplished by varying the radiation pressure on each flyer, with mirrors covering 2% of the flyer area and tiltable about an axis pointing to the flyer center. In the normal equilibrium configuration, half the mirrors would be turned so as to let the sunlight pass by and half would be set close to normal incidence to reflect back the sunlight. By appropriate rotations of the different mirrors, the lateral and angular acceleration in all six degrees of freedom can be set independently. . . . Thus, flyers can easily be held within the elliptical envelope, requiring an outward acceleration of $\approx 8 \cdot 10^{-7}$ m/sec^2 5,000 km off the axis. Shadowing could be stopped temporarily if desired by placing the flyers into halo orbits about the L1 axis.

Flyer size and design for launch at high acceleration.   The preferred option is to eliminate completely construction, assembly, or unfurling in space by having rigid flyers completely fabricated on Earth and launched in stacks. A mechanism built into the launch vehicle would be used to deal the flyers off the stack, a steady process that could take around a year. This approach avoids any requirement for space rendezvous or infrastructure of any sort, except for the local beacon system.

Although aerodynamic considerations constrain the vehicle mass density to be ≥4,000 kg/m^2, they do not favor a specific diameter. However, several factors argue for keeping the flyers small. To survive the high acceleration of launch, the smaller the flyers are, the less overhead will be needed for structural elements, and the easier it will be to make the sail-tilting mechanisms and to achieve high stacking density. A lower limit will be set ultimately by how small the control sensors and computer can be made, but a mass of no more than 0.1 g total seems reasonable. Based on these arguments, a flyer size of <1 m is adopted, to fit in a launch vehicle diameter of 1 m with cross-sectional area of 0.78 m^2 and total mass of 3,100 kg. . . .

Once rugged flyer prototypes are developed, their operation with radiation pressure control would be tested in space. They would be taken to L1 initially by conventional rocket propulsion.

The mass of 3,100 kg for the launch vehicle will break down approximately as 1 ton for the flyers, 1 ton for the armature (scaled by area from the Lipinski design), and 1 ton for the structure and remaining items. To prevent the build up of very high loads, the flyers will be stowed in a number of short stacks, each supported by a shelf to transfer the local load to the outer cylindrical wall and thence down to the armature. Each 1,000-kg payload will contain 800,000 flyers. The payload height, set by the stacking separation of 5 μm, will be 4 m plus the thickness of the shelves. The remaining elements with 1,000-kg budget will include the structure and nonstructural items whose mass was already estimated, the ablation shield ($\approx$80 kg), and the ion-propulsion fuel ($\approx$150 kg) and motor, along with the mechanism to destack and release the flyers and vehicle spacecraft elements for communications and orientation.

Discussion

None of the technical issues explored above invalidate the space sunshade concept. To take it further, more analysis and experiments are needed, and the benefits and costs must be further explored, particularly in relation to Earth-based approaches. In making such a comparison, it will be important to understand flyer lifetime. Currently, spacecraft in high orbits such as communications satellites last for $\approx$20 years, failing in part from loss of solar power of 1% a year caused by cosmic rays. Lifetimes $\geq$50 years should be achievable for the much simpler flyers, provided that radiation damage is mitigated by derating the solar cells, and the control electronics is made highly redundant. The mirror mechanisms should not be a limitation, because lifetimes >10^{10} operations are achieved by MEMS mirrors in TV displays.

At the end of their life, the flyers will have to be replaced if atmospheric carbon levels remain dangerously high. The dead ones that find their way back to Earth could present a threat to Earth-orbiting spacecraft, but hopefully no greater than the annual flux of a million, 1-g micrometeorites, or the 30 million debris objects in low-Earth orbit that weigh $\approx$1 g. This issue needs to be analyzed. Similarly, the 20 million spent armatures would be directed into solar orbit or to the moon, but a small fraction might take up eccentric orbits and eventually reach the Earth intact. It seems, however, that this threat could be held to a level no more than that presented by the ≈100 1-ton natural objects that hit the Earth annually.

The total cost of the first full sunshade implementation will include development and ground operations, as well as the flyer production and transportation. Of these, transportation is the best understood at present, although a significant cost not yet addressed will be for storing the electrical energy for release during the short launch interval. Here, because of the large scale of the project, the key parameter is the cost per launch amortized over the lifetime of the storage medium. Capacitors of the type used to store 0.3 GJ at the National Ignition Facility would be suitable, if upgraded for million shot lifetime. Flywheel storage such as used currently to deliver ≈5 GJ to the JET torus at rates up to 800 MW also could be adapted to supply high power over the 0.3-sec launch interval and should have potential for even longer lifetime. Batteries optimized for very fast discharge and long life are another possibility. A reasonable goal for cost of highly mass-produced storage with million cycle lifetime is 2¢/J. This corresponds to 7¢/kW • hr, comparable to the cost of the electrical energy itself.

To transport the total sunshade mass of 20 million tons, a total of 20 million launches will be needed, given flyer payloads of 1,000 kg. If it became necessary to complete the sunshade deployment in as little as 10 years, a number of launchers working in parallel would be needed. If each one were operated a million times on a 5-min cycle, in all, 20 would be required. To propel the 3.1-ton vehicles to escape velocity with 40% efficiency, each launcher will need 640 GJ of energy storage, which at 2¢/J will cost $13 billion. Allowing also $10 billion for the 2-km-high, largely underground launch structure, and another $6 billion for other costs such as for magnet wire and high-speed switches, then the total capital cost of each launcher would be ≈$30 billion. The first such launcher could serve not only to verify and start sunshade construction but also to test other systems requiring large mass in high orbit. (It could be used, for example, to transport a prototype space solar electric system weighing ≥100,000 tons to geosynchronous orbit, at a cost less than the National Research Council target for financial viability of $400/kg, or to deliver a similar mass of freight to the moon.) For all 20 million launchings the capital cost would be ≈$600 billion and the electrical energy cost $150 billion.

The environmental impact of launch must be considered in addition to its cost. In the worst case, if electrical energy were generated with coal, ≈30 kg would be required for each kg transported to L1. But each kilogram of the sunshade mitigates the warming effect of 30 tons of atmospheric carbon, a thousand times more. Note that if the launch were by rockets with kerosene/liquid oxygen fuel, the carbon consumed would be comparable. It takes ≈20 kg of kerosene to place 1 kg in low-Earth orbit with an efficient two-stage rocket, and likely twice this to escape the Earth. On the other hand, the fuel cost for rocket launch is much higher. Kerosene costs currently $0.73/kg, compared with ≈$0.02/kg for coal delivered to power stations. This difference underlies in part the economy of magnetic launch.

The production costs for the flyers as described here are unclear, as a completely unprecedented scale of mass-production is needed. An aggressive target would be the same $50 cost per kilogram as for launch, for $1 trillion total. To date, spacecraft have been mass-produced only in quantities ≤100. The Iridium satellites, for example, at $5 million each cost ≈$7,000/kg, an order of magnitude less than for one-off spacecraft but still over a hundred times too high. Strategies for completely automated production of 16 trillion flyers will have to draw on, but go far beyond, experience from the highest volume mass production in other fields. Some highly complex systems produced by the millions already come close to our cost target, for example, laptop computers at ≈$100/kg. At a volume a million time larger still, new economies of scale should further reduce cost, for example, mass-production of flyer mass-production lines themselves. Although further studies are needed, it seems that $50/kg for the flyers is not unreasonable. And if flyer construction and transportation costs each can be held in the region of $1 trillion total, then a project total including development and operations of <$5 trillion seems also possible. If the 50-year lifetime is achieved, the cost per year averages to $100 billion (0.2% of current world gross domestic product) and would decrease after that when only flyer and energy storage renewal is needed.

In conclusion, it must be stressed that the value of the space sunshade is its potential to avert dangerous abrupt climate change found to be imminent or in progress. It would make no sense to plan on building and replenishing ever larger space sunshades to counter continuing and increasing use of fossil fuel. The same massive level of technology innovation and financial investment needed for the sunshade could, if also applied to renewable energy, surely yield better and permanent solutions. A number of technologies hold great promise, given appropriate investment.

James R. Fleming  **NO**

The Climate Engineers

Beyond the security checkpoint at the National Aeronautics and Space Administration's Ames Research Center at the southern end of San Francisco Bay, a small group gathered in November for a conference on the innocuous topic of "managing solar radiation." The real subject was much bigger: how to save the planet from the effects of global warming. There was little talk among the two dozen scientists and other specialists about carbon taxes, alternative energy sources, or the other usual remedies. Many of the scientists were impatient with such schemes. Some were simply contemptuous of calls for international cooperation and the policies and lifestyle changes needed to curb greenhouse-gas emissions; others had concluded that the world's politicians and bureaucrats are not up to the job of agreeing on such reforms or that global warming will come more rapidly, and with more catastrophic consequences, than many models predict. Now, they believe, it is time to consider radical measures: a technological quick fix for global warming.

"Mitigation is not happening and is not going to happen," physicist Lowell Wood declared at the NASA conference. Wood, the star of the gathering, spent four decades at the University of California's Lawrence Livermore National Laboratory, where he served as one of the Pentagon's chief weapon designers and threat analysts. (He reportedly enjoys the "Dr. Evil" nickname bestowed by his critics.) The time has come, he said, for "an intelligent elimination of undesired heat from the biosphere by technical ways and means," which, he asserted, could be achieved for a tiny fraction of the cost of "the bureaucratic suppression of CO_2." His engineering approach, he boasted, would provide "instant climatic gratification."

Wood advanced several ideas to "fix" the earth's climate, including building up Arctic sea ice to make it function like a planetary air conditioner to "suck heat in from the mid-latitude heat bath." A "surprisingly practical" way of achieving this, he said, would be to use large artillery pieces to shoot as much as a million tons of highly reflective sulfate aerosols or specially engineered nanoparticles into the Arctic stratosphere to deflect the sun's rays. Delivering up to a million tons of material via artillery would require a constant bombardment—basically declaring war on the stratosphere. Alternatively, a fleet of B-747 "crop dusters" could deliver the particles by flying continuously around the Arctic Circle. Or a 25-kilometer-long sky hose could be tethered to a military superblimp high above the planet's surface to pump reflective particles into the atmosphere.

Far-fetched as Wood's ideas may sound, his weren't the only Rube Goldberg proposals aired at the meeting. Even as they joked about a NASA staffer's apology for her inability to control the temperature in the meeting room, others detailed their own schemes for manipulating earth's climate. Astronomer J. Roger Angel suggested placing a huge fleet of mirrors in orbit to divert incoming solar radiation, at a cost of "only" several trillion dollars. Atmospheric scientist John Latham and engineer Stephen Salter hawked their idea of making marine clouds thicker and more reflective by whipping ocean water into a froth with giant pumps and eggbeaters. Most frightening was the science-fiction writer and astrophysicist Gregory Benford's announcement that he wanted to "cut through red tape and demonstrate what could be done" by finding private sponsors for his plan to inject diatomaceous earth—the chalk-like substance used in filtration systems and cat litter—into the Arctic stratosphere. He, like his fellow geo-engineers, was largely silent on the possible unintended consequences of his plan.

⚬❦⚬

The inherent unknowability of what would happen if we tried to tinker with the immensely complex planetary climate system is one reason why climate engineering has until recently been spoken of only sotto voce in the scientific community. Many researchers recognize that even the most brilliant scientists have a history of blindness to the wider ramifications of their work. Imagine, for example, that Wood's scheme to thicken the Arctic icecap did somehow become possible. While most of the world may want to maintain or increase polar sea ice, Russia and some other nations have historically desired an ice-free Arctic ocean, which would liberate shipping and open potentially vast oil and mineral deposits for exploitation. And an engineered Arctic ice sheet would likely produce shorter growing seasons and harsher winters in Alaska, Siberia, Greenland, and elsewhere, and could generate super winter storms in the midlatitudes. Yet Wood calls his brainstorm a plan for "global climate stabilization," and hopes to create a sort of "planetary thermostat" to regulate the global climate.

Who would control such a "thermostat," making life-altering decisions for the planet's billions? What is to prevent other nations from undertaking unilateral climate modification? The United States has no monopoly on such dreams. In November 2005, for example, Yuri Izrael, head of the Moscow-based Institute of Global Climate and Ecology Studies, wrote to Russian president Vladimir Putin to make the case for immediately burning massive amounts of sulfur in the stratosphere to lower the earth's temperature "a degree or two"—a correction greater than the total warming since pre-industrial times.

There is, moreover, a troubling motif of militarization in the history of weather and climate control. Military leaders in the United States and other countries have pondered the possibilities of weaponized weather manipulation for decades. Lowell Wood himself embodies the overlap of civilian and military interests. Now affiliated with the Hoover Institution, a think tank at Stanford University, Wood was a protégé of the late Edward Teller, the weapons scientist who was credited with developing the hydrogen bomb and was the architect of the Reagan-era Star Wars missile defense system (which Wood worked on, too). Like Wood, Teller was known for his advocacy of controversial military and technological solutions to complex problems, including the chimerical "peaceful uses of nuclear weapons." Teller's plan to excavate an artificial harbor in Alaska using thermonuclear explosives actually came close to receiving government approval. Before his death in 2003, Teller was advocating a climate control scheme similar to what Wood proposed.

Despite the large, unanswered questions about the implications of playing God with the elements, climate engineering is now being widely discussed in the scientific community and is taken seriously within the U.S. government. The Bush administration has recommended the addition of this "important strategy" to an upcoming report of the Intergovernmental Panel on Climate Change, the UN-sponsored organization whose February study seemed to persuade even the Bush White House to take global warming more seriously. And climate engineering's advocates are not confined to the small group that met in California. Last year, for example, Paul J. Crutzen, an atmospheric chemist and Nobel laureate, proposed a scheme similar to Wood's, and there is a long paper trail of climate and weather modification studies by the Pentagon and other government agencies.

As the sole historian at the NASA conference, I may have been alone in my appreciation of the irony that we were meeting on the site of an old U.S. Navy airfield literally in the shadow of the huge hangar that once housed the ill-starred Navy dirigible U.S.S. *Macon*. The 785-foot-long *Macon*, a technological wonder of its time, capable of cruising at 87 miles per hour and launching five Navy biplanes, lies at the bottom of the Pacific Ocean, brought down in 1935 by strong winds. The Navy's entire rigid-airship program went down with it. Coming on the heels of the crash of its sister ship, the *Akron*, the *Macon's* destruction showed that the design of these technological marvels was fundamentally flawed. The hangar, built by the Navy in 1932, is now both a historic site and a Superfund site, since it has been discovered that its "galbestos" siding is leaching PCBs into the drains. As I reflected on the fate of the Navy dirigible program, the geoengineers around the table were confidently and enthusiastically promoting techniques of climate intervention that were more than several steps beyond what might be called state of the art, with implications not simply for a handful of airship crewmen but for every one of the 6.5 billion inhabitants of the planet.

Ultimate control of the weather and climate excites some of our wildest fantasies and our greatest fears. It is the stuff of age-old myths. Throughout history, we mortals have tried to protect ourselves against harsh weather. But weather *control* was reserved for the ancient sky gods. Now the power has seemingly devolved to modern Titans. We are undoubtedly facing an uncertain future. With rising temperatures, increasing emissions of greenhouse gases, and a growing world population, we may be on the verge of a worldwide climate crisis. What shall we do? Doing nothing or too little is clearly wrong, but so is doing too much.

Largely unaware of the long and checkered history of weather and climate control and the political and ethical challenges it poses, or somehow considering themselves exempt, the new Titans see themselves as heroic pioneers, the first generation capable of alleviating or averting natural disasters. They are largely oblivious to the history of the charlatans and sincere but deluded scientists and engineers who preceded them. If we fail to heed the lessons of that history, and fail to bring its perspectives to bear in thinking about public policy, we risk repeating the mistakes of the past, in a game with much higher stakes.

Three stories (there are many more) capture the recurring pathologies of weather and climate control schemes. The first involves 19th-century proposals by the U.S. government's first meteorologist and other "pluviculturalists" to make artificial rain and relieve drought conditions in the American West. The second begins in 1946 with promising discoveries in cloud seeding that rapidly devolved into exaggerated claims and attempts by cold warriors to weaponize the technique in the jungles of Vietnam. And then there is the tale of how computer modeling raised hopes for perfect forecasting and ultimate control of weather and climate—hopes that continue to inform and encourage present-day planetary engineers. . . .

Weather warfare took a macro-pathological turn between 1967 and '72 in the jungles over North and South Vietnam, Laos, and Cambodia. Using technology developed at the naval weapons testing center at China Lake, California, to seed clouds by means of silver iodide flares, the military conducted secret operations intended, among other goals, to "reduce trafficability" along portions of the Ho Chi Minh Trail, which Hanoi used to move men and materiel to South Vietnam. Operating out of Udorn Air Base, Thailand, without the knowledge of the Thai government or almost anyone else, but with the full and enthusiastic support of presidents Lyndon B. Johnson and Richard M. Nixon, the Air Weather Service flew more than 2,600 cloud seeding sorties and expended 47,000 silver iodide flares over a period of approximately five years at an annual cost of some $3.6 million. The covert operation had several names, including "POPEYE" and "Intermediary-Compatriot."

In March 1971, nationally syndicated columnist Jack Anderson broke the story about Air Force rainmakers in Southeast Asia in *The Washington Post*, a story confirmed several months later with the leaking of the Pentagon Papers and splashed on the front page of *The New York Times* in 1972 by Seymour Hersh. By 1973, despite stonewalling by Nixon administration officials, the U.S. Senate had adopted a resolution calling for an international treaty "prohibiting the use of any environmental or geophysical modification activity as a weapon of war." The following year,

Senator Claiborne Pell (D.-R.I.), referring to the field as a "Pandora's box," published the transcript of a formerly top-secret briefing by the Defense Department on the topic of weather warfare. Eventually, it was revealed that the CIA had tried rainmaking in South Vietnam as early as 1963 in an attempt to break up the protests of Buddhist monks, and that cloud seeding was probably used in Cuba to disrupt the sugarcane harvest. Similar technology had been employed, yet proved ineffective, in drought relief efforts in India and Pakistan, the Philippines, Panama, Portugal, and Okinawa. All of the programs were conducted under military sponsorship and had the direct involvement of the White House.

Operation POPEYE, made public as it was at the end of the Nixon era, was dubbed the "Watergate of weather warfare." Some defended the use of environmental weapons, arguing that they were more "humane" than nuclear weapons. Others suggested that inducing rainfall to reduce trafficability was preferable to dropping napalm. As one wag put it, "Make mud, not war." At a congressional briefing in 1974, military officials downplayed the impact of Operation POPEYE, since the most that could be claimed were 10 percent increases in local rainfall, and even that result was "unverifiable." Philip Handler, president of the National Academy of Sciences, represented the mainstream of scientific opinion when he observed, "It is grotesquely immoral that scientific understanding and technological capabilities developed for human welfare to protect the public health, enhance agricultural productivity, and minimize the natural violence of large storms should be so distorted as to become weapons of war."

At a time when the United States was already weakened by the Watergate crisis, the Soviet Union caused considerable embarrassment to the Ford administration by bringing the issue of weather modification as a weapon of war to the attention of the United Nations. The UN Convention on the Prohibition of Military or Any Other Hostile Use of Environmental Modification Techniques (ENMOD) was eventually ratified by nearly 70 nations, including the United States. Ironically, it entered into force in 1978, when the Lao People's Democratic Republic, where the American military had used weather modification technology in war only six years earlier, became the 20th signatory.

The language of the ENMOD Convention may become relevant to future weather and climate engineering, especially if such efforts are conducted unilaterally or if harm befalls a nation or region. The convention targets those techniques having "widespread, longlasting or severe effects as the means of destruction, damage, or injury to any other State Party." It uses the term "environmental modification" to mean "any technique for changing—through the deliberate manipulation of natural processes—the dynamics, composition, or structure of the Earth, including its biota, lithosphere, hydrosphere, and atmosphere, or of outer space."

⚜

A vision of perfect forecasting ultimately leading to weather and climate control was present at the birth of modern computing, well before the GE cloud seeding experiments. In 1945 Vladimir Zworykin, an RCA engineer noted for his early work in television technology, promoted the idea that electronic computers could be used to process and analyze vast amounts of meteorological data, issue timely and highly accurate forecasts, study the sensitivity of weather systems to alterations of surface conditions and energy inputs, and eventually intervene in and control the weather and climate. He wrote:

> The eventual goal to be attained is the international organization of means to study weather phenomena as global phenomena and to channel the world's weather, as far as possible, in such a way as to minimize the damage from catastrophic disturbances, and otherwise to benefit the world to the greatest extent by improved climatic conditions where possible.

Zworykin imagined that a perfectly accurate machine forecast combined with a paramilitary rapid deployment force able literally to pour oil on troubled ocean waters or even set fires or detonate bombs might someday provide the capacity to disrupt storms before they formed, deflect them from populated areas, and otherwise control the weather.

John von Neumann, the multi-talented mathematician extraordinaire at the Institute for Advanced Study in Princeton, New Jersey, endorsed Zworykin's view, writing to him, "I agree with you completely. . . . This would provide a basis for scientific approach[es] to influencing the weather." Using computer-generated predictions, von Neumann wrote, weather and climate systems "could be controlled, or at least directed, by the release of perfectly practical amounts of energy" or by "altering the absorption and reflection properties of the ground or the sea or the atmosphere." It was a project that neatly fit von Neumann's overall philosophy: "All stable processes we shall predict. All unstable processes we shall control." Zworykin's proposal was also endorsed by the noted oceanographer Athelstan Spilhaus, then a U.S. Army major, who ended his letter of November 6, 1945, with these words: "In weather control meteorology has a new goal worthy of its greatest efforts."

In a 1962 speech to meteorologists, "On the Possibilities of Weather Control," Harry Wexler, the MIT-trained head of meteorological research at the U.S. Weather Bureau, reported on his analysis of early computer climate models and additional possibilities opened up by the space age. Reminding his audience that humankind was modifying the weather and climate "whether we know it or not" by changing the composition of the earth's atmosphere, Wexler demonstrated how the United States or the Soviet Union, perhaps with hostile intent, could alter the earth's climate in a number of ways. Either nation could cool it by several degrees using a dust ring launched into orbit, for example, or warm it using ice crystals lofted into the polar atmosphere by the explosion of hydrogen bombs. And while most practicing atmospheric chemists today believe that the discovery of ozone-destroying reactions dates to the early 1970s, Wexler sketched out a scenario for destroying the ozone layer using chlorine or bromine in his 1962 speech.

"The subject of weather and climate control is now becoming respectable to talk about," Wexler claimed, apparently hoping to reduce the prospects of a geophysical arms race. He cited Soviet premier Nikita Khrushchev's mention of weather control in an address to the Supreme Soviet and a 1961 speech to the United Nations by John F. Kennedy in which the president proposed "cooperative efforts between all nations in weather prediction and eventually in weather control." Wexler was actually the source of Kennedy's suggestions, and had worked on them behind the scenes with the President's Science Advisory Committee and the State Department. But if weather control's "respectability" was not in question, its attainability—even using computers, satellites, and 100-megaton bombs—certainly was.

⋅❀⋅

In 1965, the President's Science Advisory Committee warned in a report called *Restoring the Quality of Our Environment* that increases in atmospheric carbon dioxide due to the burning of fossil fuels would modify the earth's heat balance to such an extent that harmful changes in climate could occur. This report is now widely cited as the first official statement on "global warming." But the committee also recommended geoengineering options. "The possibilities of deliberately bringing about countervailing climatic changes . . . need to be thoroughly explored," it said. As an illustration, it pointed out that, in a warming world, the earth's solar reflectivity could be increased by dispersing buoyant reflective particles over large areas of the tropical sea at an annual cost, not considered excessive, of about $500 million. This technology might also inhibit hurricane formation. No one thought to consider the side effects of particles washing up on tropical beaches or choking marine life, or the negative consequences of redirecting hurricanes, much less other effects beyond our imagination. And no one thought to ask if the local inhabitants would be in favor of such schemes. The committee also speculated about modifying high-altitude cirrus clouds to counteract the effects of increasing atmospheric carbon dioxide. It failed to mention the most obvious option: reducing fossil fuel use.

After the embarrassment of the 1978 ENMOD Convention, federal funding for weather modification research and development dried up, although freelance rainmakers continued to ply their trade in the American West with state and local funding. Until recently, a 1991 National Academy of Sciences report, *Policy Implications of Greenhouse Warming,* was the only serious document in decades to advocate climate control. But the level of urgency and the number of proposals have increased dramatically since the turn of the new century.

In September 2001, the U.S. Climate Change Technology Program quietly held an invitational conference, "Response Options to Rapid or

Severe Climate Change." Sponsored by a White House that was officially skeptical about global warming, the meeting gave new status to the control fantasies of the climate engineers. According to one participant, "If they had broadcast that meeting live to people in Europe, there would have been riots." . . .

[The] National Research Council issued a study, *Critical Issues in Weather Modification Research,* in 2003. It cited looming social and environmental challenges such as water shortages and drought, property damage and loss of life from severe storms, and the threat of "inadvertent" climate change as justifications for investing in major new national and international programs in weather modification research. Although the NRC study included an acknowledgment that there is "no convincing scientific proof of the efficacy of intentional weather modification efforts," its authors nonetheless argued that there should be "a renewed commitment" to research in the field of intentional and unintentional weather modification.

⋅❦⋅

The absence of such proof after decades of efforts has not deterred governments here and abroad from a variety of ill-advised or simply fanciful undertakings. . . .

With great fanfare, atmospheric chemist Paul J. Crutzen, winner of a 1995 Nobel Prize for his work on the chemistry of ozone depletion, recently proposed to cool the earth by injecting reflective aerosols or other substances into the tropical stratosphere using balloons or artillery. He estimated that more than five million metric tons of sulfur per year would be needed to do the job, at an annual cost of more than $125 billion. The effect would emulate the 1991 eruption of Mount Pinatubo in the Philippines, which covered the earth with a cloud of sulfuric acid and other sulfates and caused a drop in the planet's average temperature of about 0.5°C for roughly two years. Unfortunately, Mount Pinatubo may also have contributed to the largest ozone hole ever measured. The volcanic eruption was also blamed for causing cool, wet summers, shortening the growing season, and exacerbating Mississippi River flooding and the ongoing drought in the Sahel region of Africa.

Overall, the cooling caused by Mount Pinatubo's eruption temporarily suppressed the greenhouse warming effect and was stronger than the influence of the El Niño event that occurred at the same time. Crutzen merely noted that if a Mount Pinatubo-scale eruption were emulated every year or two, undesired side effects and ozone losses should not be "as large," but some whitening of the sky and colorful sunsets and sunrises would occur. His "interesting alternative" method would be to release soot particles to create minor "nuclear winter" conditions.

Crutzen later said that he had only reluctantly proposed his planetary "shade," mostly to "startle" political leaders enough to spur them to more serious efforts to curb greenhouse-gas emissions. But he may well have produced the opposite effect. The appeal of a quick and seemingly painless technological "fix" for the global climate dilemma should not be underestimated. The more practical such dreams appear, the less likely the world's citizens and political leaders are to take on the difficult and painful task of changing the destiny that global climate models foretell.

❦

These issues are not new. In 1956, F. W. Reichelderfer, then chief of the U.S. Weather Bureau, delivered an address to the National Academy of Sciences, "Importance of New Concepts in Meteorology." Reacting to the widespread theorizing and speculation on the possibilities of weather and climate control at the time, he pointed out that the crucial issue was "practicability" rather than "possibility." In 1956 it was possible to modify a cloud with dry ice or silver iodide, yet it was impossible to predict what the cloud might do after seeding and impracticable to claim any sense of control over the weather. This is still true today. Yet thanks to remarkable advances in science and technology, from satellite sensors to enormously sophisticated global climate models, the fantasies of the weather and climate engineers have only grown. Now it is possible to tinker with scenarios in computer climate models—manipulating the solar inputs, for example, to demonstrate that artificially increased solar reflectivity will generate a cooling trend in the model.

But this is a far cry from conducting a practical global field experiment or operational program with proper data collection and analysis; full accounting for possible liabilities, unintended consequences, and litigation; and the necessary international support and approval. Lowell Wood blithely declares that if his proposal to turn the polar icecap into a planetary air conditioner were implemented and didn't work, the process could be halted after a few years. He doesn't mention what harm such a failure could cause in the meantime.

There are signs among the geoengineers of an overconfidence in technology as a solution of first resort. Many appear to possess a too-literal belief in progress that produces an anything-is-possible mentality, abetted by a basic misunderstanding of the nature of today's climate models. The global climate system is a "massive, staggering beast," as oceanographer Wallace Broecker describes it, with no simple set of controlling parameters. We are more than a long way from understanding how it works, much less the precise prediction and practical "control" of global climate.

Assume, for just a moment, that climate control were technically possible. Who would be given the authority to manage it? Who would have the wisdom to dispense drought, severe winters, or the effects of storms to some so that the rest of the planet could prosper? At what cost, economically, aesthetically, and in our moral relationship to nature, would we manipulate the climate?

These questions are never seriously contemplated by the climate wizards who dream of mastery over nature. If, as history shows, fantasies of weather and climate control have chiefly served commercial and military interests, why should we expect the future to be different? . . .

When Roger Angel was asked at the NASA meeting last November how he intended to get the massive amount of material required for his space mirrors into orbit, he dryly suggested a modern cannon of the kind originally proposed for the Strategic Defense Initiative: a giant electric rail gun firing a ton or so of material into space roughly every five minutes. Asked where such a device might be located, he suggested a high mountaintop on the Equator.

I was immediately reminded of Jules Verne's 1889 novel *The Purchase of the North Pole*. For two cents per acre, a group of American investors gains rights to the vast and incredibly lucrative coal and mineral deposits under the North Pole. To mine the region, they propose to melt the polar ice. Initially the project captures the public imagination, as the backers promise that their scheme will improve the climate everywhere by reducing extremes of cold and heat, making the earth a terrestrial heaven. But when it is revealed that the investors are retired Civil War artillerymen who intend to change the inclination of the earth's axis by building and firing the world's largest cannon, public enthusiasm gives way to fears that tidal waves generated by the explosion will kill millions. In secrecy and haste, the protagonists proceed with their plan, building the cannon on Mount Kilimanjaro. The plot fails only when an error in calculation renders the massive shot ineffective. Verne concludes, "The world's inhabitants could thus sleep in peace." Perhaps he spoke too soon.

POSTSCRIPT

Is "Geoengineering" a Possible Answer to Global Warming?

Roger Angel does not suggest that climate engineering solutions such as injecting sulfur compounds into the stratosphere or orbiting reflective spacecraft should be tried *instead* of reducing greenhouse gas emissions. Rather, he suggests that such solutions should be evaluated for use *in extremis*, if greenhouse gas reductions are not sufficient or if global warming runs out of control. This position may make a good deal of sense.

However, some proposals focus on applying such measures before or instead of reducing greenhouse gas emissions. Jeff Goodell, "Can Dr. Evil Save the World?" *Rolling Stone* (November 16, 2006), discusses Lowell Wood's proposal to inject sulfur compounds, notes the expense seems low, and reports that computer simulations say it could work. However, Wood has already moved away from a strong "instead of" position. Fred C. Iklé and Lowell Wood, "Climatic Engineering," *The National Interest* (January/ February 2008), argue that "Programs should be funded to conduct serious research in climate geoengineering and to carefully evaluate the most promising options, while international efforts to curtail greenhouse gas emissions continue."

James R. Fleming, "The Pathological History of Weather and Climate Modification: Three Cycles of Promise and Hype," *Historical Studies in the Physical and Biological Sciences* (vol. 37, no. 1, 2006), finds the history of attempts to modify weather and climate so marred by excessive optimism that we should doubt the rationality of present climate engineering proposals. Thomas Sterner, et al., "Quick Fixes for the Environment: Part of the Solution or Part of the Problem?" *Environment* (December 2006), say that "Quick fixes are sometimes appropriate because they work sufficiently well and/or buy time to design longer term solutions . . . [but when] quick fixes are deployed, it is useful to tie them to long-run abatement measures." Fundamental solutions (such as reducing emissions of greenhouse gases to solve the global warming problem) are to be preferred, but they may be opposed because of "lack of understanding of ecological mechanisms, failure to recognize the gravity of the problem, vested interests, and absence of institutions to address public goods and intergenerational choices effectively."

A basic problem with solutions such as sulfate injections or reflective spacecraft is that even if they work as intended, with few or no undesirable side effects, they must be maintained indefinitely, while the underlying problem continues. If the maintenance falters, as seems reasonable to expect it will given the nature of human politics, the underlying problem will still be there. In fact, atmospheric levels of greenhouse gases will be higher than before because emissions will have continued to rise. The climate will then warm relatively suddenly, to an extent determined largely by how long we have been able to suppress the greenhouse effect.

Such solutions also fail to recognize that we face more than one problem. Fossil fuels are finite in supply. We will eventually run out of them. At that time, if we have failed to develop alternative energy sources, we will face a tremendous crisis. But if we reduce greenhouse gas emissions in part by developing alternative energy sources, that crisis will never arrive or will not be as severe when it does. One question with which human society is presently struggling is whether we can shift away from fossil fuels despite the vested interests mentioned by Sterner et al.

It is perhaps worth noting that similar climate modification schemes have also been proposed for other purposes. In the 1970s, when some people were worrying about a coming ice age, darkening polar ice with soot was suggested as a way of boosting heat absorption. More recently, adding chlorofluorocarbons to the atmosphere of Mars has been suggested as a way to warm the planet and prepare it for "terraforming." See Jeffrey Kluger, "Mars, in Earth's Image," *Discover* (September 1992).

Internet References . . .

The Future of Nuclear Power

When an "MIT faculty group decided to study the future of nuclear power because of a belief that this technology is an important option for the United States," the result was this report.

http://web.mit.edu/nuclearpower/

Nuclear Energy

The U.S. Department of Energy's Office of Nuclear Energy leads U.S. efforts to develop new nuclear energy generation technologies; to develop advanced, proliferation-resistant nuclear fuel technologies that maximize energy from nuclear fuel; and to maintain and enhance the national nuclear technology infrastructure.

http://www.ne.doe.gov/

Yucca Mountain

The U.S. Environmental Protection Agency provides a great deal of information on the proposed Yucca Mountain permanent nuclear waste repository.

http://www.epa.gov/radiation/yucca/

The La Hague Nuclear Reprocessing Plant

The AREVA NC La Hague site, located on the western tip of the Cotentin Peninsula in Normandy, France, reprocesses spent power reactor fuel to recycle reusable energy materials—uranium and plutonium—and to condition the waste into suitable final form. Virtual tours are no longer offered, due to security concerns.

http://www.lahague.areva-nc.com/scripts/areva-nc/publigen/content/templates/Show.asp?P=13&L=EN

Nuclear Power

*N*uclear power has drawbacks, but many people, including environmentalists, are concluding that it has fewer drawbacks than fossil fuels and may be essential to our energy future. However, nuclear power does not exist by itself, for it generates worrisome wastes whose handling poses additional problems. Understanding the issues in this unit of the book is essential to understanding the associated debates.

- Does Nuclear Power Need Government Help?

- Should the United States Continue to Focus Plans for Permanent Nuclear Waste Disposal Exclusively at Yucca Mountain?

- Should the United States Reprocess Spent Nuclear Fuel?

ISSUE 12

Does Nuclear Power Need Government Help?

YES: John J. Grossenbacher, from "Nuclear Power," Testimony before the U.S. House Committee on Science and Technology Hearing on Opportunities and Challenges for Nuclear Power (April 23, 2008)

NO: Thomas B. Cochran, from Testimony before the U.S. House Committee on Science and Technology Hearing on Opportunities and Challenges for Nuclear Power (April 23, 2008)

ISSUE SUMMARY

YES: John J. Grossenbacher argues that there is no realistic alternative to nuclear power as a reliable producer of massive amounts of cost-effective and carbon-emission-free electricity and process heat and that the challenges of high costs, waste disposal, and proliferation risk associated with nuclear power can be managed.

NO: Thomas B. Cochran argues that nuclear power is part of the "energy mix." But it is a mature, polluting industry that needs no federal subsidies. New nuclear power plants are not economical in the absence of strong carbon controls.

The technology of releasing the energy that holds the atom together did not get off to an auspicious start. Its first significant application was military, and the deaths associated with the Hiroshima and Nagasaki explosions have ever since tainted the technology with negative associations. It did not help that for the ensuing half-century, millions of people grew up under the threat of nuclear armageddon. But almost from the beginning, nuclear physicists and engineers wanted to put nuclear energy to more peaceful uses. Touted in the 1950s as an astoundingly cheap source of electricity, nuclear power soon proved to be expensive, and safety concerns caused delays in the approval process, prompting elaborate built-in precautions. Safety measures have worked well when needed—Three Mile Island, often cited as a horrific example of what can go wrong, released very little radioactive material to the environment. The Chernobyl disaster occurred when safety measures were ignored. In both cases, human error was more to blame than the technology itself. The related issue of nuclear waste has also raised fears and proved to add expense to the technology.

From this very brief overview, it is clear that two factors—fear and expense—impede the wide adoption of nuclear power. If both could somehow be alleviated, it might become possible to gain the benefits of the technology. Among those benefits are that nuclear power does not burn oil, coal, or any other fuel, does not emit air pollution and thus contribute to smog and haze, does not depend on foreign sources of fuel and thus weaken national independence, and does not emit carbon dioxide. The last may be the most important benefit at a time when society is concerned about global warming. The OECD's Nuclear Energy Agency ("Nuclear Power and Climate Change," [Paris, France, 1998] [http://www.nea.fr/html/ndd/climate/climate.pdf]) found that a greatly expanded deployment of nuclear power to combat global warming was both technically and economically feasible. Robert C. Morris published *The Environmental Case for Nuclear Power: Economic, Medical, and Political Considerations* (Paragon House) in 2000. *USA Today Magazine* published "A Nuclear Solution to Global Warming?" in August 2000. "The time seems right to reconsider the future of nuclear power," say James A. Lake, Ralph G. Bennett, and John F. Kotek in "Next-Generation Nuclear Power," *Scientific American* (January 2002). See also I. Fells, "Clean and Secure Energy for the Twenty-First Century," *Proceedings of the Institution of Mechanical Engineers, Part—Power & Energy* (August 1, 2002). Stephen Ansolabehere et al., "The Future of Nuclear Power," *An Interdisciplinary MIT Study* (MIT, 2003), say that greatly expanded use of nuclear power may be needed to meet future energy needs and reduce carbon emissions, but reducing costs and risks will need attention. David Talbot, "Nuclear Powers Up," *Technology Review* (September 2005), notes that "While the waste problem remains unsolved, current trends favor a nuclear renaissance. Energy needs are growing. Conventional energy sources will eventually dry up. The atmosphere is getting dirtier." Many argue that nuclear power is the one practical answer to global warming and coming shortages of fossil fuels, and is essential to a sustainable future.

In the following selections, John J. Grossenbacher, director of the Idaho National Laboratory, argues that there is no realistic alternative to nuclear power as a reliable producer of massive amounts of cost-effective and carbon-emission-free electricity and process heat and that the challenges of high costs, waste disposal, and proliferation risk associated with nuclear power can be managed. Nuclear power has a definite and valuable role to play in the future. Thomas B. Cochran, senior scientist with the Natural Resources Defense Council's Nuclear Program, argues that nuclear power is part of the "energy mix." But it is a mature, polluting industry that needs no federal subsidies. New nuclear power plants are not economical in the absence of strong carbon controls.

YES

John J. Grossenbacher

Nuclear Power

Nuclear Power 2010

The U.S. Energy Information Administration projects that U.S. electricity consumption will increase 30% by 2030. This means our nation will need hundreds of new plants to provide electricity. Rising demand for energy and electricity, pressure to reduce carbon emissions along with fair consideration of the outstanding performance and economics associated with operating U.S. nuclear power plants have spurred a nuclear energy renaissance in the U.S.

Recognizing that all sources of energy will be needed to meet energy demand, the Department of Energy launched the Nuclear Power 2010 program in 2002 as a joint government-industry cost-shared program to identify sites for new nuclear power plants, develop and bring to market advanced nuclear plant technologies, and evaluate the business case for building new nuclear power plants by demonstrating untested regulatory processes. Together with incentives enacted through the Energy Policy Act of 2005—federal loan guarantees for low emission energy technologies, federal risk insurance and production tax credits—government and industry are working together to address the last barriers associated with building new plants: the financial and regulatory risks. These federal tools will allow first movers to address and manage the risks associated with building the first few new nuclear power plants. This year's budget request seeks to significantly increase the government's share in the NP 2010 program and to extend the period during which companies can seek loan guarantees by two years. Industry has stated that loan guarantees are essential to ensuring the first new nuclear plants are ordered and built.

Industry has responded with 17 companies and consortia pursuing licenses for more than 30 nuclear power plants in states represented by 20 members of this committee. Nuclear Regulatory Commission review of the first wave of applications has already begun and industry indicates it expects to submit 11 to 15 more applications this year. At the same time, orders are starting to be placed for long-lead items such as forgings. The signing earlier this month of a contract between Georgia Power and Westinghouse for two AP1000 units is yet another signal that the nuclear energy renaissance has begun.

From U.S. House Committee on Science and Technology by John J. Grossenbacher, (April 23, 2008).

Light Water Reactor Research and Development

The combination of low operating and fuel costs which keep electricity prices down, an excellent record of performance, and clean energy benefits means that nuclear energy will remain an important source of energy for our nation's future. The design features of the Generation III and Generation III+ nuclear power plants, which include redundant systems, automatic shutdown systems and multiple layers of protection, combined with a strong safety culture and an excellent regulator means that nuclear power will continue to be a safe and reliable source of energy.

The increased electricity from existing nuclear power plants since 1990 is enough to power 29 cities the size of Atlanta or Boston each year. The outstanding performance of the existing fleet and the prospects that market pull will demand a ramping up in new nuclear plant build projects has prompted consideration of a new government-industry cost-shared initiative in FY 2009 within the Generation IV program for light water reactor research and development. This research and development would be aimed at supporting efficient construction and operation of the dozens of new plant projects anticipated over the next decade and at maximizing the contribution of the existing fleet by further extending the licenses beyond 60 years.

In February, the Electric Power Research Institute and Idaho National Laboratory issued a joint Nuclear Power Strategic Plan for Light Water Reactor Research and Development that sets forth 10 objectives, six of which are considered to be of highest priority for this initiative. These high priority objectives include:

- Transitioning to state of the art digital instrumentation and controls
- Making further advances in nuclear fuel reliability and lifetime
- Implementing broad-spectrum workforce development
- Implementing broad-spectrum infrastructure improvements for design and sustainability
- Addressing electricity infrastructure-wide problems
- Sustaining the high performance of nuclear plant materials.

This LWR strategic R&D plan presents a framework for how industry and government should work together on research and development and is the first step in identifying the specific research to be pursued. DOE's budget request includes $10M to support LWR R&D, representing the government's share in FY 2009. Both Nuclear Power 2010 and the LWR R&D initiative will enable the nation to do much to meet near-term domestic power needs, while continuing to avoid generation of the massive amounts of greenhouse gases that would be produced if our nuclear fleet were to be replaced with fossil-fuel plants.

Advanced Fuel Cycle Initiative

In much the same way that Congress has determined that it is in the best interest of our nation to boost the fuel economy of our cars, trucks, vans and SUVs—so, too, has DOE and the global nuclear industry determined that we need to raise the fuel efficiency of nuclear power, while reducing the toxicity and volume of waste that requires disposal. The Department and its system of national laboratories—working in partnership with industry and academia—are pursuing this essential goal through the Advanced Fuel Cycle Initiative.

The once-through fuel cycle used by our nation's 104 nuclear power plants is only able to extract less than five percent of the available energy from their nuclear fuel rods before they have to be replaced. By eventually closing the fuel cycle as envisioned by AFCI, much more of the available energy in nuclear fuel would be extracted, and more easily managed high-level waste would result. Admittedly, significant technology development must occur before AFCI's complete vision is realized, and additional cost analyses should be done to further understand the economics. But waiting until someone determines the economics are right to begin investing in alternate and advanced technologies tends to produce the kind of crises the world faces today with oil prices at well over $100 a barrel.

Over the near term, the AFCI program is conducting research and demonstrating technologies that have a high probability of reducing the volume, heat generation and radiotoxicity of used nuclear fuel materials requiring repository disposal. The AFCI program is developing advanced separations processes for the treatment of used nuclear fuel from current light water reactor and advanced light water reactor systems. While plutonium burning and transmutation of some of the other transuranic elements that impact repository performance can be accomplished in thermal reactors, more complete transmutation of transuranic elements is achievable in fast reactors with a much larger reduction in decay heat and radiotoxicity per unit energy produced in a nuclear power plant. This translates into a reduction in the source term per unit energy produced and hence, more effective utilization of a geologic repository. The AFCI program is conducting R&D aimed at addressing the economics of fast reactor technology and developing the advanced fuels and associated reprocessing technologies for sodiumcooled fast reactors to enable more of the energy value of used nuclear fuel to be recovered, while destroying, and extracting energy from the transuranics.

AFCI is the first DOE Office of Nuclear Energy program to implement a Technical Integration Office model to effectively and efficiently coordinate the research and development across the DOE national laboratory complex, including with universities and international research partners. Research supporting AFCI has been organized into seven campaigns and two cross-cutting functions. The seven campaigns include advanced separations technologies, advanced fuel development, systems analysis, safeguard systems development, advanced reactor design, waste form development, and grid-appropriate reactor development. The two cross-cutting functions are modeling and simulation and nuclear safety and regulatory activities. World-recognized experts at DOE's national laboratories have been assigned to lead each of the campaigns, with much of the research conducted at the Science labs.

AFCI is the domestic R&D component of the Global Nuclear Energy Partnership. GNEP is an international initiative that seeks to enable global expansion of nuclear energy in a safe and secure manner, enabling countries to enjoy the benefits of nuclear power without having to invest in expensive and sensitive enrichment and reprocessing technologies. Although GNEP is a relatively new initiative, 21 nations have formally joined the partnership and four teams comprised of some of the most capable and respected nuclear industry firms have offered approaches to DOE on how best to implement a closed fuel cycle with advanced fuel cycle technologies. In addition, industry has told DOE that meaningful steps can be taken in the near-term to close the fuel cycle by 2020 to 2025, suggesting that government take a fresh look at nuclear waste management through an integrated approach including recycling and repositories.

The bottom line is—GNEP comes at a crucial time in the global expansion of nuclear power, and is an important initiative for addressing challenges associated with nuclear waste management. It's a comprehensive proposal to close the nuclear fuel cycle in the U.S., and engage the global community to minimize proliferation risks—while providing the mechanism for international synergy in policy formation, technical support and technology and infrastructure development.

Generation IV Nuclear Energy Systems

For the long-term future, the Department is working on the next generation of nuclear energy systems, technologies that represent enhancements in economics, sustainability, reduced waste intensity and proliferation-resistance over today's technologies through the Generation IV nuclear energy systems program. Additionally, the U.S. is part of the Generation IV International Forum or GIF, a multinational effort to work collaboratively on Generation IV technologies. GIF nations are exploring six advanced systems of interest. Overall, the investment of 10 nations in collaborative R&D on Generation IV technologies is over $100M per year on the first two systems.

U.S. Generation IV research is focused on reactor systems that operate at higher temperatures than today's reactors to both improve efficiency and provide a process heat source for a wide range of energy-intensive co-located industrial processes. A mid-term version of the Generation IV Very High Temperature Reactor concept, the High Temperature Gas Reactor (HTGR) nuclear system is being pursued in the U.S. through the Next Generation Nuclear Plant (NGNP) demonstration, authorized by the Energy Policy Act of 2005. The HTGR is an advanced nuclear technology that can provide high temperature heat for industrial processes at temperatures up to 950°C. Coupled with developmental high temperature electrolytic or thermo-chemical technologies, this advanced HTGR technology can also be used in the production of hydrogen and oxygen from water for existing markets such as refinery upgrading of petroleum crude, chemical and fertilizer plants, as well as in processes such as coal-to-synthetic fuels and hydrocarbon feedstocks. Using the HTGR nuclear heat source will reduce dependence for producing process heat using fossil fuels such as natural gas and oil, for which the long-term prices are increasing and the availability is uncertain. This is achieved without carbon emissions, thus reducing the carbon footprint of these industrial processes.

As currently conceived, the commercialized HTGR will be inherently safe by design and more flexible in application than any commercial nuclear plant in history. The commercialized HTGR will secure a major role for nuclear energy for the long-term future and also provide the U.S. with a practical path toward replacing imported oil and gas with domestically produced clean and economic process heat, hydrogen and oxygen. As with Nuclear Power 2010, the Advanced Fuel Cycle Initiative and GNEP, the Generation IV program in general and the Next Generation Nuclear Plant project in particular are built on a public-private partnership foundation. DOE has recently issued a Request for Information and Request for Expression of Interest seeking input from interested parties on how best to achieve the goals and meet the requirements of the NGNP demonstration project at Idaho National Laboratory.

Idaho National Laboratory, Oak Ridge National Laboratory and The Babcock and Wilcox Company are developing TRISO-coated fuel and conducting other HTGR research. The research to improve performance of the coated particle fuel recently met an important milestone by reaching a burn-up of nine percent without any fuel failure, demonstrating that the U.S. can produce high-quality gas reactor fuel. Already, significant success has been achieved with the Department's Nuclear Hydrogen Initiative with the development and testing of high-temperature electrolysis cells that take advantage of NGNP's high process heat output to efficiently produce hydrogen and customizable carbon-neutral fuels.

Nuclear Science and Engineering Education and Facility Infrastructure

While all of the programs I've highlighted for you individually and collectively do much to advance the state of the art in nuclear science and technology, and enable the continued global expansion of nuclear power, there is a great area of challenge confronting nuclear energy's future. As with most other technologically intensive U.S. industries—it has to do with human capital and sustaining critical science and technology infrastructure. My laboratory, its fellow labs and the commercial nuclear power sector all face a troubling reality—a significant portion of our work force is nearing retirement age and the pipeline of qualified potential replacements is not sufficiently full.

Since I'm well aware of this committee's interests in science education, I'd like to update you on what the Department and its labs are doing to inspire our next generation of nuclear scientists, engineers and technicians. Fundamentally, the Office of Nuclear Energy has made the decision to invite direct university partnership in the shared execution of all its

R&D programs and will set aside a significant amount of its funds for that purpose. Already, nuclear science and engineering programs at U.S. universities are involved in the Office of Nuclear Energy's R&D, but this move will enable and encourage even greater participation in DOE's nuclear R&D programs.

In addition, all NE-supported labs annually bring hundreds of our nation's best and brightest undergraduate and graduate students on as interns or through other mechanisms to conduct real research. For example, at INL we offer internships, fellowships, joint faculty appointments and summer workshops that focus on specific research topics or issues that pertain to maintaining a qualified workforce. This year, we are offering a fuels and materials workshop for researchers and a 10-week training course for engineers interested in the field of reactor operations. Last year, DOE designated INL's Advanced Test Reactor as a national scientific user facility, enabling us to open the facility to greater use by universities and industry and to supporting more educational opportunities. ATR is a unique test reactor that offers the ability to test fuels and materials in nine different prototypic environments operated simultaneously. With this initiative, we join other national labs such as Argonne National Laboratory and Oak Ridge National Laboratory in offering nuclear science and engineering assets to universities, industry and the broader nuclear energy research community.

Finally, national laboratories face their own set of challenges in sustaining nuclear science and technology infrastructure—the test reactors, hot cells, accelerators, laboratories and other research facilities that were developed largely in support of prior missions. To obtain a more complete understanding of the status of these assets, the Office of Nuclear Energy commissioned a review by Battelle to examine the nuclear science and technology infrastructure at the national laboratories and report back later this year on findings and recommendations on a strategy for future resource allocation that will enable a balanced, yet sufficient approach to future investment in infrastructure.

Conclusion

All of the programs I've cited today—Nuclear Power-2010, the Advanced Fuel Cycle Initiative, GNEP, Generation IV, Nuclear Hydrogen Initiative—ultimately seek to make nuclear power better and safer. Realistically, we as a nation have no silver bullets that in the near- or mid-term can replace nuclear power as a reliable, 24/7 producer of massive amounts of cost-effective and carbon-emission-free baseload electric power and process heat for industrial processes to displace burning of natural gas and oil.

The challenges frequently associated with nuclear power—high costs, waste disposal and proliferation risks—can all, from a technological perspective, be managed. The high cost concerns actually have little to do with the fuel used in a nuclear reactor—they're more related to the rising costs of concrete, steel, copper, and project capital on large, lengthy projects like a nuclear power plant. Many of these same cost concerns apply to virtually every means of generating electricity we have. Nuclear Power 2010 and the other incentives available to first movers of new nuclear plants can effectively address these financial and regulatory challenges.

The waste stream from a nuclear reactor is hazardous and must be isolated—but we know how to handle it safely and we know the pathways we can take to reduce and manage it. The Nuclear Regulatory Commission has concluded that used fuel can be safely stored onsite for 100 years. An integrated approach to used fuel management offers the possibility of recycling the usable components, greater utilization of our uranium resources, and reduced toxicity and/or volume of used fuel requiring geologic disposal. Finally, proliferation. The fact is that nuclear materials can be redirected for non-peaceful purposes. President Eisenhower acknowledged that a half century ago in his Atoms for Peace address. But the nuclear genie is out of the bottle. Over 430 nuclear reactors are already in operation around the world, and dozens more are under construction or in the planning process. Do we in this country wish to disengage from the global nuclear renaissance and hope for the best—or do we want to help guide the world toward the best nuclear fuel cycle possible?

These programs maintain the viability of today's nuclear reactor fleet and prepare the way for the safe, sustainable future for this large and immediately available global power source. They address the challenges facing nuclear energy, and leverage the best minds in our national laboratories, universities and industry. . . .

Thomas B. Cochran

 **NO**

Nuclear Power

. . . Statements such as, "nuclear must be part of the mix," "I don't see how we can mitigate climate change without nuclear," "I support [or do not support nuclear power," are largely irrelevant. Nuclear is part of the current mix of power generation, and it will continue to be part of the mix for the foreseeable future. Existing nuclear power plants are contributing to climate change mitigation and will continue to do so.

The real issue for the Congress is not whether one is for or against nuclear power per se. The crucial question for Congress is whether to continue, curtail, or increase federal taxpayer subsidies to a mature, polluting industry in order to spur building new U.S. nuclear plants. As NRDC demonstrates below, the answer to this question is a resounding "no."

Why Congress should cease subsidizing the construction of new nuclear power plants.

1. New-build nuclear power plants are not economical in the absence of strong carbon controls, and even with such controls they may not compete effectively against electricity supplied by renewable sources and energy efficiency programs. Existing nuclear plants that have been largely or fully depreciated, or that acquired a new cost basis via a change in ownership at a deep discount to their original cost, are now economical to operate. The forward cost (fuel and operating and maintenance costs) average less than 2 cents per kilowatt-hour (c/kWh), and thus these plants produce some of the lowest cost electricity.

In strong contrast to existing plants, new plants are uneconomical due to their high cost of construction. In late-2003, the MIT study, "The Future of Nuclear Power" estimated that the cost of electricity generated by a new merchant nuclear plant would be some 60 percent higher than the cost of energy generated by a fossil-fueled plant. Since that report was published in 2003, the cost of fossil fuels and the capital cost of electricity generating plants have both increased significantly. In June 2007, the joint industry and non-profit Keystone Center report found that the levelized cost of electricity from new nuclear power plants was estimated to be in the range 8.3–11.1 c/kwh, up from the 6.7 to 7.0 c/kwh estimate in the 2003 MIT study. See the Keystone Report, "Nuclear Power Joint Fact-Finding," at 11. Based on more recent data supplied by utilities and energy generating companies pursuing new nuclear plants, the low end of the Keystone

From U.S. House Committee on Science and Technology by Thomas B. Cochran, (April 23, 2008).

estimate is no longer valid. Current cost estimates for several new reactors are in the range of 14 to 18 c/kwh (in 2007 dollars).

Electricity from new nuclear power plants in this cost range is not competitive with fossil-fueled baseload generation in today's marketplace, nor even with electricity supplied by waste heat co-generation, wind turbines, or freed-up by continuing pursuit of end-use efficiency programs. By the time the earliest of these new nuclear plants begin delivering power to the grid, several forms of solar power are also likely to be cheaper on a retail delivered-cost basis, and concentrating solar thermal plants will likely be competitive in the wholesale power market as well.

Implementation of a carbon cap that internalizes the true cost of burning fossil fuels is the single policy that would most benefit the nuclear industry, not because new-build nuclear power will necessarily be cheaper than other sources, but rather because it will make polluting fossil-fueled power more expensive. EPA has modeled the effect of the current version of the Lieberman-Warner climate bill to predict CO_2 prices using two different models. One model forecasts prices starting at $22/ton CO2 in 2015, rising to $28 in 2020 and $46 in 2030 and continuing up from there; the other model's prices start at $35/ton in 2015 and hit $45 and $73/ton in 2020 and 2030 respectively. In short, enacting a carbon cap could increase the value of generating electricity from nuclear plants by 2.2–3.4 c/kwh in the near term and more in later years.

Subsidizing new nuclear plants through direct federal cost sharing, a production tax credit, and tens of billions in federally subsidized and guaranteed debt will not remove new-build nuclear's cost disadvantage vis-a-vis other energy sources. Rather it will tend to disguise and even prolong these cost disadvantages, thereby penalizing and slowing investments in less costly demand-side energy management programs energy efficiency, and an array of electricity supply options that can provide carbon offsets more quickly, cheaply and safely than nuclear power. Unlike the wind and solar industries, after fifty years of operations, the nuclear reactor industry displays no consistent trend toward lower unit costs in manufacturing and construction, so it seems unlikely that further subsidies at this late date will serve to catalyze major cost reductions.

Given their high capital costs, and all the other non-carbon environmental liabilities and risks that attend reliance on the nuclear fuel cycle, new nuclear plants are obviously not the first, second, or even third option this body should turn to stem the buildup of carbon dioxide in the atmosphere. Put bluntly, anyone or any organization pushing for more taxpayer-funded largesse for nuclear power plants in a climate bill is either seeking inappropriate windfalls for their clients, or is pursuing a poison pill strategy to protect carbon polluters by trying to kill the bill.

2. International safeguards are inadequate.

As evidenced by events in Iran and North Korea, the current international safeguards regime has major vulnerabilities. Under the Treaty on the Non-Proliferation of Nuclear Weapons (NPT), International Atomic

Energy Agency (IAEA) safeguards agreements, and other elements, a non-weapon state can develop sensitive dual-purpose technologies, such as gas centrifuge enrichment plants, bring them within days or weeks of producing nuclear weapons. Moreover, "[T]he objective of safeguards is the timely detection of diversion of significant quantities of nuclear material from peaceful activities to the manufacture of nuclear weapons or of other explosive devices or for purposes unknown, and deterrence of such diversion by the risk of early detection."

In non-nuclear weapon states today, this objective cannot be met at several types of facilities used by the nuclear power industry, including commercial gas centrifuge plants, nuclear fuel reprocessing plants, mixed-oxide fuel fabrication plants, and storage facilities for separated plutonium and highly-enriched uranium. The "timely warning criteria"—detecting a diversion in time to bring diplomatic pressure to reverse the course of action—simply cannot be met if these plants are located in non-weapon states such as Iran or North Korea.

There are a number of reasons for this, including for example, IAEA "Significant Quantities" for direct use nuclear materials are technically erroneous, and in the case of plutonium are too large by roughly a factor of eight. Also, at large commercial-size bulk handling facilities—e.g., uranium enrichment plants, reprocessing plants and plutonium fuel fabrication plants (MOX plants)—inventory differences exceed the amount of material required for a nuclear explosive device. . . .

There is a significant risk that one or more of these countries will represent a future proliferation threat as Iran does today.

3. The Administration's current program for a "Global Nuclear Energy Partnership" (GNEP), built around the reprocessing and the international recycling of spent nuclear fuel, would be a disaster for international security and a multinational economic boondoggle of staggering proportions. Even if by some miracle in thirty years GNEP's development managed to succeed on a technical level, an outcome that we do not believe is at all likely, it would still drain vital capital away from more timely and practical clean energy investments that are desperately needed now to avert pollution and foster human development around the world.

The Administration originally proposed GNEP to allegedly reduce the proliferation risk posed by the future spread of conventional methods of reprocessing, and to reduce the amount of waste required for disposal by closing the nuclear fuel cycle. The center piece of the GNEP vision is an elaborate scheme involving as yet unproven techniques for spent fuel reprocessing and fabricating new types of transuranic fuels, and the "transmutation" of the long-lived transuranic isotopes in this fuel using a new class of costly fast reactors.

Of course, a simpler and cheaper way to avert the proliferation risks posed by reprocessing is not to engage in it, and strongly discourage others from doing so. GNEP is a far more elaborate scheme than the approach currently used by France , which involves reprocessing using the conventional

PUREX process and burning the recovered plutonium only once in existing thermal reactors. The French approach is already a bad idea. Implementing the grandiose GNEP vision would require a century long multinational state enterprise that would cost US and foreign taxpayers hundreds of billions of dollars, and result in the importation of thousands of tons of foreign nuclear waste into the United States. By mid-century, when the best available science says we must have stabilized global CO_2 levels at no more than twice their pre-industrial levels—we would just be wrapping up the GNEP pilot projects, having already misallocated precious tens of billions of dollars merely to get GNEP to the starting line.

In reality, the whole concept is flawed technically, economically, and politically: the proposed mixture of transuranic isotopes in the transmutation fuel would still be usable in nuclear weapons; the resulting fuel cycle would not be remotely cost-competitive with conventional nuclear power, much less other modes of electric power generation; and the rest of the world is highly unlikely to sanction another shared nuclear monopoly over the civil nuclear fuel cycle to match the one currently controlled by the select group of nuclear weapon-states under the Nuclear Nonproliferation Treaty. Both the current French and proposed GNEP approaches to closing the fuel cycle increase nuclear proliferation risks relative to and neither is preferable to the "once-through" fuel cycle currently used in the United States.

Compared to the once-through fuel cycle, the French fuel cycle costs more, has greater associated nuclear proliferation risks when replicated in non-weapon states, results in larger inventories of separated weapon-usable plutonium, is less safe, results in greater releases of routine radioactive emissions, produces greater quantities of radioactive waste when low-level and intermediate-level waste is included, provides no significant benefits in interim spent fuel and HLW storage requirements, and does not reduce the geologic repository requirements.

As noted in the recent Keystone Center report:

> No commercial reprocessing of nuclear fuel is currently undertaken in the U.S. The NJFF [Nuclear Joint Fact Finding] group agrees that while reprocessing of commercial spent fuel has been pursued for several decades in Europe, overall fuel cycle economics have not supported a change in the U.S. from a "once through" fuel cycle. Furthermore, the long-term availability of uranium at reasonable cost suggests reprocessing of spent fuel will not be cost-effective in the foreseeable future. A closed fuel cycle with any type of separations program will still require a geologic repository for long-term management of waste streams.

GNEP represents the marriage of two failed technologies reprocessing and fast reactors. Reprocessing and closed fuel cycles have resulted in the accumulation of about 250 tonnes of separated plutonium in civil nuclear programs in Europe, Japan, Russia and India. In theory the GNEP vision reduces geologic repository requirements by substituting costly reprocessing plants and costly MOX fabrication plants for costly geologic repositories.

For the GNEP vision to work an estimated 40 to 75 gigawatts (GW) of fast reactor capacity would be required for every 100 GW of thermal reactor capacity. But we already know from decades of experience with fast reactors and failed efforts to develop commercial fast breeder reactors that fast reactors are uneconomical and unreliable far more costly and far less reliable than existing thermal reactors. No energy company is going to order a fast reactor when it can purchase a less-costly, more-reliable light water reactor. GNEP is a recipe for further federalizing and increasing the cost of the nuclear fuel cycle.

Despite decades of research costing many tens of billions of dollars, the effort to develop fast breeder reactors has been a failure in the United States, France, United Kingdom, Germany, Italy, Japan and the Soviet Union. The flagship fast reactors in each these countries have been failures. The effort to develop fast reactors for naval propulsion was a failure in the United States and the Soviet Union, the only two navies that tried to introduce fast reactors into their respective submarine fleets. After investing tens of billions and decades of effort in fast breeder R&D, the Congress should ask itself why there is only one commercial-size fast reactor operating in the world today—one out of approximately 440 reactors. NRDC knows why. Fast reactors are uneconomical and unreliable.

The history of fast reactors was best summed up by the "father" of the nation's Nuclear Navy, Admiral Hyman Rickover, when he decided in 1956 to abandon the sodium-cooled fast reactor and replace it by a pressurized water reactor in the USS Seawolf (SSN 575). "In Rickover's words they were 'expensive to build, complex to operate, susceptible to prolonged shutdown as a result of even minor malfunctions, and difficult and timeconsuming to repair.'" A 1995 sodium coolant leak and fire in Japan's Monju prototype fast breeder reactor has kept the facility shut-down for the last twelve years.

To our dismay and despite the decades of evidence to the contrary, the DOE is actively signing up countries to the GNEP vision and promoting GNEP research and development worldwide. But as the Keystone Center report noted, "The GNEP program could encourage the development of hot cells and reprocessing R&D centers in non-weapon states, as well as the training of cadres of experts in plutonium chemistry and metallurgy, all of which pose a grave proliferation risk." "Could encourage" can now be changed to "is encouraging" as we are already witnessing the promotion under GNEP of closed fuel cycle R&D in South Korea.

Professor Frank von Hippel, in the most recent issue of *Scientific American,* has summarized the reasons "it makes no sense to rush into [this] expensive and potentially catastrophic undertaking." In sum, Congress should pull the plug on DOE's effort to close the close the fuel cycle and stop funding research on advanced nuclear fuel reprocessing.

4. Reactor safety is a significant concern and, to a degree not matched by any other power source, continued nuclear power generation is hostage to its worst practitioners. The most important factor affecting the safety of nuclear power plants is the safety culture at the plant. In the United

States and some OECD countries the safety culture at operating plants has improved over the past two decades. While new reactor designs have improved safety and security features, over the next two to three decades, the safety and security of nuclear plants in the United States and the rest of the world will largely be determined by the safety and security of existing reactors. Several countries that already have nuclear plants, e.g., Russia, Ukraine, China, India, and Bulgaria, have notably weaker safety cultures than the nuclear enterprise merits. This is not a situation that the United States government as a whole or this Congress can control or resolve.

Compounding the problem, expansion of nuclear power is projected to occur primarily in countries that currently have significant weaknesses in legal structure (rule of law), construction practice, operating safety and security cultures, and regulatory oversight, e.g. China and India. Securing commercial sales and "nuclear renaissance" exuberance have taken precedence over nuclear safety and non-proliferation concerns. This is evidenced by the fact that since his election in May 2007, President Nicolas Sarkozy has offered French reactors to such authoritarian, unaccountable, nontransparent, and corrupt governments as Georgia, Libya, the UAE, Saudi Arabia, Egypt, Morocco, and Algeria. Consequently, if another catastrophic nuclear reactor accident occurs during the next couple of decades, it is more likely to occur in Russia, Ukraine, China, India, or another country with a poor safety culture, than in the United States. Several countries recently expressing an interest in acquiring nuclear reactors also have very high indices of industrial accidents and official corruption.

We concur with the findings and recommendations in the excellent report by the Union of Concerned Scientists (UCS), "Nuclear Power in a Warming World" (December 2007). As noted by UCS, "The United States has strong nuclear power safety standards, but serious safety problems continue to arise at U.S. nuclear power plants because the Nuclear Regulatory Commission (NRC) is not adequately enforcing the existing standards." (p. 3) Since the United States will continue to rely on nuclear power for substantial base load electricity generation into the foreseeable future, it is essential that the safety of U.S. nuclear plants be improved.

The biggest barrier to significant improvement of U.S. nuclear plant safety is the poor safety culture of the NRC. The Congress should establish an unbiased outside commission, similar to the Kemeny Commission, to report on ways to improve the NRC's safety culture. This commission should investigate failures to enforce regulations, staff deferral of safety inspections and upgrades so as not to impinge upon reactor operating schedules, pro-nuclear bias in the selection of Commissioners, senior NRC staff management and advisory committee members, the revolving door practice of NRC staff being hired from the industry it regulates and industry hiring of NRC staff, the curtailment of public's ability to engage in discovery and cross-examination during reactor licensing hearings, and other issues identified in the UCS report.

5. After more than fifty years of nuclear power use there is no operational spent fuel or high-level waste disposal facility anywhere in the world. The proposed Yucca Mountain geologic repository site selection process has been severely damaged by its premature politicized designation as the sole site for detailed investigation. This error has been compounded by unsupportable manipulation of the licensing criteria for the site, and the credibility of the technical site investigation has been seriously undermined by charges of fraudulent data. In light of this record, the project either should be terminated, or the amount of wastes destined to the facility should be severely restricted, for example, by limiting its use to the disposal of defense high-level waste and R&D on spent fuel disposal. In either case, Congress should initiate a search for a second repository.

For fifty years, since the National Academy of Sciences first addressed this issue, the scientific consensus has been that high-level nuclear waste, and by implication spent fuel, should be permanently sequestered in deep underground geologic repositories, and by implication the primary barrier to prevent the release of the radioactivity into the biosphere should be the geology of the site. In this regard, some amount of spent fuel can be disposed of safely in Yucca Mountain. At this time we do not know whether this is greater or smaller than the statutory limit of 70,000 tons of spent fuel and high-level nuclear waste, and for reasons highlighted below, we may never know because the site selection process and the criteria for judging its long term safety have been thoroughly corrupted. . . .

The Yucca Mountain project has repeatedly failed to meet its schedule and there is a possibility that the project will be terminated by Congress. If this occurs it would represent the third failed attempt by the Federal government to solve the high-level waste/spent fuel disposal problem. The first failure being the salt vault project at Lyons, Kansas followed by the failed Retrievable Surface Storage Facility (RSSF). So where does all this leave us. We have a proposed geologic repository for spent fuel and high-level waste that was selected through a corrupted site selection process, that cannot meet the original site selection criteria, that will be judged against thoroughly corrupted licensing criteria developed in collusion with DOE, the licensee, and judged with the aid of a computer simulation model that cannot be independently checked or run by the regulators or outside experts.

The Congress should require that DOE resume a search for a second repository site. Aged spent fuel can be stored safely in dry casks until a safe geologic disposal site is identified and licensed for use. However, it has been a policy of the Federal government that we should not rely on administrative controls for more than 100 years for the management and disposal of nuclear wastes.

The Congress also should approve consolidation of spent fuel from shut down reactors, but should not support consolidation of spent fuel from operational reactors since these sites will require the on-site management of spent fuel in any case.

POSTSCRIPT

Does Nuclear Power Need Government Help?

Christine Laurent, in "Beating Global Warming with Nuclear Power?" *UNESCO Courier* (February 2001), notes that "For several years, the nuclear energy industry has attempted to cloak itself in different ecological robes. Its credo: nuclear energy is a formidable asset in the battle against global warming because it emits very small amounts of greenhouse gases. This stance, first presented in the late 1980s when the extent of [global warming] was still the subject of controversy, is now at the heart of policy debates over how to avoid droughts, downpours and floods." Laurent adds that it makes more sense to focus on reducing carbon emissions by reducing energy consumption. Robert Evans, "Nuclear Power: Back in the Game," *Power Engineering* (October 2005), reports that a number of power companies are now considering new nuclear power plants. See also Eliot Marshall, "Is the Friendly Atom Poised for a Comeback?", Daniel Clery, "Nuclear Industry Dares to Dream of a New Dawn," *Science* (August 19, 2005), and Josh Goodman, "The Nuclear Option," *Governing* (November 2006). Nuclear momentum is growing, says Charles Petit, "Nuclear Power: Risking a Comeback," *National Geographic* (April 2006), thanks in part to new technologies. John Geddes, "Harper Embraces the Nuclear Future," *Maclean's* (May 7, 2007), notes that the Canadian Prime Minister has endorsed the expanded use of nuclear power as a way to reduce fossil fuel use and greenhouse gas emissions. Karen Charman, "Brave Nuclear World? Part I" *World Watch* (May/June 2006), objects that producing nuclear fuel uses huge amounts of electricity derived from fossil fuels, so going nuclear can hardly prevent all releases of carbon dioxide (although using electricity derived from nuclear power would reduce the problem). She also notes that "Although no comprehensive and integrated study comparing the collateral and external costs of energy sources globally has been done, all currently available energy sources have them. . . . Burning coal—the single largest source of air pollution in the U.S.—causes global warming, acid rain, soot, smog, and other toxic air emissions and generates waste ash, sludge, and toxic chemicals. Landscapes and ecosystems are completely destroyed by mountaintop removal mining, while underground mining imposes high fatality, injury, and sickness rates. Even wind energy kills birds, can be noisy, and, some people complain, blights landscapes." In "Brave Nuclear World? Part II," *World Watch* (July/August 2006), she argues that nuclear power's drawbacks and the promise of clean, lower-cost, less dangerous alternatives greatly weaken the case for nuclear power.

Stephen Ansolabehere, *et al.*, "The Future of Nuclear Power," *An Interdisciplinary MIT Study* (MIT, 2003), note that in 2000 there were 352 nuclear reactors in the developed world as a whole, and a mere 15 in developing nations, and that even a very large increase in the number of nuclear power plants—to 1,000 to 1,500—will not stop all releases of carbon dioxide. In fact, if carbon emissions double by 2050 as expected, from 6,500 to 13,000 million metric tons per year, the 1,800 million metric tons not emitted because of nuclear power will seem relatively insignificant. Nevertheless, say John M. Deutch and Ernest J. Moniz, "The Nuclear Option," *Scientific American* (September 2006), such a cut in carbon emissions would be "significant." However, says Jose Goldemberg, "The Limited Appeal of Nuclear Energy," *Scientific American* (July 2007), nuclear power is likely to be of limited value to developing nations, which will need to find other options. Robert D. Furber, James C. Warf, and Sheldon C. Plotkin, "The Future of Nuclear Power," *Monthly Review: An Independent Socialist Magazine* (February 2008), call "proposals to resort massively to nuclear power as an answer to global warming . . . irrational."

Alvin M. Weinberg, former director of the Oak Ridge National Laboratory, notes in "New Life for Nuclear Power," *Issues in Science and Technology* (Summer 2003), that to make a serious dent in carbon emissions would require perhaps four times as many reactors as suggested in the MIT study. The accompanying safety and security problems would be challenging. If the challenges can be met, says John J. Taylor, retired vice president for nuclear power at the Electric Power Research Institute, in "The Nuclear Power Bargain," *Issues in Science and Technology* (Spring 2004), there are a great many potential benefits. Are new reactor technologies needed? Richard K. Lester, "New Nukes," *Issues in Science and Technology* (Summer 2006), says that better centralized waste storage is what is needed, at least in the short term. If the price of energy from other sources (such as oil and coal) rises sufficiently, government subsidies for technology development may not be necessary. However, there will surely still be pressure for government help with regulatory and insurance burdens.

Environmental groups such as Friends of the Earth are adamantly opposed, saying "Those who back nuclear over renewables and increased energy efficiency completely fail to acknowledge the deadly radioactive legacy nuclear power has created and continues to create" ("Nuclear Power Revival Plan Slammed," Press Release, April 18, 2004, http://www.foe-scotland. org.uk/press/pr20040408.html). However, there are signs that some environmentalists do not agree; see William M. Welch, "Some Rethinking Nuke Opposition," *USA Today* (March 23, 2007). Judith Lewis, "The Nuclear Option," *Mother Jones* (May/June 2008), concludes that "When rising seas flood our coasts, the idea of producing electricity from the most terrifying force ever harnessed may not seem so frightening—or expensive—at all."

ISSUE 13

Should the United States Continue to Focus Plans for Permanent Nuclear Waste Disposal Exclusively at Yucca Mountain?

YES: Spencer Abraham, from Recommendation by the Secretary of Energy Regarding the Suitability of the Yucca Mountain Site (February 2002)

NO: Gar Smith, from "A Gift to Terrorists?" *Earth Island Journal* (Winter 2002–2003)

ISSUE SUMMARY

YES: U.S. Secretary of Energy Spencer Abraham argues that the Yucca Mountain, Nevada, nuclear waste disposal site is technically and scientifically fully suitable and its development serves the national interest in numerous ways.

NO: Environmentalist writer Gar Smith argues that transporting nuclear waste to Yucca Mountain will expose millions of Americans to risks from accidents and terrorists.

Nuclear waste is generated when uranium and plutonium atoms are split to make energy in nuclear power plants, when uranium and plutonium are purified to make nuclear weapons, when nuclear wastes are reprocessed, and when radioactive isotopes useful in medical diagnosis and treatment are made and used. These wastes are radioactive, meaning that as they break down, they emit radiation of several kinds. Those that break down fastest are most radioactive; they are said to have a short half-life (the time needed for half the material to break down). Uranium-238, the most common isotope of uranium, has a half-life of 4.5 billion years and is not very radioactive at all. Plutonium-239 (bomb material) has one of 24,000 years and is radioactive enough to be hazardous to humans.

According to the U.S. Department of Energy, high-level waste includes spent reactor fuel (52,000 tons) and waste from weapons production (91 million gallons). Transuranic waste includes clothing, equipment, and other materials contaminated with plutonium and other radioactive materials

(11.3 million cubic feet, some of which has been buried in the Waste Isolation Pilot Plant salt cavern in New Mexico). Low and mixed-level waste includes waste from hospitals and research labs, remnants of decommissioned nuclear plants, and air filters (472 million cubic feet). The high-level waste is the most hazardous and poses the most severe disposal problems. In general, experts say, such materials must be kept away from people and other living things, with no possibility of contaminating air, water (including ground water), or soil for ten half-lives.

The Nuclear Age began in the 1940s. As nuclear waste accumulated, there also developed a sense of urgency about finding a place to put it where it would not threaten humans or ecosystems for a quarter million years or more. In 1982, the Nuclear Waste Policy Act called for locating candidate disposal sites for high-level wastes and choosing one by 1998. Since no state chosen as a candidate site was happy, and many sites were for various reasons less than ideal, the schedule proved impossible to meet. In 1987, Congress attempted to settle the matter by designating Yucca Mountain, Nevada, as the one site to be intensively studied and developed. It would be opened for use in 2010. Risk assessment expert D. Warner North wrote in "Unresolved Problems of Radioactive Waste: Motivation for a New Paradigm," *Physics Today* (June 1997) that the technical and political problems related to nuclear waste disposal remained formidable and a new approach was needed. Luther J. Carter and Thomas H. Pigford wrote in "Getting Yucca Mountain Right," *Bulletin of the Atomic Scientists* (March/April 1998) that those formidable problems could be defeated, given technical and congressional attention, and the Yucca Mountain strategy was both sensible and realistic. However, problems have continued to plague the project, as summarized by Chuck McCutcheon, "High-Level Acrimony in Nuclear Storage Standoff," *Congressional Quarterly Weekly Report* (September 25, 1999), and Sean Paige, "The Fight at the End of the Tunnel," *Insight on the News* (November 15, 1999). Jon Christensen, in "Nuclear Roulette," *Mother Jones* (September/October 2001), argues that one of the most basic problems is that estimates of Yucca Mountain's long-term safety are based on probabilistic computer models that are too uncertain to trust. Per F. Peterson, William E. Kastenberg, and Michael Corradini, "Nuclear Waste and the Distant Future," *Issues in Science and Technology* (Summer 2006), argue that the risks of waste disposal have been sensibly addressed by the EPA and we should be focusing more attention on other risks (such as those of global warming).

In February 2002, U.S. Secretary of Energy Spencer Abraham recommended to the president that the nation go ahead with development of the Yucca Mountain site. His report, excerpted here, makes the points that a disposal site is necessary, that Yucca Mountain has been thoroughly studied, and that moving ahead with the site best serves "our energy future, our national security, our economy, our environment, and safety." Objections to the site are not serious enough to stop the project. In the second selection, Gar Smith argues that in addition to any risks associated with Yucca Mountain itself, transporting large quantities of nuclear waste to that disposal site will expose millions of Americans to risks from accidents and terrorists.

YES

Spencer Abraham

Recommendation by the Secretary of Energy Regarding the Suitability of the Yucca Mountain Site for a Repository Under the Nuclear Waste Policy Act of 1982

Introduction

For more than half a century, since nuclear science helped us win World War II and ring in the Atomic Age, scientists have known that the Nation would need a secure, permanent facility in which to dispose of radioactive wastes. Twenty years ago, when Congress adopted the Nuclear Waste Policy Act of 1982 (NWPA or "the ACT"), it recognized the overwhelming consensus in the scientific community that the best option for such a facility would be a deep underground repository. Fifteen years ago, Congress directed the Secretary of Energy to investigate and recommend to the President whether such a repository could be located safely at Yucca Mountain, Nevada. Since then, our country has spent billions of dollars and millions of hours of research endeavoring to answer this question. I have carefully reviewed the product of this study. In my judgment, it constitutes sound science and shows that a safe repository can be sited there. I also believe that compelling national interests counsel in favor of proceeding with this project. Accordingly, consistent with my responsibilities under the NWPA, today I am recommending that Yucca Mountain be developed as the site for an underground repository for spent fuel and other radioactive wastes.

The first consideration in my decision was whether the Yucca Mountain site will safeguard the health and safety of the people, in Nevada and across the country, and will be effective in containing a minimum risk the material it is designed to hold. Substantial evidence shows that it will. Yucca Mountain is far and away the most thoroughly researched site of its kind in the world. It is a geologically stable site, in a closed groundwater basin, isolated on thousands of acres of Federal land, and farther from any

---

Recommendation by the Secretary of Energy, by Spencer Abraham (February 2002) notes omitted.

metropolitan area than the great majority of less secure, temporary nuclear waste storage sites that exist in the country today.

This point bears emphasis. We are not confronting a hypothetical problem. We have a staggering amount of radioactive waste in this country—nearly 100,000,000 gallons of high-level nuclear waste and more than 40,000 metric tons of spent nuclear fuel with more created every day. Our choice is not between, on the one hand, a disposal site with costs and risks held to a minimum, and, on the other, a magic disposal system with no costs or risks at all. Instead, the real choice is between a single secure site, deep under the ground at Yucca Mountain, or making do with what we have now or some variant of it—131 aging surface sites, scattered across 39 states. Every one of those sites was built on the assumption that it would be temporary. As time goes by, every one is closer to the limit of its safe life span. And every one is at least a potential security risk—safe for today, but a question mark in decades to come.

The Yucca Mountain facility is important to achieving a number of our national goals. It will promote our energy security, our national security, and safety in our homeland. It will help strengthen our economy and help us clean up the environment.

The benefits of nuclear power are with us every day. Twenty percent of our country's electricity comes from nuclear energy. To put it another way, the "average" home operates on nuclear-generated electricity for almost five hours a day. A government with a complacent, kick-the-can-down-the-road nuclear waste disposal policy will sooner or later have to ask its citizens which five hours of electricity they would care to do without.

Regions that produce steel, automobiles, and durable goods rely in particular on nuclear power, which reduces the air pollution associated with fossil fuels—greenhouse gases, solid particulate matter, smog, and acid rain. But environmental concerns extend further. Most commercial spent fuel storage facilities are near large populations centers; in fact, more than 161 million Americans live within 75 miles of these facilities. These storage sites also tend to be near rivers, lakes, and seacoasts. Should a radioactive release occur from one of these older, less robust facilities, it could contaminate any of 20 major waterways, including the Mississippi River. Over 30 million Americans are served by these potentially at-risk water sources.

Our national security interests are likewise at stake. Forty percent of our warships, including many of the most strategic vessels in our Navy, are powered by nuclear fuel, which eventually becomes spent fuel. At the same time, the end of the Cold War has brought the welcome challenge to our Nation of disposing of surplus weapons-grade plutonium as part of the process of decommissioning our nuclear weapons. Regardless of whether this material is turned into reactor fuel or otherwise treated, an underground repository is an indispensable component in any plan for its complete disposition. An affirmative decision on Yucca Mountain is also likely to affect other nations' weapons decommissioning, since their willingness to proceed will depend on being satisfied that we are doing so. Moving forward with the repository will contribute to our global efforts to stem the proliferation of nuclear weapons in other ways, since it will encourage nations with weaker controls over their own materials to follow a similar path of permanent, underground disposal, thereby making it more difficult for these materials to fall into the wrong hands. By moving forward with Yucca Mountain, we will show leadership, set out a roadmap, and encourage other nations to follow it.

There will be those who say the problem of nuclear waste disposal generally, and Yucca Mountain in particular, needs more study. In fact, both issues have been studied for more than twice the amount of time it took to plan and complete the moon landing. My Recommendation today is consistent with the conclusion of the National Research Council of the National Academy of Sciences—a conclusion reached, not last week or last month, but 12 years ago. The Council noted "a worldwide scientific consensus that deep geological disposal, the approach being followed by the United States, is the best option for disposing of high-level radioactive waste." Likewise, a broad spectrum of experts agrees that we now have enough information, including more than 20 years of researching Yucca Mountain specifically, to support a conclusion that such a repository can be safely located there.

Nonetheless, should this site designation ultimately become effective, considerable additional study lies ahead. Before an ounce of spent fuel or radioactive waste could be sent to Yucca Mountain, indeed even before construction of the permanent facilities for emplacement of waste could begin there, the Department of Energy (DOE or "the Department") will be required to submit an application to the independent Nuclear Regulatory Commission (NRC). There, DOE would be required to make its case through a formal review process that will include public hearings and is expected to last at least three years. Only after that, if the license were granted, could construction begin. The DOE would also have to obtain an additional operating license, supported by evidence that public health and safety will be preserved, before any waste could actually be received.

In short, even if the Yucca Mountain Recommendation were accepted today, an estimated minimum of eight more years lies ahead before the site would become operational.

We have seen decades of study, and properly so for a decision of this importance, one with significant consequences for so many of our citizens. As necessary, many more years of study will be undertaken. But it is past time to stop sacrificing that which is forward-looking and prudent on the altar of a *status quo* we know ultimately will fail us. The *status quo* is not the best we can do for our energy future, our national security, our economy, our environment, and safety—and we are less safe every day as the clock runs down on dozens of older, temporary sites.

I recommend the deep underground site at Yucca Mountain, Nevada, for development as our Nation's first permanent facility for disposing of high-level nuclear waste.

Background

History of the Yucca Mountain Project
and the Nuclear Waste Policy Act

The need for a secure facility in which to dispose of radioactive wastes has been known in this country at least since World War II. As early as 1957, a National Academy of Sciences report to the Atomic Energy Commission suggested burying radioactive waste in geologic formations. Beginning in the 1970s, the United States and other countries evaluated many options for the safe and permanent disposal of radioactive waste, including deep seabed disposal, remote island siting, dry cask storage, disposal in the polar ice sheets, transmutation, and rocketing waste into orbit around the sun. After analyzing these options, disposal in a mined geologic repository emerged as the preferred long-term environmental solution for the management of these wastes. Congress recognized this consensus 20 years ago when it passed the Nuclear Waste Policy Act of 1982.

In the Act, Congress created a Federal obligation to accept civilian spent nuclear fuel and dispose of it in a geologic facility. Congress also designated the agencies responsible for implementing this policy and specified their roles. The Department of Energy must characterize, site, design, build, and manage a Federal waste repository. The Environmental Protection Agency (EPA) must set the public health standards for it. The Nuclear Regulatory Commission must license its construction, operation, and closure.

The Department of Energy began studying Yucca Mountain almost a quarter century ago. Even before Congress adopted the NWPA, the Department had begun national site screening research as part of the National Waste Terminal Storage program, which included examination of Federal sites that had previously been used for defense-related activities and were already potentially contaminated. Yucca Mountain was one such location, on and adjacent to the Nevada Test Site, which was then under construction. Work began on the Yucca Mountain site in 1978. When the NWPA was passed, the Department was studying more than 25 sites around the country as potential repositories. The Act provided for the siting and development of two; Yucca Mountain was one of nine sites under consideration for the first repository program.

Following the provisions of the Act and the Department's siting Guidelines, the Department prepared draft environmental assessments for the nine sites. Final environmental assessments were prepared for five of these, including Yucca Mountain. In 1986, the Department compared and ranked the sites under construction for characterization. It did this by using a multi-attribute methodology—an accepted, formal scientific method used to help decision makers compare, on an equivalent basis, the many components that make up a complex decision. When all the components of the ranking decision were considered together, taking account of both preclosure and postclosure concerns, Yucca Mountain was the top-ranked site. The Department examined a variety of ways of combining the components of the ranking scheme; this only confirmed the conclusion that Yucca Mountain came out in first place. The EPA also looked at the performance of a repository in unsaturated tuff. The EPA noted that in its modeling in support of development of the standards, unsaturated tuff was one of the two geologic media that appeared most capable of limiting releases of radionuclides in a manner that keeps expected doses to individuals low.

In 1986, Secretary of Energy Herrington found three sites to be suitable for site characterization, and recommended the three, including Yucca Mountain, to President Reagan for detailed site characterization. The Secretary also made a preliminary finding, based on Guidelines that did not require site characterization, that the three sites were suitable for development as repositories.

The next year, Congress amended the NWPA, and selected Yucca Mountain as the single site to be characterized. It simultaneously directed the Department to cease activities at all other potential sites. Although it has been suggested that Congress's decision was made for purely political reasons, the record described above reveals that the Yucca Mountain site consistently ranked at or near the top of the sites evaluated well before Congress's action.

As previously noted, the National Research Council of the National Academy of Sciences concluded in 1990 (and reiterated [recently]) that there is "a worldwide scientific consensus that deep geological disposal, the approach being followed by the United States, is the best option for disposing of high-level radioactive waste." Today, many national and international scientific experts and nuclear waste management professionals agree with DOE that there exists sufficient information to support a national decision on designation of the Yucca Mountain site.

The Nuclear Waste Policy Act and the Responsibilities of the Department of Energy and the Secretary

Congress assigned to the Secretary of Energy the primary responsibility for implementing the national policy of developing a deep underground repository. The Secretary must determine whether to initiate the next step laid out in the NWPA—a recommendation to designate Yucca Mountain as the site for development as a permanent disposal facility. . . . Briefly, I first must determine whether Yucca Mountain is in fact technically and scientifically suitable to be a repository. A favorable suitability determination is indispensable for a positive recommendation of the site to the President. Under additional criteria I have adopted above and beyond the statutory requirements, I have also sought to determine whether, when other relevant considerations are taken into account, recommending it is in the overall national interest and, if so, whether there are countervailing arguments so strong that I should nonetheless decline to make the Recommendation.

The Act contemplates several important stages in evaluating the site before a Secretarial recommendation is in order. It directs the Secretary to develop a site characterization plan, one that will help guide test programs for the collection of data to be used in evaluating the site. It directs the Secretary to conduct such characterization studies as may be necessary to evaluate the site's suitability. And it directs the Secretary to hold hearings in the vicinity of the prospective site to inform the residents and receive their comments. It is at the completion of these stages that the Act directs the Secretary, if he finds the site suitable, to determine whether to recommend it to the President for development as a permanent repository.

If the Secretary recommends to the President that Yucca Mountain be developed, he must include with the Recommendation, and make available to the public, a comprehensive statement of the basis for his determination. If at any time the Secretary determines that Yucca Mountain is not a suitable site, he must report to Congress within six months his recommendations for further action to assure safe, permanent disposal of spent nuclear fuel and high-level radioactive waste.

Following a Recommendation by the Secretary, the President may recommend the Yucca Mountain site to Congress "if . . . [he] considers [it] qualified for application for a construction authorization. . . ." If the President submits a recommendation to Congress, he must also submit a copy of the statement setting forth the basis for the Secretary's Recommendation.

A Presidential recommendation takes effect 60 days after submission unless Nevada forwards a notice of disapproval to the Congress. If Nevada submits such a notice, Congress has a limited time during which it may nevertheless give effect to the President's recommendation by passing, under expedited procedures, a joint resolution of siting approval. If the President's recommendation takes effect, the Act directs the Secretary to submit to the NRC a construction license application.

The NWPA by its terms contemplated that the entire process of siting, licensing, and constructing a repository would have been completed more than four years ago, by January 31, 1998. Accordingly, it required the Department to enter into contracts to begin accepting waste for disposal by that date.

Decision

The Recommendation

After over 20 years of research and billions of dollars of carefully planned and reviewed scientific field work, the Department has found that a repository at Yucca Mountain brings together the location, natural barriers, and design elements most likely to protect the health and safety of the public, including those Americans living in the immediate vicinity, now and long into the future. It is therefore suitable, within the meaning of the NWPA, for development as a permanent nuclear waste and spent fuel repository.

After reviewing the extensive, indeed unprecedented, analysis the Department has undertaken, and in discharging the responsibilities made incumbent on the Secretary under the Act, I am recommending to the President that Yucca Mountain be developed as the Nation's first permanent, deep underground repository for high-level radioactive waste. A decision to develop Yucca Mountain will be a critical step forward in addressing our Nation's energy future, our national defense, our safety at home, and protection for our economy and environment.

What This Recommendation Means, and What It Does Not Mean

Even after so many years of research, this Recommendation is a preliminary step. It does no more than start the formal safety evaluation process. Before a license is granted, much less before repository construction or waste emplacement may begin, many steps and many years still lie ahead. The DOE must submit an application for a construction license; defend it through formal review, including public hearings; and receive authorization from the NRC, which has the statutory responsibility to ensure that any repository built at Yucca Mountain meets stringent tests of health and safety. The NRC licensing process is expected to take a minimum of three years. Opposing viewpoints will have every opportunity to be heard. If the NRC grants this first license, it will only authorize initial construction. The DOE would have then have to seek and obtain a second operating license from the NRC before any wastes could be received. The process altogether is expected to take a minimum of eight years.

The DOE would also be subject to NRC oversight as a condition of the operating license. Construction, licensing, and operation of the repository would also be subject to ongoing Congressional oversight.

At some future point, the repository is expected to close. EPA and NRC regulations require monitoring after the DOE receives a license amendment authorizing the closure, which would be from 50 to about 300 years after waste emplacement begins, or possibly longer. The repository would also be designed, however, to be able to adapt to methods future generations might develop to manage high-level radioactive waste. Thus, even after completion of waste emplacement, the waste could be retrieved to take advantage of its economic value or usefulness to as yet undeveloped technologies.

Permanently closing the repository would require sealing all shafts, ramps, exploratory boreholes, and other underground openings connected to the surface. Such sealing would discourage human intrusion and prevent water from entering through these openings. DOE's site stewardship would include maintaining control of the area, monitoring and testing, and implementing security measures against vandalism and theft. In addition, a network of permanent monuments and markers would be erected around the site to alert future generations to the presence and nature of the buried waste. Detailed public records held in multiple places would identify the location and layout of the repository and the nature and potential hazard of the waste it contains. The Federal Government would maintain control of the site for the indefinite future. Active security systems would prevent deliberate or inadvertent human intrusion and any other human activity that could adversely affect the performance of the repository. . . .

Nuclear Science and the National Interest

Our country depends in many ways on the benefits of nuclear science: in the generation of twenty percent of the Nation's electricity; in the operation of many of the Navy's most strategic vessels; in the maintenance of the Nation's nuclear weapons arsenal; and in numerous research and development projects, both medical and scientific. All these activities produce radioactive wastes that have been accumulating since the mid-1940s. They are currently scattered among 131 sites in 39 states, residing in temporary surface storage facilities and awaiting final disposal. In exchange for the many benefits of nuclear power, we assume the cost of managing its byproducts in a responsible, safe, and secure fashion. And there is a near-universal consensus that a deep geologic facility is the only scientifically credible, long-term solution to a problem that will only grow more difficult the longer it is ignored.

Energy Security

Roughly 20 percent of our country's electricity is generated from nuclear power. This means that, on average, each home, farm, factory, and business in America runs on nuclear fuel for a little less than five hours a day.

A balanced energy policy—one that makes use of multiple sources of energy, rather than becoming dependent entirely on generating electricity from a single source, such as natural gas—is important to economic growth. Our vulnerability to shortages and price spikes rises in direct proportion to our failure to maintain diverse sources of power. To assure that we will continue to have reliable and affordable sources of energy, we need to preserve our access to nuclear power.

Yet the Federal government's failure to meet its obligation to dispose of spent nuclear fuel under the NWPA—as it has been supposed to do starting in 1998—is placing our access to this source of energy in jeopardy. Nuclear power plants have been storing their spent fuel on site, but many are running out of space to do so. Unless a better solution is found, a growing number of these plants will not be able to find additional storage space and will be forced to shut down prematurely. Nor are we likely to see any new plants built.

Already we are facing a growing imbalance between our projected energy needs and our projected supplies. The loss of existing electric generating capacity that we will experience if nuclear plants start going off-line would significantly exacerbate this problem, leading to price spikes and increased electricity rates as relatively cheap power is taken off the market. A permanent repository for spent nuclear fuel is essential to our continuing to count on nuclear energy to help us meet our energy demands.

National Security

Powering the Navy Nuclear Fleet
A strong Navy is a vital part of national security. Many of the most strategically important vessels in our fleet, including submarines and aircraft carriers, are nuclear powered. They have played a major role in every significant military action in which the United States has been involved for some 40 years, including our current operations in Afghanistan. They are also essential to our nuclear deterrent. In short, our nuclear-powered Navy is indispensable to our status as a world power.

For the nuclear Navy to function, nuclear ships must be refueled periodically and the spent fuel removed. The spent fuel must go someplace. Currently, as part of a consent decree entered into between the State of Idaho and the Federal Government, this material goes to temporary surface storage facilities at the Idaho National Environmental and Engineering Laboratory. But this cannot continue indefinitely, and indeed the agreement specifies that the spent fuel must be removed. Failure to establish a permanent disposition pathway is not only irresponsible, but could also create serious future uncertainties potentially affecting the continued capability of our Naval operations.

Allowing the Nation to Decommission Its Surplus Nuclear Weapons and Support Nuclear Non-Proliferation Efforts
A decision now on the Yucca Mountain repository is also important in several ways to our efforts to prevent the proliferation of nuclear weapons. First, the end of the Cold War has brought the welcome challenge to our country of disposing of surplus weapons-grade plutonium as part of the process of decommissioning weapons we no longer need. Current plans call for turning the plutonium into "mixed-oxide" or "MOX" fuel. But creating MOX fuel as well as burning the fuel in a nuclear reactor will generate spent nuclear fuel, and other byproducts which themselves will require somewhere to go. A geological repository is critical to completing disposal of these materials. Such complete disposal is important if we are to expect other nations to decommission their own weapons, which they are unlikely to do unless persuaded that we are truly decommissioning our own.

A respository is important to non-proliferation for other reasons as well. Unauthorized removal of nuclear materials from a repository will be difficult even in the absence of strong institutional controls. Therefore, in countries that lack such controls, and even in our own, a safe repository is essential in preventing these materials from falling into the hands of rogue nations. By permanently disposing of nuclear weapons materials in a facility of this kind, the United States would encourage other nations to do the same.

Protecting the Environment

An underground repository at Yucca Mountain is important to our efforts to protect our environment and achieve sustainable growth in two ways. First, it will allow us to dispose of the radioactive waste that has been building up in our country for over fifty years in a safe and environmentally sound manner. Second, it will facilitate continued use and potential expansion of nuclear power, one of the few sources of electricity currently available to us that emits no carbon dioxide or other greenhouse gases.

As to the first point: While the Federal government has long promised that it would assume responsibility for nuclear waste, it has yet to start implementing an environmentally sound approach for disposing of this material. It is past time for us to do so. The production of nuclear weapons at the end of the Second World War and for many years thereafter has resulted in a legacy of high-level radioactive waste and spent fuel, currently located in Tennessee, Colorado, South Carolina, New Mexico, New York, Washington, and Idaho. Among these wastes, approximately 100,000,000 gallons of high-level liquid waste are stored in, and in some instances have leaked from, temporary holding tanks. In addition to this high-level radioactive waste, about 2,100 metric tons of solid, unreprocessed fuel from a plutonium-production reactor are stored at the Hanford Nuclear Reservation, with another 400 metric tons stored at other DOE sites.

In addition, under the NWPA, the Federal government is also responsible for disposing of spent commercial fuel, a program that was to have begun in 1998, four years ago. More than 161 million Americans, well more than half the population, reside within 75 miles of a major nuclear facility—and, thus, within 75 miles of that facility's aging and temporary capacity for storing this material. Moreover, because nuclear reactors require abundant water for cooling, on-site storage tends to be located near rivers, lakes, and seacoasts. Ten closed facilities, such as Big Rock Point, on the banks of Lake Michigan, also house spent fuel and incur significant annual costs without providing any ongoing benefit. Over the long-term, without active management and monitoring, degrading surface storage facilities may pose a risk to any of 20 major U.S. lakes and waterways, including the Mississippi River. Millions of Americans are served by municipal water systems with intakes along these waterways. In recent letters, Governors Bob Taft of Ohio and John Engler of Michigan raised concerns about the advisability of long-term storage of spent fuel in temporary systems so close to major bodies of water. The scientific consensus is that disposal of this material in a deep underground repository is not merely the safe answer and the right answer for protecting our environment but the *only* answer that has any degree of realism.

In addition, nuclear power is one of only a few sources of power available to us now in a potentially plentiful and economical manner that could drastically reduce air pollution and greenhouse gas emissions caused by the generation of electricity. It produces no controlled air pollutants, such as sulfur and particulates, or greenhouse gases. Therefore, it can help keep our air clean, avoid generation of ground-level ozone, and prevent acid rain. A repository of Yucca Mountain is indispensable to the maintenance and potential expansion of the use of this environmentally efficient source of energy. . . .

Summary

In short, there are important reasons to move forward with a repository at Yucca Mountain. Doing so will advance our energy security by helping us to maintain diverse sources of energy supply. It will advance our national security by helping to provide operational certainty to our nuclear Navy and by facilitating the decommissioning of nuclear weapons and the secure disposition of nuclear materials. It will help us clean up our environment by allowing us to close the nuclear fuel cycle and giving us greater access to a form of energy that does not emit greenhouse gases. And it will help us in our efforts to secure ourselves against terrorist threats by allowing us to remove nuclear materials from scattered above-ground locations to a single, secure underground facility. Given the site's scientific and technical suitability, I find that compelling national interests counsel in favor of taking the next step toward siting a repository at Yucca Mountain.

Gar Smith   # NO

A Gift to Terrorists?

America's atomic powerplants are burdened with growing stockpiles of spent fuel-rods and other radioactive wastes. "Temporary" fuel storage ponds at most reactors were filled long ago and, as aging reactors face the end of their operating (and revenue-generating) lives, the atomic power industry is running short of space, time and patience.

After years of opposition by antinuclear activists, environmentalists and the governors of all the affected states, the [George W.] Bush administration is prepared to start shipping 70,000 tons of radioactive wastes from nearly 100 nuclear powerplants nationwide to an "interim" storage site at Yucca Mountain, Nevada.

When the nuclear power business first got its start in the 1960s, the Department of Energy (DOE) promised to assume final responsibility for each and every spent nuclear fuel rod. The DOE was supposed to start picking up and parking Big Nuke's hot rods on January 31, 1998. It didn't happen.

Back in the 1960s, nuclear power advocates believed that they could generate electricity "too cheap to meter." The hope was that, by the time the powerplants needed to be shut down, future scientists would have discovered how to store radioactive waste safely for the next 24,000 years.

Forty years later, science still hasn't solved the problem.

With storage pools brim-full, US facilities have been forced to start packing used fuel rods above-ground in "dry cask" storage. The operators of the Maine Yankee nukeplant recently invested $60 million to build a new fuel-rod storage facility. These surface "parking lots" will store uranium-filled rods in two-story-tall casks, stacked in rows. Though fenced in and protected by armed guards, the casks will still be exposed to the open sky. By 2005, there may be as many as 50 such parking lots scattered about the country.

Hiroshima on Wheels

The White House's nuclear waste transport plan (dubbed "Mobile Chernobyl" by its critics) would send caravans of casks filled with High Level Waste (HLW) rolling down highways and rail lines near major cities in 43 states. Fifty-two million Americans live within a mile of the proposed routes.

From *Earth Island Journal*, Winter 2002–2003, pp. 41–44. Copyright © 2003 by Gar Smith. Reprinted by permission of the author.

Any casks that survived the trip would not be buried in the belly of Yucca Mountain, however. The facility is not expected to be open for business until 2010 at the earliest. Instead, the casks would be placed in another temporary above-ground parking lot—a federalized version of the dry-cask scenario.

Nearly 80,000 truck and 13,000 rail shipments would be required to ship used nuclear fuel rods and assorted rad-waste from decommissioned nuke plants. The shipments would continue day and night for 30–40 years.

The radiation aboard a single truck would be equal to 40 times the radiation released by the US A-bomb dropped on the Japanese city of Hiroshima. Each atomic cask traveling by rail would contain 240 Hiroshimas.

The Politics of Nuclear Waste

In 1986, the DOE began examining three potential sites that might be used as nuclear dumps. The sites were located in Texas, Nevada and Washington state.

But something strange happened in Congress. Legislation was crafted to eliminate the sites in Texas and Washington. Was it coincidental that the Speaker of the House at that time was Texas Representative Jim Wright and the House Majority Leader was Washington's Tom Foley? Robert Loux, the head of Nevada's Agency for Nuclear Projects, thinks not. "Congress acted on political, not scientific criteria in choosing this site," Loux charges.

Government geologists have since discovered that Yucca Mountain sits between two active earthquake faults, 12 miles from the epicenter of a 5.6 Richter scale quake that struck in 1992. A 4.4 quake rattled the region in June [2002].

Another drawback: Yucca Mountain is located atop a major Western aquifer. Millions of tiny fissures in the volcanic rock would allow water to drip onto the stored casks. The canisters will have to be retrofitted with titanium drip shields.

Government engineers claim these casks can last 270,000 years, but Loux's studies show the casks could corrode within as few as 500 years.

If any of the casks were to crack, the wastes would move inexorably toward the aquifer.

Does any of this concern the White House, whose resident-in-chief insists that his judgements will be made on the basis of "the best science, not politics"? Apparently not. On February 14, Bush agreed with his advisors' recommendation: "We've found nothing so far that would disqualify the site. . . . There are no show stoppers."

Highways to Hell

The government admits there could be as many as 900 accidents involving these nuclear shipments over 30 years. Department of Energy officials confide radioactive shipping accidents are "inevitable."

If a single truck were to spill its radioactive load, federal studies estimate, it would contaminate 42 square miles. Decontaminating a single square mile would take four years.

If the accident happened in a rural location, federal studies estimate cleanup costs could reach $620 million. If the accident occurred in an urban location, the entire city would be rendered uninhabitable. The decontamination costs would top $9.5 billion.

Truck accidents and train derailments are in the news nearly every day. The DOE, however, says there is little danger, as its casks are crash- and fire-proof. The US Conference of Mayors is not reassured. On June 18, the mayors called on the DOE to halt its plans to ship waste to Yucca Mountain, noting that the casks "have never undergone full-scale physical testing to determine if they can withstand likely transportation accident and terrorism scenarios."

If the shipments are to go ahead, the mayors stated, Congress must first pass legislation requiring "adequate funds, training and equipment to protect the public health and safety in the event of an accident."

On July 18, 2001, a CSX railroad train caught fire in the Howard Street tunnel beneath the streets of downtown Baltimore. It was an hour before the fire departments were notified, and nearly three before the public was warned. The inferno raged for five days and reached temperatures of 1,500°F—hot enough to have melted the DOE's "impregnable" casks within a few hours.

According to studies conducted by the New York-based Radioactive Waste Management Associates, had that train been hauling HLW, 390,388 residents would have been exposed to the radioactive cloud. Tens of thousands might have died of cancer as a result. The cleanup costs would have approached $14 billion.

Despite calls for heightened security in the wake of 9/11, the Department of Transportation (DOT) and the Nuclear Regulatory Commission (NRC) are planning to relax safety regulations governing these nuclear shipments. The NRC concedes the new rules will reduce public health and safety.

Under the joint DOT/NRC plan, hundreds of radioactive isotopes would be exempted from regulatory controls. The plan would allow the industry to ship the wastes in cheaper, stripped down single-shell casks instead of the sturdier double-shell models currently required.

Agency officials explain the scheme to deregulate nuclear waste shipments was written before September 11. Nonetheless, NRC officials have refused to abandon plans to loosen security in the post 9/11 world. Their response is that these unforeseen new threats will be addressed "later."

The agency entrusted with safeguarding these rolling terror targets is the DOE's Transportation Security Division (TSD). In simulations run to assess the TSD's readiness to protect the cargo against terrorist attack, the Project On Government Oversight . . . reports, TSD defenders "were annihilated in ten seconds after an attack was started."

An internal DOE memo dated December 12, 1998 reported on the results of a computerized Joint Tactical Simulation of TSD's readiness. The results of the first test: three losses and no wins. The results of the second simulation: three losses and one win. At that point, all further simulations were cancelled.

DOE decided to purchase fleets of armored Humvees to help TSD's troopers patrol the shipments. That was before the Security Director at DOE's Pantex nuclear weapons assembly plant in Texas pointed out the Humvees were motorized death traps and it would be "just as effective to buy Yugos."

The problem? Armor-piercing incendiary rounds could penetrate the Humvees, turning the passengers into toast. A Government Accounting Office investigation has revealed the Pentagon has released more than 100,000 of these deadly surplus rounds for sale on the open market.

The shipping casks could be equally vulnerable. According to the Nuclear Information and Resource Service . . . the White House has been informed "rocket launchers that are for retail sale . . . around the world are capable of penetrating a shipping cask, releasing deadly amounts of radioactivity." As NIRS spokesperson Kevin Kamps observes: "Providing security over a 30-year period for tens of thousands of moving targets is not realistic."

In July, the US Senate voted 60–39 to override Nevada's veto of the Yucca Mountain nuclear waste dump. This does not mean Yucca Mountain will ever open; instead, it sets the stage for years of courtroom activity, Nuclear Regulatory Commission (NRC) licensing proceedings, continued Congressional action, and an increased likelihood of large protests and blockades of highways and railways.

POSTSCRIPT

Should the United States Continue to Focus Plans for Permanent Nuclear Waste Disposal Exclusively at Yucca Mountain?

As Secretary Abraham notes, the state of Nevada has the right to object to his recommendation. Not surprisingly, Nevada Governor Kenny Guinn did exactly that on April 8, 2002. On May 8, the U.S. House of Representatives promptly voted to set aside the veto, and on July 9, the Senate voted to do the same. News reports said this ends "years of political debate over nuclear waste disposal." But the debate continued. Senator Hillary Clinton said in testimony before the Senate Environment and Public Works Committee on October 31, 2007, that she thought it was time to scrap both the work done so far and the controversy and start over. In February 2008, Senator James Inhofe introduced a bill intended to speed up the licensing process for Yucca Mountain. Journalist Chuck Muth, "Nevada Kids, They Glow in the Dark," *Las Vegas Business Press* (January 7, 2008), says that waste deposited at Yucca Mountain could be very valuable if the nation chooses to reprocess waste and that Nevada could wind up being "the nuclear research and reprocessing capital of the world."

Even those who favor using Yucca Mountain for high-level nuclear waste disposal admit that in time the site is bound to leak. The intensity of the radioactivity emitted by the waste will decline rapidly as short-half-life materials decay, and by 2300 AD, when the site is expected to be sealed, that intensity will be less than 5 percent of the initial level. After that, however, radiation intensity will decline much more slowly. The nickel-alloy containers for the waste are expected to last at least 10,000 years, but they will not last forever. The Department of Energy's (DOE) computer simulations predict that the radiation released to the environment will rise rapidly after about 100,000 years, with a peak annual dose after 400,000 years that is about double the natural background exposure. Whether the site can be protected for any significant fraction of such time periods arouses considerable skepticism among those who point out that 10,000 years is about the same length of time as has passed since humans built their first cities, and 400,000 years is about twice as long as modern *Homo sapiens* has existed.

On June 3, 2008, the DOE submitted a license application to the U.S. Nuclear Regulatory Commission, seeking authorization to construct a deep geologic repository for disposal of high-level radioactive waste at Yucca Mountain, Nevada; see http://www.nrc.gov/waste/hlw-disposal.html.

The Waste Isolation Pilot Plant in New Mexico started receiving transuranic waste in 1999. It is worth noting that it too was surrounded by controversy, as summarized by Chris Hayhurst in "WIPP Lash: Doubts Linger about a Controversial Underground Nuclear Waste Storage Site," *E—The Environmental Magazine* (January–February 1998). Its website is at http://www.wipp.energy.gov/.

For a good summary of the nuclear waste problem and the disposal controversy, see Michael E. Long, "Half Life: The Lethal Legacy of America's Nuclear Waste," *National Geographic* (July 2002). Gary Taubes, in "Whose Nuclear Waste?" *Technology Review* (January/February 2002), argues that a whole new approach may be necessary. One such approach is an interim, above-ground storage facility for commercial nuclear waste at Yucca Mountain. This has been urged as a way to create commitment to continue developing the Yucca Mountain site and to meet government responsibilities to deal with commercial waste. This facility was part of legislation that would approve the Yucca Mountain site, but it was removed before Congress passed the bill in March 2000, and President Clinton vetoed the bill.

Steven Ashley, in "Divide and Vitrify," *Scientific American* (June 2002), describes work on potential methods of separating the most hazardous components of nuclear waste. One such approach is to expose nuclear waste to neutrons from particle accelerators or special nuclear reactors and thereby greatly hasten the process of radioactive decay.

ISSUE 14

Should the United States Reprocess Spent Nuclear Fuel?

YES: Phillip J. Finck, from Statement before the House Committee on Science, Energy Subcommittee, Hearing on Nuclear Fuel Reprocessing (June 16, 2005)

NO: Frank N. von Hippel, from "Rethinking Nuclear Fuel Recycling," *Scientific American* (May 2008)

ISSUE SUMMARY

YES: Phillip J. Finck argues that by reprocessing spent nuclear fuel, the United States can enable nuclear power to expand its contribution to the nation's energy needs while reducing carbon emissions, nuclear waste, and the need for waste repositories such as Yucca Mountain.

NO: Frank N. von Hippel argues that reprocessing nuclear spent fuel is expensive and emits lethal radiation. There is also a worrisome risk that the increased availability of bomb-grade nuclear materials will increase the risk of nuclear war and terrorism.

$\mathbf{A}$s nuclear reactors operate, the nuclei of uranium-235 atoms split, releasing neutrons and nuclei of smaller atoms called fission products, which are themselves radioactive. Some of the neutrons are absorbed by uranium-238, which then becomes plutonium. The fission product atoms eventually accumulate to the point where the reactor fuel no longer releases as much energy as it used to. It is said to be "spent." At this point, the spent fuel is removed from the reactor and replaced with fresh fuel.

Once removed from the reactor, the spent fuel poses a problem. Currently it is regarded as high-level nuclear waste that must be stored on the site of the reactor, initially in a swimming pool–sized tank and later, once the radioactivity levels have subsided a bit, in "dry casks." There is a plan to dispose of the casks permanently in a subterranean repository being built at Yucca Mountain, Nevada (see Issue 13), but spent fuel still contains useful components. Not all the uranium-235 has been burned up, and the plutonium created as fuel is burned can itself be used as fuel. When spent fuel is treated as waste, these components of the waste are discarded.

Early in the Nuclear Age, it was seen that if these components could be recovered, the amount of waste to be disposed of could be reduced. The fuel supply could also be extended, and in fact, since plutonium is made from otherwise useless uranium-238, new fuel could be created. Reactors designed to maximize plutonium creation, known as "breeder reactors because they "breed" fuel, were built and are still in use as power plants in Europe. In the United States, breeder reactors have been built and operated only by the Department of Defense, because plutonium extracted from spent fuel is required for making nuclear bombs. They have not seen civilian use in part because of fear that bomb-grade material could fall into the wrong hands.

The separation and recycling of unused fuel from spent fuel is known as reprocessing. In the United States, a reprocessing plant operated in West Valley, New York, from 1966 to 1972 (see "Plutonium Recovery from Spent Fuel Reprocessing by Nuclear Fuel Services at West Valley, New York, from 1966 to 1972" [DOE, 1996; https://www.osti.gov/opennet/forms.jsp?formurl=document/purecov/nfsrepo.html]). After the Nuclear Nonproliferation Treaty went into force in 1970, it became U.S. policy not to reprocess spent nuclear fuel and thereby to limit the availability of bomb-grade material. As a consequence, spent fuel was not recycled, it was regarded as high-level waste to be disposed of, and the waste continued to accumulate.

The Yucca Mountain nuclear waste disposal site has proven to be controversial, and there remains a great deal of resistance to storing waste there. But the need to dispose of nuclear waste is not about to go away, especially if the United States expands its reliance on nuclear power (see Issue 12). This simple truth drives much of the discussion of nuclear fuel reprocessing. In the following selections, Phillip J. Finck, deputy associate laboratory director, Applied Science and Technology and National Security, Argonne National Laboratory, argues that by reprocessing spent nuclear fuel, the United States can enable nuclear power to expand its contribution to the nation's energy needs while reducing carbon emissions, nuclear waste, and the need for waste repositories such as Yucca Mountain. Frank N. von Hippel argues that reprocessing nuclear spent fuel is expensive and emits lethal radiation. There is also a worrisome risk that the increased availability of bomb-grade nuclear materials will increase the risk of nuclear war and terrorism. Prudence demands that spent fuel be stored until the benefits or reprocessing exceed the risks (if they ever do).

YES

Phillip J. Finck

Statement before the House Committee on Science, Energy Subcommittee, Hearing on Nuclear Fuel Reprocessing

Summary

Management of spent nuclear fuel from commercial nuclear reactors can be addressed in a comprehensive, integrated manner to enable safe, emissions-free, nuclear electricity to make a sustained and growing contribution to the nation's energy needs. Legislation limits the capacity of the Yucca Mountain repository to 70,000 metric tons from commercial spent fuel and DOE defense-related waste. It is estimated that this amount will be accumulated by approximately 2010 at current generation rates for spent nuclear fuel. To preserve nuclear energy as a significant part of our future energy generating capability, new technologies can be implemented that allow greater use of the repository space at Yucca Mountain. By processing spent nuclear fuel and recycling the hazardous radioactive materials, we can reduce the waste disposal requirements enough to delay the need for a second repository until the next century, even in a nuclear energy growth scenario. Recent studies indicate that such a closed fuel cycle may require only minimal increases in nuclear electricity costs, and are not a major factor in the economic competitiveness of nuclear power (The University of Chicago study, "The Economic Future of Nuclear Power," August 2004). However, the benefits of a closed fuel cycle can not be measured by economics alone; resource optimization and waste minimization are also important benefits. Moving forward in 2007 with an engineering-scale demonstration of an integrated system of proliferation-resistant, advanced separations and transmutation technologies would be an excellent first step in demonstrating all of the necessary technologies for a sustainable future for nuclear energy.

Nuclear Waste and Sustainability

World energy demand is increasing at a rapid pace. In order to satisfy the demand and protect the environment for future generations, energy sources must evolve from the current dominance of fossil fuels to a

From United States Senate by Phillip J. Finck, (June 16, 2005).

more balanced, sustainable approach. This new approach must be based on abundant, clean, and economical energy sources. Furthermore, because of the growing worldwide demand and competition for energy, the United States vitally needs to establish energy sources that allow for energy independence.

Nuclear energy is a carbon-free, secure, and reliable energy source for today and for the future. In addition to electricity production, nuclear energy has the promise to become a critical resource for process heat in the production of transportation fuels, such as hydrogen and synthetic fuels, and desalinated water. New nuclear plants are imperative to meet these vital needs.

To ensure a sustainable future for nuclear energy, several requirements must be met. These include safety and efficiency, proliferation resistance, sound nuclear materials management, and minimal environmental impacts. While some of these requirements are already being satisfied, the United States needs to adopt a more comprehensive approach to nuclear waste management. The environmental benefits of resource optimization and waste minimization for nuclear power must be pursued with targeted research and development to develop a successful integrated system with minimal economic impact. Alternative nuclear fuel cycle options that employ separations, transmutation, and refined disposal (e.g., conservation of geologic repository space) must be contrasted with the current planned approach of direct disposal, taking into account the complete set of potential benefits and penalties. In many ways, this is not unlike the premium homeowners pay to recycle municipal waste.

The spent nuclear fuel situation in the United States can be put in perspective with a few numbers. Currently, the country's 103 commercial nuclear reactors produce more than 2000 metric tons of spent nuclear fuel per year (masses are measured in heavy metal content of the fuel, including uranium and heavier elements). The Yucca Mountain repository has a legislative capacity of 70,000 metric tons, including spent nuclear fuel and DOE defense-related wastes. By approximately 2010 the accumulated spent nuclear fuel generated by these reactors and the defense-related waste will meet this capacity, even before the repository starts accepting any spent nuclear fuel. The ultimate technical capacity of Yucca Mountain is expected to be around 120,000 metric tons, using the current understanding of the Yucca Mountain site geologic and hydrologic characteristics. This limit will be reached by including the spent fuel from current reactors operating over their lifetime. Assuming nuclear growth at a rate of 1.8% per year after 2010, the 120,000 metric ton capacity will be reached around 2030. At that projected nuclear growth rate, the U.S. will need up to nine Yucca Mountain-type repositories by the end of this century. Until Yucca Mountain starts accepting waste, spent nuclear fuel must be stored in temporary facilities, either storage pools or above ground storage casks.

Today, many consider repository space a scarce resource that should be managed as such. While disposal costs in a geologic repository are currently quite affordable for U.S. electric utilities, accounting for only a few percent of the total cost of electricity, the availability of U.S. repository space will likely remain limited.

Only three options are available for the disposal of accumulating spent nuclear fuel:

- Build more ultimate disposal sites like Yucca Mountain.
- Use interim storage technologies as a temporary solution.
- Develop and implement advanced fuel cycles, consisting of separation technologies that separate the constituents of spent nuclear fuel into elemental streams, and transmutation technologies that destroy selected elements and greatly reduce repository needs.

A responsible approach to using nuclear power must always consider its whole life cycle, including final disposal. We consider that temporary solutions, while useful as a stockpile management tool, can never be considered as ultimate solutions. It seems prudent that the U.S. always have at least one set of technologies available to avoid expanding geologic disposal sites.

Spent Nuclear Fuel

The composition of spent nuclear fuel poses specific problems that make its ultimate disposal challenging. Fresh nuclear fuel is composed of uranium dioxide (about 96% U238, and 4% U235). During irradiation, most of the U235 is fissioned, and a small fraction of the U238 is transmuted into heavier elements (known as "transuranics"). The spent nuclear fuel contains about 93% uranium (mostly U238), about 1% plutonium, less than 1% minor actinides (neptunium, americium, and curium), and 5% fission products. Uranium, if separated from the other elements, is relatively benign, and could be disposed of as low-level waste or stored for later use. Some of the other elements raise significant concerns:

- The fissile isotopes of plutonium, americium, and neptunium are potentially usable in weapons and, therefore, raise proliferation concerns. Because spent nuclear fuel is protected from theft for about one hundred years by its intense radioactivity, it is difficult to separate these isotopes without remote handling facilities.
- Three isotopes, which are linked through a decay process (Pu241, Am241, and Np237), are the major contributors to the estimated dose for releases from the repository, typically occurring between 100,000 and 1 million years, and also to the long-term heat generation that limits the amount of waste that can be placed in the repository.
- Certain fission products (cesium, strontium) are major contributors to the repository's shortterm heat load, but their effects can be mitigated by providing better ventilation to the repository or by providing a cooling-off period before placing them in the repository.
- Other fission products (Tc99 and I129) also contribute to the estimated dose.

The time scales required to mitigate these concerns are daunting: several of the isotopes of concern will not decay to safe levels for hundreds of thousands of years. Thus, the solutions to long-term disposal of spent nuclear fuel are limited to three options: the search for a geologic environment that will remain stable for that period; the search for waste forms that can contain these elements for that period; or the destruction of these isotopes. These three options underlie the major fuel cycle strategies that are currently being developed and deployed in the U.S. and other countries.

Options for Disposing of Spent Nuclear Fuel

Three options are being considered for disposing of spent nuclear fuel: the once-through cycle is the U.S. reference; limited recycle has been implemented in France and elsewhere and is being deployed in Japan; and full recycle (also known as the closed fuel cycle) is being researched in the U.S., France, Japan, and elsewhere.

1. Once-through Fuel Cycle

This is the U.S. reference option where spent nuclear fuel is sent to the geologic repository that must contain the constituents of the spent nuclear fuel for hundreds of thousands of years. Several countries have programs to develop these repositories, with the U.S. having the most advanced program. This approach is considered safe, provided suitable repository locations and space can be found. It should be noted that other ultimate disposal options have been researched (e.g., deep sea disposal; boreholes and disposal in the sun) and abandoned. The challenges of long-term geologic disposal of spent nuclear fuel are well recognized, and are related to the uncertainty about both the long-term behavior of spent nuclear fuel and the geologic media in which it is placed.

2. Limited Recycle

Limited recycle options are commercially available in France, Japan, and the United Kingdom. They use the PUREX process, which separates uranium and plutonium, and directs the remaining transuranics to vitrified waste, along with all the fission products. The uranium is stored for eventual reuse. The plutonium is used to fabricate mixed-oxide fuel that can be used in conventional reactors. Spent mixed-oxide fuel is currently not reprocessed, though the feasibility of mixed-oxide reprocessing has been demonstrated. It is typically stored or eventually sent to a geologic repository for disposal. Note that a reactor partially loaded with mixed-oxide fuel can destroy as much plutonium as it creates. Nevertheless, this approach always results in increased production of americium, a key contributor to the heat generation in a repository. This approach has two significant advantages:

- It can help manage the accumulation of plutonium.
- It can help significantly reduce the volume of spent nuclear fuel (the French examples indicate that volume decreases by a factor of 4).

Several disadvantages have been noted:

- It results in a small economic penalty by increasing the net cost of electricity a few percent.
- The separation of pure plutonium in the PUREX process is considered by some to be a proliferation risk; when mixed-oxide use is insufficient, this material is stored for future use as fuel.
- This process does not significantly improve the use of the repository space (the improvement is around 10%, as compared to a factor of 100 for closed fuel cycles).
- This process does not significantly improve the use of natural uranium (the improvement is around 15%, as compared to a factor of 100 for closed fuel cycles).

3. Full Recycle (The Closed Fuel Cycle)

Full recycle approaches are being researched in France, Japan, and the United States. This approach typically comprises three successive steps: an advanced separations step based on the UREX+ technology that mitigates the perceived disadvantages of PUREX, partial recycle in conventional reactors, and closure of the fuel cycle in fast reactors.

The first step, UREX+ technology, allows for the separations and subsequent management of highly pure product streams. These streams are:

- Uranium, which can be stored for future use or disposed of as low-level waste.
- A mixture of plutonium and neptunium, which is intended for partial recycle in conventional reactors followed by recycle in fast reactors.
- Separated fission products intended for short-term storage, possibly for transmutation, and for long-term storage in specialized waste forms.
- The minor actinides (americium and curium) for transmutation in fast reactors.

The UREX+ approach has several advantages:

- It produces minimal liquid waste forms, and eliminates the issue of the "waste tank farms."
- Through advanced monitoring, simulation and modeling, it provides significant opportunities to detect misuse and diversion of weapons-usable materials.
- It provides the opportunity for significant cost reduction.

- Finally and most importantly, it provides the critical first step in managing all hazardous elements present in the spent nuclear fuel.

The second step—partial recycle in conventional reactors—can expand the opportunities offered by the conventional mixed-oxide approach. In particular, it is expected that with significant R&D effort, new fuel forms can be developed that burn up to 50% of the plutonium and neptunium present in spent nuclear fuel. (Note that some studies also suggest that it might be possible to recycle fuel in these reactors many times—i.e., reprocess and recycle the irradiated advanced fuel—and further destroy plutonium and neptunium; other studies also suggest possibilities for transmuting americium in these reactors. Nevertheless, the practicality of these schemes is not yet established and requires additional scientific and engineering research.) The advantage of the second step is that it reduces the overall cost of the closed fuel cycle by burning plutonium in conventional reactors, thereby reducing the number of fast reactors needed to complete the transmutation mission of minimizing hazardous waste. This step can be entirely bypassed, and all transmutation performed in advanced fast reactors, if recycle in conventional reactors is judged to be undesirable.

The third step, closure of the fuel cycle using fast reactors to transmute the fuel constituents into much less hazardous elements, and pyroprocessing technologies to recycle the fast reactor fuel, constitutes the ultimate step in reaching sustainable nuclear energy. This process will effectively destroy the transuranic elements, resulting in waste forms that contain only a very small fraction of the transuranics (less than 1%) and all fission products. These technologies are being developed at Argonne National Laboratory and Idaho National Laboratory, with parallel development in Japan, France, and Russia.

The full recycle approach has significant benefits:

- It can effectively increase use of repository space by a factor of more than 100.
- It can effectively increase the use of natural uranium by a factor of 100.
- It eliminates the uncontrolled buildup of all isotopes that are a proliferation risk.
- The fast reactors and the processing plant can be deployed in small co-located facilities that minimize the risk of material diversion during transportation.
- The fast reactor does not require the use of very pure weapons usable materials, thus increasing their proliferation resistance.
- It finally can usher the way towards full sustainability to prepare for a time when uranium supplies will become increasingly difficult to ensure.
- These processes would have limited economic impact; the increase in the cost of electricity would be less than 10% (ref: OECD).

- Assuming that demonstrations of these processes are started by 2007, commercial operations are possible starting in 2025; this will require adequate funding for demonstrating the separations, recycle, and reactor technologies.
- The systems can be designed and implemented to ensure that the mass of accumulated spent nuclear fuel in the U.S. would always remain below 100,000 metric tons—less than the technical capacity of Yucca Mountain—thus delaying, or even avoiding, the need for a second repository in the U.S.

Conclusion

A well engineered recycling program for spent nuclear fuel will provide the United States with a long-term, affordable, carbon-free energy source with low environmental impact. This new paradigm for nuclear power will allow us to manage nuclear waste and reduce proliferation risks while creating a sustainable energy supply. It is possible that the cost of recycling will be slightly higher than direct disposal of spent nuclear fuel, but the nation will only need one geologic repository for the ultimate disposal of the residual waste.

Rethinking Nuclear Fuel Recycling

Although a dozen years have elapsed since any new nuclear power reactor has come online in the U.S., there are now stirrings of a nuclear renaissance. The incentives are certainly in place: the costs of natural gas and oil have skyrocketed; the public increasingly objects to the greenhouse gas emissions from burning fossil fuels; and the federal government has offered up to $8 billion in subsidies and insurance against delays in licensing (with new laws to streamline the process) and $18.5 billion in loan guarantees. What more could the moribund nuclear power industry possibly want?

Just one thing: a place to ship its used reactor fuel. Indeed, the lack of a disposal site remains a dark cloud hanging over the entire enterprise. The projected opening of a federal waste storage repository in Yucca Mountain in Nevada (now anticipated for 2017 at the earliest) has already slipped by two decades, and the cooling pools holding spent fuel at the nation's nuclear power plants are running out of space.

Most nuclear utilities are therefore beginning to store older spent fuel on dry ground in huge casks, each typically containing 10 tons of waste. Every year a 1,000-megawatt reactor discharges enough fuel to fill two of these casks, each costing about $1 million. But that is not all the industry is doing. U.S. nuclear utilities are suing the federal government, because they would not have incurred such expenses had the U.S. Department of Energy opened the Yucca Mountain repository in 1998 as originally planned. As a result, the government is paying for the casks and associated infrastructure and operations—a bill that is running about $300 million a year.

Under pressure to start moving the fuel off the sites, the DOE has returned to an idea that it abandoned in the 1970s—to "reprocess" the spent fuel chemically, separating the different elements so that some can be reused. Vast reprocessing plants have been running in France and the U.K. for more than a decade, and Japan began to operate its own $20-billion facility in 2006. So this strategy is not without precedent. But, as I discuss below, reprocessing is an expensive and dangerous road to take.

The Element from Hell

Grasping my reasons for rejecting nuclear fuel reprocessing requires nothing more than a rudimentary understanding of the nuclear fuel cycle and a dollop of common sense. Power reactors generate heat—which makes steam to turn electricity-generating turbines—by maintaining a nuclear chain reaction that splits (or "fissions") atoms. Most of the time the fuel is uranium, artificially enriched so that 4 to 5 percent is the chain-reacting isotope uranium 235; virtually all the rest is uranium 238. At an enrichment of only 5 percent, stolen reactor fuel cannot be used to construct an illicit atom bomb.

In the reactor, some of the uranium 238 absorbs a neutron and becomes plutonium 239, which is also chain-reacting and can in principle be partially "burned" if it is extracted and properly prepared. This approach has various drawbacks, however. One is that extraction and processing cost much more than the new fuel is worth. Another is that recycling the plutonium reduces the waste problem only minimally. Most important, the separated plutonium can readily serve to make nuclear bombs if it gets into the wrong hands; as a result, much effort has to be expended to keep it secure until it is once more a part of spent fuel.

These drawbacks become strikingly clear when one examines the experiences of the nations that have embarked on reprocessing programs. In France, the world leader in reprocessing technology, the separated plutonium (chemically combined with oxygen to form plutonium dioxide) is mixed with uranium 238 (also as an oxide) to make a "mixed oxide," or MOX, fuel. After being used to generate more power, the spent MOX fuel still contains about 70 percent as much plutonium as when it was manufactured; however, the addition of highly radioactive fission products created inside a reactor makes this plutonium difficult to access and make into a bomb. The used MOX fuel is shipped back to the reprocessing facility for indefinite storage. Thus, France is, in effect, using reprocessing to move its problem with spent fuel from the reactor sites to the reprocessing plant.

Japan is following France's example. The U.K. and Russia simply store their separated civilian plutonium—about 120 tons between them as of the end of 2005, enough to make 15,000 atom bombs.

Until recently, France, Russia and the U.K. earned money by reprocessing the spent fuel of other nations, such as Japan and Germany, where domestic antinuclear activists demanded that the government either show it had a solution for dealing with spent fuel or shut down its reactors. Authorities in these nations found that sending their spent fuel abroad for reprocessing was a convenient, if costly, way to deal with their nuclear wastes—at least temporarily.

With such contracts in hand, France and the U.K. were easily able to finance new plants for carrying out reprocessing. Those agreements specified, however, that the separated plutonium and any highly radioactive waste would later go back to the country of origin. Russia has recently adopted a similar policy. Hence, governments that send spent fuel abroad need eventually to arrange storage sites for the returning radioactive waste. That reality took a while to sink in, but it has now convinced almost all nations that bought foreign reprocessing services that they might as well store their spent fuel and save the reprocessing fee of about $1 million per ton (10 times the cost of dry storage casks).

So France, Russia and the U.K. have lost virtually all their foreign customers. One result is that the U.K. plans to shut down its reprocessing plants within the next few years, a move that comes with a $92-billion price tag for cleaning up the site of these facilities. In 2000 France considered the option of ending reprocessing in 2010 and concluded that doing so would reduce the cost of nuclear electricity. Making such a change, though, might also engender acrimonious debates about nuclear waste— the last thing the French nuclear establishment wants in a country that has seen relatively little antinuclear activism.

Japan is even more politically locked into reprocessing: its nuclear utilities, unlike those of the U.S., have been unable to obtain permission to expand their on-site storage. Russia today has just a single reprocessing plant, with the ability to handle the spent fuel from only 15 percent of that country's nuclear reactors. The Soviets had intended to expand their reprocessing capabilities but abandoned those plans when their economy collapsed in the 1980s.

During the cold war, the U.S. operated reprocessing plants in Washington State and South Carolina to recover plutonium for nuclear weapons. More than half of the approximately 100 tons of plutonium that was separated in those efforts has been declared to be in excess of our national needs, and the DOE currently projects that disposing of it will cost more than $15 billion. The people who were working at the sites where this reprocessing took place are now primarily occupied with cleaning up the resulting mess, which is expected to cost around $100 billion.

In addition to those military operations, a small commercial reprocessing facility operated in upstate New York from 1966 to 1972. It separated 1.5 tons of plutonium before going bankrupt and becoming a joint federal-state cleanup venture, one projected to require about $5 billion of taxpayers' money.

With all the problems reprocessing entailed, one might rightly ask why it was pursued at all. Part of the answer is that for years after civilian nuclear power plants were first introduced, the U.S. Atomic Energy Commission (AEC) promoted reprocessing both domestically and abroad as essential to the future of nuclear power, because the industry was worried about running out of uranium (a concern that has since abated).

But that was before the security risks of plutonium production went from theoretical to real. In 1974 India, one of the countries that the U.S. assisted in acquiring reprocessing capabilities, used its first separated plutonium to build a nuclear weapon. At about this time, the late Theodore B. Taylor, a former U.S. nuclear weapons designer, was raising an alarm about the possibility that the planned separation and recycling of thousands of tons of plutonium every year would allow terrorists to steal enough of this material to make one or more nuclear bombs.

Separated plutonium, being only weakly radioactive, is easily carried off—whereas the plutonium in spent fuel is mixed with fission products that emit lethal gamma rays. Because of its great radioactivity, spent fuel can be transported only inside casks weighing tens of tons, and its plutonium can only be recovered with great difficulty, typically behind thick shielding using sophisticated, remotely operated equipment. So unseparated plutonium in spent fuel poses a far smaller risk of ending up in the wrong hands.

Having been awakened by India to the danger of nuclear weapons proliferation through reprocessing, the Ford administration (and later the Carter administration) reexamined the AEC's position and concluded that reprocessing was both unnecessary and uneconomic. The U.S. government therefore abandoned its plans to reprocess the spent fuel from civilian reactors and urged France and Germany to cancel contracts under which they were exporting reprocessing technology to Pakistan, South Korea and Brazil.

The Reagan administration later reversed the Ford-Carter position on domestic reprocessing, but the U.S. nuclear industry was no longer interested. It, too, had concluded that reprocessing to make use of the recovered plutonium would not be economically competitive with the existing "once-through" fueling system. Reprocessing, at least in the U.S., had reached a dead end, or so it seemed.

Rising from Nuclear Ashes

The current Bush administration has recently breathed life back into the idea of reprocessing spent nuclear fuel as part of its proposal to deploy a new generation of nuclear reactors. According to this vision, transuranics (plutonium and other similarly heavy elements extracted from conventional reactor fuel) would be recycled not once but repeatedly in the new reactors to break them down through fission into lighter elements, most of which have shorter half-lives. Consequently, the amount of nuclear waste needing to be safely stored for many millennia would be reduced [see "Smarter Use of Nuclear Waste," by William H. Hannum, Gerald E. Marsh and George S. Stanford; SCIENTIFIC AMERICAN, December 2005]. Some scientists view this new scheme as "technically sweet," to borrow a phrase J. Robert Oppenheimer once used to describe the design for the hydrogen bomb. But is it really so wise?

The proposal to recycle U.S. spent fuel in this way is not new. Indeed, in the mid-1990s the DOE asked the U.S. National Academy of Sciences (NAS) to carry out a study of this approach to reducing the amount of long-lived radioactive waste. The resulting massive report, Nuclear Wastes: Technologies for Separation and Transmutation, was very negative. The NAS panel concluded that recycling the transuranics in the first 62,000 tons of spent fuel (the amount that otherwise would have been stored in Yucca Mountain) would require "no less than $50 billion and easily could be over $100 billion"—in other words, it could well cost something like $500 for every person in the U.S. These numbers would have to be doubled to deal with the entire amount of spent fuel that existing U.S. reactors are expected to discharge during their lifetimes.

Why so expensive? Because conventional reactors could not be employed. Those use water both for cooling and for slowing down the neutrons given off when the uranium nuclei in the fuel break apart; this slowing allows the neutrons to induce other uranium 235 atoms to split, thereby sustaining a nuclear chain reaction. Feeding recycled fuel into such a reactor causes the heavier transuranics (plutonium 242, americium and curium) to accumulate. The proposed solution is a completely different type of nuclear reactor, one in which the neutrons get slowed less and are therefore able to break down these hard-to-crack atoms.

During the 1960s and 1970s the leading industrial countries, including the U.S., put the equivalent of more than 50 billion of today's dollars into efforts to commercialize such fast-neutron reactors, which are cooled by molten sodium rather than water. These devices were also called breeder reactors, because they were designed to generate more plutonium than they consumed and therefore could be much more efficient in using the energy in uranium. The expectation was that breeders would quickly replace conventional water-cooled reactors. But sodium-cooled reactors proved to be much more costly to build and troublesome to operate than expected, and most countries abandoned their efforts to commercialize them.

It is exactly this failed reactor type that the DOE now proposes to develop and deploy—but with its core reconfigured to be a net plutonium burner rather than a breeder. The U.S. would have to build between 40 and 75 1,000-megawatt reactors of this type to be able to break down transuranics at the rate they are being generated in the nation's 104 conventional reactors. If each of the new sodium-cooled reactors cost $1 billion to $2 billion more than one of its water-cooled cousins of the same capacity, the federal subsidy necessary would be anywhere from $40 billion to $150 billion, in addition to the $100 billion to $200 billion required for building and operating the recycling infrastructure. Given the U.S. budget deficit, it seems unlikely that such a program would actually be carried through.

If a full-scale reprocessing plant were constructed (as the DOE until recently was proposing to do by 2020) but the sodium-cooled reactors did not get built, virtually all the separated transuranics would simply go into indefinite storage. This awkward situation is exactly what befell the U.K., where the reprocessing program, started in the 1960s, has produced about 80 tons of separated plutonium, a legacy that will cost tens of billions of dollars to dispose of safely.

Reprocessing spent fuel and then storing the separated plutonium and radioactive waste indefinitely at the reprocessing plant is not a disposal strategy. Rather it is a strategy for disaster, because it makes the separated plutonium much more vulnerable to theft. In a 1998 report the U.K.'s Royal Society (the equivalent of the NAS), commenting on the growing stockpile of civilian plutonium in that country, warned that "the chance that the stocks of plutonium might, at some stage, be accessed for illicit weapons production is of extreme concern." In 2007 a second Royal Society report reiterated that "the status quo of continuing to stockpile a very dangerous material is not an acceptable long-term option."

Clearly, prudence demands that plutonium should not be stored at a reprocessing facility in a form that could readily be stolen. Indeed, common sense dictates that it should not be separated at all. Until a long-term repository is available, spent reactor fuel can remain at the sites of the nuclear power plants that generated it.

Would such storage be dangerous? I would argue that keeping older fuel produced by the once-through system in dry storage casks represents a negligible addition to the existing nuclear hazard to the surrounding population. The 10 kilowatts of radioactive heat generated by the 10 tons of 20-year-old fuel packed in a dry storage cask is carried off convectively as it warms the air around it. Terrorists intent on doing harm might attempt to puncture such a cask using, say, an antitank weapon or the engine of a crashing aircraft, but under most circumstances only a small mass of radioactive fuel fragments would be scattered about a limited area. In contrast, if the coolant in the nearby reactor were cut off, its fuel would overheat and begin releasing huge quantities of vaporized fission products within minutes. And if the water were lost in a storage pool containing spent fuel, the zirconium cladding of the fuel rods would be heated up to ignition temperature within hours. Seen in this light, dry storage casks look pretty benign.

Is there enough physical room to keep them? Yes, there is plenty of space for more casks at U.S. nuclear power plants. Even the oldest operating U.S. reactors are having their licenses extended for another 20 years, and new reactors will likely be built on the same sites. So there is no reason to think that these storage areas are about to disappear. Eventually, of course, it will be necessary to remove the spent fuel and put it elsewhere, but there is no need to panic and adopt a policy of reprocessing, which would only make the situation much more dangerous and costly than it is today.

Fear and Loathing in Nevada

The long-term fate of radioactive waste in the U.S. hinges on how the current impasse over Yucca Mountain is resolved. Opinion on the site is divided. The regulatory requirements are tough: the DOE has to show that the mountain will contain the waste well enough to prevent significant off-site doses for a million years.

Demonstrating safety that far into the future is not easy, but the risks from even a badly designed repository are negligible in comparison with those from a policy that would make nuclear weapons materials more accessible. From this perspective, it is difficult to understand why the danger of local radioactive pollution 100,000 or a million years hence has generated so much more political passion in the U.S. than the continuing imminent danger from nuclear weapons.

Part of the problem is the view in Nevada that the Reagan administration and Congress acted unfairly in 1987 when they cut short an objective evaluation of other candidate sites and designated Yucca Mountain as the location for the future nuclear waste repository. To overcome this perception, it may be necessary to reopen deliberations for choosing an additional site. Such a move should not be difficult. Indeed, the Nuclear Waste Policy Act of 1987 requires the secretary of energy to report to Congress by 2010 on the need for a second storage facility. Given the disastrous record of the DOE in dealing with radioactive waste, however, consideration should also be given to establishing a more specialized and less politicized agency for this purpose.

In the meantime, spent fuel can be safely stored at the reactor sites in dry casks. And even after it is placed in a geologic repository, it would remain retrievable for at least a century. So in the unlikely event that technology or economic circumstances change drastically enough that the benefits of reprocessing exceed the costs and risks, that option would still be available. But it makes no sense now to rush into an expensive and potentially catastrophic undertaking on the basis of uncertain hopes that it might reduce the long-term environmental burden from the nuclear power industry.

POSTSCRIPT

Should the United States Reprocess Spent Nuclear Fuel?

The nuclear waste disposal problem is real, and it must be dealt with. If it is not, we may face the same kinds of problems created by the former Soviet Union, which disposed of some nuclear waste simply by dumping it at sea. For a summary of the nuclear waste problem and the disposal controversy, see Michael E. Long, "Half Life: The Lethal Legacy of America's Nuclear Waste," *National Geographic* (July 2002). The need for care in nuclear waste disposal is underlined by Tom Carpenter and Clare Gilbert, "Don't Breathe the Air," *Bulletin of the Atomic Scientists* (May/June 2004); they describe the Hanford Site in Hanford, Washington, where wastes from nuclear weapons production were stored in underground tanks. Leaks from the tanks have contaminated groundwater, and an extensive cleanup program is under way. But cleanup workers are being exposed to both radioactive materials and toxic chemicals, and they are falling ill. And in June 2004, the U.S. Senate voted to ease cleanup requirements. Per F. Peterson, William E. Kastenberg, and Michael Corradini, "Nuclear Waste and the Distant Future," *Issues in Science and Technology* (Summer 2006), argue that the risks of waste disposal have been sensibly addressed and we should be focusing more attention on other risks (such as those of global warming). Behnam Taebi and Jan Kloosterman, "To Recycle or Not to Recycle? An Intergenerational Approach to Nuclear Fuel Cycles," *Science & Engineering Ethics* (June 2008), argue that the question of whether to accept reprocessing comes down to choosing between risks for the present generation and risks for future generations.

In November 2005, President Bush signed the budget for the Department of Energy, which contained $50 million to start work toward a reprocessing plant; see Eli Kintisch, "Congress Tells DOE to Take Fresh Look at Recycling Spent Reactor Fuel," *Science* (December 2, 2005). By April 2008, Senator Pete Domenici of the U.S. Senate Energy and Natural Resources Committee was working on a bill that would set up the nation's first government-backed commercialized nuclear waste reprocessing facilities. Reprocessing spent nuclear fuel will be expensive, but the costs may not be great enough to make nuclear power unacceptable; see "The Economic Future of Nuclear Power," University of Chicago (August 2004) (http://www. anl.gov/Special_Reports/NuclEconSumAug04.pdf).

In February 2006, the United States Department of Energy announced the Global Nuclear Energy Partnership, to be operated by the United States, Russia, Great Britain, and France. It would lease nuclear fuel to other nations, reprocess spent fuel without generating material that could be diverted to making nuclear bombs, reduce the amount of waste that must be disposed of, and help meet future energy needs. See Stephanie Cooke, "Just Within Reach?" *Bulletin of the Atomic Scientists* (July/August 2006), and Jeff Johnson, "Reprocessing Key to Nuclear Plan," *Chemical & Engineering News* (June 18, 2007). Critics such as Karen Charman ("Brave Nuclear World, Parts I and II," *World Watch* (May/June and July/August 2006), insist that nuclear power is far too expensive and carries too serious risks of breakdown and exposure to wastes to rely upon, especially when cleaner, cheaper, and less dangerous alternatives exist.

It is an unfortunate truth that the reprocessing of nuclear spent fuel does indeed increase the risks of nuclear proliferation. On February 28, 2004, *The Economist* ("The World Wide Web of Nuclear Danger") wrote that "the risk that someone, somewhere, might detonate a bomb in anger is arguably greater than at any time since the 1962 Cuban missile crisis brought the cold-war world soberingly close to the brink." Both nations and terrorists itch to possess nuclear weapons, whose destructive potential makes present members of the "nuclear club" tremble. Can the risk be controlled? John Deutch, Arnold Kanter, Ernest Moniz, and Daniel Poneman, in "Making the World Safe for Nuclear Energy," *Survival* (Winter 2004/2005), argue that present nuclear nations could supply fuel and reprocess spent fuel for other nations; nations that refuse to participate would be seen as suspect and subject to international action.

Internet References . . .

The National Renewable Energy Laboratory

The National Renewable Energy Laboratory is the nation's primary laboratory for renewable energy and energy efficiency research and development. Among other things, it works on wind power and biofuels.

http://www.nrel.gov/learning/re_basics.html

American Wind Energy Association

The American Wind Energy Association is the national trade association for wind power project developers, equipment suppliers, services providers, parts manufacturers, utilities, researchers, and advocates.

http://www.awea.org/

Army Corps of Engineers

The Army Corps of Engineers discusses its role in the management of the nation's water resources on this site.

http://www.vtn.iwr.usace.army.mil/

American Rivers

American Rivers advocates for the protection of rivers as vital to our health, safety, and quality of life. It addresses pollution cleanup, dam removal, and heritage activities.

http://www.americanrivers.org

Alternative Energy Sources

*F*ossil fuels and nuclear power are not the only options. Alternatives discussed here are wind and hydroelectric power, biofuels and hydrogen. Others include tidal power, geothermal power, and solar power. All require funding to develop and deploy, and all have impacts on the environment and people nearby. Some enthusiasts tout the promise of various kinds of free or infinite energy, such as zero point and vacuum energy, but physicists warn that thanks to the laws of thermodynamics, "There Ain't No Such Thing as a Free Lunch." We need energy, but we will always have to pay for it.

- Is Wind Power Green?

- Do Biofuels Enhance Energy Security?

- Can Hydropower Play a Role in Preventing Climate Change?

- Will Hydrogen Replace Fossil Fuels for Cars?

- Is There Any Such Thing as "Free Energy"?

ISSUE 15

Is Wind Power Green?

YES: Charles Komanoff, from "Whither Wind?" *Orion* (September–October 2006)

NO: Jon Boone, from "Wayward Wind," Speech Given in the Township of Perry, near Silver Lake, Wyoming County, New York (June 19, 2006)

ISSUE SUMMARY

YES: Charles Komanoff argues that the energy needs of civilization can be met without adding to global warming if we both conserve energy and deploy large numbers of wind turbines.

NO: Jon Boone argues that wind power is better for corporate tax avoidance than for providing environmentally friendly energy. It is at best a placebo for our energy dilemma.

For centuries, windmills have exploited the pressure exerted by blowing wind to grind grain and pump water. On U.S. farms, before rural electrification programs brought utility power, windmills provided small amounts of electricity. These windmills fell out of favor when the powerlines arrived, bringing larger amounts of electricity more reliably (even when the wind was not blowing). The sources of electricity became hydroelectric dams, coal and oil-fired power plants, and even nuclear power plants.

The oil crisis of the 1970s brought new attention to wind and other renewable energy sources. Today, high oil prices and concern about global warming caused by the carbon dioxide emitted by the burning of fossil fuels are renewing that attention. Researchers are looking for ways to reduce carbon emissions (see Jay Apt, David W. Keith, and M. Granger Morgan, "Promoting Low-Carbon Electricity Production," *Issues in Science and Technology,* Spring 2007). Low-carbon techniques include capturing carbon dioxide instead of releasing it, biofuels, nuclear power, hydroelectric power, wind power, and geothermal power, all of which play minor roles at present. At present, "the electric power industry is the single largest emitter of carbon dioxide in the United States, accounting for 40% of emissions of CO_2 in 2006, up from 36% in 1990 and 25% in 1970."

Wind power is growing rapidly. According to Ryan H. Wiser of Lawrence Berkeley National Laboratory, testifying before the Senate Finance Committee on March 29, 2007, "recent growth in the U.S. renewable electricity sector has been led by wind power. In fact, the year 2006 was the largest on record in the U.S. for wind power capacity additions, with over 2,400 MW of capacity added to the U.S. grid. And, for the second consecutive year, this made wind power the second largest new resource added to the U.S. electrical grid in capacity terms, well behind new natural gas plants, but ahead of coal. New wind plants contributed roughly 19% of the new capacity added to the U.S. grid in 2006, compared to 12% in 2005. On a worldwide basis, 15,200 MW of wind capacity was added in 2006, up from 11,500 MW in 2005, for a cumulative total of 74,200 MW." Yet these advances are not without resistance. Wind turbines take up space and affect views. They provide fatal obstacles to birds and bats. They make noise, and some people find that noise objectionable (see Johann Tasker, "Wind Farm Noise Is Driving Us Out of Our House," *Farmers Weekly,* January 12, 2007). Yet they do generate electricity without burning fossil fuels and emitting CO_2 (or other pollutants). The question is whether they offer enough advantages to be worth their price.

In the following selections, Charles Komanoff argues that the energy needs of civilization can be met without adding to global warming if we both conserve energy and deploy large numbers of wind turbines. Acceptance of wind farms, he says, could be "our generation's way of avowing our love for the next." Jon Boone argues that wind power is better for corporate tax avoidance than for providing environmentally friendly energy. It is at best a placebo for our energy dilemma. "The only environmentally responsible short-range solution to the problem of our dependence upon fossil fuels must combine effective conservation with much higher efficiency standards."

YES

Charles Komanoff

Whither Wind?

It was a place I had often visited in memory but feared might no longer exist. Orange slabs of calcified sandstone teetered overhead, while before me, purple buttes and burnt mesas stretched over the desert floor. In the distance I could make out southeast Utah's three snowcapped ranges—the Henrys, the Abajos, and, eighty miles to the east, the La Sals, shimmering into the blue horizon.

No cars, no roads, no buildings. Two crows floating on the late-winter thermals. Otherwise, stillness. . . . Now, perched on a precipice above Goblin Valley, stoked on endorphins and elated by the beauty before me, I had what might seem a strange, irrelevant thought: I didn't want windmills here.

Not that any windmills are planned for this Connecticut-sized expanse—the winds are too fickle. But wind energy is never far from my mind these days. As Earth's climate begins to warp under the accumulating effluent from fossil fuels, the increasing viability of commercial-scale wind power is one of the few encouraging developments.

Encouraging to me, at least. As it turns out, there is much disagreement over where big windmills belong, and whether they belong at all.

Fighting fossil fuels, and machines powered by them, has been my life's work. In 1971, shortly after getting my first taste of canyon country, I took a job crunching numbers for what was then a landmark exposé of U.S. power plant pollution, *The Price of Power.* The subject matter was drier than dust—emissions data, reams of it, printed out on endless strips of paper by a mainframe computer. Dull stuff, but nightmarish visions of coal-fired smokestacks smudging the crystal skies of the Four Corners kept me working 'round the clock, month after month.

A decade later, as a New York City bicycle commuter fed up with the oil-fueled mayhem on the streets, I began working with the local bicycle advocacy group, Transportation Alternatives, and we soon made our city a hotbed of urban American anti-car activism. The '90s and now the '00s have brought other battles—"greening" Manhattan tenement buildings through energy efficiency and documenting the infernal "noise costs" of Jet Skis, to name two—but I'm still fighting the same fight.

Why? Partly it's knowing the damage caused by the mining and burning of fossil fuels. And there's also the sheer awfulness of machines gone wild, their groaning, stinking combustion engines invading every corner of life. But now the stakes are immeasurably higher. As an energy analyst, I can tell you that the science on global warming is terrifyingly clear: to have even a shot at fending off climate catastrophe, the world must reduce carbon dioxide emissions from fuel burning by at least 50 percent within the next few decades. If poor countries are to have any room to develop, the United States, the biggest emitter by far, needs to cut back by 75 percent.

Although automobiles, with their appetite for petroleum, may seem like the main culprit, the number one climate change agent in the U.S. is actually electricity. The most recent inventory of U.S. greenhouse gases found that power generation was responsible for a whopping 38 percent of carbon dioxide emissions. Yet the electricity sector may also be the least complicated to make carbon free. Approximately three-fourths of U.S. electricity is generated by burning coal, oil, or natural gas. Accordingly, switching that same portion of U.S. electricity generation to nonpolluting sources such as wind turbines, while simultaneously ensuring that our ever-expanding arrays of lights, computers, and appliances are increasingly energy efficient, would eliminate 38 percent of the country's CO_2 emissions and bring us halfway to the goal of cutting emissions by 75 percent.

To achieve that power switch entirely through wind power, I calculate, would require 400,000 windmills rated at 2.5 megawatts each. To be sure, this is a hypothetical figure, since it ignores such real-world issues as limits on power transmission and the intermittency of wind, but it's a useful benchmark just the same.

What Would That Entail?

To begin, I want to be clear that the turbines I'm talking about are huge, with blades up to 165 feet long mounted on towers rising several hundred feet. Household wind machines like the 100-foot-high Bergey 10-kilowatt BWC Excel with 11-foot blades, the mainstay of the residential and small business wind turbine market, may embody democratic self-reliance and other "small is beautiful" virtues, but we can't look to them to make a real dent in the big energy picture. What dictates the supersizing of windmills are two basic laws of wind physics: a wind turbine's energy potential is proportional to the square of the length of the blades, and to the cube of the speed at which the blades spin. I'll spare you the math, but the difference in blade lengths, the greater wind speeds higher off the ground, and the sophisticated controls available on industrial-scale turbines all add up to a market-clinching five-hundred-fold advantage in electricity output for a giant General Electric or Vestas wind machine.

How much land do the industrial turbines require? The answer turns on what "require" means. An industry rule of thumb is that to maintain adequate exposure to the wind, each big turbine needs space around it of about 60 acres. Since 640 acres make a square mile, those 400,000 turbines would need 37,500 square miles, or roughly all the land in Indiana or Maine.

On the other hand, the land actually occupied by the turbines—their "footprint"—would be far, far smaller. For example, each 3.6-megawatt Cape Wind turbine proposed for Nantucket Sound will rest on a platform roughly 22 feet in diameter, implying a surface area of 380 square feet—the size of a typical one-bedroom apartment in New York City. Scaling that up by 400,000 suggests that just six square miles of land—less than the area of a single big Wyoming strip mine—could house the bases for all of the windmills needed to banish coal, oil, and gas from the U.S. electricity sector.

Of course, erecting and maintaining wind turbines can also necessitate clearing land: ridgeline installations often require a fair amount of deforestation, and then there's the associated clearing for access roads, maintenance facilities, and the like. But there are also now a great many turbines situated on farmland, where the fields around their bases are still actively farmed.

Depending, then, on both the particular terrain and how the question is understood, the land area said to be needed for wind power can vary across almost four orders of magnitude. Similar divergences of opinion are heard about every other aspect of wind power, too. Big wind farms kill thousands of birds and bats . . . or hardly any, in comparison to avian mortality from other tall structures such as skyscrapers. Industrial wind machines are soft as a whisper from a thousand feet away, and even up close their sound level would rate as "quiet" on standard noise charts . . . or they can sound like "a grinding noise" or "the shrieking sound of a wild animal," according to one unhappy neighbor of an upstate New York wind farm. Wind power developers are skimming millions via subsidies, state-mandated quotas, and "green power" scams . . . or are boldly risking their own capital to strike a blow for clean energy against the fossil fuel Goliath.

Some of the bad press is warranted. The first giant wind farm, comprising six thousand small, fast-spinning turbines placed directly in northern California's principal raptor flyway, Altamont Pass, in the early 1980s rightly inspired the epithet "Cuisinarts for birds." The longer blades on newer turbines rotate more slowly and thus kill far fewer birds, but bat kills are being reported at wind farms in the Appalachian Mountains; as many as two thousand bats were hacked to death at one forty-four-turbine installation in West Virginia. And as with any machine, some of the nearly ten thousand industrial-grade windmills now operating in the U.S. may groan or shriek when something goes wrong. Moreover, wind power does benefit from a handsome federal subsidy; indeed, uncertainty over renewal of the "production tax credit" worth 1.9 cents per kilowatt-hour nearly brought wind power development to a standstill a few years ago.

At the same time, however, there is an apocalyptic quality to much anti-wind advocacy that seems wildly disproportionate to the actual harm, particularly in the overall context of not just other sources of energy but modern industry in general. New York State opponents of wind farms call their website "Save Upstate New York," as if ecological or other damage from wind turbines might administer the coup de grace to the state's rural provinces that decades of industrialization and pollution, followed by outsourcing, have not. In neighboring Massachusetts, a group called Green Berkshires argues that wind turbines "are enormously destructive to the environment," but does not perform the obvious comparison to the destructiveness of fossil fuel-based power. Although the intensely controversial Cape Wind project "poses an imminent threat to navigation and raises many serious maritime safety issues," according to the anti-wind Alliance to Protect Nantucket Sound, the alliance was strangely silent when an oil barge bound for the region's electric power plant spilled ninety-eight thousand gallons of its deadly, gluey cargo into Buzzards Bay three years ago.

Of course rhetoric is standard fare in advocacy, particularly the environmental variety with its salvationist mentality—environmentalists always like to feel they are "saving" this valley or that species. It all comes down to a question of what we're saving, and for whom. You can spend hours sifting through the anti-wind websites and find no mention at all of the climate crisis, let alone wind power's potential to help avert it.

In fact, many wind power opponents deny that wind power displaces much, if any, fossil fuel burning. Green Berkshires insists, for example, that "global warming [and] dependence on fossil fuels . . . will not be ameliorated one whit by the construction of these turbines on our mountains."

This notion is mistaken. It is true that since wind is variable, individual wind turbines can't be counted on to produce on demand, so the power grid can't necessarily retire fossil fuel generators at the same rate as it takes on windmills. The coal- and oil-fired generators will still need to be there, waiting for a windless day. But when the wind blows, those generators can spin down. That's how the grid works: it allocates electrons. Supply more electrons from one source, and other sources can supply fewer. And since system operators program the grid to draw from the lowest-cost generators first, and wind power's "fuel," moving air, is free, wind-generated electrons are given priority. It follows that more electrons from wind power mean proportionately fewer from fossil fuel burning.

What about the need to keep a few power stations burning fuel so they can instantaneously ramp up and counterbalance fluctuations in wind energy output? The grid requires this ballast, known as spinning reserve, in any event both because demand is always changing and because power plants of any type are subject to unforeseen breakdowns. The additional variability due to wind generation is slight—wind speeds don't suddenly drop from strong to calm, at least not for every turbine in a wind farm and certainly not for every wind farm on the grid. The clear verdict of the engineers responsible for grid reliability—a most conservative lot—is that the current level of wind power development will not require additional spinning reserve, while even much larger supplies of wind-generated electricity could be accommodated through a combination of energy storage technologies and improved models for predicting wind speeds.

With very few exceptions, then, wind output can be counted on to displace fossil fuel burning one for one. No less than other nonpolluting technologies like bicycles or photovoltaic solar cells, wind power is truly an anti-fossil fuel.

I made my first wind farm visit in the fall of 2005. I had seen big wind-mills up close in Denmark, and I had driven through the big San Gorgonio wind farm that straddles Highway I-10 near Palm Springs, California. But this trip last November had a mission. After years of hearing industrial wind turbines in the northeastern United States characterized as either monstrosities or crowns of creation, I wanted to see for myself how they sat on the land. I also wanted to measure the noise from the turning blades, so I brought the professional noise meter I had used in my campaign against Jet Skis.

Madison County occupies the broad middle of New York State, with the Catskill Mountains to the south, Lake Ontario to the northwest, and the Adirondacks to the northeast. Its rolling farms sustain seventy thousand residents and, since 2001, two wind farms, the 20-windmill Fenner Windpower Project in the western part of the county and the 7-windmill Madison Windpower Project twenty miles east.

At the time of my visit Fenner was the state's largest wind farm, al-though that distinction has since passed to the 120-windmill Maple Ridge installation in the Tug Hill region farther north. It was windy that day, though not unusually so, according to the locals. All twenty-seven tur-bines were spinning, presumably at their full 1.5-megawatt ratings. For me the sight of the turning blades was deeply pleasing. The windmills, sleek, white structures more than three hundred feet tall sprinkled across farmland, struck me as graceful and marvelously useful. I thought of a story in the *New York Times* about a proposed wind farm near Coopers-town, New York, in which a retiree said that seeing giant windmills near your house "would be like driving through oil derricks to get to your front door." To my eye, the Fenner turbines were anti-derricks, oil rigs running in reverse.

For every hour it was in full use, each windmill was keeping a cou-ple of barrels of oil, or an entire half-ton of coal, in the ground. Of course wind turbines don't generate full power all the time because the wind doesn't blow at a constant speed. The Madison County turbines have an average "capacity factor," or annual output rate, of 34 percent, meaning that over the course of a year they generate about a third of the electricity they would pro-duce if they always ran at full capacity. But that still means an average three thousand hours a year of full output for each turbine. Multiply those hours by the twenty-seven turbines at Fenner and Madison, and a good 200,000 barrels of oil or 50,000 tons of coal were being kept underground by the two wind farms each year—enough to cover an entire sixty-acre farm with a six-inch-thick oil slick or pile of coal.

The windmills, spinning easily at fifteen revolutions per minute—that's one leisurely revolution every four seconds—were clean and elegant in a way that no oil derrick or coal dragline could ever be. The nonlinear arrangement of the Fenner turbines situated them comfortably among the traditional farmhouses, paths, and roads, while at Madison, a grassy hill-side site, the windmills were more prominent but still unaggressive. Un-like a ski run, say, or a power line cutting through the countryside, the windmills didn't seem like a violation of the landscape. The turning vanes called to mind a natural force—the wind—in a way that a cell phone or microwave tower, for example, most certainly does not.

They were also relatively quiet. My sound readings, taken at distances ranging from one hundred to two thousand feet from the tower base, topped out at 64 decibels and went as low as 45—the approximate noise range given for a small-town residential cul-de-sac on standard noise charts. It's fair to say that the wind turbines in Madison County aren't terribly noisy even from up close and are barely audible from a thousand feet or more away. The predominant sound was a low, not unpleasant hum, or hvoohmm, like a distant seashore, but perhaps a bit thicker.

Thinking back on that November day, I've come to realize that a windmill, like any large structure, is a signifier. Cell-phone towers signify the intrusion of quotidian life—the reminder to stop off at the 7-Eleven, the unfinished business at the office. The windmills I saw in upstate New York signified, for me, not just displacement of destructive fossil fuels, but acceptance of the conditions of inhabiting the Earth. They signified, in the words of environmental lawyer and MIT research affiliate William Shutkin, "the capacity of environmentalists—of citizens—to match their public positions with the private choices necessary to move toward a more environmentally and economically sustainable way of life."

The notion of choices points to another criticism of wind turbines: the argument that the energy they might make could be saved instead through energy-efficiency measures. The Adirondack Council, for example, in a statement opposing the 10-windmill Barton Mines project on a former mountaintop mine site writes, "If the Barton project is approved, we will gain 27 to 30 megawatts of new, clean power generation. Ironically, we could save more than 30 megawatts of power in the Adirondack Park through simple, proven conservation methods in homes and businesses."

The council's statement is correct, of course. Kilowatts galore could be conserved in any American city or town by swapping out incandescent light bulbs in favor of compact fluorescents, replacing inefficient kitchen appliances, and extinguishing "vampire" loads by plugging watt-sucking electronic devices into on-off power strips. If this notion sounds familiar, it's because it has been raised in virtually every power plant dispute since the 1970s. But the ground has shifted, now that we have such overwhelming proof that we're standing on the threshold of catastrophic climate change.

Those power plant debates of yore weren't about fuels and certainly not about global warming, but about whether to top off the grid with new megawatts of supply or with "negawatts"—watts that could be saved through conservation. It took decades of struggle by legions of citizen advocates and hundreds of experts (I was one) to embed the negawatt paradigm in U.S. utility planning. But while we were accomplishing that, inexorably rising fossil fuel use here and around the world was overwhelming Earth's "carbon sinks," causing carbon dioxide to accumulate in the atmosphere at an accelerating rate, contributing to disasters such as Hurricane Katrina and Europe's 2003 heat wave, and promising biblical-scale horrors such as a waning Gulf Stream and disappearing polar icepacks.

The energy arena of old was local and incremental. The new one is global and all-out. With Earth's climate, and the world as we know and love it, now imperiled, topping off the regional grid pales in comparison to the task at hand. In the new, ineluctable struggle to rescue the climate from fossil fuels, efficiency and "renewables" (solar and biomass as well as wind) must all be pushed to the max. Those thirty negawatts that lie untapped in the kitchens and TV rooms of Adirondack houses are no longer an alternative to the Barton wind farm—they're another necessity.

In this new, desperate, last-chance world—and it is that, make no mistake—pleas like the Adirondack Council's, which once would have seemed reasonable, now sound a lot like fiddling while the Earth burns. The same goes for the urgings by opponents of Cape Wind and other pending wind farms to "find a more suitable site"; those other suitable wind farm sites (wherever they exist) need to be developed in addition to, not instead of, Nantucket Sound, or Barton Mines, or the Berkshires.

There was a time when the idea of placing immense turbines in any of these places would have filled me with horror. But now, what horrifies me more is the thought of keeping them windmill free. . . .

Intruding the unmistakable human hand on any landscape for wind power is, of course, a loss in local terms, and no small one, particularly if the site is a verdant ridgeline. Uplands are not just visible markers of place but fragile environments, and the inevitable access roads for erecting and serving the turbines can be damaging ecologically as well as symbolically. In contrast, few if any benefits of the wind farm will be felt by you in a tangible way. If the thousands of tons of coal a year that your wind farm will replace were being mined now, a mile from your house, it might be a little easier to take. Unfortunately, our society rarely works that way. The bread you cast upon the waters with your vote will not come back to you in any obvious way—it will be eaten in Wyoming, or Appalachia. . . .

But what if the big push for wind power simply "provides more energy for people to waste?" as Carl Safina, an oceanographer who objects to the Cape Wind project, asked me recently. Safina is unusual among Cape Wind opponents, not just because he is a MacArthur Fellow and prize-winning author (*Song for the Blue Ocean*, *Voyage of the Turtle*), but because he is completely honest about the fact that his objections are essentially aesthetic.

"I believe the aesthetics of having a national seashore with a natural view of the blue curve of the planet are very important," he wrote in an e-mail from coastal Long Island, where he lives. "I think turbines and other structures should be sited in places not famed for natural beauty"—a statement that echoed my feelings about Utah's Goblin Valley. . . .

Yet for all his fierce attachment to that view, Safina says he might give it up if doing so made a difference. "If there was a national energy strategy that would make the U.S. carbon neutral in fifty years," he wrote, "and if Cape Wind was integral and significant, that might be a worthwhile sacrifice." But the reality, as Safina described in words that could well have been mine, is that "Americans insist on wasting energy and needing more. We will affect the natural view of a famously beautiful piece of America's ocean and still not develop a plan to conserve energy."

Safina represents my position and, I imagine, that of others on both sides of the wind controversy when he pleads for federal action that could justify local sacrifice for the greater good. If Congress enacted an energy policy that harnessed the spectrum of cost-effective energy efficiency together with renewable energy, thereby ensuring that fossil fuel use shrank starting today, a windmill's contribution to climate protection might actually register, providing psychic reparation for an altered viewshed. And if carbon fuels were taxed for their damage to the climate, wind power's profit margins would widen, and surrounding communities could extract bigger tax revenues from wind farms. Then some of that bread upon the waters would indeed come back—in the form of a new high school, or land acquired for a nature preserve.

It's very human to ask, "Why me? Why my ridgeline, my seascape, my viewshed?" These questions have been difficult to answer; there has been no framework—local or national—to guide wind farm siting by ranking potential wind power locales for their ecological and community suitability. That's a gap that the Appalachian Mountain Club is trying to bridge, using its home state of Massachusetts as a model.

According to AMC research director Kenneth Kimball, who heads the project, Massachusetts has ninety-six linear miles of "Class 4" ridgelines, where wind speeds average fourteen miles per hour or more, the threshold for profitability with current technology. Assuming each mile can support seven to nine large turbines of roughly two megawatts each, the state's uplands could theoretically host 1,500 megawatts of wind power. (Coastal areas such as Nantucket Sound weren't included in the survey.)

Kimball's team sorted all ninety-six miles into four classes of governance—Appalachian Trail corridor or similar lands where development is prohibited; other federal or state conservation lands; Massachusetts open space lands; and private holdings. They then overlaid these with ratings denoting conflicts with recreational, scenic, and ecological values. The resulting matrix suggests the following rankings of wind power suitability:

1. *Unsuitable*—lands where development is prohibited (Appalachian Trail corridors, for example) or "high conflict" areas: 24 miles (25 percent).
2. *Less than ideal*—federal or state conservation lands rated "medium conflict": 21 miles (22 percent).
3. *Conditionally favorable*—Conservation or open space lands rated "low conflict," or open space or private lands rated "medium conflict": 27 miles (28 percent).

4. *Most favorable*—Unrestricted private land and "low conflict" areas: 24 miles (25 percent).

Category 4 lands are obvious places to look to for wind farm development. Category 3 lands could also be considered, says the AMC, if wind farms were found to improve regional air quality, were developed under a state plan rather than piecemeal, and were bonded to assure eventual decommissioning. If these conditions were met, then categories 3 and 4, comprising approximately fifty miles of Massachusetts ridgelines, could host four hundred wind turbines capable of supplying nearly 4 percent of the state's annual electricity—without grossly endangering wildlife or threatening scenic, recreational, or ecological values (e.g., critical habitat, roadless areas, rare species, old growth, steep slopes).

Whether that 4 percent is a little or a lot depends on where you stand and, equally, on where we stand as a society. You could call the four hundred turbines mere tokenism against our fuel-besotted way of life, and considering them in isolation, you'd be right. But you could also say this: Go ahead and halve the state's power usage, as could be done even with present-day technology, and "nearly 4 percent" doubles to 7–8 percent. Add the Cape Wind project and other offshore wind farms that might follow, and wind power's statewide share might reach 20 percent, the level in Denmark.

Moreover, the windier and emptier Great Plains states could reach 100 percent wind power or higher, even with a suitability framework like the AMC's, thereby becoming net exporters of clean energy. But even at 20 percent, Massachusetts would be doing its part to displace that 75 percent of U.S. electricity generated by fossil fuels. If you spread the turbines needed to achieve that goal across all fifty states, you'd be looking to produce roughly eight hundred megawatt-hours of wind output per square mile—just about what Massachusetts would be generating in the above scenario. And the rest of New England and New York could do the same, affording these "blue" states a voice in nudging the rest of the country greenward.

So goes my notion, anyway. You could call it wind farms as signifiers, with their value transcending energy-share percentages to reach the realm of symbols and images. That is where we who love nature and obsess about the environment have lost the high ground, and where *Homo americanus* has been acting out his (and her) disastrous desires—opting for the "manly" SUV over the prim Prius, the macho powerboat over the meandering canoe, the stylish halogen lamp over the dorky compact fluorescent.

Throughout his illustrious career, wilderness champion David Brower called upon Americans "to determine that an untrammeled wildness shall remain here to testify that this generation had love for the next." Now that all wild things and all places are threatened by global warming, that task is more complex.

Could a windmill's ability to "derive maximum benefit out of the site-specific gift nature is providing—wind and open space," in the words of aesthetician Yuriko Saito, help Americans bridge the divide between pristine landscapes and sustainable ones? Could windmills help Americans subscribe to the "higher order of beauty" that environmental educator David Orr defines as something that "causes no ugliness somewhere else or at some later time"? Could acceptance of wind farms be our generation's way of avowing our love for the next?

I believe so. Or want to.

Jon Boone  **NO**

The Wayward Wind

Introduction

The United States east of the Mississippi River has about 5% of the nation's onshore wind potential. If industrial wind developers achieve their goals, the region will be saturated with approximately 300,000 wind turbines spread over millions of acres. New York, with .3 of 1% of the nation's onshore wind, could be saturated with about 20,000 400 foot tall machines, covering more than a thousand miles of terrain. Wyoming County alone could absorb around 400, of which 105 have already been proposed. Although most of the country's wind-rich lands are in the upper Midwest, relatively inexpensive access to existing transmission lines makes eastern states such as New York attractive for wind development, spurred by the state's renewable portfolio law. Despite a desire by many to reduce our reliance on fossil fuels in order to shrink the rate of carbon dioxide emissions that are a by-product of burning fossil fuels, demand for electricity has increased 2% each year since 1975; at this rate, we will double current usage in about thirty years. Nationally, fossil fuels produce nearly 75% of our electricity. Because it is perceived as non-polluting and renewable, wind energy has become popular with the public and with politicians. If all these wind turbines are constructed, what will it mean to ordinary people, to energy policy and to an improved environment?

Nearly four years ago, I set out to investigate these questions. In a number of forums, I examined the claims of wind industry developers, their trade organization, the American Wind Energy Association, and the National Renewable Energy Lab, an agency of the US Department of Energy. I'll share with you how those claims withstand the evidence of real world experience. At first, I'd hoped to support wind energy because, as an environmentalist, I have long been concerned about our society's addiction to fossil fuels and such malignant coal mining practices as mountaintop removal. I'm alarmed at such statistics as the number of asthma cases in the nation doubling every five years. High levels of mercury contamination in our rivers and oceans are also by-products of fossil fuel consumption. However, I seek effective solutions for these and other environmental problems. Although I support efforts to reduce demand by living off the grid with small-scale wind and solar power, I'm mindful of the initial costs of doing so, making this kind of enterprise difficult to apply at industrial scale.

As a student of history and science, I wanted to understand the nature of "renewable" energy, and to provide some context for wind energy. The quest for renewable energy has a long history. A few hundred years ago, timber seemed inexhaustible, but our demand made short work of the supply. Coal, too, is renewable, but again, our demand will at some time overrun supply—and our meager lifespan won't extend the tens of millions of years necessary to replenish it. A few generations ago, hydroelectric dams were all the rage. Although these do produce a lot of electricity from a renewable source, they are so environmentally damaging that many are now being dismantled around the country, at taxpayer expense. Because time seems to be running out on fossil fuels and the lure of non-polluting wind energy is so seductive, some people are now promoting wind energy initiatives at any cost, without investigating potential negative consequences—and with no apparent knowledge of even recent environmental history. . . .

Wind developers and their supporters make a number of claims for wind facilities, stating they lessen dependence on foreign oil; improve air quality; reduce global warming by replacing fossil-fueled power plants; and improve public health; while providing electrical power for many thousands of homes and adding significant revenue and jobs to local economies. They also promise their technology will not pose much risk to wildlife, nor will it alter the landscape in perceptible ways, nor decrease the value for surrounding properties, nor introduce disturbances that might jeopardize the right of neighbors to quietly enjoy their property. Conversely, they never mention the extraordinary subsidies that taxpayers and ratepayers provide, *subsidies not indexed to reductions in CO_2 and various toxic emissions.*

Throughout my experience, I could not substantiate a single claim developers made for industrial wind energy, including the one justifying its existence: that massive wind installations would meaningfully reduce our reliance on fossil fuels. When you understand this, you realize the wind business is not really that complex. But there are a lot of complicated issues swirling around it that obscure and distract from this main point, issues such as global warming, property values, the nature of wind leases, local revenues and taxes, wildlife, natural views, and a host of others. So how does one know the truth of it all? How does one go about separating the reality from spin?

Perhaps you'll agree that if something seems too good to be true, it almost always is. You should ask good questions and demand solid proof, not relying upon unsecured promises—and realize that the responsibility for substantiation lies with those making the claim. I could address all the complications surrounding this issue, but that would take far too much time. Consequently, I'll touch on a few prominent ones, then focus on wind energy effectiveness and economics, showing what we might get, and what we would have to give, for industrial wind energy, examining the two windplant operations presently targeting Wyoming County.

Property Values

Do you believe industrial facilities stretching many miles across your landscape, with 105 spinning skyscraper sized structures creating a cascade of noise, are not going to negatively affect property values for those in the neighborhood, as the wind industry maintains a government study proves? One of the most validated real estate precepts is that prominent natural views and historic scenery have premium value, and intrusions restricting those views erode value.

Independent inquiry in Britain, Denmark, and New England suggests the likelihood of significant property devaluations. In his June 10, 2005 direct testimony before the Wisconsin Public Service Commission, Kevin Zarem, an appraiser, estimated that residential property near a proposed windplant "will likely be in the 17%–20% loss range." And this based solely upon visual impact. He did not assess potential loss due to wind turbine noise, motion, or shadows. Russell Bounds, one of western Maryland's leading realtors in large property transactions, has already lost sales in the area of proposed windplants. Mr. Bounds testified in a PSC hearing that, over the last several years, he has had at least 25 people who expressed interest in buying land in the area targeted by wind developers. However, when he advised them about the plans for wind facilities, not one of those people expressed further interest.

Wind Turbine Noise

Developers claim modern wind turbines make little noise beyond the sound of "wind rustling through the leaves," pointing to their own studies showing low decibel levels and the experience of observers who've been taken directly under a wind turbine. However, the reality for people living near a windplant does not substantiate this claim. Turbine noise is so irritating and disconcerting that it can cause people to seek medical attention, as Rodger Hutzell of Meyersdale, Pennsylvania, had to do. The problem is so acute in Europe that the world's first International Wind Turbine Noise conference was convened in Berlin last fall. A Malone, New York, physician, Nina Pierpont, who has studied the symptoms of several families, especially the d'Entremont family of Nova Scotia, has called for systematic medical study of what she has termed Wind Turbine Noise Syndrome.

An explanation for turbine noise was published earlier this year by a Dutch researcher, G.P. van den Berg of the University of Groningen in the Netherlands. Van den Berg demonstrated that loud aerodynamic sounds are generated when the moving propeller blade passes the turbine's tower mast, creating sound pressure fluctuations. Such fluctuations may not be great from an individual turbine, but when several turbines operate together, the pulses amplify each other, greatly magnifying the sound. Van den Berg also noted a "distinct audible difference between the night and daytime sound at some distance [more than one mile] from the turbines." . . .

There are windplant-generated nuisances that have been verified across three continents. The failure of many local governments to provide appropriate leadership on this issue is appalling. After-the-fact lawsuits brought because of predictable nuisances are difficult, expensive, and time consuming. These massive windplants precipitate incivility, pitting neighbor against neighbor. A major reason for government to exist is to anticipate and mitigate this incivility. Recent changes to the Perry Township Wind Ordinance strongly suggest they were prepared under the guidance, if not the dictation, of the wind industry, without consulting any comprehensive plan that honors the rural integrity of this region. This is a prescription for discord.

Safety for Birds, Bats and Other Wildlife

The wind industry asserts its technology is safe for migrating wildlife, using avian experts and industry-sponsored studies to bolster its claims. None of these have withstood the scrutiny of independent inquiry. Tall structures—buildings, cell and communication towers—are responsible for annually killing millions of migrating birds. Wind turbines, each more than 400 feet tall—with propeller blades moving at nearly 160 miles per hour at their tips and placed atop prominent ridges where large numbers of birds concentrate in migration—kill birds of prey, songbirds, and especially bats. Despite industry insistence this won't happen, it already has. When confronted with this reality, the industry argument morphs into a ten wrongs make a right scenario: "Cats and communication towers kill millions of birds annually, and we won't kill that many." When challenged about the appropriateness of this defense, the industry shifts gears once more: "The need for clean energy justifies the loss of wildlife," implying that wind energy will displace significant fossil fuel production. Some might recall this same ends justifies the means rationale promoted use of DDT.

Recent radar studies—one in Vermont, one in Virginia—documented significant potential problems for migratory wildlife. Last week, I also talked with graduate students from Frostburg University in Maryland who recently used radar to chart numbers of birds and bats flying overhead along the mountains of Western Maryland. The preliminary data shows that wind turbines may pose a high risk to bird and bat populations. On many nights during the season as many as 300,000 birds and bats flew low enough to collide with huge wind turbines. Last year, Ed Arnett, a biologist with Bat Conservation International, released his study of two Florida Power and Light windplants in Pennsylvania and West Virginia. His research reaffirmed earlier studies showing major bat mortality. Faced with the news that its wind turbines were killing thousands of bats, Florida Power and Light reacted quickly. It barred scientists from pursuing follow-up work, removed its $75,000 contribution from the research cooperative studying bat mortality and ended the doctoral work of a graduate student who had produced two years of data showing unusually high rates of bat death at the Pennsylvania and

West Virginia sites. Although Florida Power and Light has pulled the plug on further research into avian and bat mortality on its properties, the company plans to construct hundreds more turbines in the mountainous areas of the region.

Braddock Bay near Rochester along Lake Ontario is a major destination point for thousands of birds of prey, many of which use the ridges along Silver Lake to help guide their spring migration. The July issue of *Wildbird* (2006) contains an excellent article about Braddock Bay and raptor migration. When I told Donald Heintzelman, one of this country's leading bird of prey specialists, about plans to construct several large windplants in this part of New York, he expressed concern. Avian migration is an extremely complex phenomenon, with many influencing factors, including the changing conditions of weather and climate over many years. Adequate preconstruction study for wind projects does not mean that, because such study is made, therefore windplants can be built. Rather, risk studies should be made to determine whether or not they should be built at all. Wind developers plan thousands of turbines along major avian migration flyways from Georgia through New Hampshire, creating a gauntlet of risk for birds and bats, some species of which have extremely vulnerable populations. We should take great care to avoid the unintended adverse consequence wrought by uninformed decisions of the well intentioned.

Not Here There

Just how clean, green, functional and effective is wind energy? Is it worth the high level of public subsidy sustaining it? On a per kilowatt-hour basis, wind is the most heavily subsidized source of industrial power in the nation, according to John Sherwell, spokesman for Maryland's Power Plant Research Program. Conventional power producers enjoy a high level of public subsidy, but they also provide significant, reliable electricity.

Presently, Horizon Wind seeks to place 65 turbines around the county. Orion Wind has stated it wants to put 40 turbines here—for a total of 105. The rated capacity of each Horizon turbine is 2 MW; Orion's turbines may be rated at 1.5 MW. These 105 turbines would have a combined rated capacity of 190 MW. *Rated capacity* means the amount of electricity a wind turbine could put into the electricity grid over a year's time *if* it were working at full strength all the time.

Engineers use the term *capacity factor* to assess what percentage of its rated capacity a power plant will actually deliver over a specified time. Wind turbines don't begin generating electricity until wind speeds hit around 8 mph and they shut off at wind speeds exceeding 55 mph to avoid damage. They achieve rated capacity typically at wind speeds of 32–37 mph. Because of wind's unpredictable intermittency and wide fluctuations, along with the downtime for maintenance, no windplants located in the eastern United States have achieved a capacity factor of more than 30%. Consequently, Horizon/Orion's combined windplants might contribute on average 57 MW of sporadic energy annually to the electricity grid, which is 30% of their rated capacity. Although no conventional power plants work at peak capacity all the time, this is due to operator choice, not because of the limitations of their power source.

Conventional units must pass stringent tests for reliability and effectiveness. Generators that satisfy basic levels of demand, such as nuclear, large coal plants, and hydro, have capacity factors approaching 100%. Smaller, more flexible load balancing units, which may be used only a few hours a year, may have capacity factors of less than 5%. But the random, desultory nature of the wind, which rapidly changes the energy level contributed to the electricity grid at frequent intervals, limits what wind machinery can do, condemning wind turbines to *intrinsically* low capacity factors. Moreover, the wind typically blows hardest at night, at times of least demand, and much less during the afternoon, at times of peak demand. And in summer months, when demand for electricity is greatest, there may be no wind at all. The *capacity credit* for wind technology, a measure of the percentage of time wind technology can be relied upon to have energy available when needed to meet demand, is in the low single digits. Conversely, the capacity credit for conventional units approaches certainty.

An electricity *grid* is a complex network of regional power sources to supply demand for a variety of customers—residential, commercial, industrial, along with public and quasi-public operations like police, schools, hospitals, traffic control. The grid management creates and maintains a dynamic equilibrium between demand and supply, fine-tuning it on a second-by-second basis to within +/– 1%. The New York grid is known as the New York Independent System Operator, and it serves over 19 million people with a required annual installed capacity of 37,534 MW. Coal generates around 15% of its power; nuclear—27%; hydro—19 %; natural gas—20%; and petroleum—15%. All of these conventional fuels provide steady, reliable power, and are carefully orchestrated to achieve effective responses at reasonable cost; their predictable performance provides *capacity*, a measure of firm generation and transmission capability.

No one knows what hours in a day the wind will blow sufficiently to produce electricity; or when the wind will blow at speeds providing only a fraction of a plant's rated capacity; or when wind will stop suddenly or change direction. One minute a wind facility may be producing 80% of its rated capacity and in the next produce nothing. A few minutes later, it may hit the grid with 10% of its rated capacity and, a bit later, jump up to 40%, and a few minutes after that, come back down to zero. Since electricity produced at industrial scales cannot be stored and must be used immediately, the grid, to assure reliability and stability, must enlist compensatory companion generation to follow and balance wind's skittering activity. This typically consists of smaller, very flexible conventional generators such as hydro or natural gas, which, unlike large coal and nuclear plants, can be throttled forward and back quickly, giving grid operators the kind of rapid response they must have to "smooth" the ongoing flux.

As wind developers are quick to say, grid operators already are engaged in the process of balancing the fluctuations of demand, which occurs continually as people turn on and off their appliances. The number and variety of power sources on the grid and the fluctuations of demand do indeed provide a real challenge for grid operators to integrate and balance all of this activity, even without the addition of highly fluctuating wind energy, which is many times more unpredictable and volatile than the time-tested patterns of demand flux. Paradoxically, fluctuating wind energy is treated as grid operators treat sudden shifts caused by people turning on and off their lights unexpectedly. *It is treated as if it were fluctuating demand, and not as a source of supply that can be relied upon to satisfy demand.*

According to energy expert Tom Hewson, wind technology generates energy, not capacity—that is, reliable energy on demand. It is therefore inimical to the process by which power grids work to insure reliability and system security at reasonable cost. Moreover, since it has virtually no capacity credit, it cannot obviate the need for new reliable conventional generating plants, especially in light of increasing demand. Most of this new generation would likely be in the form of coal, since there is so little discretionary hydro (most of it is used to supply either basic demand or to follow and balance demand flux), and natural gas is so expensive, much of it diverted for heating purposes, while new nuclear plants do not seem to be an option anywhere in this country.

Because wind energy must be followed and balanced second-by-second by conventional generation, typically flexible fossil-fueled units, to achieve functional integration within the grid, this creates higher costs in the form of increased rates (someone must pay for the accompanying generation) and in the form of increased CO_2 emissions, since those wind-following fossil-fueled units are operating extremely inefficiently. For example, the Judith Gap wind-plant in Montana, producing in one hour 80 MW of electricity, and falling to 20 MW the next, is causing major headaches for the grid, even though the amount of wind energy relative to the grid's total supply is minute. The Montana utility was forced to buy more short-term power than expected from other energy sources to balance the grid's supply, driving costs upward.

If wind energy's electricity approaches, say, 10% of the grid's online supply, it would threaten the grid's ability to function. What would happen if the grid had insufficient supply to compensate for a sudden loss of wind power at this level of production? The same kind of blackout that occurred recently in Spain. What would happen if a sudden burst of high energy hit the grid because the wind increased unexpectedly? Such a power surge at 10% of the grid's total would shut the grid down. These situations demonstrate why E.On Netz, Germany's largest utility, has concluded that if wind penetration approaches 5%–10% of the grid's actual generation, *additional* conventional power must be added to the system at 90% of the wind installations' rated capacity—to protect the grid from wind's higher levels of fluctuating volatility.

Several sobering observations emerge from all this. First, any CO_2 emission saving that wind production creates is offset to some degree by the need for accompanying and backup generation, since much of that would come from "dirty" power sources working overtime. It is not clear whether wind energy creates even more CO_2 emissions throughout the grid because of this factor, given the need to continuously ramp the various companion power sources up and down, using more fuel much in the way a car engine does in stop-and-go traffic. Generally, fossil-fueled generators operating even 2% less efficiently than they were designed to do for following demand flux produce 16% more carbon emissions. No independent, peer-reviewed analyses measuring the operation of existing wind facilities have been conducted to show how—or whether—wind-produced electricity actually reduces CO_2 emissions throughout a grid system. If hydro units, which emit no hydrocarbons, balance the variability of wind turbines, that wind energy cannot be considered green, given how destructive hydro plants are to sensitive ecosystems. If fossil-fueled generators follow and balance wind flux, these wind facilities can hardly be considered clean or green.

Second, no unpredictably intermittent, highly variable power source can, of itself, provide power for anyone, given modern expectations of reliability and performance—despite all the media puffery implying it can. Wyoming County's two proposed wind facilities might contribute, on a hit-or-miss basis, an annual average of 57 MW to the NYISO's annual installed capacity of more than 37,000 MW, which would be little more than one tenth of 1% of the grid's current total. Since we increase our demand for electricity at 2% a year (and New York is presently doing so at more than 3%), these 57 MW would be swallowed up within the first three weeks of the new demand year. And this is if everything works the way the wind industry hopes it will. If this amount of power were generated by coal or nuclear, with capacity factors approaching 90% and with a predictable and constant stream of energy, it would service about 50,000 homes. However, because of the intermittent, unpredictable nature of wind, no homes would be powered by this source. How will such energy stabilize natural gas prices or serve to "diversify" the mix of power sources, as wind developers claim?

An electricity grid generally accepts wind energy not because it works well, but because it has to, the result of political decisions to legislate Renewable Portfolio Standards that now exist in over 20 states, requiring utilities to purchase a certain percentage of renewable energy. The only two renewables capable of achieving industrial levels of electricity are hydro and wind—and no one outside China and some third world countries is constructing new hydro facilities.

Industrial Wind and Climate Change

I'd also like to dispel an untruth that wind developers spread to generate support among environmental groups: that wind energy will contravene the forces contributing to global warming and reduce dependence on foreign oil. Wind only generates electricity. Electricity generation is only part of our energy production. More than 60% of the nation's energy use does not involve the making of electricity. Coal and gas-fired electricity power plants do pollute the air with hydrocarbons. But the sheer volume of automobile exhausts and an insatiable demand for heat are the major contributors to the problem. It is folly to suggest that thousands of wind turbines blanketing the eastern US would do anything to mitigate these other energy uses. Nationally, oil contributes only 3% of our electricity production. Even if industrial wind generated 10% of the nation's electricity, it would not staunch the fossil fuel emissions thought to be involved in accelerating global warming, given our nation's increasing energy consumption and given that wind can only intermittently address the electricity portion of our energy production problem—the minor portion. Since wind energy only produces electricity and we use so little oil for the production of electricity, even if large numbers of wind turbines displaced the 3% of our electricity now powered by oil, we would still be heavily dependent on coal and gas—and we would still be mightily dependent on foreign oil.

These realities doom wind technology as anything other than a Rube Goldberg operation. To reduce fossil-fueled companion and back-up power generation for wind energy, we would have to build three windplants for every one, each in a separate geographical area to provide statistical redundancy for the intermittent flux of wind—and, even then, we would have to spend billions for new grid equipment to provide the lowest level capacity value. By this reckoning, about 6000-2.5 MW turbines would be needed to equal the output of one 1600 MW coalplant—and perhaps 8000 or more to compensate for the low wind capacity credit during the summer months, when, of course, demand is greatest. This far-fetched scenario might minimize windplant-induced CO_2 emissions at the operational level. However, energy expert Tom Tanton has calculated that, to compensate for the CO_2 emissions required for the concrete pads necessary to anchor each wind turbine, a large windplant would have to operate CO_2 free for at least seven years. There is no free lunch with the laws of thermodynamics.

To me, this is the smoking gun that challenges notions that wind energy may be a splendid idea. For wind-rich areas in the East, industrial wind is a non-starter anywhere in the region because, although the industry will have reasonably easy access to transmission lines, it's not going to produce enough reliable power to dent a grape in the scheme of things. Contrary to a wind developer's claim that our choice is between the belching smoke-stacks of coal and the twirling blades of huge wind turbines, we'll have both. Even if these turbines were fully deployed in the uplands of the East, coal plants would still be puffing away, their numbers actually increasing, while many thousands of gigantic wind machines would glut the landscape—killing wildlife, destroying culturally significant viewsheds, devaluing property, and creating major disturbances for those who live nearby. And, because the air would be getting dirtier, people everywhere would be getting sicker while paying more in rates and taxes.

In the Midwest, however, and certainly in the deep oceans, there is enough wind resource to make a big difference. European nations such as

Denmark, Germany, Spain, and the Netherlands, each of which has encountered a political uproar about onshore windplants, are now seriously examining offshore wind potential. The problem is that, because of the need for
redundancy and our ever-increasing demand for electricity, millions of turbines must be constructed and linked to new transmission systems, as well as
retooled grid systems—at a cost of trillions of dollars. The ecological implications would be enormous.

Wind Economics

A discussion of the wind industry's vast array of public subsidies would
fill a book. In a nutshell, Kenneth Lay's Enron, the "energy" company
that, before its demise, owned and operated the nation's largest collection of wind facilities, cultivated them; Enron pioneered the tax shelter
as a commodity. Publicly funded tax avoidance schemes reimburse wind
energy developers as much as two-thirds of the capital cost of each $2
million turbine, with many states creating incentives to cover on average an additional 10% of these costs. A recent Beacon Hill Institute study
showed that such incentive programs would allow the Cape Wind project
to be reimbursed up to 78% of its capital costs over the life of the facility.
Windplant owners can use these tax shelters themselves, or sell them, or
enter into "equity partnerships" with other companies—all to reduce their
corporate tax obligations by tens of millions each year, as the Marriott Corporation did a few years ago with a similar clean energy scheme, within
a year reducing its corporate tax obligations from 36% to 6%—generating
tax credits worth $159 million and a return of 246% on its investment in
just one year.

The Florida Power and Light Group, the parent of FPL Energy, paid no
federal income tax in 2002 and 2003, according to Citizens for Tax Justice,
despite having revenues of $2.2 billion during those years. The FPL Group
made large investments in wind energy during that time and now claims to
be one of the nation's leading wind energy producers. It is also the parent
company of Meyersdale Wind in Pennsylvania and Mountaineer Wind in
West Virginia, both of which have delivered only a fraction of promised local
taxes to date.

Wind is the perfect vehicle for tax shelter generation. Its unearned
environmental credit brings a public relations cachet while trading in
wind's renewable energy credits allows outfits like Florida Power and Light,
GE, AES, and BP, which collectively own most of the nation's wind facilities, to avoid cleaning up their dirtiest burning plants. And the politicians
who support all this give the appearance of challenging the status quo
when in reality they're reinforcing it, especially since more wind facilities very likely will result in more coal plants. These costs to the federal
treasury, which are actually transfers of wealth from average tax and ratepayers to a few corporate investors, aren't worth the benefits accruing to a
handful of full time employees and to undisclosed annual lease payments
for a very few property owners. Many new reliable conventional plants

will be needed in the next 30 years. The subsidies for each will encourage efficient, dependable, cost effective electricity. The subsidies for dysfunctional industrial wind energy, which can provide virtually no capacity to the system and can deliver only sporadic energy, will be used to make ineffective and uneconomical technology falsely appear to be effective and economical. . . .

Carl Sagan once said, "Extraordinary claims require extraordinary proof." I have never seen an independent peer-reviewed analysis in a reputable scientific publication substantiating any of the claims made for wind energy. Reports from wind developers, their trade association, and from the Renewable Energy Lab, all of which stand to gain from the "enhancement" of wind technology, do not stem from the rigorous science enabling good public policy.

I have worked to understand this issue from a citizen's perspective, reasoning from basic principles, knowing when answers I've been given are unresponsive, and saying, like the boy in the story about the emperor's new clothes, that I don't see the evidence when it was not provided. As citizens interested in more effective energy solutions, I trust you will do the same. One can be concerned about how our fossil fuel combustion practices may help accelerate the process of global warming and injure public health without agreeing that the intrusive and ineffectual nature of wind energy technology is even a partial solution to the problem. For me, the harsh reality is that massive wind turbines are much more functional (and lucrative) as corporate tax avoidance generators than they are as environmentally friendly producers of energy, symbolic not of a more enlightened energy future but rather of our continuing attraction to the forces of ignorance and greed. They represent at best a placebo for our energy dilemma, distracting from the level of discourse—and political action—necessary for achieving genuinely effective responses. There are no magic bullets, unfortunately. The environmentally responsible short-range solution to the problem of our dependence upon fossil fuels must combine effective conservation with much higher efficiency standards—heavy lifting indeed for the most wasteful culture in the history of the planet.

POSTSCRIPT

Is Wind Power Green?

Despite the rapid growth of wind power, the debate over its benefits is far from over. Yet the debate centers more on industrial-scale wind farms, which deploy large numbers of large wind turbines, than on small home-scale systems. According to Jennifer Alsever, "Wind Power, The Home Edition," *Business 2.0* (January/February 2007), a dozen U.S. companies are offering wind turbines to be installed next to private homes. The Skystream costs about $10,000. Glen Salas, "A Great Wind Is Blowing," *Professional Builder* (January 2007), says that home builders can cater to "a lot of people [who] are willing to spend the extra money to generate their own electricity" and notes that "Over its life, a small residential wind turbine can offset about 1.2 tons of air pollutants and 200 tons of greenhouse gases, according to the American Wind Energy Association" (which offers fact sheets and more at http://www.awea.org/).

Oil tycoon T. Boone Pickens now sees wind as the only "source of energy that's going to make a substantial difference for this country" (Philip Klein, "Energy's Prevailing Winds," *American Spectator,* May 2008). Utilities are investing in major wind farms, both on land and at sea. Objections have included damage to the view and interference with navigation and fishing. A more novel proposal is to use kites that could lift wind turbines into the jet stream, where the wind is very fast; see "Getting Wind Farms off the Ground," *Economist* (June 9, 2007). Another proposal, described by Todd Woody in "Tower of Power," *Business 2.0* (August 2006), calls for a 1,600-foot tall tower that will exploit the temperature difference between the bottom and the top to set a powerful wind flowing up the tower. EnviroMission, the Australian company behind the idea, says the tower will yield 50 megawatts of electricity, and larger versions are in the planning stages.

Like standard wind farms, both kites and towers will surely provoke protests. It is worth bearing in mind that no matter how humanity generates energy in the future, there will be environmental impacts. The only way to avoid that is to stop using energy, which is not a practical proposal. On the other hand, reducing energy use through conservation and efficiency is practical, and as Komanoff writes, it is an essential part of the solution. One of the primary exponents of efficiency is Amory B. Lovins, whose "More Profit with Less Carbon," *Scientific American* (September 2005), urges that "Using energy more efficiently offers an economic bonanza—not because of the benefits of stopping global warming but because saving fossil fuel is a lot cheaper than buying it." Lovins is profiled by Elizabeth Kolbert in "Mr. Green," *New Yorker* (January 22, 2007).

ISSUE 16

Do Biofuels Enhance Energy Security?

YES: Bob Dinneen, from Testimony before Committee on Senate Energy and Natural Resources (April 12, 2007)

NO: Robbin S. Johnson and C. Ford Runge, from "Ethanol: Train Wreck Ahead," *Issues in Science and Technology* (Fall 2007)

ISSUE SUMMARY

YES: Bob Dinneen, president and CEO of the Renewable Fuels Association, the national trade association representing the U.S. ethanol industry, argues that government support of the renewable fuels industry has created jobs, saved consumers money, and reduced oil imports. The industry's potential is great, and continued support will contribute to ensuring America's future energy security.

NO: Consultant Robbin S. Johnson and Professor C. Ford Runge argue that the U.S. government's bias in favor of corn-based ethanol rigs the market against more efficient alternatives. It also leads to rising food prices, which particularly affects the world's poor.

The threat of global warming has spurred a great deal of interest in finding new sources of energy that do not add to the amount of carbon dioxide in the air. Among other things, this has meant a search for alternatives to fossil fuels, which modern civilization uses to generate electricity, heat homes, and power transportation. Finding alternatives for electricity generation (which relies much more on coal than on oil or natural gas) or home heating (which relies more on oil and natural gas) is easier than finding alternatives for transportation (which relies on oil, refined into gasoline and diesel oil). In addition, the transportation infrastructure, consisting of refineries, pipelines, tank trucks, gas stations, and an immense number of cars and trucks that will be on the road for many years, is well designed for handling liquid fuels. It is not surprising that industry and government would like to find non-fossil liquid fuels for cars and trucks (as well as ships and airplanes).

There are many suitably flammable liquids. Among them are the so-called biofuels or renewable fuels, plant oils and alcohols that can be distilled from plant sugars. According to Daniel M. Kammen, "The Rise of Renewable Energy," *Scientific American* (September 2006), the chief biofuel in the United States so far is ethanol, distilled from corn and blended with gasoline. Production is subsidized with $2 billion of federal funds, and "when all the inputs and outputs were correctly factored in, we found that ethanol" contains about 25 percent more energy (to be used when it is burned as fuel) than was used to produce it. At least one study says the "net energy" is actually less than the energy used to produce ethanol from corn. If other sources, such as cellulose-rich switchgrass or cornstalks, can be used, the "net energy" is much better; see Evan Ratliff, "The Switchgrass Solution," *Wired* (October 2007), and Joel K. Bourne, Jr., "Green Dreams," *National Geographic* (October 2007). However, generating ethanol requires first converting cellulose to fermentable sugars, which so far is an expensive process. A significant additional concern is the amount of land needed for growing crops to be turned into biofuels; in a world where hunger is widespread, this means land is taken out of food production. If additional land is cleared to grow biofuel crops, this must mean loss of forests and wildlife habitat, increased erosion, and other environmental problems. See "Ethanol: Energy Well Spent, A Survey of Studies Published since 1990," Natural Resources Defense Council and Climate Solutions [February 2006] (http://www.nrdc.org/air/transportation/ethanol/ethanol.pdf).

Under the Energy Policy Act of 2005, the U.S. Environmental Protection Agency (EPA) requires that gasoline sold in the United States contain a minimum volume of renewable fuel. Under the Renewable Fuel Program (also known as the Renewable Fuel Standard [RFS] Program), that volume will increase over the years, reaching 7.5 billion gallons by 2012. According to the EPA (http://www.epa.gov/otaq/renewablefuels/), "the RFS program was developed in collaboration with refiners, renewable fuel producers, and many other stakeholders." However, some think it is premature to put so much emphasis on biofuels. Pat Thomas, introducing *The Ecologist*'s special report on biofuels in the March 2007 issue (http://www.theecologist.org/archive_detail. asp?content_id=838), wrote that "the science is far from complete, the energy savings far from convincing and, although many see biofuels as a way to avoid the kind of resource wars currently raging in the Middle East and elsewhere, going down that road may in the end provoke a wider series of resource wars—this time over food, water and habitable land."

In the following selections, Bob Dinneen, president and CEO of the Renewable Fuels Association, the national trade association representing the U.S. ethanol industry, argues that government support of the renewable fuels industry has created jobs, saved consumers money, and reduced oil imports. The industry's potential is great, and continued support will contribute to ensuring America's future energy security. Consultant Robbin S. Johnson and Professor C. Ford Runge argue that the U.S. government's bias in favor of corn-based ethanol rigs the market against more efficient alternatives. It also leads to rising food prices, which particularly affects the world's poor.

YES

Bob Dinneen

Biofuels

. . . I am pleased to be here to discuss the future of our nation's ethanol industry and how the bipartisan Biofuels for Energy Security and Transportation Act of 2007 (S. 987) can help our country achieve its energy security goals.

Due to the visionary and invaluable work of this Committee in the 109th Congress, the Energy Policy Act of 2005 (EPAct 2005) put our nation on a new path toward greater energy diversity and national security through the RFS [Renewable Fuel Standard Program]. EPAct 2005 has stimulated unprecedented investment in the U.S. ethanol industry. Since January of 2006, when the RFS went into effect, no fewer than 15 new ethanol biorefineries have begun operation, representing some 1.2 billion gallons of new production capacity. These new gallons represent a direct investment of more than $1.8 billion and the creation of more than 22,000 new jobs in small communities across rural America.

The RFS has done exactly what Congress intended. It provided our industry with the opportunity to grow with confidence. It convinced the petroleum industry that ethanol would be a significant part of future motor fuel markets and moved them toward incorporating renewable fuels into their future plans. It persuaded the financial community that biofuels companies are growth market opportunities, encouraging significant new investment from Wall Street and other institutional investors. If a farmer in Des Moines doesn't want to invest in the local co-op, he can choose to invest in a publicly traded ethanol company through the stock market. As can a schoolteacher in Boston, or a receptionist in Seattle. Americans coast-to-coast have the opportunity to invest in our domestic energy industry, and not just in ethanol, but biodiesel and bio-products.

In addition to the RFS, many of the other programs authorized by EPAct 2005, such as the loan guarantee and grant programs, will accelerate the commercialization of cellulosic ethanol and make the new goals set forth in S. 987 absolutely achievable. Many of the provisions included in S. 987 build upon the programs designed by this Committee and included in EPAct 2005 to further expand the domestic renewable fuels industry. The Senate Energy and Natural Resources Committee will have an invaluable role to play in making sure our nation successfully moves toward increasing the use of domestic, renewable energy sources.

From Testimony before Committee on Senate Energy and Natural Resources by Bob Dinneen (for Renewable Fuels Association), (April 12, 2007).

Background

Today's ethanol industry consists of 115 biorefineries located in 19 different states with the capacity to process almost 2 billion bushels of grain into 5.7 billion gallons of high octane, clean burning motor fuel, and more than 12 million metric tons of livestock and poultry feed. It is a dynamic and growing industry that is revitalizing rural America, reducing emissions in our nation's cities, and lowering our dependence on imported petroleum.

Ethanol has become an essential component of the U.S. motor fuel market. Today, ethanol is blended in more than 46% of the nation's fuel, and is sold virtually from coast to coast and border to border. The almost 5 billion gallons of ethanol produced and sold in the U.S. last year contributed significantly to the nation's economic, environmental and energy security.

According to an analysis completed for the RFA1, the approximately 5 billion gallons of ethanol produced in 2006 resulted in the following impacts:

- Added $41.1 billion to gross output;
- Created 160,231 jobs in all sectors of the economy;
- Increased economic activity and new jobs from ethanol increased household income by $6.7 billion, money that flows directly into consumers' pockets;
- Contributed $2.7 billion of tax revenue for the Federal government and $2.3 billion for State and Local governments; and,
- Reduced oil imports by 170 million barrels of oil, valued at $11.2 billion.

In addition to providing a growing and reliable domestic market for American farmers, the ethanol industry also provides the opportunity for farmers to enjoy some of the value added to their commodity by further processing. Farmer-owned ethanol plants account for 43 percent of the U.S. fuel ethanol plants and almost 34 percent of industry capacity.

There are currently 79 biorefineries under construction. With seven existing biorefineries expanding, the industry expects more than 6 billion gallons of new production capacity to be in operation by the end of 2009. The following is our best estimate of when this new production will come online.

To date, the U.S. ethanol industry has grown almost exclusively from grain processing. As a result of steadily increasing yields and improving technology, the National Corn Growers Association (NCGA) projects that by 2015, corn growers will produce 15 billion bushels of grain. According to the NCGA analysis, this will allow a portion of that crop to be processed into 15 billion gallons of ethanol without significantly disrupting other markets for corn. Ethanol also represents a growing market for other grains, such as grain sorghum. Ethanol production consumed approximately 26 percent of the nation's sorghum crop in 2006 (domestic use).

Research is also underway on the use of sweet and forage sorghum for ethanol production. In fact, the National Sorghum Producers believe that as new generation ethanol processes are studied and improved, sorghum's role will continue to expand.

In the future, however, ethanol will be produced from other feedstocks, such as cellulose. Ethanol from cellulose will dramatically expand the types and amount of available material for ethanol production, and ultimately dramatically expand ethanol supplies. Many companies are working to commercialize cellulosic ethanol production. Indeed, there is not an ethanol biorefinery in production today that does not have a very aggressive cellulose ethanol research program. The reason for this is that today's ethanol producers all have cellulose already coming into the plant in the form of corn fiber. Producers are making good use of all parts of the corn kernel—beyond just the starch. Several ethanol producers are working on technology to turn the fiber in a corn kernel into ethanol through fermentation. Since fiber represents 11 percent of the kernel, this could lead to dramatic increases in ethanol production efficiency. If today's producers can process these cellulosic materials into ethanol, they will have a significant marketplace advantage. The RFA believes cellulose ethanol will be commercialized first by current producers who have these cellulosic feedstocks at their grain-based facilities. It is essential to the advancement of the ethanol industry that these "bridge technology" cellulosic feedstocks be included in the definition of advanced biofuels.

Further, biotechnology will play a significant role in meeting our nation's future ethanol needs.

Average yield per acre is not static and will increase incrementally, especially with the introduction of new biotech hybrid varieties. According to NCGA, corn yields have consistently increased an average of about 3.5 bushels per year over the last decade. Based on the 10-year historical trend, corn yield per acre could reach 180 bushels by 2015. For comparison, the average yield in 1970 was about 72 bushels per acre. Agricultural companies like Monsanto believe we can achieve corn yields of up to 300 bushels per acre by 2030. It is not necessary to limit the potential of any feedstock—existing or prospective. Ultimately, the marketplace will determine which feedstocks are the most economically and environmentally feasible.

While there are indeed limits to what we will be able to produce from grain, cellulose ethanol production will augment, not replace, grain-based ethanol. The conversion of feedstocks like corn stover, corn fiber and corn cobs will be the "bridge technology" that leads the industry to the conversion of other cellulosic feedstocks and energy crops such as wheat straw, switchgrass, and fast-growing trees. Even the garbage, or municipal solid waste, Americans throw away today will be a future source of ethanol.

Research & Development, Deployment and Commercialization of New Technologies

The ethanol industry today is on the cutting edge of technology, pursuing new processes, new energy sources and new feedstocks that will make tomorrow's ethanol industry unrecognizable from today's. Ethanol companies are already utilizing cold starch fermentation, corn fractionation, and corn oil extraction. Companies are pursuing more sustainable energy sources, including biomass gasification and methane digesters. And, as stated, there is not an ethanol company represented by the RFA that does not have a cellulose-to-ethanol research program.

These cutting edge technologies are reducing energy consumption and production costs, increasing biorefinery efficiency, improving the protein content of feed co-products, utilizing new feedstocks such as cellulose, and reducing emissions by employing best available control technologies.

The technology exists to process ethanol from cellulose feedstocks; however, commercialization of cellulosic ethanol remains a question of economics. The capital investment necessary to build cellulosic ethanol facilities remains about five times that of grain-based facilities. Those costs will, of course, come down once the first handful of cellulosic facilities are built, the bugs in those "first mover" facilities are worked out, and the technology continues to advance. The enzymes involved in the cellulosic ethanol process remain a significant cost, as well. While there has been a tremendous amount of progress over the past few years to bring the cost of those enzymes down, it is still a significant cost relative to processing grain-based ethanol.

To continue this technological revolution, however, continued government support will be critically important. The biomass, bioresearch, and biorefinery development programs included in S. 987 will be essential to developing these new technologies and bringing them to commercialization. Competitively awarded grants and loan guarantees that build upon the existing programs authorized in EPAct 2005 and enhanced in S. 987 will allow technologically promising cellulosic ethanol projects [that] move the industry forward [to] become a reality.

Infrastructure

Ethanol today is largely a blend component with gasoline, adding octane, displacing toxics and helping refiners meet Clean Air Act specifications. But the time when ethanol will saturate the blend market is on the horizon, and the industry is looking forward to new market opportunities.

As rapidly as ethanol production is expanding, it is possible the industry will saturate the existing blend market before a meaningful E-85 market develops. In such a case, it would be most beneficial to allow refiners to blend ethanol in greater volumes, e.g., 15 or 20 percent. The ethanol industry today is engaged in testing on higher blend levels of ethanol, beyond E-10.

There is evidence to suggest that today's vehicle fleet could use higher blends. An initial round of testing is underway, and more test programs will be needed. A study of increased blend levels of ethanol, included in S. 987, will be an essential and necessary step to moving to higher blend levels with our current vehicle fleet. Higher blend levels would have a significant positive impact on the U.S. ethanol market, without needing to install new fuel pumps and wait for a vehicle fleet to turn over in the next few decades. It would also allow for a smoother transition to E-85 by growing the infrastructure more steadily.

Enhancing incentives to gasoline marketers to install E-85 refueling pumps will continue to be essential. There are now more than 1,000 E-85 refueling stations across the country, more than doubling in number since the passage of EPAct 2005. The RFA also supports the concept of regional "corridors" that concentrate the E-85 markets first where the infrastructure already exists, which is reflected in S. 987 in the infrastructure pilot program for renewable fuels.

Over the past several years, the ethanol industry has worked to expand a "Virtual Pipeline" through aggressive use of the rail system, barge and truck traffic. As a result, we can move product quickly to those areas where it is needed. Many ethanol plants have the capability to load unit trains of ethanol for shipment to ethanol terminals in key markets. Unit trains are quickly becoming the norm, not the exception, which was not the case just a few years ago.

Railroad companies are working with our industry to develop infrastructure to meet future demand for ethanol. We are also working closely with terminal operators and refiners to identify ethanol storage facilities and install blending equipment. We will continue to grow the necessary infrastructure to make sure that in any market we need to ship ethanol there is rail access at gasoline terminals, and that those terminals are able to take unit trains. Looking to the future, studying the feasibility of transporting ethanol by pipeline from the Midwest to the East and West coasts, as proposed in S. 987, will be critical.

As flexible fuel vehicle (FFV) production is ramped up, it is important to encourage the use of the most efficient technologies. Some FFVs today experience a reduction in mileage when ethanol is used because of the differences in BTU content compared to gasoline. But the debit can be easily addressed through continued research and development. For example, General Motors has introduced a turbo-charged SAAB that experiences no reduction in fuel efficiency when E-85 is used. There is also technology being developed that utilizes "variable compression ratio engines" that would adjust the compression ratio depending on the fuel used.

Thus, if the car's computer system recognized E-85 was being used, it would adjust the compression ratio to take full advantage of ethanol's properties. RFA supports the further study of how best to optimize technologies of alternative fueled vehicles to use E-85 fuel as included in S. 987. The study of new technologies could dramatically improve E-85 economics by eliminating or substantially reducing the mileage penalty associated with existing FFV technology.

Conclusion

The continued commitment of the 110th Congress, this Committee, and the introduction of legislation such as S. 987 will all contribute to ensuring America's future energy security. Chairman Bingaman and Ranking Member Domenici, you have made clear your commitment to the hardworking men and women across America who are today's newest energy producers.

There have been numerous bills introduced in the first few months of the 110th Congress to further expand the rapidly growing domestic biofuels industry that will soon eclipse the current RFS. Many of the sound provisions included in those bills to move the industry forward and create new market opportunities for biofuels are incorporated in S. 987. With minimal modifications, S. 987 strikes the right balance between incentivizing cellulosic ethanol technologies, developing the necessary infrastructure, moving beyond existing blend markets for ethanol, and capitalizing on the momentum created by EPAct 2005. The RFA looks forward to working with you to further develop this important legislation.

**Robbin S. Johnson and
C. Ford Runge**

 **NO**

Ethanol: Train Wreck Ahead?

The new vogue in energy policy is plant-derived alternative fuels. Corn-based ethanol, and to a lesser extent oilseed-based biodiesel, have emerged from the margins to take center stage. However, although ethanol and biodiesel will surely play a role in our energy future, the rush to embrace them has overlooked numerous obstacles and untoward implications that merit careful assessment. The current policy bias toward corn-based ethanol has driven a run-up in the prices of staple foods in the United States and around the world, with particularly hurtful consequences for poor consumers in developing countries. U.S. ethanol policies rig the market against alternatives based on the conversion of cellulosic inputs such as switchgrass and wood fibers. Moreover, the environmental consequences of corn-based ethanol are far from benign, and indeed are negative in a number of important respects. Given the tremendous growth in the corn-based ethanol market, it should no longer be considered an infant industry deserving of tax breaks, tariff protection, and mandates.

In place of current approaches, we propose initiatives that would cool the overheated market and encourage more diversified investment in cellulosic alternatives and energy conservation. First, we would freeze current mandates for renewable fuels to reduce overinvestment in and overreliance on corn-based ethanol. Second, we would replace current ethanol tax breaks with a sliding scale that would reduce incentives to produce ethanol when corn prices are high and thus slow the diversion of corn from food to fuel. Third, we would implement a wide-ranging set of federal fees and rebates that discourage energy consumption and encourage conservation. Fourth, we would shift federal investment in cellulosic alternatives from subsidies for inefficient production facilities and direct them instead to upstream investment in R&D to improve conversion technologies. Together, these four changes would still retain a key role for biofuels in our energy future, while eliminating many of the distortions that current policy has created.

Infant Industry No More

Since 1974, when the first federal legislation to promote corn-based ethanol as a fuel was approved, ethanol has been considered an infant industry and provided with increasingly generous government subsidies and mandates.

Ethanol's first big boost came in the late 1970s in response to rising oil prices and abundant corn surpluses. A tax credit for blending corn-based ethanol with gasoline created a reliable market for excess corn production, which was seen as an alternative to uncertain export markets.

But the real momentum for ethanol resulted from environmental concerns about the use of lead to boost the octane rating of gasoline. The phase-out of lead as an additive began in 1973, and ethanol replaced it as a cleaner-burning octane enhancer. In recent years, it has replaced the oxygen additive MTBE, which was phased out because of concerns about groundwater pollution. Ethanol's increasing value as a gasoline additive has allowed it to receive a premium price, and by 2005 corn-based ethanol production in the United States reached 3.9 billion gallons.

More recently, increases in oil prices during the past two years brought ethanol into national prominence. From $52 a barrel in November 2005 to more than $70 in mid-2007, higher oil prices coincided at first with cheap corn: a prescription for supernormal ethanol profits. Investment in new capacity took off, and 2006 production topped 5 billion gallons.

Although high oil prices have given ethanol the headroom it needs to compete, the industry is built on federal subsidies to both the corn farmer and the ethanol producer. Direct corn subsidies equaled $8.9 billion in 2005, but fell in 2006 and 2007 as high ethanol-driven corn prices reduced subsidy payments. These payments may soon be dwarfed by transfers to ethanol producers resulting from production mandates, tax credits, grants, and government loans under 2005 energy legislation and U.S. farm policy. In addition to a federal ethanol tax allowance of 51 cents per gallon, many states provide additional subsidies or have imposed their own mandates.

In the 2005 energy bill, Congress mandated the use of 7.5 billion gallons of biofuels by 2012, and there is strong political support for raising the mandate much higher. President Bush, in his January 2007 State of the Union speech, called for increasing renewable fuel production to 35 billion gallons by 2017. Such an amount, if it were all corn-derived ethanol, would require about 108% of total current U.S. corn production.

In addition to providing domestic subsidies, Congress has also shielded U.S. producers from foreign competition. Brazil currently produces about as much ethanol as the United States (most of its derived from sugarcane instead of corn) at a significantly lower cost, but the United States imposes a 54-cent-a-gallon tariff on imported ethanol.

Negative Effects

As the ethanol industry has spiked, a larger and larger share of the U.S. corn crop has gone to feed the huge mills that produce it. According to the Renewable Fuels Association, there were 110 U.S. ethanol refineries in operation at the end of 2006, another 73 were under construction, and many existing plants were being expanded. When completed, this ethanol capacity will reach an estimated 11.4 billion gallons per year by the end of 2008, requiring 35% of the total U.S. corn crop even with a good harvest. More alarming estimates predict that ethanol plants could consume up to half of domestic corn supplies within a few years. Yet, from the standpoint of energy independence, even if the entire U.S. corn crop were used to make ethanol, it would displace less gasoline usage than raising fleet fuel economy five miles per gallon, readily achievable with existing technologies.

As biofuels increasingly impinge on the supply of corn, and as soybeans and other crops are sacrificed to grow still more corn, a food-versus-fuel debate has broken out. Critics note that domestic and international consumers of livestock fed with grains face steadily rising prices. In July 2007, the Organization for Economic Cooperation and Development issued an outlook for 2007–2016, saying that biofuels had introduced global structural shifts in food markets that would raise food costs during the next 10 years. Especially for the 2.7 billion people in the world living on the equivalent of less than $2 per day and the 1.1 billion surviving on less than $1, even marginal increases in the cost of staple grains can be devastating. Put starkly: Filling the 25-gallon tank of a sport utility vehicle with pure ethanol would require more than 450 pounds of corn, enough calories to feed one poor person for a year.

The enormous volume of corn required by the ethanol industry is sending shock waves through the food system. The United States accounts for some 40% of the world's total corn production and ships on average more than half of all corn exports. In June 2007, corn futures rose to over $4.25 a bushel, the highest level in a decade. Like corn, wheat and rice prices have surged to 10-year highs, encouraging farmers to plant more acres of corn and fewer acres of other crops, especially soybeans. The proponents of corn-based ethanol argue that yields and acreage can increase to satisfy the rising demand. However, U.S. corn yields have been trending upward by a little less than 2% annually during the past 10 years. Even a doubling of yield gains would not be enough to meet current increases in demand. If substantial additional acres are to be planted with corn, the land will have to be pulled from other crops and the Conservation Reserve Program, as well as other environmentally fragile areas.

In the United States, the explosive growth of the biofuels sector and its demand for raw stocks of plants has triggered run-ups in the prices not only of corn, other grains, and oilseeds, but also of crops and products less visible to analysts and policymakers. In Minnesota, land diverted to corn to feed the ethanol maw is reducing the acreage planted to a wide range of other crops, especially soybeans. Food processors with contracts with farmers to grow crops such as peas and sweet corn have been forced to pay higher prices to keep their supplies secure. Eventually, these costs will appear in the prices of frozen and canned vegetables. Rising feed prices are also hitting the livestock and poultry industries. Some agricultural economists predict that Iowa's pork producers will be driven out of business as they are forced to compete with ethanol producers for corn.

It is in the rest of the world, however, where biofuels may have their most untoward and devastating effects. The evidence of these effects is already clear in Mexico. In January 2007, in part because of the rise in U.S. corn prices from $2.80 to $4.20 in less than four months, the price of tortilla flour in some parts of Mexico rose sharply. The connection was that 80% of Mexico's corn imports, which account for a quarter of its consumption, are from the United States, and U.S. corn prices had risen, largely because of surges in demand to make ethanol. About half of Mexico's 107 million people live in poverty; for them, tortillas are the main source of calories. By December 2006, the price of tortillas had doubled in a few months to eight pesos ($0.75) or more per kilogram. Most tortillas are made from homegrown white corn. However, industrial users of imported yellow corn in Mexico (for animal feed and processed foods) shifted to using white corn rather than imported yellow, because of the latter's sharp price increase. The price increase of tortillas was exacerbated by speculation and hoarding. In January 2007, public outcry forced Mexico's new President, Felipe Calderón, to set limits on the price of corn products.

The International Food Policy Research Institute (IFPRI), in Washington, DC, has monitored the run-up in the demand for biofuels and provides some sobering estimates of their potential global impact. IFPRI's Mark Rosegrant and his colleagues estimated the displacement of gasoline and diesel by biofuels and its effect on agricultural market prices. Given rapid increases in current rates of biofuels production with existing technologies in the United States, the European Union, and Brazil, and continued high oil prices, global corn prices are projected to be pushed upward by biofuels by 20% by 2010 and 41% by 2020. As more farmers substitute corn for other commodities, prices of oilseeds, including soybeans, rapeseed, and sunflower seed, are projected to rise 26% by 2010 and 76% by 2020. Wheat prices rise 11% by 2010 and 30% by 2020. Finally, and significantly for the poorest parts of sub-Saharan Africa, Asia, and Latin America where it is a staple, cassava prices rise 33% by 2010 and 135% by 2020.

Is Ethanol Competitive?

Although there are possible alternatives to corn and soybeans as feedstocks for ethanol and biodiesel, these two crops are likely, in the United States at least, to remain the primary inputs for many years. Politics will play a major role in keeping corn and soybeans at center stage. Cellulosic feedstocks are still more than twice as expensive to convert to ethanol as is corn, although they use far fewer energy resources to grow. And corn and soybean growers and ethanol producers have not lavished 35 years of attention and campaign contributions on Congress and presidents to give the store away to grass.

Yet because of the panoply of tax breaks and mandates lavished on the industry, the competitive position of the biofuels industry has never been tested. Today, however, the pressures and distortions it has created encourage perverse incentives: For ethanol to profit, either oil prices must remain high, further draining U.S. foreign exchange for petroleum imports, or corn prices must come off their market highs, allowing reasonable margins in the corn ethanol business. But high oil prices are what allow ethanol producers to pay a premium for corn. Hence, oil and corn prices are ratcheting up together, heedless of the effects on consumers and inflation. Bruce Babcock, in a study for the Center for Agricultural and Rural Development at Iowa State University, predicted in June 2007 that ethanol's impact on corn prices could make corn ethanol itself unprofitable by 2008.

Apart from ethanol-specific subsidies, tax breaks, and mandates, it is also important to recall that the ethanol market has been made in large part by shifts in U.S. transportation and clean air policies. When these policies are considered, it is clear that ethanol is not really competitive with petroleum, but has served instead as its complement. As increased production capacity allows ethanol to move beyond its traditional role as a gasoline enhancer (now a roughly 6-billion-gallon market) and become a gasoline replacement, several major concerns have arisen.

One critical factor involves a key ethanol liability: its energy content. Because it will drive a car only two-thirds as far as gasoline, its value as a gasoline replacement (rather than a gasoline additive) will probably gravitate toward two-thirds of gasoline's price. A lower ethanol price would then lower the breakeven price that ethanol producers could pay for corn. Meanwhile, the domestic market for corn has been transformed from chronic surplus stocks and carryforwards into bare shelves. Tighter supplies have led to higher prices, even in good-weather years. And what if dry hot weather produces a short corn crop? A 2007 report for the U.S. Department of Agriculture by Iowa State's Center for Agricultural and Rural Development estimated that with a 2012 mandate of 14.7 billion gallons, corn prices would be driven 42% higher and soybean prices 22% higher by a short crop similar to that of 1988. Corn exports, meanwhile, would tumble 60%. In short, ethanol is switching from a demand-builder to a demand-diverter.

Another factor involves energy efficiency. If net energy efficiency is thought of as a dimension of competitiveness, a recent Argonne National Laboratory ethanol study summarized by the U.S. Department of Energy is revealing. It showed that ethanol on average uses 0.74 million BTUs of fossil energy for each 1 million BTUs of ethanol delivered to the pump. In addition, the total energy used to produce corn-based ethanol, including the solar energy captured by photosynthesis, is 1.5 to 2 million BTUs for each 1 million BTUs of ethanol delivered to a pump. If corn for ethanol is just an additional user of land, it is fair to ignore the "free" solar energy that grows the corn. But if corn-based ethanol is diverting solar energy from food or feed to fuel through subsidies or mandates, policymakers cannot so easily ignore it. Similarly, because ethanol has only two-thirds the energy content of gasoline, its greenhouse gas emissions per mile traveled (rather than per gallon) are comparable to those of conventional gasoline.

Yet another concern is the net environmental effect of ethanol. It takes from one to three gallons of water to produce a gallon of ethanol, which raises concerns about ground and surface water supplies. Although ethanol has some advantages over conventional gasoline in terms of its contribution to air pollution, it also has some disadvantages. One is its higher volatile organic compounds (VOCs) emissions, which contribute to ozone formation. Ethanol also increases concentration of acetaldehyde, which is a carcinogen. In addition, corn and soybeans are row crops that encourage the runoff of fertilizers and pesticides into streams, rivers, and lakes. As acres come out of soybeans and into corn (of the 12 million acres of new corn planted in 2007, three-fourths came out of soybeans), they require more nitrogen fertilizer. This nitrogen runs off into waters, encouraging algae blooms that choke off oxygen for fish and other creatures. All of the above belie ethanol's reputation as "greener" than gasoline.

Finally, the logic behind the renewable fuels standard is that the raw material used—such as corn for ethanol—is renewable. Corn is renewable in the sense that it is harvested annually. But corn production and processing consume fossil fuels. So what is the net renewable benefit? Most estimates place the net renewable energy contribution from corn-based ethanol at 25% to 35%. Using a midpoint of 30%, that means that a mandate of 7.5 billion gallons, if filled by corn-based ethanol, yields a net renewable energy gain of only 2.25 billion gallons. Other products or processes may be more cost-effective in replacing gasoline.

As these problems become clearer, so does the appeal of cellulose as the feedstock for ethanol. The best role for corn-based ethanol then becomes simply building a bridge to the more promising world of cellulosic ethanol. But it is not clear why building a corn-based ethanol industry much beyond its current size as a producer of a gasoline additive makes sense as a prelude to cellulosic ethanol, for a number of reasons, First, technological progress in producing corn-based ethanol is not likely to be relevant to the technology challenges facing cellulosic ethanol. Second, growing areas for cellulose may well be different than for corn; if switchgrass is to be grown on current corn acres, it will have to beat high current corn prices in profitability. Third, the low energy density of cellulosic materials suggests that the handling and processing infrastructure they need is likely to be different in scale than for corn-based ethanol. Fourth, the economics of cellulosic ethanol are currently very high cost, with many other petroleum substitutes likely to be attractive before cellulosic ethanol. Finally, land-use conflicts—between food/feed and fuel or between conservation and fuel—differ in degree, not kind, between corn and cellulose and are likely to constrain a cellulosic industry's capacity to well below the 35 billion gallons called for by President Bush. And whatever plant material is used to make biofuels, an estimate in the August 17, 2007 issue of *Science* suggested that substituting just 10% of U.S. fuel needs with biofuels would require 43% of U.S. cropland.

In short, there is enough uncertainty about ethanol's supply and demand prospects to argue for a pause in the headlong rush into ethanol production. Turning corn surpluses into a gasoline additive was a strategy that made food and fuel complementary. But turning a tightening corn market into a less rewarding gasoline-replacement strategy heightens the conflict between food and fuel uses, with major environmental externalities and limited environmental benefits.

Fundamental Change Needed

If we are to avoid a situation in which ethanol becomes a demand diverter for corn, a fundamental reorientation in farm and energy policies is required. The alternative policy model will require replacing the mandates, subsidies, and tariffs designed to help an infant industry with a new set of policy instruments intended to broaden the portfolio of energy alternatives and to create market-driven growth in renewable energy demand.

Today, politicians compete with one another to raise the biofuels mandate. Little apparent consideration is given to the potential consequences of building markets on political fiat rather than sound finances. The result is that capacity is built too fast, at uneconomic scale, and in the wrong locations. Competing interests such as domestic feeders and foreign consumers can get trampled in the process, especially during a short crop, when the mandate functions as an embargo on other uses. Eventually, competing suppliers take over the traditional markets imperiled by ill-considered mandates. As this scenario unfolds, the burden of false economics and competitive responses may become too much to bear, and the shaky superstructure will crash, stranding assets and bankrupting many. In order to avoid such a crash, the United States should not increase the biofuels mandate beyond the current level of 7.5 billion gallons.

Next, consider subsidies to ethanol. The blender's tax credit of 51 cents per gallon enabled ethanol to compete with gasoline in a market characterized by low gasoline prices and surplus corn supplies. That market no longer exists. Gasoline prices have skyrocketed because of high petroleum prices. The fixed per-gallon subsidy generated high profit margins for ethanol producers, which led to excessive growth in production. Some suggest correcting for this effect by replacing the fixed subsidy with a variable one that would decline as oil prices rose. This approach essentially would link ethanol to the volatile petroleum market.

Linking to the demand side of the equation, however, may not be the best avenue for reconciling food and fuel uses. We should consider the subsidy's effect on the supply side of the equation. To the extent that an ethanol subsidy reduces surpluses, it is likely to enjoy continued and significant political support. But if it creates shortages and diverts corn from food and feed to fuel uses, it will become increasingly controversial and politically vulnerable, as will the tariff walls erected to keep cheaper Brazilian ethanol out of the U.S. market.

For these reasons, we should replace today's fixed subsidy policy with a variable subsidy linked to corn supplies. As corn prices rise, the subsidy should be phased down. This would provide an incentive to convert corn to energy when supplies are ample, while allowing food and feed (and other industrial) uses to compete on an equal footing as supplies tighten and prices rise. When corn prices rise above some set level, the subsidy would fall to zero. At the same time, we should lower the tariff on imported ethanol.

An approach to ethanol incentives along these lines has three distinct advantages over current policy. First, it will function more like a shock absorber for corn producers and corn users; in contrast, a fixed subsidy in a volatile petroleum market functions like a shock transmitter that amplifies the effect of price swings. Second, it should largely disarm the emerging food-versus-fuel and environment-versus-fuel debates by letting market forces play a larger role in the industry's future expansion. Finally, it preserves incentives for developing fuel uses in surplus markets, which would encourage continued technological progress in the breeding, production, processing, and use of corn for ethanol. Such developments should continue to improve corn-based ethanol's competitive position.

Now consider energy policy. With better throttle control on ethanol's role in the farm-food-feed economy, a fresh approach could also be taken toward U.S. energy policy and ethanol's place within it. Current policy is too dependent on the political process: picking winners and losers and anointing technologies such as ethanol as favored approaches. Such an approach confronts two huge risks. The first resembles the risk Alan Greenspan foresaw in the U.S. stock market at the beginning of this century: an "irrational exuberance." In the case of ethanol, the concern is that the enthusiasm for ethanol's political rewards may run ahead of the logic that governs its economic realities.

A third element in our proposed mix of policies would be the creation of a wide-ranging set of fees and rewards to discourage energy inefficiencies and encourage conservation. Milton Friedman once proposed a negative income tax in which at a certain base income, taxes would be zero and below which subsidies would be paid to families. We propose a broad-based set of fees on energy uses that are carbon-loading and inefficient, but we would subsidize energy efficiency improvements that exceed a national standard. Simple examples would be progressive taxes on automobile horsepower and rebates to hybrid vehicles; fees on housing spaces in excess of 3,500 square feet; and rebates for energy-compliant, economical use of housing space. These "negative pollution taxes" would encourage conservation, while discouraging energy-guzzling cars, trucks, and homes. In particular, these policies could help encourage full–life-cycle energy accounting, tilting the economy toward the use of renewable fuels based on cellulosic alternatives to corn.

Finally, instead of subsidizing the current generation of inadequate cellulosic or coal gasification technologies, we would invest government resources in upstream R&D to bring further innovation and lower costs to these technologies so that they could compete in the market.

To move from our current devotion to corn-based ethanol and toward a new set of policies for renewable fuels will require bravery on the part of those who lead the reforms. The courage to admit that current policies have stoked the ethanol engine to an explosive heat may be in short supply. But unless the ethanol train slows down, it is likely to go off the tracks.

POSTSCRIPT

Do Biofuels Enhance Energy Security?

In March 2007, President Bush visited Brazil, which meets much of its need for vehicle fuel with ethanol from sugarcane, and agreed to work with Brazil in developing and promoting biofuels. According to the U.S. State Department, the agreement "reassures small countries in Central America and the Caribbean that they can reduce their dependence on foreign oil." In both Europe and the United States, governments are rushing to encourage the production and use of biofuels. L. Pelmans et al., "European Biofuels Strategy," *International Journal of Environmental Studies* (June 2007), attempts to classify nations according to their strategies so that "the formulation of a strategy to support the advancement of biofuels and alternative motor fuels in general should become more manageable." Corporations and investors see huge potential for profit, and many environmentalists see benefits for the environment.

However, there *are* problems with biofuels, and those problems are getting a great deal of attention. Robin Maynard, "Against the Grain," *The Ecologist* (March 2007), stresses that when food and fuel compete for farmland, food prices will rise, perhaps drastically. The poor will suffer, as will rainforests. Renton Righelato, "Forests or Fuel," *The Ecologist* (March 2007), reminds us that when forests are cleared, they no longer serve as "carbon sinks"; thus, deforestation adds to the global warming problem, and it may take a century for the benefit of biofuels to show itself. Harriet Williams, "How Green Is My Tank?" *The Ecologist* (March 2007), calls biofuels a dangerous distraction. Heather Augustyn, "A Burning Issue," *World Watch* (July/August 2007), describes the impact of forest fires to clear land for oil palm plantations in Indonesia. Palm oil holds great promise as a biofuel, but the plantations displace natural ecosystems and destroy habitat for numerous species, as well as for indigenous peoples. Despite the drawbacks, Robert Zubrin, "In Defense of Biofuels," *The New Atlantis* (Spring 2008), argues that biofuels are a net gain, and Congress should stimulate the market in their favor "by passing a bill mandating that all new cars sold in the United States be flexible-fueled—that is, able to run on any combination of gasoline, ethanol, or methanol. Such cars already exist and only cost about $100 more than comparable non-flex-fuel models."

Laura Venderkam, "Biofuels or Bio-Fools?" *American: A Magazine of Ideas* (May/June 2007), describes the huge amounts of money being invested in companies planning to bring biofuels to market. A great deal of research is also going on, including efforts to use genetic engineering to produce enzymes that can cheaply and efficiently break cellulose into its component sugars (see Matthew L. Wald, "Is Ethanol for the Long Haul?" *Scientific American,* January 2007, and Michael E. Himmel et al., "Biomass Recalcitrance: Engineering Plants and Enzymes for Biofuels Production," *Science,* February 9, 2007), make bacteria or yeast that can turn a greater proportion of sugar into alcohol (see Francois Torney et al., "Genetic Engineering Approaches to Improve Bioethanol Production from Maize," *Current Opinion in Biotechnology,* June 2007), and even bacteria that can convert sugar or cellulose into hydrocarbons that can easily be turned into gasoline or diesel fuel (see Neil Savage, "Building Better Biofuels," *Technology Review,* July/August 2007; and David Rotman, "The Price of Biofuels," *Technology Review,* January/February 2008). If these efforts succeed, the price of biofuels may drop drastically, leading investors to abandon the field. Such a price drop would, of course, benefit the consumer and lead to wider use of biofuels. It would also, say C. Ford Runge and Benjamin Senauer, in "How Biofuels Could Starve the Poor," *Foreign Affairs* (May/June 2007), ease the impact on food supply.

ISSUE 17

Can Hydropower Play a Role in Preventing Climate Change?

YES: Alain Tremblay, Louis Varfalvy, Charlotte Roehm, and Michelle Garneau, from "The Issue of Greenhouse Gases from Hydroelectric Reservoirs: From Boreal to Tropical Regions," United Nations Symposium on Hydropower and Sustainable Development, Beijing, China (October 27–29, 2004)

NO: American Rivers, from "Hydropower: Not the Answer to Preventing Climate Change," (http://www.americanrivers.org) (2007)

ISSUE SUMMARY

YES: Alain Tremblay, Louis Varfalvy, Charlotte Roehm, and Michelle Garneau, researchers with Hydro-Quebec and the University of Quebec in Montreal, argue that hydropower is a very efficient way to produce electricity, with emissions of greenhouse gases between a tenth and a hundredth of the emissions associated with using fossil fuels.

NO: American Rivers, a nonprofit organization dedicated to the protection and restoration of North America's rivers, argues that suggesting that hydropower is the answer to global warming hurts opportunities for alternative renewable energy technologies such as solar and wind and distracts from the most promising solution, energy efficiency.

Dams have long been an icon of civilization. Building dams of all sizes, from those that hold back village mill ponds to the giant Hoover Dam, was a crucial step in the settling and development of America. They supplied mills with the mechanical power generated when flowing water spun waterwheels. Combined with locks and canals, dams improved the navigability of waterways in the days before railroads. They provided water for irrigation, reduced flooding, and generated electricity. In other parts of the world, building dams for these benefits has been an important step in moving from "undeveloped" to "developing" to "developed" status. See

Ibrahim Yuksel, "Hydropower in Turkey for a Clean and Sustainable Energy Future, *Renewable & Sustainable Energy Reviews* (August 2008).

In the United States, the Army Corps of Engineers (ACE) built almost all hydroelectric power systems until the late 1970s. Today, according to the ACE pamphlet, "Hydropower: Value to the Nation" (http://www.vtn.iwr.usace.army.mil/pdfs/Hydropower.pdf), the ACE is the single largest owner and operator of hydroelectric power plants in the country and one of the largest in the world. Its 75 power plants produce nearly 100 billion kilowatt-hours per year. Hydroelectric power is renewable, efficient, and clean. It does not generate air or water pollution, and it emits no greenhouse gases to contribute to global warming.

Does this mean that building more hydroelectric power plants could help solve the global warming crisis? In the United States, most good sites for large hydropower plants have already been developed. In the rest of the world, the best sites, such as China's Three Gorges project, are rapidly being developed. Unfortunately, many people see problems in these projects. Mara Hvistendahl's "China's Three Gorges Dam: An Environmental Catastrophe?" *Scientific American* online (March 25, 2008) (http://www.sciam.com/article.cfm?id=chinas-three-gorges-dam-disaster), is indicative. Because dams flood the land behind them, they destroy forests, farmland, and villages and displace thousands—even millions—of people. Species decline and vanish. Sediment trapped behind the dam no longer reaches the sea to nourish fisheries. Diseases change their patterns. When a dam breaks, the resulting sudden, immense flood can do colossal damage downstream. And one subject of debate has been whether dams really help with reducing the addition of greenhouse gases to the atmosphere and the consequent global warming. According to the International Hydropower Association (http://hydropower.org), the lakes behind dams do emit greenhouse gases, and the land covered by the lake no longer grows trees that absorb carbon dioxide from the atmosphere, but before the lake existed, the land emitted greenhouse gases, not all such lands grew trees, and lake sediments can store large amounts of organic matter. The real issue is the *net* effect, which is ignored by those who wish to discredit hydroelectric power, who also focus on the worst cases, which tend to be in tropical environments.

The net emissions of greenhouse gases from hydropower impoundments is an area of ongoing research. In Canada, one such research program focuses on the large Eastmain-1 impoundment in northwestern Quebec, near James Bay. Commissioned in April 2007, it can generate 480 megawatts of electricity. Annual output is expected to average 2700 gigawatt-hours (2.7 billion kilowatt-hours). Alain Tremblay is the coordinator of the Reservoirs' Net Greenhouse Gas Emissions project at the site. In the following selections, he and coauthors Louis Varfalvy, Charlotte Roehm, and Michelle Garneau argue that hydropower is a very efficient way to produce electricity, with emissions of greenhouse gases between a tenth and a hundredth of the emissions associated with using fossil fuels. American Rivers, a nonprofit organization dedicated to the protection and restoration of North America's rivers, argues that suggesting that hydropower is the answer to global warming hurts opportunities for alternative renewable energy technologies such as solar and wind and distracts from the most promising solution, energy efficiency.

The Issue of Greenhouse Gases from Hydroelectric Reservoirs: From Boreal to Tropical Regions

Abstract

The role of greenhouse gas emissions (GHG) from freshwater reservoirs and their contribution in increasing atmospheric GHG concentrations is actually well discussed worldwide. The amount of GHGs emitted at the air-water interface of reservoirs varies over time. The maximum is attained within 3 to 5 years after impoundment. In reservoirs older >10 years in boreal and semi-arid regions, GHG emissions are similar than those of natural lakes. In tropical regions, the time to return to natural values may be longer depending on the water quality conditions. Hydropower is a very efficient way to produce electricity, showing emission factors between one and two orders of magnitude lower than the thermal alternatives.

1.0 Introduction

The major greenhouse gases are carbon dioxide (CO_2), methane (CH_4) and nitrous oxide (N_2O). These gases are emitted from both natural aquatic (lakes, rivers, estuaries, wetlands) and terrestrial ecosystems (forest, soils) as well as from anthropogenic sources. According to both the European Environment Agency and the United States Environmental Protection Agency, CO_2 emissions account for the largest share of GHGs equivalent of ±80–85% of the emissions. Fossil fuel combustion for transportation and electricity generation are the main source of CO_2 contributing to more than 50% of the emissions. Thermal power plants represents 66% of the world's electric generation capacity. Hydropower represents about 20% of the world's electricity generation capacity and emits 35 to 70 times less GHGs per TWh than thermal power plants. Nevertheless, for the last few years GHG emissions from freshwater reservoirs and their contribution to the increase of GHGs in the atmosphere are actually at the heart of a

From *United Nations Symposium on Hydropower and Sustainable Development,* by Alain Tremblay, Louis Varfalvy, Charlotte Roehm, and Michelle Garneau (UN Economic & Social Affairs, 27–29 October, 2004). Reprinted by permission of the author. www.un.org/esa/sustdev/sdissues/energy/op/hydro_tremblaypaper.pdf

worldwide debate concerning the electricity generating sector. However, to our knowledge, there are few emission measurements available from these environments although they are at the heart of the debate concerning methods of energy production.

In this context, Hydro-Québec and its partners have adapted a technique to measure gross GHG emissions at the air-water interface that allows for a high rate of sampling in a short period of time, while increasing the accuracy of the results and decreasing the confidence intervals of the average flux measured. These measurements were done in order to compare the results with those obtained by other methods, and to better assess the gross emissions of GHG from aquatic ecosystems in boreal (northern climate), semi-arid and tropical regions. This was done also to adequately estimate the contribution of reservoirs compared to natural water bodies in these regions, as well as to compare properly various options of electricity generation.

2.0 Adapting a Simple CO2 and CH4 Emission Measuring Technique

Measuring equipment consists of a one piece Rubbermaid box (polyethylene container) with a surface area of $0.2 \, m^2$ and a height of 15 cm, of which 2 cm is placed below the water surface. The air is sampled through an opening at the top of the floating chamber and it is returned at the opposite end of the chamber. The inlet and the outlet at opposite ends of the chamber allows the trapped air to be continuously mixed. This brings for a more representative measurement of gas concentrations. Air is analysed with a NDIR (Non-Dispersive Infrared) instrument (PP-System model Ciras-SC) or a FTIR (Fourier Transform Infrared) instrument. The accuracy of the instrument in the 350–500 ppm range is of 0.2 to 0.5 ppm for the NDIR and 3 to 5 ppm for the FTIR. The instrument takes continuous reading and the data logger stores a value every 20 seconds over a period of 5 to 10 minutes. All samples are plotted on a graph to obtain a slope and calculate the flux of CO_2 or CH_4 per m^2.

3. Results and Discussion

The results come from a sampling program that was conducted since 2001 in many boreal Canadian provinces, in the semi-arid western region of the United States of America and in tropical region of Panama and French Guiana. The results and conclusions also benefit from the Synthesis "Greenhouse Gas Emissions: Fluxes and Processes, Hydroelectric Reservoirs and Natural Environments." One must keep in mind, that most of the data on GHG from hydroelectric reservoirs come from research and measurements in boreal regions and, to a lesser extent, from a follow-up environmental program of Petit Saut reservoir in tropical French Guiana and a few Brazilian reservoirs.

The chemical, morphological and biological processes determining the fate of carbon in reservoirs are similar to those occurring in natural aquatic ecosystems. However, some of these processes might be temporally modified in reservoirs due to the flooding of terrestrial ecosystems which results from the creation of reservoirs. In boreal reservoirs, environmental follow-up programs have clearly shown that these changes generally last less than 10 years. However in tropical reservoirs, these changes can extend over a longer period of time according to the conditions of impoundment.

In the case of reservoirs, it is known that the amount of GHGs emitted at the air-water interface varies over time. In fact, there is an initial peak which occurs immediately after impoundment.

Fluxes of GHG in boreal reservoirs are usually 3 to 6 times higher than those from natural lakes when they reach their maximum at 3 to 5 years after impoundment. In boreal reservoirs older than 10 years (10 years for CO_2 and 4 years for CH_4), CO_2 fluxes ranged between -1800 to 11200 mg $CO_2 \cdot m^{-2} \cdot d^{-1}$ and are similar to those of natural systems with flux ranged from -460 to 10800 mg $CO_2 \cdot m^{-2} \cdot d^{-1}$. Generally, degassing and ebullition emissions are not reported for boreal regions because diffusive emissions are considered the major pathway. Methane emissions are very low in these ecosystems; however, they can be substantial in some tropical areas where the ebullition pathway is important.

Despite fewer data available, similar patterns are observed in most of the studied reservoirs in boreal (Finland, British-Columbia, Manitoba, New Foundland–Labrador), semi-arid (Arizona, New Mexico, Utah) and tropical regions (Panama, Brazil, French Guiana). In tropical regions, the time to return to natural values is sometimes longer depending on the water quality conditions. For example, when anoxic conditions occur CH_4 production decreases slowly and might be maintained for longer periods by carbon input from the drainage basin. However, such situations are rare in most of the studied reservoirs.

The increase of GHG emissions in reservoirs shortly after flooding is related to the release of nutrients, enhanced bacterial activity and decomposition of labile carbon. Magnitude of emissions for both reservoirs and natural aquatic systems depend on physico-chemical characteristics of the water body and on the incoming carbon from the watershed.

There is a convergence in the results that clearly illustrates that, in both boreal and tropical reservoirs, the contribution of flooded soils of the reservoir carbon pool is important in the first few years following impoundment. After this period, terrestrial allochthonous (drainage basin level) input of dissolved organic matter (DOC) can exceed, by several times, the amount of particulate organic matter and DOC produced within the reservoir through soil leaching or primary production. In reservoirs, this is particularly important since the water residence time is generally shorter, from a few weeks to a few months, in comparison to several years to many decades in the case of lakes.

Advantages of Hydroelectricity

There is a convergence in the results, from both boreal and tropical reservoirs, that clearly illustrates that reservoirs do emit GHGs for a period of about 10–15 years. Therefore, according to the GHG emission factors reported for hydro reservoirs both by IAEA and by various studies performed during the last decade on a variety and a great number of reservoirs, it can be concluded that the energy produced with the force of water is very efficient, showing emission factors between one and two orders of magnitude lower than the thermal alternatives (Table 1). However in some cases, tropical reservoirs, such as the Petit Saut reservoir in French Guiana or some Brazilian reservoirs, GHG emissions could, during a certain time period, significantly exceed emissions from thermal alternatives. Similar values have been reported in the literature. With respect to GHG emissions from hydropower, we can provide the following general observations:

- GHG emission factors from hydroelectricity generated in boreal regions are significantly smaller than corresponding emission factors from thermal power plants alternatives (i.e. from < 2% to 8% of any kind of conventional thermal generation alternative);
- GHG emission factors from hydroelectricity generated in tropical regions cover a much wider range of values (for example, a range of more than 2 order of magnitude for the 9 Brazilian reservoirs). Based on a 100 year lifetime, these emissions factors could either reach very low or very high values, varying from less than 1%

Table 1

Full Energy Chain Greenhouse Gas Emission Factors in g CO_2 equiv./kWh(e) h^{-1} (modified from IAEA 1996).

Energy Source	Emission Factor* g CO_2 equiv./kWh(e).h
Coal (lignite and hard coal)	940–1340
Oil	690–890
Gas (natural and LNG)	650–770
Nuclear Power	8–27
Solar (photovoltaic)	81–260
Wind Power	16–120
Hydro Power	4–18
Boreal reservoirs (La Grande Complexe)[1]	~33
Average boreal reservoirs[2]	~15
Tropical reservoirs (Petit-Saut)[3]	~455 (gross)/~327 (net)
Tropical reservoirs (Brazil)[4]	~6 to 2100 (average: ~160)

*: Rounded to the next unit or the next tenth respectively for values < or > 100 g CO_2 equiv./kWh(e) h^{-1}.
1: La Grande Complexe, Quebec, 9 reservoirs, 15 784 MW, ~ 174 km^2/TWh, (Hydro-Québec 2000).
2: According to average reservoir characteristics of 63 km^2/TWh, (Hydro-Québec 2000).
3: Petit-Saut, French Guiana, 115 MW, 0.315 MW/km^2 (Chap. 12).
4: 9 Brazilian reservoirs from 216 to 12 600 MW, total power = 23 518 MW, total surface = 7867 km^2.

to more than 200% of the emission factors reported for thermal power plant generation;
- Net GHG emission factors for hydro power, should be at first sight 30% to 50% lower than the emission factors currently reported.

The vast majority of hydroelectric reservoirs built in boreal regions are emitting very small amounts of GHGs, and represent therefore one of the cleanest way to generate electricity. In some tropical reservoirs, anoxic conditions could lead to larger emissions. Therefore, GHG emissions from tropical reservoirs should be considered on a case by case base level.

References

Cole JJ, Caraco FC, Kling GW, Kratz TK (1994). Carbon dioxide supersaturation in the surface waters of lakes. Science 265:1568–1570.

Fearnside PM (1996). Hydroelectric dams in Brazilian Amazonia: response to Rosa, Schaeffer and dos Santos. Environ Conserv 23:105–108.

Gagnon L, Chamberland A (1993). Emissions from hydroelectric reservoirs and comparison of hydroelectric, natural gas and oil. Ambio 22:568–569.

Gagnon L, van de Vate JF (1997). Greenhouse gas emissions from hydropower, the state of research in 1996. Ener Pol 25:7–13.

Hope D, Billet MF, Cressner MS (1994). A review of the export of carbon in river water: fluxes and processes. Environ Pollut 84:301–324.

IAEA, Hydro-Québec (1996). Assessment of greenhouse gas emissions from the full energy chain for hydropower, nuclear power and other energy sources. Working material: papers presented at IAEA advisory group meeting jointly organized by Hydro-Québec and IAEA (Montréal, 12–14 March, 1996), Montréal, International Atomic Energy Agency et Hydro-Québec.

St. Louis VL, Kelly CA, Duchemin E, Rudd JWM, Rosenberg DM (2000). Reservoirs surfaces as sources of greenhouse gases to the atmosphere: a global estimate. BioScience 50:766–775.

Tremblay, A., Lambert, M and Gagnon, L., 2004a. CO_2 Fluxes from Natural Lakes and Hydroelectric Reservoirs in Canada. Environmental Management, Volume 33, Supplément 1: S509–S517.

Tremblay, A., Varfalvy, L., Roehm, C., and Garneau, M. (Eds.), 2004b. Greenhouse gas Emissions: Fluxes and Processes, Hydroelectric Reservoirs and Natural Environments. Environmental Science Series, Springer, Berlin, Heidelberg, New York, 731 pages.

Hydropower: Not the Answer to Preventing Climate Change

Scientists from around the world have sounded the alarm that climate change (a.k.a. global warming) is one of the greatest long-term threats facing the natural and human environment today.

Although it is difficult to predict precisely how and when the impacts of human caused climate change will manifest, likely consequences could include catastrophic storms, severe droughts, wide-spread epidemics, loss of crops, and massive species extinctions.

The river conservation community is equally concerned about climate change. The impacts that this phenomenon will have on the planet are not something that we take lightly and we adamantly support efforts to reduce this pressing threat. However, we need not sacrifice the health of our nation's rivers to prevent climate change.

The leading cause of climate change is the accumulation of atmospheric carbon dioxide which causes an increase in global temperatures through a "greenhouse effect."

The greatest contributor of human made carbon dioxide is the burning of fossil fuels, such as coal and oil, for the generation of electricity. Hydropower is often promoted as the answer to the world's greenhouse woes due to its "emissions free" generation.

It is true that generation of hydropower does not create significant air pollution or greenhouse gases but the climate benefits of hydropower do not come without significant environmental costs. Boosting U.S. hydropower generation—either through building new dams or relaxing environmental controls at existing dams—would not generate a significant amount of extra power, and would come at a terrible cost to rivers, fish, and wildlife and recreation.

Suggesting that hydropower is the answer to the climate change problem not only hurts opportunities for emerging renewable technologies such as solar and wind, but it also distracts us from the most promising solutions to this dilemma—energy efficiency.

Is Hydropower Renewable?

No. Moving Water May Be Renewable But Endangered River Species Are Not.

It is true that generation of hydropower does not create significant air pollution or greenhouse gases but this power generation definitely has environmental impacts. Of the 3.5 million river miles in the United States, almost 600,000 or 20 percent are impounded by dams, with thousands more miles indirectly affected downstream. Only recently have we begun to recognize the price that these dams have wrought on our environment.

According to The Nature Conservancy, fresh water aquatic species are up to 10 times more endangered than their terrestrial or avian cousins, in no small measure due to dams. In addition, valuable fisheries throughout the country have been adversely affected by dams. Dams create physical barriers, corrupt natural flows, and alter water chemistry and temperature as evidenced in the Columbia, Colorado, Mississippi, and Missouri River basins. On the Columbia River, salmon runs are only 2% of their historic levels.

Do We Need More Hydropower to Meet the Kyoto Treaty Targets? No!

According to the treaty on Climate Change signed in December 1997 in Kyoto, Japan, the United States is obligated to reduce its emissions to 7% below 1990 levels. The Energy Information Administration's 1997 preliminary estimates for carbon emissions show we are currently emitting close to 10% above 1990 levels, meaning that the U.S. must reduce emissions by 17% from today's current output.

Data from the Energy Information Administration suggests that hydropower currently makes up only 10% of the nation's annual electric generation, with approximately half of that coming from the nation's 2,000 non-federal owned hydropower dams. Existing hydropower can continue to make a contribution to the nation's energy needs as a source of electricity with very limited climate impact, we must not—and have no need to—sacrifice our free-flowing rivers, fish and wildlife in the process.

Damming more rivers to produce more hydropower, however, is not a realistic option for meeting the Kyoto targets. For the most part, the good dam sites in the U.S. are already dammed. Those river reaches that remain undammed are either prohibitively expensive, protected lands and waterways, or have a far greater value as recreational, aesthetic, or environmental resources.

Are Environmental Regulations Severely Reducing Hydropower's Generating Capacity? No.

The operation of these dams is regulated by the Federal Energy Regulatory Commission (FERC), which grants 30 to 50 year licenses to dam owners to operate and profit from the public's waterways. When a dam owner's license expires, the operator must apply for a new license from FERC. As part of this relicensing process, FERC can impose new conditions to protect fish and wildlife as well as accommodate other uses of the river such as recreation. A dam owner can also decide not to seek a new license, or FERC could deny the application for a new license and order the dam removed.

Some in the hydropower industry argue that by imposing environmental conditions, the government is cutting hydropower production and therefore leading to further emissions of greenhouse gases. According to FERC however, the changed license conditions of the 273 dam licenses which expired in 1993 resulted in an average loss of only 1% of annual generation. In fact, according to statistics kept by the Energy Information Administration, hydropower generation is at an all-time high despite environmental regulation imposed during the last several years of relicensing.

Over the next 12 years, more than 500 dams or approximately half of FERC-regulated hydropower capacity (2.5% of the annual generation of the United States), will come up for relicensing. Based on FERC's experience from their 1993 class of dams, we can expect about a 1% reduction in the annual generation of these projects and therefore a 0.025% reduction in the nation's over-all annual generation.

That is only enough energy to meet the country's needs for 2.2 hours of an entire year!!! This 0.025% reduction of annual generation is significantly less than the 5% average fluctuation of energy demand caused by factors such as weather, fuel prices, and technology. This small loss could be made up by retrofitting one out of every 30 homes in the nation with just one energy efficient compact fluorescent light bulb!

Is This Small Loss in Power Really Worth It? Yes.

The licensing requirements that lead to losses in power generation at hydropower dams put water back into stream channels, restoring valuable fisheries, improving flood control, and ensuring compliance with state water quality standards. Given the perilous state of rivers and riverine species, and the ability of rivers to heal themselves once natural flows are restored, the cost of regulation is not only a small price to pay, it is a necessary one.

Relicensing of FERC regulated hydropower dams can and has rehabilitated rivers. For example, on the Deerfield River, a settlement signed in October 1994, between the New England Power Company and state, federal and resource agencies enhanced thirty-three river miles and returned water to twelve miles of river, which had been previously de-watered by diversions. This same project was recently sold at a price well above what was expected by market analysts. Along the Au Sable, Manistee, and Muskegon Rivers, license conditions calling for restoration of a more natural flow regime have already resulted in significant increases in natural fish reproduction.

Operational changes can also guarantee equal use of the public's rivers for what are often more profitable recreational interests. In 1996,

29 million anglers spent nearly $31 billion on fishing related products and services. In 1992, the economic value from power production of hydropower Project #3 on the Kern River in California was $17,000 per day. By contrast, the total economic benefit from commercial rafting on the Kern was in excess of $35,000 per day. Mitigation efforts at each of these dams will continue to improve fish and wildlife habitat and water quality while maintaining profitable operations for the dam owner.

But Won't These Reductions in Hydropower Generation Make a Significant Contribution to Climate Change? No.

Even assuming that this small amount of power would need to be replaced—and it is unclear that it would—it is likely that, given the current market, most new generation will consist of natural gas turbines. While these facilities do emit greenhouse gases and use non-renewable fossil fuels, they are 35% more efficient than coal and emit 40% less carbon dioxide.

Emerging technologies such as solar, wind, and cogeneration are becoming increasingly cost competitive and are likely to meet growing demand. But conservation and efficiency are perhaps the greatest untapped resource in meeting the energy needs of the future. None of these substitutes will add significantly to greenhouse gas emissions. Thus, any fear that lost generation would be made up from the dirtiest coal-fired power plant is unrealistic and unfounded.

Won't Interest in Dam Removal Lead to Dramatic Decreases in Hydropower Capacity? No.

No one is advocating the decommissioning and removal of all hydropower dams in this country. The vast majority of dam removal in this country will affect small, non-generating dams that no longer serve their original purpose. Beyond those, the Hydropower Reform Coalition supports the removal of a small number of economically unviable hydropower dams and a handful of projects that cause acute environmental harm, which cannot be mitigated.

The generating capacity of those non-federal projects that the Coalition has identified add up to less than 100 MW and accounts for less than 0.2% of total non-federal hydropower capacity. Only 0.006% of carbon emissions from natural gas or coal generation would be saved if the projects remained in production. These dam removals will result in big river benefits with virtually no negative climate impacts.

How Will We Meet the Kyoto Targets? Efficiency and Renewables.

Cutting back environmental protection at existing hydropower dams will not get us where we need to be to meet the Kyoto targets; neither will development of the few marginal sites left in this country. Natural gas provides an interim solution, but is not sustainable in the long run and can also have adverse impacts on rivers through water withdrawals and thermal pollution. During this interim period the U.S. should focus research and development on truly renewable sources of energy, such as solar, wind, and new technologies like fuel cells. There is still an enormous amount of growth potential in these technologies.

However, the best and most immediate answers lie not with new generation sources but instead with more efficient use of existing resources. Rather than continue pouring water into a leaky bucket, we need to patch the holes! According to the Rocky Mountain Institute, an energy think-tank, we can easily halve what we currently use while improving our standard of living through additional use of more efficient lighting, heating, cooling, building, and industrial processes.This is not futuristic talk of technologies on the horizon. We have the capability—all we need are the right incentives.

Buildings—Energy and carbon savings can be made at no additional cost by implementing energy efficient building practices, such as those advocated by the 1995 modern energy codes, which include selecting appropriate building materials and strategically placing windows and doors to reduce the need for heating and cooling systems and light fixtures.

Lighting—The initial costs of compact fluorescent light bulbs and Energy Star light fixtures are balanced by long-term economic and environmental benefits. Already this program is saving more than 70 billion kilowatt-hours annually (about a quarter of the conventional hydroelectric generation in the U.S. or 4% of annual coal generation).

Insulation—Ceiling, wall, and foundation insulation in existing buildings is saving the United States about 12 quads—that's 15 percent of the U.S. national energy bill—and another 2.2 quads could be saved insulating all new and existing buildings to the levels recommended by modern energy codes.

Investing in wind and photovoltaic technologies—Wind generation and photovoltaics are two efficient and consumer-friendly alternatives to hydropower generation. Since the 1980's, wind power prices have dropped to near competitive rates (44/kWh) and are in high demand in markets across the country. Thirty-seven U.S. states have a wind resource that could support development of utility-scale wind plants—13 of these exceed the wind resource available in California, which is the world's leader in wind energy development. Photovoltaics are advantageous because of their easy installation, adaptability to consumers needs, and their independence from electric transmission systems. Manufacturing photovoltaic cells could provide an excellent opportunity for high-tech companies adapting to shrinking military contracts.

Does Reducing the Threat of Global Climate Change Have to Harm Rivers? No.

The nation's solution to the climate change problem need not involve trading jobs or economic prosperity for the environment. Nor should it mean that we trade healthy rivers for clean air and reduced threat of climate change. We can meet and surpass our climate treaty obligations by 2010 at low or no cost per unit saved by building better buildings, using better lights, using insulation, improving industrial practices, constructing combined cycle gas turbines, and investing in wind and photovoltaic technologies.

When people incorporate energy-efficient appliances and heating and cooling systems into their homes and businesses they save money and the environment. The future economic and environmental benefits outweigh the initial costs of making the transition to more energy-efficient systems and living practices. In our effort to reduce the threat of climate change we must continue to protect the health of our nation's rivers.

POSTSCRIPT

Can Hydropower Play a Role in Preventing Climate Change?

A year after Tremblay et al. gave their talk at the United Nations Symposium on Hydropower and Sustainable Development, Beijing, China, they published *Greenhouse Gas Emissions—Fluxes and Processes: Hydroelectric Reservoirs and Natural Environments* (Springer, 2005). The research continues today (see Suzanne Pritchard, "Emitting the Truth," *International Water Power and Dam Construction* (January 16, 2008), but even though hydropower seems a relatively benign energy source, the objections also continue. Sara Phelan, "Bubbling Waters," *Earth Island Journal* (Autumn 2007), notes reports that suggest that any gains in regard to carbon emissions are offset by methane emissions. Hydropower also has genuine undesirable environmental effects. There is thus a tension between real benefits and real drawbacks, as discussed by R. Sternberg in "Hydropower: Dimensions of Social and Environmental Coexistence," *Renewable & Sustainable Energy Reviews* (August 2008).

Fortunately, it is possible to get energy from water without building lakes. Tidal power requires dams across estuaries; at high tide, water flows upstream through turbines; at low tide, the turbines are reversed to extract energy as the water flows downstream. Turbines can also be placed on the sea floor to take advantage of tidal (and other) currents. See Jonathon Porritt, "Catch the Tide," *Green Futures* (January 2008) and David Kerr, "Marine Energy," *Philosophical Transactions: Mathematical, Physical & Engineering Sciences* (April 2007). In North America, a number of tidal power projects are being started in the Bay of Fundy; see Colin Woodard, "On US Border, a Surge in Tidal-Power Projects," *Christian Science Monitor* (August 15, 2007).

There is also wave power, which uses the motion of waves to work special arrangements of pistons, levers, and air chambers to extract energy. See Ewen Callaway, "To Catch a Wave," *Nature* (November 8, 2007), David C. Holzman, "Blue Power: Turning Tides into Electricity," *Environmental Health Perspectives* (December 2007), and Elisabeth Jeffries, "Ocean Motion Power," *World Watch* (July/August 2008). Yet even this can draw attention from environmentalists, who fear that the equipment may interfere with marine animals and that associated electromagnetic fields may harm sensitive species such as sharks and salmon; see Stiv J. Wilson, "Wave Power," *E—The Environmental Magazine* (May/June 2008). However, Urban Henfridsson et al., "Wave Energy Potential in the Baltic Sea and the Danish Part of the North Sea, with Reflections on the Skagerrak," *Renewable Energy: An International Journal* (October 2007), note that the potential contribution of wave energy to civilization's needs is large. To take advantage of that potential requires "Sound engineering, in combination with producer, consumer and broad societal perspective."

ISSUE 18

Will Hydrogen Replace Fossil Fuels for Cars?

YES: David L. Bodde, from "Fueling the Future: The Road to the Hydrogen Economy," Statement Presented to the Committee on Science, Subcommittee on Research and Subcommittee on Energy, U.S. House of Representatives (July 20, 2005)

NO: Michael Behar, from "Warning: The Hydrogen Economy May Be More Distant Than It Appears," *Popular Science* (January 2005)

ISSUE SUMMARY

YES: Professor David L. Bodde argues that there is no question whether hydrogen can satisfy the nation's energy needs. The real issue is how to handle the transition from the current energy system to the hydrogen system.

NO: Michael Behar argues that the public has been misled about the prospects of the "hydrogen economy." We must overcome major technological, financial, and political obstacles before hydrogen can be a viable alternative to fossil fuels.

The 1973 "oil crisis" heightened awareness that the world—even if it was not yet running out of oil—was extraordinarily dependent on that fossil fuel (and therefore on supplier nations) for transportation, home heating, and electricity generation. Recent rapid price increases have repeated the lesson. Since the supply of oil and other fossil fuels is clearly finite, some people have worried that there would come a time when demand could not be satisfied, and our dependence would leave us helpless. At the same time, we became acutely aware of the many unfortunate side-effects of fossil fuels, including air pollution, strip mines, oil spills, global warming, and more.

The 1970s saw the modern environmental movement gain momentum. The first Earth Day was in 1970. Numerous government steps were taken to deal with air pollution, water pollution, and other environmental problems. In response to the oil crisis, a great deal of public money went into developing alternative energy supplies. The emphasis was on "renewable" energy, meaning conservation, wind, solar, and fuels such as hydrogen gas (which when burned with pure oxygen produces only water vapor as exhaust). However, when the crisis passed and oil supplies were once more ample (albeit it did cost more to fill a gasoline tank), most public funding for alternative-energy research and demonstration projects vanished. What work continued was at the hands of a few enthusiasts and those corporations that saw future opportunities. In 2001, the World-Watch Institute published Seth Dunn's *Hydrogen Futures: Toward a Sustainable Energy System*. In 2002, MIT Press published Peter Hoffman's *Tomorrow's Energy: Hydrogen, Fuel Cells, and the Prospects for a Cleaner Planet*.

What drives the continuing interest in hydrogen and other alternative or renewable energy systems is the continuing problems associated with fossil fuels, concern about dependence and potential political instability, rising oil and gasoline prices, and the growing realization that the availability of petroleum will peak in the near future (see Issue 1). Will that interest come to anything? There are, after all, a number of other ways to meet the need. Coal can be converted into oil and gasoline (though the air pollution and global warming problems remain). Cars can be made more efficient (and mileage efficiency is much greater than it was in the seventies despite the popularity of SUVs) (see Issue 3). Cars can be designed to use natural gas or battery power; "hybrid" cars use combinations of gasoline and electricity, and some are already on the market. See Mark K. Solheim, "How Green Is My Hybrid?" *Kiplinger's Personal Finance* (May 2006), and Seth Fletcher, "Tomorrow's Hybrid," *Popular Science* (April 2008).

Perhaps people are just waiting for hydrogen. The hydrogen enthusiasts remain. In the selections that follow, Clemson University professor David L. Bodde argues that there is no question whether hydrogen can satisfy the nation's energy needs. The real issue is how to handle the transition from the current energy system to the hydrogen system. He recommends research, education, and support for entrepreneurs. Journalist Michael Behar argues that the public has been misled about the prospects of the "hydrogen economy." Before it can arrive, we must overcome major technological, financial, and political obstacles.

YES

David L. Bodde

Fueling the Future: The Road to the Hydrogen Economy

Thank you, ladies and gentlemen, for this opportunity to discuss the *Road to the Hydrogen Economy*, a road I believe we must travel if we are to ensure a world well supplied with clean, affordable energy derived from secure sources. I will speak to this from the perspective of motor vehicle transportation and address the questions posed by the Committee within the framework of three basic ideas.

First, research policy should view the hydrogen transition as a marketplace competition. For the next several decades, three rival infrastructures will compete for a share of the world auto market: (a) the current internal combustion engine and associated fuels infrastructure; (b) the hybrid electric vehicles, now emerging on the market; and (c) the hydrogen fueled vehicles, now in early demonstration. We can judge policy alternatives and applied research investments by their ability to accelerate the shift in market share among these competing infrastructures.

Second, and in parallel with the marketplace transition, fundamental research should focus on sustaining the hydrogen economy into the far future. Key issues include: (a) storing hydrogen on-board vehicles at near-atmospheric pressure; (b) sequestering the carbon-dioxide effluent from manufacturing hydrogen from coal; (c) sharply reducing the cost of hydrogen produced from non-coal resources, especially nuclear, photobiological, photoelectrochemical, and thin-film solar processes; (d) improving the performance and cost of fuel cells; and (e) storing electricity on-board vehicles in batteries that provide both high energy performance and high power performance at reasonable cost.

And third, the results of this research must be brought swiftly and effectively to the marketplace. This requires economic policies that encourage technology-based innovation, both by independent entrepreneurs and those operating from the platform of established companies. Clemson University, through its International Center for Automotive Research and its Arthur M. Spiro Center for Entrepreneurial Leadership, intends to become a major contributor to this goal.

In what follows, I will set out my reasoning and the evidence that supports these three basic ideas.

From Statement Presented to the Committee on Research and Subcommittee on Energy, U.S. House of Representatives by David L. Bodde, (July 20, 2005).

The Hydrogen Transition: A Marketplace Competition

Much thinking about the hydrogen economy concerns "what" issues, visionary descriptions of a national fuels infrastructure that would deliver a substantial fraction of goods and services with hydrogen as the energy carrier. And yet, past visions of energy futures, however desirable they might have seemed at the time, have not delivered sustained action, either from a public or private perspective. The national experience with nuclear power, synthetic fuels, and renewable energy demonstrates this well.

The difficulty arises from insufficient attention to the transition between the present and the desired future—the balance between forces that lock the energy economy in stasis and the entrepreneurial forces that could accelerate it toward a more beneficial condition.

In effect, the present competes against the future, and the pace and direction of any transition will be governed by the outcome. Viewing the transition to a hydrogen economy through the lens of a competitive transition can bring a set of "how" questions to the national policy debate—questions of how policy can rebalance the competitive forces so that change prevails in the marketplace.

A Model of the Competitive Transition

The competitive battle will be fought over a half century among three competing infrastructures:[1]

- The internal combustion engine (ICE), either in a spark-ignition or compression-ignition form, and its attendant motor fuels supply chain;
- The hybrid electric vehicle (HEV), now entering the market, which achieves superior efficiency by supplementing an internal combustion engine with an electric drive system and which uses the current supply chain for motor fuels; and,
- The hydrogen fuel cell vehicle (HFCV), which requires radically distinct technologies for the vehicle, for fuel-production, and for fuel distribution.

Figure 1 shows one scenario, based on the most optimistic assumptions, of how market share could shift among the contending infrastructures (NRC 2004). Several aspects of this scenario bear special mention. First, note the extended time required for meaningful change: these are long-lived assets built around large, sunk investments. They cannot be quickly changed under the best of circumstances. Second, the road to the hydrogen economy runs smoothest through the hybrid electric vehicle. The HEV offers immediate gains in fuel economy and advances technologies that will eventually prove useful for hydrogen fuel cell vehicles, especially battery and electric system management technologies. Although this scenario shows significant market penetration for the HEV, its success

Figure 1

Competition for Market Share

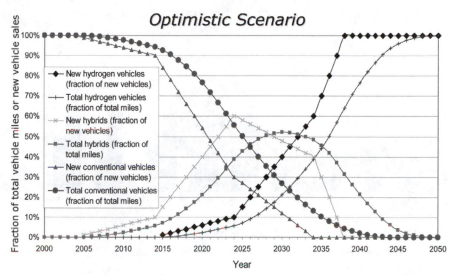

Optimistic Scenario

- Complete replacement of ICE and HEV vehicles with fuel cell vehicles in 2050

Source: NRC 2004

cannot be assured. The HEV might remain a niche product, despite its current popularity if consumers conclude that the value of the fuel savings does not compensate for the additional cost of the HEV. Or, its gains in efficiency might be directed toward vehicle size and acceleration rather than fuel economy. Either circumstance would make an early hydrogen transition even more desirable.

Any transition to a HFCV fleet, however, will require overcoming a key marketplace barrier that is unique to hydrogen—widely available supplies of fuel. And to this we now turn.

The Chicken and the Egg[2]

Most analyses suggest that large-scale production plants in a mature hydrogen economy can manufacture fuel at a cost that competes well with gasoline at current prices (NRC 2004). However, investors will not build these plants and their supporting distribution infrastructure in the absence of large-scale demand. And, the demand for hydrogen will not be forthcoming unless potential purchasers of hydrogen vehicles can be assured widely available sources of fuel. Variants of this "chicken and egg" problem have limited the

Figure 2

A Supply Chain Infrastructure

Delivered H₂ Costs of Alternative Technologies

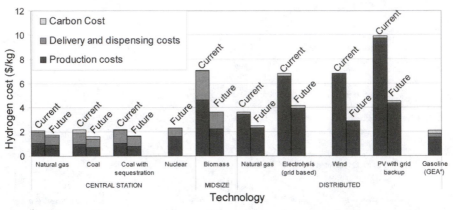

* GEA = Gasoline Efficiency Adjusted – scaled to hybrid vehicle efficiency

Source: NRC 2004

market penetration of other fuels, such as methanol and ethanol blends (M85 and E85) and compressed natural gas. This issue—the simultaneous development of the supply side and demand sides of the market—raises one of the highest barriers to a hydrogen transition.

Distributed Hydrogen Production for the Transition

To resolve this problem, a committee of the National Academy of Sciences (NRC 2004) recommended an emphasis on distributed production of hydrogen. In this model, the hydrogen fuel would be manufactured at dispensing stations conveniently located for consumers. Once the demand for hydrogen fuel grew sufficiently, then larger manufacturing plants and logistic systems could be built to achieve scale economies. However, distributed production of hydrogen offers two salient challenges.

The first challenge is cost. Figure 2, shows the delivered cost of molecular hydrogen for a variety of production technologies. The "distributed" technologies, to the right in Figure 2, offer hydrogen at a cost between 2 and 5 times the cost of the large-scale, "central station" technologies, on the left in Figure 2. Technological advances can mitigate, but not remove entirely, this cost disadvantage.

The second challenge concerns the environment. Carbon capture and sequestration do not appear practical in distributed production. During the opening stage of a hydrogen transition, we might simply have to accept some carbon releases in order to achieve the later benefits.

Research to Accelerate a Transition by Distributed Hydrogen Production

A study panel convened by the National Academy of Sciences (NAS) recently recommended several research thrusts that could accelerate distributed production for a transition to hydrogen (NRC 2004). These include:

- Development of hydrogen fueling "appliance" that can be manufactured economically and used in service stations reliably and safely by relatively unskilled persons—station attendants and consumers.
- Development of an integrated, standard fueling facility that includes the above appliance as well as generation and storage equipment capable of meeting the sharply varying demands of a 24-hour business cycle.
- Advanced technologies for hydrogen production from electrolysis, essentially a fuel cell operated in reverse, to include enabling operation from intermittent energy sources, such as wind.
- Research on breakthrough technologies for small-scale reformers to produce hydrogen from fossil feedstocks.

The Department of Energy has adopted the NAS recommendations and modified its programs accordingly. It remains too early to judge progress, but in any case these technologies should receive continued emphasis as the desired transition to hydrogen nears. However, progress in research is notoriously difficult to forecast accurately. This suggests consideration be given to interim strategies that would work on the demand side of the marketplace, either to subsidize the cost of distributed hydrogen production while demand builds or to raise the cost of the competition, gasoline and diesel fuels. Such actions would relieve the research program of the entire burden for enabling the transition.

Fundamental Research to Sustain a Hydrogen Economy

At the same time that the marketplace transition advances, several high-payoff (but also high-risk) research campaigns should be waged. These include:

- Storing hydrogen on-board vehicles at near-atmospheric pressure;
- Sequestering the carbon-dioxide effluent from manufacturing hydrogen from coal;
- Sharply reducing the cost of hydrogen produced from non-coal resources, especially nuclear, photobiological, photoelectrochemical, and thin-film solar processes;
- Improving the performance and cost of fuel cells; and,
- Storing electricity on-board vehicles in batteries that provide both high energy performance and high power performance at reasonable cost.

On-Vehicle Hydrogen Storage

The most important long-term research challenge is to provide a more effective means of storing hydrogen on vehicles than the compressed gas or cryogenic liquid now in use. In my judgment, failure to achieve this comes closer to a complete "show-stopper" than any other possibility. I believe this true for two reasons: hydrogen leakage as the vehicle fleet ages, and cost.

With regard to leakage, high pressure systems currently store molecular hydrogen on demonstration vehicles safely and effectively. But these are new and specially-built, and trained professionals operate and maintain. What can we expect of production run vehicles that receive the casual maintenance afforded most cars? A glance at the oil-stained pavement of any parking lot offers evidence of the leakage of heavy fluids stored in the current ICE fleet at atmospheric pressure. As high pressure systems containing the lightest element in the universe age, we might find even greater difficulties with containment. With regard to cost, the energy losses from liquefaction and even compression severely penalize the use of hydrogen fuel, especially when manufactured at distributed stations.

The NAS Committee, cited earlier (NRC 2004), strongly supported an increased emphasis on game-changing approaches to on-vehicle hydrogen storage. One alternative could come from novel approaches to generating the hydrogen on board the vehicle.[3] Chemical hydrides, for example, might offer some promise here, such as the sodium borohydride system demonstrated by Daimler-Chrysler.

Carbon Sequestration

Domestic coal resources within the United States hold the potential to relieve the security burdens arising from oil dependence—but only if the environmental consequences of their use can be overcome. Further, as shown in Figure 2, coal offers the lowest cost pathway to a hydrogen-based energy economy, once the transient conditions have passed. Thus, the conditions under which this resource can be used should be established as soon as possible. The prevailing assumption holds that the carbon effluent from hydrogen manufacturing can be stored as a gas (carbon dioxide, or CO_2) in deep underground formations. Yet how long it must be contained and what leakage rates can be tolerated remain unresolved issues (Socolow 2005). Within the Department of Energy, the carbon sequestration program is managed separately from hydrogen and vehicles programs. The NAS committee recommended closer coordination between the two as well as an ongoing emphasis on carbon capture and sequestration (NRC 2004).

Producing Hydrogen Without Coal

Manufacturing hydrogen from non-fossil resources stands as an important hedge against future constraints on production from coal, or even from natural gas. And under any circumstance, the hydrogen economy will be more robust if served by production from a variety of domestic sources.

The non-fossil resource most immediately available is nuclear. Hydrogen could be produced with no CO_2 emissions by using nuclear heat and electricity in the high-temperature electrolysis of steam. Here the technology issues include the durability of the electrode and electrolyte materials, the effects of high pressure, and the scale-up of the electrolysis cell. Alternatively, a variety of thermochemical reactions could produce hydrogen with great efficiency. Here the needed research concerns higher operating temperatures (700°C to 1000°C) for the nuclear heat as well as research into the chemical cycles themselves. In both cases, the safety issues that might arise from coupling the nuclear island with a hydrogen production plant bear examination (NRC 2004).

In addition, hydrogen production from renewable sources should be emphasized, especially that avoiding the inefficiencies of the conventional chain of conversions: (1) from primary energy into electricity; (2) from electricity to hydrogen; (3) from hydrogen to electricity on-board the vehicle; (4) from electricity to mobility, which is what the customer wanted in the first place. Novel approaches to using renewable energy, such as photobiological or photoelectrochemical, should be supported strongly (NRC 2004).

Improved Fuel Cells

The cost and performance of fuel cells must improve significantly for hydrogen to achieve its full potential. To be sure, molecular hydrogen can be burned in specially designed internal combustion engines. But doing so foregoes the efficiency gains obtainable from the fuel cell, and becomes a costly and (from an energy perspective) inefficient process. The NAS Committee thought the fuel cell essential for a hydrogen economy to be worth the effort required to put it in place. They recommended an emphasis on long-term, breakthrough research that would dramatically improve cost, durability, cycling capacity, and useful life.

Improved Batteries

The battery is as important to a hydrogen vehicle as to a hybrid because it serves as the central energy management device. For example, the energy regained from regenerative braking must be stored in a battery for later reuse. Though energy storage governs the overall operating characteristics of the battery, a high rate of energy release (power) can enable the electric motor to assist the HEV in acceleration and relieve the requirements for fuel cells to immediately match their power output with the needs of the vehicle. Thus, advanced battery research becomes a key enabler for the hydrogen economy and might also expand the scope of the HEV.

Entrepreneurship for the Hydrogen Economy

For the results of DoE research to gain traction in a competitive economy, entrepreneurs and corporate innovators must succeed in bringing hydrogen-related innovations to the marketplace. In many cases, independent entrepreneurs provide the path-breaking innovations that lead to radical improvements in performance, while established companies provide continuous, accumulating improvement. The federal government, in partnership with states and universities, can become an important enabler of both pathways to a hydrogen economy.

Federal Policies Promoting Entrepreneurship

From the federal perspective, several policies could be considered to build an entrepreneurial climate on the "supply" side of the market. These include:

- Special tax consideration for investors in new ventures offering products relevant to fuel savings. The intent would be to increase the amount of venture capital available to startup companies.
- Commercialization programs might enable more entrepreneurs to bring their nascent technologies up to investment grade. For example, an enhanced and focused *Small Business Innovation Research* (SBIR) program might increase the number of participating entrepreneurs participating in fuel-relevant markets. A portion of the *Advanced Technology Program* (ATP) could be focused in like manner.
- Outreach from the National Laboratories to entrepreneurs might be improved. Some laboratories, the National Renewable Energy Laboratory (NREL) for example, offer small, but effective programs. But more systematic outreach, not to business in general, but to entrepreneurial business, would also increase the supply of market-ready innovations.

On the demand side, any policy that increases consumer incentives to purchase fuel efficient vehicles will provide an incentive for ongoing innovation—provided that the policy is perceived as permanent. Entrepreneurs and innovators respond primarily to opportunity; but that opportunity must be durable for the 10 year cycle required to establish a new, high-growth company.

States and Universities as Agents of Innovation/Entrepreneurship

Innovation/entrepreneurship is a contact sport, and that contact occurs most frequently and most intensely within the context of specific laboratories and specific relationships. I will use Clemson's International Center for Automotive Research (ICAR) to illustrate this principle. Most fundamentally, the ICAR is a partnership among the State of South Carolina, major auto makers,[4] and their Tier I, Tier II, and Tier III suppliers. The inclusion of these suppliers will be essential for the success of ICAR or any similar research venture. This is because innovation in the auto industry has evolved toward a global, networked process, much as it has in other industries like microelectronics. The "supply chain" is more accurately described as a network, and network innovation will replace the linear model.

For these reasons, the ICAR, when fully established, will serve as a channel for research and innovation to flow into the entire cluster of auto-related companies in the Southeast United States. We anticipate drawing together and integrating the best technology from a variety of sources:

- Research performed at Clemson University and at the ICAR itself;
- Research performed at the Savannah River National Laboratory and the University of South Carolina; and,
- Relevant science and technology anywhere in the world.

Beyond research, the ICAR will include two other components of a complete innovation package: education, and entrepreneur support. With regard to education, the Master of Science and PhD degrees offered through the ICAR will emphasize the integration of new technology into vehicle design, viewing the auto and its manufacturing plant as an integrated system. In addition, courses on entrepreneurship and innovation, offered through Clemson's Arthur M. Spiro Center for Entrepreneurial Leadership, will equip students with the skills to become effective agents of change within the specific context of the global motor vehicle industry.

With regard to entrepreneur support, the ICAR will host a state-sponsored innovation center to nurture startup companies that originate in the Southeast auto cluster and to draw others from around the world into that cluster. In addition, the ICAR innovation center will welcome teams from established companies seeking the commercial development of their technologies. The State of South Carolina has provided significant support through four recent legislative initiatives. The Research University Infrastructure and the Research Centers of Economic Excellence Acts build the capabilities of the state's universities; and the Venture Capital Act and Innovation Centers Act provide support for entrepreneurs.

None of these elements can suffice by itself; but taken together they combine to offer a package of technology, education, and innovation that can serve the hydrogen transition extraordinarily well.

A Concluding Observation

Revolutionary technological change of the kind contemplated here is rarely predictable and never containable. Every new technology from the computer to the airplane to the automobile carries with it a chain of social and economic consequences that reach far beyond the technology itself. Some of these consequences turn out to be benign; some pose challenges that must be overcome by future generations; but none have proven foreseeable.

For example, a hydrogen transition might bring prolonged prosperity or economic decline to the electric utility industry depending upon which path innovation takes. A pathway that leads through plug-hybrids to home appliances that manufacture hydrogen by electrolysis would reinforce the current utility business model. A pathway in which hydrogen fuel cell vehicles serve as generators for home electric energy would undermine that model. The same holds true for the coal industry. A future in which carbon sequestration succeeds will affect coal far differently from one in which it cannot be accomplished.

The only certainty is that the energy economy will be vastly different from that which we know today. It will have to be.

Notes

1. Another concept, the battery electric vehicle (BEV), offers an all-electric drivetrain with all on-board energy stored in batteries, which would be recharged from stationary sources when the vehicle is not in operation. I have not included this among the competitors because battery technology has not advanced rapidly enough for it to compete in highway markets. In contrast, BEV have proven quite successful in the personal transportation niche.

2. Alternatively framed: "Which comes first, the vehicle or the fuel?"

3. I do not include on-board reforming of fossil feedstocks, like gasoline, among these. These systems offer little gain beyond that achievable with the HEV, and most industrial proponents appear to have abandoned the idea.

4. BMW was the founding OEM and most significant supporter of the ICAR.

References

Socolow, Robert H. "Can We Bury Global Warming?" *Scientific American,* July 2005, pp. 49–55.

Sperling, Daniel and James D. Cannon, *The Hydrogen Transition,* Elsevier Academic Press, 2004.

U.S. National Research Council, *The Hydrogen Economy: Opportunities, Costs, Barriers, and R&D Needs,* The National Academies Press, 2004.

Michael Behar

Warning: The Hydrogen Economy May Be More Distant Than It Appears

In the presidential campaign of 2004, Bush and Kerry managed to find one piece of common ground: Both spoke glowingly of a future powered by fuel cells. Hydrogen would free us from our dependence on fossil fuels and would dramatically curb emissions of air pollutants, including carbon dioxide, the gas chiefly blamed for global warming. The entire worldwide energy market would evolve into a "hydrogen economy" based on clean, abundant power. Auto manufacturers and environmentalists alike happily rode the bandwagon, pointing to hydrogen as the next big thing in U.S. energy policy. Yet the truth is that we aren't much closer to a commercially viable hydrogen-powered car than we are to cold fusion or a cure for cancer. This hardly surprises engineers, fuel cell manufacturers and policymakers, who have known all along that the technology has been hyped, perhaps to its detriment, and that the public has been misled about what Howard Coffman . . . describes as the "undeniable realities of the hydrogen economy." These experts are confident that the hydrogen economy will arrive—someday. But first, they say, we have to overcome daunting technological, financial and political roadblocks. Herewith, our checklist of misconceptions and doubts about hydrogen and the exalted fuel cell.

1. Hydrogen Is an Abundant Fuel

True, hydrogen is the most common element in the universe; it's so plentiful that the sun consumes 600 million tons of it every second. But unlike oil, vast reservoirs of hydrogen don't exist here on Earth. Instead, hydrogen atoms are bound up in molecules with other elements, and we must expend energy to extract the hydrogen so it can be used in fuel cells. We'll never get more energy out of hydrogen than we put into it.

"Hydrogen is a currency, not a primary energy source," explains Geoffrey Ballard, the father of the modern-day fuel cell and co-founder of Ballard Power Systems, the world's leading fuel-cell developer. "It's a means of getting energy from where you created it to where you need it."

2. Hydrogen Fuel Cells Will End Global Warming

Unlike internal combustion engines, hydrogen fuel cells do not emit carbon dioxide. But extracting hydrogen from natural gas, today's primary source, does. And wresting hydrogen from water through electrolysis takes tremendous amounts of energy. If that energy comes from power plants burning fossil fuels, the end product may be clean hydrogen, but the process used to obtain it is still dirty.

Once hydrogen is extracted, it must be compressed and transported, presumably by machinery and vehicles that in the early stages of a hydrogen economy will be running on fossil fuels. The result: even more CO_2. In fact, driving a fuel cell car with hydrogen extracted from natural gas or water could produce a net increase of CO_2 in the atmosphere. "People say that hydrogen cars would be pollution-free," observes University of Calgary engineering professor David Keith. "Light-bulbs are pollution-free, but power plants are not."

In the short term, nuclear power may be the easiest way to produce hydrogen without pumping more carbon dioxide into the atmosphere. Electricity from a nuclear plant would electrolyze water—splitting H_2O into hydrogen and oxygen. Ballard champions the idea, calling nuclear power "extremely important, unless we see some other major breakthrough that none of us has envisioned."

Critics counter that nuclear power creates long-term waste problems and isn't economically competitive. An exhaustive industry analysis entitled "The Future of Nuclear Power," written last year by 10 professors from the Massachusetts Institute of Technology and Harvard University, concludes that "hydrogen produced by electrolysis of water depends on low-cost nuclear power." As long as electricity from nuclear power costs more than electricity from other sources, using that energy to make hydrogen doesn't add up.

3. The Hydrogen Economy Can Run on Renewable Energy

Perform electrolysis with renewable energy, such as solar or wind power, and you eliminate the pollution issues associated with fossil fuels and nuclear power. Trouble is, renewable sources can provide only a small fraction of the energy that will be required for a full-fledged hydrogen economy.

From 1998 to 2003, the generating capacity of wind power increased 28 percent in the U.S. to 6,374 megawatts, enough for roughly 1.6 million homes. The wind industry expects to meet 6 percent of the country's electricity needs by 2020. But economist Andrew Oswald of the University of Warwick in England calculates that converting every vehicle in the U.S. to hydrogen power would require the electricity output of a million wind turbines—enough to cover half of California. Solar panels would likewise require huge swaths of land.

Water is another limiting factor for hydrogen production, especially in the sunny regions most suitable for solar power. According to a study done by the World Resources Institute, a Washington, D.C.-based nonprofit organization, fueling a hydrogen economy with electrolysis would require 4.2 trillion gallons of water annually—roughly the amount that flows over Niagara Falls every three months. Overall, U.S. water consumption would increase by about 10 percent.

4. Hydrogen Gas Leaks Are Nothing to Worry About

Hydrogen gas is odorless and colorless, and it burns almost invisibly. A tiny fire may go undetected at a leaky fuel pump until your pant leg goes up in flames. And it doesn't take much to set compressed hydrogen gas alight. "A cellphone or a lightning storm puts out enough static discharge to ignite hydrogen," claims Joseph Romm, author of *The Hype about Hydrogen: Fact and Fiction in the Race to Save the Climate* and founder of the Center for Energy and Climate Solutions in Arlington, Virginia.

A fender bender is unlikely to spark an explosion, because carbon-fiber-reinforced hydrogen tanks are virtually indestructible. But that doesn't eliminate the danger of leaks elsewhere in what will eventually be a huge network of refineries, pipelines and fueling stations. "The obvious pitfall is that hydrogen is a gas, and most of our existing petrochemical sources are liquids," says Robert Uhrig, professor emeritus of nuclear engineering at the University of Tennessee and former vice president of Florida Power & Light. "The infrastructure required to support high-pressure gas or cryogenic liquid hydrogen is much more complicated. Hydrogen is one of those things that people have great difficulty confining. It tends to go through the finest of holes."

To calculate the effects a leaky infrastructure might have on our atmosphere, a team of researchers from the California Institute of Technology and the Jet Propulsion Laboratory in Pasadena, California, looked at statistics for accidental industrial hydrogen and natural gas leakage—estimated at 10 to 20 percent of total volume—and then predicted how much leakage might occur in an economy in which everything runs on hydrogen. Result: The amount of hydrogen in the atmosphere would be four to eight times as high as it is today.

The Caltech study "grossly overstated" hydrogen leakage, says Assistant Secretary David Garman of the Department of Energy's Office of Energy Efficiency and Renewable Energy. But whatever its volume, hydrogen added to the atmosphere will combine with oxygen to form water vapor, creating noctilucent clouds—those high, wispy tendrils you see at dawn and dusk. The increased cloud cover could accelerate global warming.

5. Cars Are the Natural First Application for Hydrogen Fuel Cells

"An economically sane, cost-effective attack on the climate problem wouldn't start with cars," David Keith says. Cars and light trucks contribute roughly

20 percent of the carbon dioxide emitted in the U.S., while power plants burning fossil fuels are responsible for more than 40 percent of CO_2 emissions. Fuel cells designed for vehicles must cope with harsh conditions and severe limitations on size and weight.

A better solution to global warming might be to hold off building hydrogen cars, and instead harness fuel cells to generate electricity for homes and businesses. Plug Power, UTC, FuelCell Energy and Ballard Power Systems already market stationary fuel-cell generators. Plug Power alone has 161 systems in the U.S., including the first fuel-cell-powered McDonald's. Collectively, however, the four companies have a peak generating capacity of about 69 megawatts, less than 0.01 percent of the total 944,000 megawatts of U.S. generating capacity.

6. The U.S. Is Committed to Hydrogen, Pouring Billions into R&D

Consider this: President George W. Bush promised to spend $1.2 billion on hydrogen. Yet he allotted $1.5 billion to promote "healthy marriages." The monthly tab for the war in Iraq is $3.9 billion—a total of $121 billion through last September. In 2004 the Department of Energy spent more on nuclear and fossil fuel research than on hydrogen.

The federal government's FreedomCAR program, which funds hydrogen R&D in conjunction with the big three American carmakers, requires that the companies demonstrate a hydrogen-powered car by 2008—but not that they sell one.

"If you are serious about [hydrogen], you have to commit a whole lot more money," contends Guenter Conzelmann, deputy director of the Center for Energy, Environmental and Economic Systems Analysis at Argonne National Laboratory near Chicago. Conzelmann develops computer models to help the energy industry make predictions about the cost of implementing new technology. His estimate for building a hydrogen economy: more than $500 billion, and that's if 60 percent of Americans continue to drive cars with internal combustion engines.

Shell, ExxonMobil and other oil companies are unwilling to invest in production, distribution, fueling facilities and storage if there are just a handful of hydrogen cars on the road. Nor will automakers foot the bill and churn out thousands of hydrogen cars if drivers have nowhere to fill them up. Peter Devlin, head of the Department of Energy's hydrogen-production research group, says, "Our industry partners have told us that unless a fourth to a third of all refueling stations in the U.S. offer hydrogen, they won't be willing to take a chance on fuel cells."

To create hydrogen fueling stations, California governor Arnold Schwarzenegger, who drives a Hummer, has championed the Hydrogen Highway Project. His plan is to erect 150 to 200 stations—at a cost of at least $500,000 each—along the state's major highways by the end of the decade. So that's one state. Now what about the other 100,775 filling stations in the rest of the U.S.? Retrofitting just 25 percent of those with hydrogen fueling systems would cost more than $13 billion.

7. If Iceland Can Do It, So Can We

Iceland's first hydrogen fueling station is already operating on the outskirts of Reykjav'k. The hydrogen, which powers a small fleet of fuel cell buses, is produced onsite from electrolyzed tap water. Meanwhile the recently formed Icelandic New Energy—a consortium that includes automakers, Royal Dutch/Shell and the Icelandic power company Norsk Hydro—is planning to convert the rest of the island nation to a hydrogen system.

Impressive, yes. But 72 percent of Iceland's electricity comes from geothermal and hydroelectric power. With so much readily available clean energy, Iceland can electrolyze water with electricity directly from the national power grid. This type of setup is impossible in the U.S., where only about 15 percent of grid electricity comes from geothermal and hydroelectric sources, while 71 percent is generated by burning fossil fuels.

Another issue is the sheer scale of the system. It could take as few as 16 hydrogen fueling stations to enable Icelanders to drive fuel cell cars anywhere in the country. At close to 90 times the size of Iceland, the U.S. would require a minimum of 1,440 fueling stations. This assumes that stations would be strategically placed to collectively cover the entire U.S. with no overlap and that everyone knows where to find the pumps.

8. Mass Production Will Make Hydrogen Cars Affordable

Simply mass-producing fuel cell cars won't necessarily slash costs. According to Patrick Davis, the former leader of the Department of Energy's fuel cell research team, "If you project today's fuel cell technologies into high-volume production—about 500,000 vehicles a year—the cost is still up to six times too high."

Raj Choudhury, operations manager for the General Motors fuel cell program, claims that GM will have a commercial fuel cell vehicle ready by 2010. Others are doubtful. Ballard says that first there needs to be a "fundamental engineering rethink" of the proton exchange membrane (PEM) fuel cell, the type being developed for automobiles, which still cannot compete with the industry standard for internal combustion engines—a life span of 15 years, or about 170,000 driving miles. Because of membrane deterioration, today's PEM fuel cells typically fail during their first 2,000 hours of operation.

Ballard insists that his original PEM design was merely a prototype. "Ten years ago I said it was the height of engineering arrogance to think that the architecture and geometry we chose to demonstrate the fuel cell in automobiles would be the best architecture and geometry for a commercial automobile," he remarks. "Very few people paid attention to that statement. The truth is that the present geometry isn't getting the price down to where it is commercial. It isn't even entering into the envelope that will allow economies of scale to drive the price down."

In the short term, conventional gasoline-burning vehicles will be replaced by gas-electric hybrids, or by vehicles that burn clean diesel, natural gas, methanol or ethanol. Only later will hydrogen cars make sense, economically and environmentally. "Most analysts think it will take several decades for hydrogen to make a large impact, assuming hydrogen technologies reach their goals," notes Joan Ogden, an associate professor of environmental science and policy at the University of California at Davis and one of the world's leading researchers of hydrogen energy.

9. Fuel Cell Cars Can Drive Hundreds of Miles on a Single Tank of Hydrogen

A gallon of gasoline contains about 2,600 times the energy of a gallon of hydrogen. If engineers want hydrogen cars to travel at least 300 miles between fill-ups—the automotive-industry benchmark—they'll have to compress hydrogen gas to extremely high pressures: up to 10,000 pounds per square inch.

Even at that pressure, cars would need huge fuel tanks. "High-pressure hydrogen would take up four times the volume of gasoline," says JoAnn Milliken, chief engineer of the Department of Energy's Office of Hydrogen, Fuel Cells and Infrastructure Technologies.

Liquid hydrogen works a bit better. GM's liquid-fueled HydroGen3 goes 250 miles on a tank roughly double the size of that in a standard sedan. But the car must be driven every day to keep the liquid hydrogen chilled to –253 degrees Celsius—just 20 degrees above absolute zero and well below the surface temperature of Pluto—or it boils off. "If your car sits at the airport for a week, you'll have an empty tank when you get back," Milliken says.

10. If Not Hydrogen, Then *What*?

The near-future prospects for a hydrogen economy are dim, concludes *The Hydrogen Economy: Opportunities, Costs, Barriers, and R&D Needs*, a major government-sponsored study published last February by the National Research Council. Representatives from ExxonMobil, Ford, DuPont, the Natural Resources Defense Council and other stakeholders contributed to the report, which urges lawmakers to legislate tougher tailpipe-emission standards and to earmark additional R&D funding for renewable energy and alternative fuels. It foresees "major hurdles on the path to achieving the vision of the hydrogen economy" and recommends that the Department of Energy "keep a balanced portfolio of R&D efforts and continue to explore supply-and-demand alternatives that do not depend on hydrogen."

Of course, for each instance where the study points out how hydrogen falls short, there are scores of advocates armed with data to show how it can succeed. Physicist Amory Lovins, who heads the Rocky Mountain Institute, a think tank in Colorado, fastidiously rebuts the most common critiques of hydrogen with an armada of facts and figures in his widely circulated white paper "Twenty Hydrogen Myths." But although he's a booster of hydrogen, Lovins is notably pragmatic. "A lot of silly things have been written both for and against hydrogen," he says. "Some sense of reality is lacking on both sides." He believes that whether the hydrogen economy arrives at the end of this decade or closer to midcentury, interim technologies will play a signal role in the transition.

The most promising of these technologies is the gas-electric hybrid vehicle, which uses both an internal combustion engine and an electric motor, switching seamlessly between the two to optimize gas mileage and engine efficiency. U.S. sales of hybrid cars have been growing steadily, and the 2005 model year saw the arrival of the first hybrid SUVs—the Ford Escape, Toyota Highlander and Lexus RX400h.

Researchers sponsored by the FreedomCAR program are also investigating ultralight materials—plastics, fiberglass, titanium, magnesium, carbon fiber—and developing lighter engines made from aluminum and ceramic materials. These new materials could help reduce vehicle power demands, bridging the cost gap between fossil fuels and fuel cells.

Most experts agree that there is no silver bullet. Instead the key is developing a portfolio of energy-efficient technologies that can help liberate us from fossil fuels and ease global warming. "If we had a wider and more diverse set of energy sources, we'd be more robust, more stable," says Jonathan Pershing, director of the Climate, Energy and Pollution Program at the World Resources Institute. "The more legs your chair rests on, the less likely it is to tip over."

Waiting for hydrogen to save us isn't an option. "If we fail to act during this decade to reduce greenhouse gas emissions, historians will condemn us," Romm writes in *The Hype about Hydrogen*. "And they will most likely be living in a world with a much hotter and harsher climate than ours, one that has undergone an irreversible change for the worse."

POSTSCRIPT

Will Hydrogen Replace Fossil Fuels for Cars?

Hydrogen as a fuel offers definite benefits. As Joan M. Ogden notes in "Hydrogen: The Fuel of the Future?" *Physics Today* (April 2002), the technology is available, and compared to the alternatives, it "offers the greatest potential environmental and energy-supply benefits." To put hydrogen to use, however, will require massive investments in facilities for generating, storing, and transporting the gas, as well as manufacturing hydrogen-burning engines and fuel cells. Currently, large amounts of hydrogen can easily be generated by "reforming" natural gas or other hydrocarbons. Hydrolysis—splitting hydrogen from water molecules with electricity—is also possible, and in the future this may use electricity from renewable sources such as wind or from nuclear power. The basic technologies are available right now. See Thammy Evans, Peter Light, and Ty Cashman, "Hydrogen—A Little PR," *Whole Earth* (Winter 2001). Daniel Sperling notes in "Updating Automotive Research," *Issues in Science and Technology* (Spring 2002), that "Fuel cells and hydrogen show huge promise. They may indeed prove to be the Holy Grail, eventually taking vehicles out of the environmental equation," but making that happen will require research, government assistance in building a hydrogen distribution system, and incentives for both industry and car buyers. First steps along these lines are already visible in a few places; see Bill Keenan, "Hydrogen: Waiting for the Revolution," *Across the Board* (May/June 2004), and Annie Birdsong, "California Drives the Future of the Automobile," *World Watch* (March/April 2005). M. Z. Jacobson, W. G. Colella, and D. M. Golden, "Cleaning the Air and Improving Health with Hydrogen Fuel-Cell Vehicles," *Science* (June 24, 2005), conclude that if all onroad vehicles are replaced with fuel-cell vehicles using hydrogen generated by wind power, both air pollution and human health impacts will be reduced, and overall costs will be less than for gasoline. Joan Ogden, "High Hopes for Hydrogen," *Scientific American* (September 2006), agrees that the potential is great but stresses that the transition to a hydrogen future will take decades. Tim Moran, "Fuel for the Future," *Automotive News* (November 20, 2006), describes General Motors' plans to bring hydrogen-fueled cars to market. Michael K. Heiman and Barry D. Solomon, "The Hydrogen Economy and Its Alternatives," *Environment* (October 2007), argue that hydrogen may serve as a bridge to the future in some ways, but it is not likely to play much role in the transportation sector.

Jeremy Rifkin, "Hydrogen: Empowering the People," *Nation* (December 23, 2002), says local production of hydrogen could mean a much more decentralized energy system. He may be right, as John A. Turner makes clear in "Sustainable Hydrogen Production," *Science* (August 13, 2004), but Henry Payne and Diane Katz, "Gas and Gasbags . . . or, the Open Road and Its Enemies," *National Review* (March 25, 2002), contend that a major obstacle to hydrogen is market mechanisms that will keep fossil fuels in use for years to come, local hydrogen production is unlikely, and adequate supplies will require that society invest heavily in nuclear power. Jim Motavalli, "Hijacking Hydrogen," *E—The Environmental Magazine* (January–February 2003), worries that the fossil fuel and nuclear industries will dominate the hydrogen future. The former wish to use "reforming" to generate hydrogen from coal, and the latter see hydrolysis as creating demand for nuclear power. In Iceland, Freyr Sverrisson, "Missing in Action: Iceland's Hydrogen Economy," *World Watch* (November/December 2006), notes that the demand of industry for electricity has shifted plans to develop hydrogen to the development of hydroelectric dams instead.

In January 2003, President George W. Bush proposed $1.2 billion in funding for making hydrogen-powered cars an on-the-road reality. Gregg Easterbrook, "Why Bush's H-Car Is Just Hot Air," *New Republic* (February 24, 2003), thinks it would make much more sense to address fuel-economy standards; Bush should "leave futurism to the futurists." Peter Schwartz and Doug Randall, "How Hydrogen Can Save America," *Wired* (April 2003), commend Bush's proposal but say the proposed funding is not enough. We need, they say, "an Apollo-scale commitment to hydrogen power. The fate of the republic depends on it."

The difficulty of the task is underlined by Robert F. Service in "The Hydrogen Backlash," *Science* (August 13, 2004) (the lead article in a special section titled "Toward a Hydrogen Economy"). In the summer of 2008, Honda introduced the FCX Clarity, a car that runs on hydrogen (with fuel cells and a battery) and is twice as efficient as a gas-electric hybrid. However, Robert Zubrin, "The Hydrogen Hoax," *The New Atlantis* (Winter 2007), contends that so far hydrogen-fueled vehicles are little better than display models. What is needed is legislation to mandate that all new cars sold in the United States be "flex-fueled"—able to burn any mixture of gasoline and alcohol. (See Issue 16 for the debate over biofuels.)

ISSUE 19

Is There Any Such Thing as "Free Energy"?

YES: Thomas Valone, from "Introduction to Zero Point Energy," *Infinite Energy*, http://www.integrityresearchinstitute.org/ (July/August 2007)

NO: Robert Park, from *Voodoo Science* (Oxford University Press, 2000)

ISSUE SUMMARY

YES: Thomas Valone argues that the solution to the world's need for large amounts of energy lies in "zero-point energy" (ZPE), a sea of energy that pervades all space. We need but develop means to tap this energy.

NO: Physicist Robert Park argues that though many inventors have claimed to have working "free energy" devices, none of them work or can work. Their proponents are guilty of "voodoo science."

It is sad but true that as the twenty-first century gets under way, energy supply, availability, and price, as well as the side-effects of its use, have become huge concerns. The concern is not new except in degree, because human beings have used energy in one form or another for a long time. Large amounts of effort and money have gone toward devising steam engines, internal combustion engines, electric motors, nuclear reactors, and many more of the machines that bend energy to human purposes such as transportation, lighting, air conditioning, and war. Money, effort, and even lives have been spent to bring energy to these machines in the form of coal and oil, impounded water, and uranium. Worry has been spent as well, because energy technologies have side-effects such as global warming, and fuels such as coal and oil are finite in supply. Can there be such a thing as an energy technology without side-effects? Can there be energy sources that are not finite?

Side-effects are probably inescapable. Since the universe itself is finite, so must be all possible energy sources. But are there sources that are much less finite than those we are accustomed to, that will last as long as humans need them, and—perhaps—that will cost less in effort and money? Such questions have driven a great deal of research work. The results have included nuclear power, whose fuel—uranium—can last much longer than coal, at least if we choose to develop breeder reactors. Thermonuclear fusion, the process that fuels the stars, relies on even more plentiful raw materials (hydrogen and deuterium) and could meet human needs for eons. But despite much effort, researchers have so far been unable to domesticate it (work continues; see, for example, "International Thermonuclear Experimental Reactor," *Advanced Materials & Processes,* February 2008; Wayt Gibbs, "Plan B for Energy," *Scientific American,* September 2006, discusses fusion and other advanced energy technologies).

Some of this work has led to what initially seemed astonishingly promising results. In 1989, Stanley Pons and Martin Fleischmann, researchers at the University of Utah, announced their discovery of "cold fusion," a version of fusion that worked without the colossal temperatures and pressures found inside stars and without the extraordinarily expensive apparatus of other fusion schemes. In fact, cold fusion happened in a jar or beaker on a lab bench, and it released large amounts of energy. Or did it? Despite many attempts to repeat the work in other labs, no one has been able to get the results Pons and Fleischmann claimed. On the other hand, there have been enough hints that something interesting was going on to keep the attention of a number of researchers; see Charles Platt, "What If Cold Fusion Is Real?" *Wired* (November 1998).

People have been inventing ways to generate abundant and free or cheap energy for a long time. Many have received press attention and enlisted enthusiasts, who maintain many Internet sites such as Patrick J. Kelly's "Practical Guide to Free-Energy Devices" (http://www.free-energy-info.co.uk/). However, not one has proved capable of lighting a home or powering a car.

In the following selections, engineer Thomas Valone argues that the solution to the world's need for large amounts of energy lies in "zero point energy" (ZPE), a sea of energy that pervades all space. We need but develop means to tap this energy. University of Maryland professor of physics Robert Park argues that though many inventors have claimed to have working "free energy" devices, none of them work or can work. Their proponents are guilty of "voodoo science."

YES

Thomas Valone

Introduction to Zero Point Energy

Overview

Zero point energy is the sea of energy that pervades all of space, often called by scientists "the physical vacuum." Perhaps a realization of the old aether theory or the Biblical firmament, it just happens to be the biggest sea of energy that is known to exist. Not only is it big but its energy is estimated to exceed nuclear energy densities. Even a small piece of it is "worth its weight in gold." What is it? It is "the kinetic energy retained by the molecules of a substance at a temperature of absolute zero." Still, most people are not sure what this "zero point energy" (ZPE) is and whether it can be useful for human energy needs.

Does it offer a source of unlimited energy for homes, cars, and space travel? Depending on whom we talk to, ZPE can do everything and ZPE can do nothing useful. How can the energy be converted to produce electricity? It may be our primitive twentieth century upbringing that stops us from putting a paddlewheel in this sea. What is the basic explanation of ZPE? *Space is quantized and virtual particles abound.* What are the new discoveries that have rocked the U.S. Patent Office, NASA, *Physical Review, Scientific American, Discover, New Scientist,* and the *New York Times*? What are some of the ZPE concepts that we should know about? These are the questions that this book will answer in the following chapters (not published here). . . .

What Is Zero Point Energy?

Maybe ZPE can shoot from a gun, like in the movie. "The Incredibles." Some scientists like to talk about the vast field of zero point energy pervading all space, as the zero point field (ZPF).We can envision the ZPF as a big sea in which we are all submerged. Contrasted with that is ZPE that locally involves energetic stuff on a microscale, which we can measure. Thus, ZPE is the energy that comprises the ZPF. Dr. Fred Wolf explains:

No matter how cool we make the chamber as we compress the gas, we would find that we could not obtain total order. Greater confinement

From chapter 1 of *Zero Point Energy: The Fuel of the Future,* by Thomas Valone; as seen in *Infinite Energy,* July/August 2007, pp. 25–30 (notes omitted). Copyright © 2007 by Integrity Research Institute. Reprinted by permission.

of each molecule would produce, according to the uncertainty principle, a greater uncertainty in its possible speed and therefore less certainty about its individual behavior. The gas would exhibit what is called zero-point energy. Even though its temperature was reduced to absolute zero, the molecules would still continue to move. Each molecule, however, would no longer be able to occupy a single position at a single time. Instead each would "spread out" throughout the whole volume of the chamber.

With the discovery of ZPE, scientists find that space is rich with activity from virtual particles and full of energy. Therefore, physicists like to call it the "physical vacuum" when they want to talk about ZPE. Furthermore, the vacuum also vibrates and "fluctuates." In fact, that is the very essence of ZPE. Vacuum fluctuations are even predicted by a branch of physics, started by Albert Einstein, Neils Bohr, and Werner Heisenberg, called quantum mechanics. "Vacuum fluctuations" will be regarded as the same thing as ZPE, which are "a disturbance in the Force, Luke."

Another aspect of both ZPE and ZPF is that the "empty vacuum" is involved somehow. This is the only "leap of faith" that is required of the reader: to keep an open mind to the fact that theory and experiment agrees that the vacuum is not empty. Instead, it is full of activity and, most importantly, it can spill over into the real world. As explained in later chapters, classical physics predicts the presence of zero point energy. The way it was discovered involved emptying a container of everything including the matter, gas, and any heat energy. The only thing left in that container, as the heat energy approaches the absolute zero point (0°K) will be the vacuum itself. This is why it is called zero point energy. . . .

Scientists have come within "microdegrees" (less than 1°K) of the absolute zero point of temperature. A famous experiment proving the existence of ZPE involves cooling helium to within microdegrees of absolute zero temperature (between –272°C and absolute the zero point of –273°C). Amazingly, it will still remain a liquid! Only ZPE can account for the source of energy that is preventing helium from freezing.

Besides the classical explanation of zero-point energy referred to above, there are rigorous derivations from quantum physics that prove its existence. One quantum mechanics text states, "It is possible to get a fair estimate of the zero point energy using the uncertainty principle alone." Because the uncertainty principle is so simple and fundamental, this implies that ZPE is also the same: simple and fundamental.

Infinite Energy

Everything about zero point energy is amazing. This apparently keeps physicists in a state of incredulity, unable to grasp its significance. For example, there is the question of whether the ZPF is conservative. (Unlike politics, conservative fields in physics are those that conserve energy, thus obeying the First Law of Thermodynamics.) If ZPE is not conservative, then we can extract "an infinite amount of energy" from the vacuum, according to Dr. Robert Forward. However, if it is proven that the ZPF is a conservative field, we can still extract energy from it. It is just that we would have to put energy in and store it somehow to get it out again.

The evidence seems to favor a nonconservative ZPF so far, with arguments still raging on both sides. In addition, the capability of ZPF storage and retrieval has convincingly been presented by Dr. Forward, as presented in the next chapters. An article entitled "Energy Unlimited" appeared a few years ago when Professor Jordan Maclay received a NASA grant to try to extract ZPE from elongated, oscillating, tiny metal boxes. A physics journal article points out, "However, vacuum fluctuations remain a matter of debate, mainly because their energy is infinite." More strikingly, their energy per unit volume is infinite. Interestingly, this seems to create intellectual difficulties which can only be artificially eliminated. "Problems with the infinite energy of vacuum fluctuations has led to the view that vacuum energy may be forced to vanish by definition . . . [from] the need to regularize the infinite energy-momentum tensor." However, this causes even more complications: "This procedure gives rise to ambiguities and anomalies, that lead to a breakdown at the quantum level of usual symmetry properties of the energy-momentum tensor."

Some physicists, for example, believe in the infinite energy theory because presently there is no known limit to how small an electromagnetic vibration can be. Therefore, they argue that there has to be infinite possible electromagnetic vibrations in the ZPF. This logically leads to the conclusion that infinite vibrations yield infinite energy content. However, this argument relates more to energy density rather than total energy content. "The zero-point energy of the vacuum is infinite in any finite volume." "A charged particle in the vacuum will therefore always see a zero-point field of infinite energy density."

For example, imagine what is the smallest vibration that could exist. That vibration has to resonate with a correspondingly high frequency. This calculation still leads to very high energy density and a really big number for the total ZPE available in the universe. We will call this the "limited" ZPF as opposed to the "unlimited" ZPF that yields infinite energy density. . . .

> In an interview taped for television on PBS's "Scientific American Frontiers," which aired in November (1997), Harold E. Puthoff, the director of the Institute for Advanced Studies, observed: "For the chauvinists in the field like ourselves, we think the 21st century could be the zero-point-energy age." That conceit is not shared by the majority of physicists; some even regard such optimism as pseudoscience that could leech funds from legitimate research. The conventional view is that the energy in the vacuum is miniscule.

Ten years later, this skeptical viewpoint is unfortunately still held by the majority of physicists and scientists.

Contrary to this pessimistic, irrational belief, the actual estimate of energy density of even the *limited* ZPF (bounded by a maximum frequency) is astounding. It is much more than we humans normally can comprehend. For example, if we presume that the minimum possible wavelength is limited to the size of the proton, the famous Nobel Prize winning physicist, Richard Feynman, calculated that the energy density of the ZPF would be 10^{108} *joules* per cubic centimeter (J/cc). Today, physicists want to look at even smaller vibration units like subatomic particles, etc. This makes the ZPF energy density escalate even more. Just as a comparison, if we converted energy to mass using $E = mc^2$, we find that the equivalent "mass density" of the ZPF is 10^{94} grams per cubic centimeter (g/cc). Compare that with typical nuclear densities of 10^{14} g/cc. Therefore, gram for gram, ZPE offers almost 10^{80} times more energy for the same amount of space as nuclear reactors. Therefore, if we presume similar energy conversion efficiency, 1 ZPE Engine = 10^{80} Nukes. This leads to a surprising conclusion: Space itself contains more energy than matter.

Free Energy

This raises the exciting and controversial issue of "free energy," which is "one of the world's twenty greatest unsolved problems," according to a new book that devotes an entire chapter to free energy. Historically, when natural gas (1950s) and again when nuclear power (1960s) was introduced to society, "cheap energy" was their advertising slogan. Back in 1903, Nikola Tesla completed the Wardenclyffe Tower on Long Island, in order to broadcast cheap electrical energy to Europe. Tesla was stopped by J.P. Morgan, who wanted to know how he could possibly put a meter on it. This caused Tesla's free energy dream to be suppressed. Today this movement is still a suppressed, popular conviction held by the majority opposed to the high cost and slavery of electrical grid power and ridiculed by mainstream physics. In 1995, I was the technical consultant to a bold, pioneering video "Free Energy: The Race to Zero Point," which introduced ZPE with state of the art graphics and a professional narrator. It also contains examples of promising inventions that showed characteristics of self-powered operation, though no endorsement was made of their outcome.

Now with the advent of ZPE, localized free energy looks much more promising than ever before. In 2001, *Popular Mechanics* featured an article talking about putting "free energy to work" moving a nanoscale seesaw (see Figure 9.1 in book, not reprinted here). In 1998, a physicist with the Jet Propulsion Laboratory invented a nanoscale ZPE engine that pumps electrons, with the help of a tiny laser, just like an electrical generator. Dr. Fabrizio Pinto states:

> In the event of no other alternative explanations, one should conclude that major technological advances in the area of endless, by-product free-energy production could be achieved.

Pinto's accomplishment has brought much more needed legitimacy to the ZPE conversion arena. Another exciting endorsement has come from the prophetic Arthur C. Clarke, who was recently overheard talking to Astronaut Buzz Aldrin in Sri Lanka, broaching the issue of zero point energy:

> I'm now convinced that there are new forms of energy, which we are tapping, and they make even nuclear energy look trivial in comparison. And when we control those energy sources, the universe will open up.

The Need for ZPEED

Today the need for a non-polluting, abundant energy source is greater than ever. Our world is battling another energy crisis of unprecedented proportions. However, the present levels of greenhouse gases that are by-products of fossil fuel energy are already impacting the climate and weather. The environmentalists' demand to reduce carbon emissions by 60% to 80%, in order to stabilize the earth's atmosphere, clashes sharply with the public's increasing demand for energy. While the world relies heavily on an oil-based energy that experts say is at peak production, new futuristic energy sources are still out of reach.

Fortunately, the ultimate goal of ZPE vacuum engineers is none other than free energy (with a single capital investment and unlimited amounts of electrical power). Zero point energy is the much-anticipated promise of the future. It is the omnipresent bulwark of nature's machinery, and the most abundant energy source in the universe. It already powers a surprising number of processes from quasars to atoms, while also linked by theoretical physicists to inertia and gravity. The applications of ZPE are limitless. We just need to design effective transducers to put the energy to use.

Dr. Marc Millis, at NASA's Breakthrough Propulsion Physics Program, calls zero point energy the "leading candidate" for interstellar travel. It also is much more convenient for interplanetary travel than NASA's overgrown firecrackers, invented by the Chinese over one thousand years ago.

Facing the future with knowledge and forethought will empower us to find success in the midst of our dilemma. The questions are simply:

(1) How can energy be used anywhere without burning something?
(2) How can we travel quickly in space without exploding something?

Zero point energy is the only long-term solution to these questions. . . .

Summary

Talking about ZPE may seem to be bordering on fantasy for most people, irrespective of whether you are a physicist or not. All of us want to be assured that any new source of energy is real and will help to cook our eggs or run our cars. Otherwise, scientists tend to treat new concepts as a black hole where lots of theory goes in and nothing comes out.

In the following chapters, a whole universe of zero point energy facts and ideas will open up for the reader. So compelling is the information that I believe you will be challenged to take it seriously and plan your energy-abundant future accordingly. I predict that third world countries will finally have their basic needs met with small, portable energy units distributed everywhere. With that capability comes a necessary burden to use this new emerging energy source wisely and constructively.

My suggestion is for civilian scientists and entrepreneurs to grab hold of the opportunity, share it with overseas colleagues and get it to market, before the military declares it classified. You may laugh but this is the best strategy, tested and proven by inventor Ken Shoulders. For a few years, his discovery of "electron charge clusters," with estimates of several times overunity, was ranked #2 on the National Critical Issues List, just under stealth bombers. Ken told me that when the officer arrived at his door with the classification papers, he told him it was too late because he had already sent it overseas in the form of a few hardcover books. It worked so well that the officer was extremely angry as he had to retreat in defeat. To this day, electron charge clusters remain available for civilian applications.

Another example also demonstrates the keen interest the military has in new energy. As many remember, cold fusion was prematurely announced at a press conference at the University of Utah in 1989 by Dr. Stanley Pons and Dr. Martin Fleischmann. Years later, Dr. Fleischmann told a small group of us at a meeting in Washington, D.C. that on his way back to England he missed a connecting flight in San Francisco and unexpectedly had to check into a hotel room. As he opened the door to his room, the phone rang. The caller said, "This is Edward Teller. Don't hang up. I have a few questions for you." The first question he was asked was, "Can you make a bomb from cold fusion?" A strict pacifist, Fleischmann denied any possibility of a runaway, positive feedback event that could result in an explosion. However, he also told me that he wished the whole project had been classified so that he and Dr. Pons could have worked without press and public interference. The question of explosive potential has also been asked of ZPE, but to benefit the human race, for its ultimate survival and for the sake of the planet, this book emphasizes basic ZPE electricity and propulsion generators for public use rather than making more bombs for military use only.

Robert Park  **NO**

It's Not News, It's Entertainment in Which the Media Covers Voodoo Science

Joe Newman and the Energy Machine

I called Joe Newman at his home in Lucedale, Mississippi. I was surprised when he answered the phone; I had tried several times before and always got a recorded message offering his book, *The Energy Machine of Joseph W. Newman,* for $74.95. I explained that I was writing a book about ideas that are not generally accepted by scientists, and it would not be complete without a full account of the Energy Machine. He seemed suspicious. "It's all in my book," he snapped. I told him I'd read his book at the time of his 1986 Senate hearing, but I wondered if his ideas had changed over the years. His voice softened. Well, he said, the book had been expanded and I should buy a new copy, but he still stood by everything he'd said before about how the Energy Machine works.

I waited through a long silence while he thought about what else he should tell me. Then he began talking. The big change since the Senate hearing was that Joe Newman had found God. Raised in a Methodist orphans' home until he ran away at fourteen, Joe became an atheist because he didn't believe a God would permit little children to suffer that much. But he now realized that the Energy Machine was meant to relieve human suffering, and that God had chosen Joe Newman to make the discovery because "he knew Joe Newman would be a good steward for his gift."

It saddened Newman that, in spite of his efforts, the benefits from the Energy Machine were still not reaching the people of the world. "I do it for the human race," he said, "but the people I trusted most betrayed me and the human race." His patent lawyer, the company that supplied the batteries for his machine, even those who had testified on his behalf in court and in the Senate hearing had all used or sold his ideas. There are motors based on his ideas on the market right now, he assured me, that are more than 100 percent efficient; the manufacturers refuse to admit it so they won't have to pay him royalties. He didn't mind his ideas being stolen, if that meant they would be turned into things that would help the world, but these people were hiding the truth about his discovery. "They don't care about humanity," he said sadly.

There was a flash of the old Joe Newman when he vowed to sue his betrayers. The refusal of the U.S. Patent and Trademark Office to grant him a patent for "an unlimited source of energy" no longer mattered, he explained; he had patented the Energy Machine in Mexico, and because of the NAFTA and GATT agreements, his patent is now good all over the world. "A jury will bury these people," he assured me.

Meanwhile, a lot of people continue to believe that Joe Newman really has found a way to generate unlimited amounts of energy. Newman told me he was still demonstrating his Energy Machine around Mississippi and Louisiana and appearing from time to time on radio talk shows. He said they like him on talk radio, "not because they believe me, but because I'm good for ratings. Creative people," Joe sighed, "die poor." There was another long pause. "The people of Mississippi have not stood up behind this technology as they should have," he told me. "I'm leaving the state and heading west. People out there are very concerned about pollution; they'll recognize what this technology can do."

How much of this does Joe Newman really believe? Even now it's impossible to tell. Perhaps not even Joe Newman knows. But he has bounced back before. I first heard about him and his Energy Machine on January 11, 1984, on the CBS *Evening News*. "What's the answer to the energy crisis?" Dan Rather was asking, "Suppose a fellow told you the answer was in a machine he has developed? Before you scoff, take a look with Bruce Hall." CBS reporter Bruce Hall had traveled to the rural hamlet of Lucedale. A mile down a dirt road, past the KEEP OUT and NO TRESPASSING signs, Hall stood with Joseph Wesley Newman in front of his garage workshop. He described Newman as "a brilliant self-educated inventor." An intense, handsome man in his forties, dressed in work clothes, his dark hair combed straight back, the plainspoken mechanic looked directly into the eyes of the viewers. He declared that his Energy Machine could produce ten times the electrical energy it took to run it. "Put one in your home," he said, "and you'll never have to pay another electric bill."

It's the sort of story Americans love. A backwoods wizard who never finished high school makes a revolutionary scientific discovery. He is denied the fruits of his genius by a pompous scientific establishment and a patent examiner who rejects his application for a patent on "an unlimited source of energy" without even examining it, on the grounds that all alleged inventions of perpetual motion machines are refused patents. Not a man to be pushed around, Joseph Wesley Newman takes on the U.S. government, filing suit in federal court against the Patent and Trademark Office. It's the little man battling a gigantic, impersonal system.

There was no one on the CBS *Evening News* to challenge Newman's claim. On the contrary, the report included endorsements from two "experts" who had examined Newman's Energy Machine. Roger Hastings, a boyish-looking Ph.D. physicist with the Sperry Corporation, declared, "It's possible his theory could be correct and that this could revolutionize society." Milton Everett, identified as an engineer with the Mississippi Department of Transportation, told viewers, "Joe's an original thinker. He's gone beyond what you can read in textbooks." Watching the CBS broadcast that evening, most viewers must have been left wondering how the Patent Office could be so certain Joe Newman was wrong.

The Patent Office based its judgment on the long and colorful history of failed attempts to build perpetual motion machines, going back at least to the seventeenth century. Waterwheels had been used in Europe for centuries to grind flour, but many areas lacked suitable streams for a mill. Farmers in those areas were forced to transport their grain to distant mills and then lug the meal back. In 1618 a famous London physician named Robert Fludd wondered if a way could be found to run a mill without depending on nature to provide the stream. Dr. Fludd was, like Joe Newman, endowed with boundless self-confidence and a wide-ranging imagination . . . . It occurred to Dr. Fludd that the waterwheel could be used to drive a pump, as well as to grind flour. The water that had turned the wheel could then be pumped back up into the millrace. That way, he reasoned, a reservoir of water could be used to run the mill indefinitely.

Dr. Fludd's idea failed, but his failure helped to lead others to one of the greatest scientific insights in history, paving the way for the industrial revolution. The amount of work a waterwheel can perform is measured by the weight of the water that comes out of the millrace, multiplied by the distance the water descends in turning the wheel. For Dr. Fludd's idea to work, the water would have to be lifted back up the same distance it fell in turning the wheel. All the energy generated in turning the wheel would be needed just to raise the water back to the reservoir. There would be no energy left over to grind the flour.

But the concept of energy or "work" as a measurable quantity did not exist in the seventeenth century. It would be another two hundred years before the flaw in Dr. Fludd's machine would be stated in the form of a fundamental law of nature: *energy is conserved*. Written as a mathematical equation, it is known as the *First Law of Thermodynamics*. There is no firmer pillar of modern science. It is the law that explains why a ball, no matter what it's made of, never bounces higher than the point from which it's dropped. The conservation of energy is consistent with our everyday experience: you can't get something for nothing.

Even if it ground no flour, however, Dr. Fludd's waterwheel could not be kept turning. Energy losses, including the heat generated by friction in the machinery, are inevitable. Without adding energy, any real machine, no matter how well it's built, would gradually slow down and stop. That's embodied in the *Second Law of Thermodynamics*. Our bouncing ball, no matter what it's made of, can in fact never bounce quite as high as the point from which it's dropped. The first law says you can't win; the second law says you can't even break even.

In the nearly four hundred years since Robert Fludd's idea failed, hundreds of inventors around the world have tried to beat the laws of thermodynamics. The laws of thermodynamics always won. In frustration, and perhaps embarrassment, many inventors ended up resorting to fraud, constructing complex devices with cleverly concealed sources of energy to keep them running. Each failure, each fraud exposed, established the laws of thermodynamics more firmly. In 1911, the U.S. patent commissioner, annoyed that so much Patent Office time was being spent on impossible ideas, ruled that a patent application for a perpetual motion machine could not be submitted until one year after an actual operating model of the machine was filed with the Patent Office. If the machine was still running at the end of a year, the application would be accepted. None of the devices turned out to be quite that perpetual, and the new ruling seemed to bring an end to patent applications for perpetual motion machines.

None of this background was touched on in the CBS News story, which ended with a final camera shot of Joe Newman, his jaw set, declaring, "I'll keep fightin' and I'll fight till Hell freezes over." There was something compelling about this man. Whatever charisma is, Joe Newman had it. No matter, I thought; no one will take him seriously. It was the last I would ever see of Joseph Newman and his Energy Machine.

I was wrong, of course. Viewers with little knowledge of the conservation of energy had no reason to scoff. The experts had vouched for Newman, and Dan Rather, a trusted guest in millions of homes, had invited people to take the story seriously. Tens of thousands did. Joe Newman is a colorful American classic in the mold of Elmer Gantry, and whatever his faults, Americans like Elmer Gantry. They wanted Joe Newman to be right.

CBS News had transformed Joe Newman into a celebrity. He appeared on the Johnny Carson show and rented the Superdome in New Orleans for a week, where thousands of fans paid a dollar each to watch him demonstrate his Energy Machine. The crude five-hundred-pound device, with its huge armatures that he and his wife had laboriously wound by hand in their kitchen, was now tucked out of sight under the hood of a sleek red Sterling sports car, which Newman would drive around the floor of the Superdome at a stately four miles per hour while the crowd applauded.

Emerging triumphant from the Sterling, looking like the winner of the Indy 500, he tells the crowd that it could have kept going forever. Applause turns to cheering. "This machine is going to change the world!" he proclaims. "You know how I can say that? It's simple. Truth is like a high-intensity laser beam, and it will burn through garbage." He has them worked up now. "Do y'all believe this car was running on the current of a single transistor battery? Let me hear from you," he shouts, holding a tiny transistor-radio battery above his head. The crowd roars its approval; whistles and rebel yells mix with the cheers. Newman is ready with his final volley. He challenges any Ph.D. physicist in the crowd to come down and debate him. The spectators fall momentarily silent. They begin to titter as Newman shades his eyes, pretending to look in vain for some physicist coming out of the stands.

Most scientists, however, simply ignored Joe Newman. The prospect of someone with little education and no record of scientific accomplishment overturning the most basic laws of physics, laws that have withstood every challenge, seemed much too unlikely to bother with. They looked the other way while science was being abused. But could they have prevented it? Perhaps the most endearing characteristic of Americans is their sympathy for the underdog. They resent arrogant scientists who talk down to them in unfamiliar language, and government bureaucrats who hide behind rules. Moreover, Joe Newman's claim invoked one of the most persistent myths of the industrialized world—free energy. Who has not heard stories of the automobile that runs on ordinary water? Suppressed, of course, by the oil industry. The public never tires of that story.

We will keep coming back to the dream of free energy—and we will keep running into Joe Newman. Maybe we will come to understand him. But the Energy Machine of Joe Newman is just one small example of the abuse of science. It's all around us.

Voodoo Science

Science fascinates us by its power to surprise. Unexpected results that appear to violate accepted laws of nature can portend revolutionary advances in human knowledge. In the past century, such scientific discoveries doubled our life span, freed us from the mind-numbing drudgery that had been the lot of ordinary people for all of history, revealed the vastness of the universe, and put all the knowledge of the world at our fingertips. As a new century begins, molecular biology is unraveling the secrets of life itself, and physicists dare to dream of a "final theory" that would make sense of the entire universe.

Alas, many "revolutionary" discoveries turn out to be wrong. Error is a normal part of science, and uncovering flaws in scientific observations or reasoning is the everyday work of scientists. Scientists try to guard against attributing significance to spurious results by repeating measurements and designing control experiments. But even eminent scientists have have had their careers tarnished by misinterpreting unremarkable events in a way that is so compelling that they are thereafter unable to free themselves of the conviction that they have made a great discovery. Moreover, scientists, no less than others, are inclined to see what they expect to see, and an erroneous conclusion by a respected colleague often carries other scientists along on the road to ignominy. This is *pathological science*, in which scientists manage to fool themselves.

If scientists can fool themselves, how much easier is it to craft arguments deliberately intended to befuddle jurists or lawmakers with little or no scientific background? This is *junk science*. It typically consists of tortured theories of what *could be* so, with little supporting evidence to prove that it *is* so.

Sometimes there is no evidence at all. Two hundred years ago, educated people imagined that the greatest contribution of science would be to free the world from superstition and humbug. It has not happened. Ancient beliefs in demons and magic still sweep across the modern landscape, but they are now dressed in the language and symbols of science: a best-selling health guru explains that his brand of spiritual healing is firmly grounded in quantum theory; half the population believes Earth is being visited by space aliens who have mastered faster-than-light travel; and educated people wear magnets in their shoes to draw energy from the Earth. This is *pseudoscience*. Its practitioners may believe it to be science, just as witches and faith healers may truly believe they can call forth supernatural powers.

What may begin as honest error, however, has a way of evolving through almost imperceptible steps from self-delusion to fraud. The line between foolishness and fraud is thin. Because it is not always easy to tell when that line is crossed, I use the term *voodoo science* to cover them all: pathological science, junk science, pseudoscience, and fraudulent science. . . .

POSTSCRIPT

Is There Any Such Thing as "Free Energy"?

Most "free energy" inventions have followed the pattern of the Steorn company's (http://www.steorn.com/) Orbo technology, based on "time variant magneto-mechanical interactions," which may, thinks inventor Sean McCarthy, tap the zero point energy. Steorn claims that "Orbo produces free, clean and constant energy. . . . By free we mean that the energy produced is done so without recourse to external source. By clean we mean that during operation the technology produces no emissions. By constant we mean that with the exception of mechanical failure the technology will continue to operate indefinitely." In July 2007, a much-anticipated public demonstration in London was stymied by "technical difficulties." Despite promises, the technology has not yet been successfully demonstrated. Physicists think it cannot be, because it amounts to a "perpetual motion machine" that violates a fundamental law of nature, the Law of Conservation of Energy, also known as the First Law of Thermodynamics. See Eric Ash, "The Perpetual Myth of Free Energy," *BBC News* (July 9, 2007) (http://news.bbc.co.uk/2/hi/technology/6283374.stm).

The search for inexpensive, long-lasting energy sources goes on, as it has since at least the 1400s (Allan A. Mills, "Leonardo da Vinci and Perpetual Motion," *Leonardo,* vol. 41, no. 1, 2008). It seems more likely that work on such things as improved methods of capturing solar energy will pay off in the near future. Work on thermonuclear fusion may pay off in the longer term. In the more distant future, other technologies may be realized. Modern physics really does offer such concepts as zero point and vacuum energy, as well as even more exotic ideas. If we have no idea how to make them work today, that does not mean that we will *never* be able to make them work. Nor does it mean that we should reject out of hand new "free energy" inventions. In science (and technology), the practical test—the experiment or demonstration—is what matters. As Eric Ash notes in the BBC item, "the fact that a device or an invention looks too marvelous to be true is not conclusive evidence that it isn't."

However, the track record for "free energy" devices is not good, despite the title of Thomas Valone's more recent book, *Practical Conversion of Zero-Point Energy,* 3rd ed. (Integrity Research Institute, 2005). We need what they promise, but to get it will continue to require that we rely on external sources of energy (coal, oil, wind, sun, etc.) and worry about waste products and other side-effects.

Contributors to This Volume

EDITOR

THOMAS A. EASTON is a professor of science at Thomas College in Waterville, Maine, where he has been teaching environmental science; science, technology, and society; emerging technologies; and computer science since 1983. He received a B.A. in biology from Colby College in 1966 and a Ph.D. in theoretical biology from the University of Chicago in 1971. He writes and speaks frequently on scientific and futuristic issues. His books include *Focus on Human Biology*, 2nd ed., coauthored with Carl E. Rischer (HarperCollins, 1995), *Careers in Science*, 4th ed. (VGM Career Horizons, 2004), *Taking Sides: Clashing Views in Science, Technology, and Society,* 8th ed. (McGraw-Hill, 2008), and *Classic Edition Sources: Environmental Studies,* 3rd ed. (McGraw-Hill, 2009). Dr. Easton is also a well-known writer and critic of science fiction.

AUTHORS

SPENCER ABRAHAM was sworn in as the tenth Secretary of Energy on January 20, 2001. Before that, he was a Republican senator from Michigan and co-chairman of the National Republican Congressional Committee.

JAMES ALLEN is a research analyst at Climate Change Capital, a London investment banking group that aims "to make the world's environment cleaner while delivering attractive financial returns."

AMERICAN RIVERS (http://www.americanrivers.org) is a national organization that protects and promotes rivers as vital to health, safety, and quality of life.

ROGER ANGEL is professor of astronomy and optical sciences at the University of Arizona, where he also serves as the director of the Steward Observatory Mirror Laboratory and the Center for Astronomical Adaptive Optics.

MICHAEL BEHAR is a freelance writer and editor based in Washington, D.C. His beat includes environmental issues and scientific innovations.

JEFF BINGAMAN (D-NM) is the chair of the Senate Committee on Energy and Natural Resources.

DAVID L. BODDE is professor and senior fellow at the International Center for Automotive Research, Arthur M. Spiro Center for Entrepreneurial Leadership, at Clemson University.

JON BOONE is a retired university administrator and the producer and director, with David Beaudoin, of the documentary video, *Life Under a Windplant* (http://www.stopillwind.org/). A lifelong environmentalist, he helped found the North American Bluebird Society and is a consultant with the Roger Tory Peterson Institute in New York. He is currently writing a book on the Dutch artist, Johannes Vermeer. He has no financial involvement with wind power but does seek informed, effective public policy.

MARIA CANTWELL (D-WA) is a member of the Senate Committee on Energy and Natural Resources. She also serves on the Senate Committees on Commerce, Science, and Transportation, Finance, Indian Affairs, and Small Business and Entrepreneurship.

RALPH J. CICERONE, president of the National Academy of Sciences, is an atmospheric scientist whose research in atmospheric chemistry and climate change has involved him in shaping science and environmental policy at the highest levels nationally and internationally.

THOMAS B. COCHRAN is a senior scientist with the Nuclear Program of the Natural Resources Defense Council.

CHARLI E. COON is senior policy analyst, Thomas A. Roe Institute for Economic Policy Studies, The Heritage Foundation.

JON STEVENS CORZINE left the Senate (where he served as a member of the Senate Committee on Energy and Natural Resources) to become the governor of New Jersey.

BOB DINNEEN is president and CEO of the Renewable Fuels Association, the national trade association representing the U.S. ethanol industry.

BYRON DORGAN (D-ND) is a member of the Senate Committee on Energy and Natural Resources. He also chairs the Committee on Indian Affairs and is a member of the Committees on Appropriations and on Commerce, Science, and Transportation.

MYRON EBELL is director of energy and global warming policy at the Competitive Enterprise Institute (CEI), a Washington, D.C.–based public policy organization dedicated to advancing the principles of free enterprise and limited government.

DIANNE FEINSTEIN (D-CA) currently serves on the Senate Committees on Rules and Administration, the Judiciary, and Appropriations, and the Senate Select Committee on Intelligence.

PHILLIP J. FINCK is deputy associate laboratory director, Applied Science and Technology and National Security, Argonne National Laboratory.

JAMES R. FLEMING, professor of science, technology, and society at Colby College in Waterville, Maine, is a public policy scholar at the Wilson Center and holds the American Association for the Advancement of Science's Roger Revelle Fellowship in Global Environmental Stewardship.

NINA FRENCH is the director, Clean Coal Technology, ADA Environmental Solutions.

DAVID FRIEDMAN is research director at the Union of Concerned Scientists.

MICHELLE GARNEAU is a professor in the Department of Geography at the University of Quebec in Montreal. She studies the impact of climate change.

ERIC GHOLZ is assistant professor of public affairs at the University of Texas, Austin.

JOHN J. GROSSENBACHER is the director of the U.S. Department of Energy's Idaho National Laboratory.

RICHARD N. HAASS is the president of the Council on Foreign Relations. From 2001 to 2003, he was the director of policy planning for the United States Department of State.

DAVID G. HAWKINS is the director of the Climate Center of the Natural Resources Defense Council.

FRANK N. VON HIPPEL is a nuclear physicist and a professor of public and international affairs in Princeton University's Program on Science and Global Security. He served as assistant director for national security in the White House Office of Science and Technology Policy in 1993–94.

ROBBIN S. JOHNSON is a consultant and former senior vice president of corporate affairs at Cargill Inc.

TIM JOHNSON (D-SD) is a member of the Senate Committee on Energy and Natural Resources. He is also a member of the Committees on Appropriations, Indian Affairs, and Banking, Housing, and Urban Affairs.

CHARLES KOMANOFF is an internationally known energy-economist and transport-economist and an environmental activist in New York City.

DWIGHT R. LEE is the Ramsey Professor of Economics in the Terry College of Business at the University of Georgia.

SUSAN MORAN teaches magazine journalism at the University of Colorado at Boulder's School of Journalism and Mass Communication.

IAIN MURRAY is a senior fellow at the Competitive Enterprise Institute (CEI), a Washington, D.C.–based public policy organization dedicated to advancing the principles of free enterprise and limited government.

IVAN OSORIO is editorial director at the Competitive Enterprise Institute (CEI), a Washington, D.C.–based public policy organization dedicated to advancing the principles of free enterprise and limited government.

ROBERT PARK is professor of physics and former chair of the Department of Physics at the University of Maryland. His books include *Voodoo Science: The Road from Foolishness to Fraud* (Oxford, 2000) and *Superstition: Belief in the Age of Science* (Princeton, 2008). His website, http://www.bobpark.org/, often takes a debunking approach to science news.

DARYL G. PRESS is associate professor of government at Dartmouth College in Hanover, New Hampshire.

PAUL ROBERTS is the author of *The End of Oil* (Houghton Mifflin, 2004) and *The End of Food* (Houghton Mifflin, 2008).

CHARLOTTE ROEHM is currently a postdoctoral researcher in the Department of Ecology and Environmental Science at Umea University in northern Sweden.

C. FORD RUNGE is Distinguished McKnight University Professor of Applied Economics and Law and director of the Center for International Food and Agricultural Policy at the University of Minnesota.

KENNETH L. SALAZAR (D-CO) is a member of the Senate Committee on Energy and Natural Resources.

CHARLES W. SCHMIDT is a freelance science writer specializing in the environment, genomics, and information technology, among other topics. In 2002, he won the National Association of Science Writers' Science-in-Society Journalism Award for his reporting on hazardous electronic waste exports to developing countries.

GAR SMITH, a former editor of Earth Island Journal, cofounded Environmentalists Against War (http://www.envirosagainstwar.org). He currently edits the weekly eco-zine The Edge (http://www.earthisland.org/the-edge).

ROY W. SPENCER is principal research scientist at the Earth System Science Center, University of Alabama in Huntsville.

SIR NICHOLAS STERN is head of the British Government Economics Service and adviser to the British Government on the economics of climate change and development.

JOHN STONE is a former Treasury Secretary and senator of Australia. He comments frequently on public affairs for the Council for the National Interest's *National Observer*.

MIMI SWARTZ is an executive editor of *Texas Monthly* and coauthor, with Sherron Watkins, of *Power Failure: The Inside Story of the Collapse of Enron* (Doubleday, 2004).

BRIAN TOKAR, an ecological activist since the 1970s, is a faculty member and Biotechnology Project Director at the Institute for Social Ecology in Vermont. His latest book, *Gene Traders: Biotechnology, World Trade and the Globalization of Hunger*, was published in 2004 by Toward Freedom in Burlington, Vermont. He was the recipient of a 1999 Project Censored award for his investigative history of the Monsanto company (*The Ecologist*, September/October 1998).

ALAIN TREMBLAY is the coordinator of the Reservoirs' Net Greenhouse Gas Emissions project at Hydro-Quebec's Eastmain-1 site.

THE UNION OF CONCERNED SCIENTISTS (UCS) is an independent nonprofit alliance of more than 100,000 concerned citizens and scientists. It was founded in 1969 by faculty members and students at the Massachusetts Institute of Technology who were concerned about the misuse of science and technology in society. Their statement called for the redirection of scientific research to pressing environmental and social problems. From that beginning, UCS has become a powerful voice for change.

THOMAS VALONE is the president of Integrity Research Institute and editor of the *Future Energy* newsletter. He has authored six books and numerous studies, articles, and papers related to energy in all forms. He holds a PhD in engineering.

LOUIS VARFALVY is a researcher with Hydro-Quebec.

ANTHONY WHITE is managing director of market development and chairman of advisory at Climate Change Capital, a London investment banking group that aims "to make the world's environment cleaner while delivering attractive financial returns." He was a founding member of the UK Government's Energy Advisory Panel and is a current member of the UK Government's Commission on Environmental Markets and Economic Performance. He also sits on the advisory boards of the UK Energy Research Centre and Sussex University's Energy Group.

RON WYDEN (D-OR) is a member of the Senate Committee on Energy and Natural Resources. He is also a member of the Senate Select Committee on Intelligence and serves on the Committees on Finance, Aging, and Budget.